Tearing Down the Gates

TEARING DOWN THE GATES

CONFRONTING THE CLASS
DIVIDE IN AMERICAN EDUCATION

Peter Sacks

UNIVERSITY OF CALIFORNIA PRESS
BERKELEY   LOS ANGELES   LONDON

University of California Press, one of the most distinguished university presses in the United States, enriches lives around the world by advancing scholarship in the humanities, social sciences, and natural sciences. Its activities are supported by the UC Press Foundation and by philanthropic contributions from individuals and institutions. For more information, visit www.ucpress.edu.

A Caravan Book
For more information, visit www.caravanbooks.org.

University of California Press
Berkeley and Los Angeles, California

University of California Press, Ltd.
London, England

Library of Congress Cataloging-in-Publication Data

Sacks, Peter.
    Tearing down the gates : confronting the class divide in American education / Peter Sacks.
        p.   cm.
    Includes bibliographical references and index.
    ISBN 978-0-520-24588-4 (cloth : alk. paper)
    1. Educational equalization—United States.
2. Discrimination in education—United States.
3. Social classes—United States.   I. Title.

LC213.2.S23   2007
379.2'60973—dc22   2006036216

Manufactured in the United States of America

15   14   13   12   11   10   09   08   07
10   9   8   7   6   5   4   3   2   1

The paper used in this publication meets the minimum requirements of ANSI/NISO Z39.48–1992 (R 1997) (*Permanence of Paper*).

Contents

Figures and Tables

FIGURES

TABLES

APPENDIX A: SUPPLEMENTARY FIGURES

APPENDIX B: SUPPLEMENTARY TABLES

Acknowledgments

I am obliged to the dozens of people who kindly lent their time and expertise at various stages of this project, including Brian K. Fitzgerald, William Boyd, Richard Kahlenberg, Thomas Mortenson, Edward P. St. John, and George Kuh. My thanks go out to the many parents, students, and teachers whom I interviewed, including several whose compelling stories did not make it into this book. I am also indebted to my editor at the University of California Press, Naomi Schneider, whose steady support for this undertaking has been an inspiration. Making a book is a team effort, and I am especially grateful to UC Press senior project editor Dore Brown and copyeditor Mary Renaud for their patient expertise and close attention to detail. My wife, Kathleen Romito, has been at my side throughout the project, for which I am especially thankful. All errors and omissions are mine alone.

INTRODUCTION

Lost Illusions

Tearing Down the Gates is about injustice. It is about the staggering economic inequalities that open the gates of opportunity for the children of affluent and well-educated families and slam the gates shut for children born without social and economic privilege. While we often hear about the widening economic divide between the rich and the poor in modern America, this book attempts to locate the fountainhead of this growing economic disparity in one of our most cherished democratic institutions: our education system.

Ashlea Jackson is a high school junior who would like to attend college and perhaps study journalism.[1] She's hard-working, eager, and smart. Ashlea, who is white, grew up in a trailer park. Two of her brothers have already been in trouble with the law; both have served time in juvenile detention. Her mother is homebound because of illness, and her father, who never finished high school, works at whatever manual labor he can find.

My wife, Kathleen, has been Ashlea's Big Sister through the Big Brothers Big Sisters program for the past several years. We decided that we wanted to set up a modest college scholarship for Ashlea, giving her money for college as long as she kept up a certain grade point average in high school. When we broached the scholarship idea with her dad, who was proud of his daughter's plans for college, he had to ask us, "What's a GPA?" As people who had monitored the progress of our GPAs and test scores like stock analysts through various graduate and professional schools, we were dumbstruck by the question.

We've watched Ashlea struggle in the school system, not because she isn't capable but because she must overcome obstacles associated with her class background that many of her more privileged classmates would never encounter. When she was a freshman, she had an assignment to write a small research paper, but there were no books on her chosen subject in the school library. Her trailer park was miles from the nearest library, and her parents didn't have a car to take her to the public library over the weekend. She had no computer and no Internet connection, and there were no books to speak of at home. Ashlea did her best, but her report was late because she had trouble simply obtaining the basic information for her paper. The scolding teacher, ignoring this larger picture, docked her paper a grade. After all, the other kids, who happened to have those Internet connections and books at home, turned in their papers on time.

We can learn a lot about the American class system from Ashlea's experience and that of her family. One recent Christmas, when the family's 1970-something Dodge van was still running, Ashlea's parents took her and her younger brother for a drive to see the Christmas lights in the foothills above the city, with the elegant houses and their extravagant holiday displays. As the family was driving around in their beat-up old van, a resident called the police. An officer stopped the family and questioned them about stealing Christmas lights. Their crime, it seems, was that they were driving around in an old van in a fancy neighborhood.

As Americans, we want to believe that we are a nation of upwardly mobile individuals, unfettered by the class structures that plague other societies. We like to think that one rises to the top of American society owing to "luck and pluck"—the Horatio Alger ideal that has become embedded into the American consciousness. We often talk about American higher education being a meritocracy and our society as one in which individuals succeed on the basis of hard work and talent. We are endlessly sunny about these matters—to the point of foolishness, it would seem.

Many Americans like to believe that once poor children enter the school system—a school system sanctioned and supported by the public—they are placed on an equal footing with all their peers and that their achievements in school will determine their future opportunities, with the best and brightest winning the race. We want our schools, colleges, and universities to be the Great Equalizers that help to erase social and economic inequality, not institutions that facilitate the Great Sorting of Americans from the day they enter kindergarten. We prefer to ignore the reality that our schools and colleges in fact reproduce, reinforce, and legitimize inequality.

Several years ago, I taught at a community college in a working-class and ethnically diverse suburb in the Seattle area. Most of my students were struggling to find a modest piece of the American Dream. There is one image from those days of teaching that still haunts me: I recall occasionally seeing my students donning Harvard or Yale sweatshirts, oblivious to the bitter irony that they were proudly displaying the emblems of an exclusive club that would never admit them as members.

Consider Ashlea's life in comparison with the lives of other families and kids I know. Their far different circumstances make a mockery of dearly held beliefs about American society as a meritocracy, where all kids supposedly have a chance to compete on relatively equal terms. My eyes open even wider every couple of years, when my wife and I attend an informal reunion of a handful of her close friends from medical school. Now mostly in their late thirties, these are graduates of institutions such as Yale, the University of California at Berkeley, and MIT. Their spouses are accomplished health care professionals, business executives, and other highly skilled experts; and their parents include university professors, scientists, and executives. Virtually all of these highly educated people consider themselves socially and politically progressive.

Most of these young physicians are now raising families of their own, and many of their children will likely bypass public schools altogether for expensive private schools with highly selective admissions policies. By the time their children are teenagers, in sixth or seventh grade—or even sooner—our friends will begin to talk to them about the SAT admissions test and will even start practicing sample SAT questions with their kids. These parents will push schools and teachers to ensure that their children are placed in the most enriched curriculum programs.

By their junior year in high school, the kids will be pressured in earnest to devote their attention to the SAT and to preparing their applications to the nation's most selective and desirable universities—their efforts aided and supported by a formidable network of parents, teachers, and school counselors. Their teachers, either at private high schools or wealthy suburban public schools—whose reputations and fundraising capabilities depend on placing their graduates in the Ivy League and similarly prestigious colleges—will steadfastly prep the high schoolers for the SAT, providing them training in test-taking skills and an insider's knowledge of the test's characteristics. These privileged children will be advised by expert college counselors, themselves graduates of prestigious colleges and universities, who may well personally know members of the admissions staff at similar colleges.

Still, many of our friends would call themselves politically progressive. But any concern that they might have for kids like Ashlea and the daunting educational inequities they encounter may be rendered moot by the desire of well-to-do parents to protect their own, at seemingly any price. Youthful passion for equity and justice is too often overshadowed by the demands of an education system that, even in the public realm, has been structured around private interests to the exclusion of the public interest. Affluent parents, it seems, have been led to believe that educational quality is a zero-sum game: that if schools help kids like Ashlea, then their own children will lose.

Compared to Ashlea and her family, our friends might as well be living on a different planet. When you add it all up, the network of elite schools, teachers, counselors, parents, grandparents and siblings, uncles and aunts, and college admissions officials who themselves are graduates of top colleges works, often in relatively unconscious ways, to sustain the culture of privilege, effectively passing it on from generation to generation. But here's the irony: this inherited culture of elite advantage is undergirded by a powerful belief system, held even by ordinary people just like Ashlea's family, that portrays America as a nation of equal opportunity in which anybody can rise to the top with enough talent and hard work. A few years ago, for example, a Time/CNN poll found that an astounding 40 percent of Americans believe they are or soon will be in the top 1 percent of the country's income distribution.[2]

These stories we tell ourselves may be comforting, but they don't align especially well with reality. It's unsettling to learn just how badly the odds are stacked against kids like Ashlea even attending college, let alone earning a college degree. "Who gets a bachelor's degree from college by age 24 is largely determined at birth," asserts Tom Mortenson, a senior scholar at the Center for the Study of Equal Opportunity in Higher Education, who bases this somewhat startling conclusion on U.S. Census data. Indeed, no more than 6 percent of college-age kids from families earning $35,000 a year and less—the Ashleas of the nation—earn a bachelor's degree by their twenty-fourth birthday. In sharp contrast, more than half of the kids from affluent families, those in the top quarter of the nation's income ladder, earn a bachelor's degree by age twenty-four. "This is the hand one is dealt from the deck of cards of life at birth—a deck of cards heavily and increasingly stacked against those unlucky enough to be born into low-income families," Mortenson says.[3]

Some may respond to this situation simply by noting, "Life's not fair. It's too bad Ashlea doesn't have the advantages of those doctors' kids, but she must play with the cards she's been dealt, as we all do."

I challenge this way of thinking. This commonly held belief feeds and legitimizes a fatalism that sustains an unnecessary and irrational degree of inequality, an inequality that is neither legitimate nor ethically defensible, based as it is on illusions. Chief among these illusions is that children who grow up poor simply can't compete with their more affluent and fortunate peers, that their academic merit, as measured by SAT scores and the like, makes them unable to handle the rigors of top colleges and universities.

As citizens in a democracy, it should anger us when kids like Ashlea are excluded from opportunities that others have in abundance, simply because they were unlucky enough to be born into poor families. It should anger us when those with the most advantages from birth continue to reap outsized rewards for no other reason than that they were born into privileged families. It should anger us when kids from poor and working-class families are relegated to the most boring and least challenging schools and teaching methods—the "slow" and rote academic tracks—while their more affluent peers are chosen for the accelerated tracks and treated to the most enriching and interesting learning environments.

America's education system is driven by class distinctions to a degree most Americans don't acknowledge and perhaps don't even comprehend. When we do talk about equal opportunity, we often talk about gender and race—justifiably so. We have created far-reaching public policies, such as affirmative action, in the hope of rectifying past injustices related to these sources of inequality in college admissions and hiring for jobs. But as Americans, we somehow believe we are immune from the same harsh class differences that have plagued other societies. We don't talk much about class and the staggering inequalities of class that divide us. We have not put class on an equal footing with race or gender when designing public policies such as affirmative action in college admissions. The nearly complete sublimation of class in our equity debates and policy considerations stands out as a glaring oddity of the social history of the last generation.

Americans have heard time and again the old saw that the rich are getting richer and the poor poorer. Not a year goes by without another new study coming out to confirm that the cliché is, indeed, true. But economic inequality is about far more than tax cuts for the rich. It's about more than lavish lifestyles of celebrities and executives. It's about more than another government report about how the rich are getting richer.

Indeed, a far more insidious and damaging inequality is spreading like a cancer in American society, a kind of inequality that rarely makes headlines or sensational news stories. It is an inequality of basic opportunity that young children find in front of them from birth—and even before. And that inequality is getting worse, not better. In terms of the class divide, the United States is not as equitable a nation as it was even a few decades ago, and the whole country will pay the price of that inequality on the global stage. We are competing with socially and economically dynamic countries that will outsmart us, quite literally. If we do not find better ways to let human talent blossom and to mitigate our growing inequality, then we all will lose.

Our education system is the very democratic institution that Americans see as the last stand against economic inequality, and yet it is suffering from this cancer. But like my former community college students unconsciously displaying the emblems of an exclusive club that would never admit them as members, most Americans seem blissfully unaware of it.

Tearing Down the Gates is about confronting this taboo subject of social class in American society and our education system in particular. This book is about exposing the creeping, insidious damage that classism inflicts on us individually and as a nation. It is about bringing class, at long last, to the forefront of our discussions of equal opportunity. It is about creating a new kind of "affirmative action," one that recognizes the gifts and talents of the many people among us who, in the past, have been excluded from opportunities as a result of entrenched rules of the game that have rewarded those with privilege and punished those without it.

This book is about tearing down the gates that have been erected on illusions.

———

Part 1, "Rich Families, Poor Families," explores the role of the family in the American opportunity structure. How does the human capital that parents provide to their children, from family wealth to the number of books in the house, influence a child's chances for higher education? Chapter 1 presents the stories of two young women, Ashlea from Boise and Gillian from Santa Monica, whose opportunity horizons are worlds apart, owing to differences in the cultural and financial resources they acquire from their families. Chapter 2 examines the interplay of family social class and schools in Boise, Idaho, and argues that the line separating affluent families and their schools has become increasingly fuzzy, with public schools being transformed into private spaces that service the wealthy and their children.

With unprecedented gains in wealth at the top of the income distribution, affluent parents are competing as never before to give their children an edge, pressing schools to carve out havens of privilege with gifted and talented programs, accelerated classes, and other methods of separating students in ways that reward upper-class status. Part 2, "Struggle for the Soul of Public Schools," delves more deeply into this theme. Chapters 3 and 4 of this section include a case study of one such struggle taking place in Berkeley, California. Chapter 5 synthesizes the case studies of Boise and Berkeley into a general discussion of how the privatization of the public sphere, at the behest of well-to-do families, is playing out across the country.

Part 3, "Affirmative Action for the Rich," investigates the class lines of American higher education. Although inequities along racial and gender lines have significantly lessened in recent decades in the United States, the opportunity gap between advantaged and disadvantaged social classes has not diminished over the past thirty years, as chapter 6 shows. Chapters 7 and 8 explore how colleges and universities themselves promote and profit from admissions and financial aid systems that favor elites. By playing this prestige game in an unholy alliance with rankings compilers such as U.S. News and World Report, colleges and universities wind up fueling social class inequalities and shirking their responsibilities to the public good. Chapter 9 argues that recent trends in college financial aid have deepened inequality, as institutions and the government have begun to give more aid to students who don't require it at the expense of students who can't afford college without it.

Examples of public schools and universities that are effectively tearing down the gates of restricted opportunities along class lines make up part 4, "Experiments in Gatecrashing and Backlash of the Elites." Chapter 10 describes the efforts of one urban high school to create a college-going culture among its disadvantaged students. Some larger public universities are reassessing their views of academic merit and reforming their admissions systems to improve the college-going prospects of disadvantaged students, as chapter 11 explains, although they may face a backlash of elites asserting political power to maintain the status quo. Chapter 12 recounts the story of a budding young scientist, Melissa

Morrow, which highlights the absence of easy solutions for closing the opportunity gap.

In the final part, "American Dreams," chapter 13 reviews those aspects of U.S. economic history since the Great Depression that have given rise in recent years to a new Gilded Age, with unprecedented gains in wealth at the top of the income distribution. Chapter 14 explores American's uncomfortable and confused relationship with class and how this confusion impedes frank discussion and the formulation of clear public policies. Finally, chapter 15 analyzes the economic imperatives for breaking down class barriers to educational opportunity. This conclusion attempts to explain why class questions became separated from race in political discourse and argues that class and race must be rejoined in a new political calculus that attacks inequality at its source. It also poses the key question: is America ready for a new political consensus on class-based remedies to educational inequality?

PART 1

RICH FAMILIES, POOR FAMILIES

ONE

ASHLEA AND GILLIAN

Ashlea Jackson remembers the moment she decided to choose a different path than her troubled brothers had followed. She was in fourth grade, and one day, walking down the hallway, she looked up when she heard some girls call out her older brother Justin's nickname, "Jay Jay."

"They were saying, 'Bye, Jay Jay,' and I turned around and saw my brother being taken out of the school in handcuffs by two cops, and that is when I knew I didn't want to end up like my older brother," Ashlea told me. "He was in fifth grade. He was eleven or twelve. I mean, that is something I will never forget. Because that was the first time I'd ever seen anyone in handcuffs."[1]

This happened at Whittier Elementary, a school in Boise, Idaho, which draws virtually all its students from Garden City, a geographically strange and often-forgotten enclave, out of sight of most Boiseans, where Ashlea lived for several years. Garden City includes some of the Boise area's poorest families. Surrounded by the city of Boise, Garden City itself has no public school, and so the largely Hispanic and poor children from its many trailer parks are bused to Whittier, which is part of the Boise school district. In any given year, more than 90 percent of Whittier's three hundred students are eligible for the school's free lunch program.

Debbie Bailey is Whittier's principal of two years. Before that, she served as principal of a far more affluent elementary school in Boise for seven years. Earlier in her career, she received special training at the Cooperative Urban Teacher Education Program in Kansas City and taught in a number of urban schools before returning to her home state of Idaho.

Bailey took the job at Whittier because she missed the sorts of kids who go to schools like this one. But she was also painfully aware of the challenges of keeping Whittier afloat in the era of No Child Left Behind, with its mandate to meet annual test score targets or face closure by the government. Bailey knows where her students come from, and she knows all too well that she and her staff are limited in what they can do for these kids, who start the academic race so far behind their peers in other schools—peers who start out and grow up with all the opportunities that their well-to-do families and schools provide.

She described Garden City's trailer parks this way to me: "The majority of our kids are bused from Garden City. I live right up the hill from there, and the trailer parks down there were eye-opening to me. They're horrible. They're a ghetto. They are Boise's ghetto."[2]

———

In truth, I do not know many kids like Ashlea, living where I do and knowing the people I know. I first met Ashlea when she was twelve or thirteen through my wife, Kathleen, who is her Big Sister. When I spoke with her over a period of several months for this book, Ashlea was in her junior year of high school. Over the years, I've watched her struggle with school and with life, facing difficulties associated with growing up poor that are unimaginable to children in most middle-class families. The difficulties she faces come with being poor, but they also come from the lack of something far more intangible: the cultural, social, and economic "capital" that upper- and middle-class families routinely provide their children. The benefits of such capital manifest themselves in a multitude of both highly visible and often subtle ways that make going to college, and going to good colleges, a common destiny for the children of wealthier families.

After being escorted out of Whittier Elementary by the police at age eleven, Ashlea's older brother would spend several years in and out of juvenile detention at various facilities across the state. By the age of eighteen, he was married and living with his wife and the child of a former girlfriend, although he soon would be divorced.

Her younger brother wound up at an alternative school for troubled kids. "His biggest problem is that he does not want to go to school,"

Ashlea explained. "And, basically, they are saying if you do not go to school, then you go to Juvie, pretty much."

When Ashlea realized that she didn't want to end up like her brothers, staying out of trouble became a conscious choice that she made daily, because trouble was all around her in the Garden City trailer parks. "There were always a lot of problems," she says. "There were always cops."

When Ashlea was in elementary school, being from Garden City wasn't a big deal, because all the students at Whittier were bused in from Garden City. But when she moved to junior high at Riverglen, surrounded by nice houses in middle-class neighborhoods, Garden City became a place of shame for her.

"I didn't let on that I lived in Garden City, because I was ashamed of it," Ashlea admitted. "Nobody knew that I lived in Garden City. When someone asked me where I lived, I would say I lived up the hill. There were like two hills, so nobody really knew."

During these years, I heard how the family became homeless after they confronted a slumlord in their Garden City trailer park over holes in the walls of their rented trailer. I heard about the family getting kicked out of a homeless shelter because Ashlea's mother and father refused the humiliation of being split up according to the shelter's single-sex rules.

During her sophomore year, Ashlea tried to commit suicide in a bout of severe depression, and school officials tried to remove her from school—just two weeks before the end of the school year—claiming she had too many absences after her suicide attempt. I watched Kathleen, loath to interfere in Ashlea's life in ways that might be inappropriate for a Big Sister, draw the line at this heavy-handed move by the school.

As a physician, Kathleen knew what Ashlea's parents might not have realized: schools were organizations run by people who could be influenced. Kathleen got on the phone with Ashlea's high school counselors, school officials, coordinators at Big Brothers Big Sisters, private counselors she knew from her medical practice, and others in order to keep Ashlea in school.

During all this, Kathleen said more than once to me that the school would have treated a middle-class child far differently than it treated Ashlea, and she wasn't going to stand for it. In effect, Kathleen did what most highly educated and affluent parents would have done in a similar situation, deploying whatever knowledge, information, contacts, political clout, stature in the community, and financial resources she had to ensure that Ashlea's interests were protected—drawing on her own cultural and social capital to help Ashlea in ways that the Jacksons didn't know how to do or perhaps weren't in a position to do.

————

Families matter when it comes to the academic success of children, and the social class background of children matters. That much is given. But these things matter far more than the recent approaches to education policy at the federal and state levels—which have an inveterate obsession with schools as the agent of social change—would lead most people to think. Indeed, the nation's preoccupation in recent years with standardized test scores and public school accountability belies more than forty years of social research, which underscores that schools themselves contribute insignificantly to student achievement relative to what children bring with them to school from the first day of kindergarten—derived largely from the social class background of their parents and grandparents and from other aspects of their life beyond school.

The 1966 Coleman Report first staked out this ground. Titled *Equality of Educational Opportunity,* this far-reaching study, headed by prominent sociologist James S. Coleman, grew out of the 1964 Civil Rights Act. The report's fundamental finding was that families' social and economic status, the stuff that children bring to school, trumped just about all else in accounting for students' educational achievements and prospects.

Coleman summarized that report:

> Taking all these results together, one implication stands out above all. That schools bring little influence to bear on a child's achievement that is independent of his background and general social context; and that this very lack of an independent effect means that the inequalities imposed on children by their home, neighborhood, and peer environment are carried along to become the inequalities with which they confront adult life at the end of school. For equality of educational opportunity through the schools must imply a strong effect of schools that is independent of the child's immediate social environment, and that strong independent effect is not present in American schools.[3]

The unavoidable policy implications are that good schools can go only so far in raising the achievement levels of disadvantaged children and that attacking the problem with policies that improve the social and economic conditions of individuals and families will be more effective than creating policies aimed just at schools. (I should note, however, that, in addition to the influence of family on individual student achievement, the socioeconomic characteristics of a student's peers also had a powerful effect on Coleman's data. Ironically, these peer effects were weakest for the very advantaged groups whose parents might be most conscious of choosing the "right" schools for their children. But for disadvantaged students, the socioeconomic background of other students at the school they attended was of considerable importance.)

In one way or another, the basic findings of the Coleman Report have been reiterated in the research literature ever since. About thirty years later, *The Black-White Test Score Gap*, edited by Christopher Jencks and Meredith Phillips, documented that fully two-thirds of the gap in school achievement between white and black students could be explained when the researchers accounted for the full range of social and economic conditions of individual students, a range that went far beyond the conventional factors of education and income and included such intergenerational resources as those passed on by grandparents to their heirs.[4]

In trying to pinpoint the source of the class advantages that affluent parents provide children, researchers in recent years have paid considerable attention to the concept of "cultural capital," a term widely attributed to the French sociologist Pierre Bourdieu.[5] His notion of cultural capital, explains Patricia McDonough in her book *Choosing Colleges,* "is precisely the knowledge that elites value yet schools do not teach. . . . Cultural capital is of no intrinsic value. Its utility comes in using, manipulating, and investing it for socially valued and difficult-to-secure purposes and resources."[6] In Bourdieu's analysis, various types of human capital can be converted into other forms. Family wealth, for example, produces cultural and social capital for children: the children of well-to-do families are able to attend museums, study art, or acquire useful social networks. Such parents provide their children with skills, resources, and—perhaps most important—a sense of social power in the world. What's more, schools and the larger society reward and reinforce that social power, all under the guise of supposedly merit-based selection methods that favor the most culturally privileged—a self-reinforcing system that reproduces social class advantage.

Indeed, this ineffable sense of social power and confidence that wealthy parents pass on to children showed up vividly in Coleman's data. Along with schools, families, peers, and other possible influences on student achievement, the Coleman Report examined the extent to which student attitudes explained differences in academic performance. Coleman discovered that students' motivation, interest in school, self-concept, and sense of control over the environment—all intimately related to one's class background—produced surprisingly strong effects on academic achievement.

"For children from advantaged groups, achievement or lack of it appears closely related to their self concept: what they believe about themselves," Coleman wrote. "For children from disadvantaged groups, achievement or lack of achievement appears closely related to what they believe about their environment: whether they believe the environment will respond to reasonable efforts, or whether they believe it is instead merely random or immovable."

But schools seemed largely powerless to affect these attitudes, according to Coleman's findings: "This study provides little evidence concerning the effect of school factors on these attitudes," he wrote. "If family background characteristics are controlled, almost none of the remaining variance in self concept and control of the environment is accounted for by the school factors measured in this survey. . . . It appears reasonable that these attitudes depend more on the home than the school."[7]

Conservatives have taken Coleman's conclusion to suggest that student attitudes are simply a question of individual choice, as if parents can just choose success or failure for their children by providing them with the right values. But the research evidence paints a far more complicated picture. Attitudes are situated in economics and the social tastes acquired from one's class position. A family can, in effect, "buy" the right values for its children with sufficient wealth, income, time, and knowledge.

For example, in their ethnographic study of children from working-class and middle-class neighborhoods, Tiffani Chin and Meredith Phillips discovered stark differences among children in terms of summer activities and vacations—differences that stemmed not from parental values but from family resources. While working-class children's summer activities tended to be unorganized and nonacademic, affluent parents variously organized book clubs, involved children in university research projects, arranged piano lessons, and provided many similar sorts of enrichment.

"Even though children's summer experiences are stratified by social class, most parents from all social classes aspire to develop their children's skills and talents," Chin and Phillips write in *Sociology of Education*. "Most parents from all social classes believed that they should actively nurture their children's development, and most tried to do so. Yet, relative to the working class and poor parents, the middle-class parents tended to be more successful in constructing highly stimulating summers for their children because they tended to have greater financial resources, more flexible jobs, and more knowledge about how to match particular activities to their children's skills and interests." They continue, "These social-class differences probably produce both a 'talent development gap' and a 'cultural exposure gap,' which, if exacerbated each summer, contribute to disparities in children's future life chances."[8]

While there's little doubt that a child's family circumstances account for most of his or her chances of success in school, the exact sources of this family effect are uncertain. Does family income matter more or less than, say, providing children with lots of learning opportunities, such as puzzles, games, and a daily newspaper? Does cultural capital matter more or less than a family's financial capital?

One recent international study, for example, found that a child's cultural capital at home trumped family economics in predicting school success. Researchers Yang Yang and Jan-Eric Gustafsson examined some sixty-two thousand students in twenty-three countries in order to see how student resources and possessions at home, such as having books, newspapers, and computers, compared to family financial resources in predicting reading achievement. "The results show the cultural aspects of home background to be more important than the economic aspects in accounting for individual differences in reading achievement," the researchers conclude.[9]

Indeed, the powerful effects of cultural capital suggest that standard measures of socioeconomic status, such as parents' salary income and their education levels, probably underestimate the effect of family background on children's school chances. It turns out that wealth itself matters. Wealth, the economic assets that parents own, allows families to create the stores of cultural capital that seem to be essential to their children's success in school.

For example, in a study that examined differences in math achievement between white and black children, Amy J. Orr found that family wealth, particularly a family's income-producing financial assets, such as stocks and bonds, was a powerful predictor of math achievement, even after accounting for the parents' annual income and level of education.

But wealth lost explanatory power in Orr's model once several mediating variables associated with cultural capital, including books, newspapers, museum trips, and such, were accounted for. This model provides a fairly neat proof of Bourdieu's theory that the forms of human capital are mutable. As Orr concludes, "The effect of wealth on achievement is explained mainly by the effect of wealth on the amount of cultural capital to which a child is exposed. This finding supports Bourdieu's (1986) notion of capital: Economic capital (wealth) can be converted into other forms of capital (in this case, cultural capital) to reproduce status."[10]

After Kathleen's intervention with school officials, Ashlea was able to return to school. Although she had to make up some classes during the summer, she bounced back emotionally and academically.

As a sophomore, Ashlea discovered journalism after an English teacher read one of her essays and encouraged her to join the school's newspaper staff. In journalism, Ashlea seemed to have found a calling, one that tapped into her ingrained sense of social justice. Once, for instance, she became angry when kids on the school bus were harassing a boy who suffered from Asperger's syndrome, and she challenged the bus driver to do something about it.

"The boy was constantly picked on, and the bus driver really didn't pay attention to it," Ashlea told me. "He knew what was going on, but he wouldn't say anything about it. I felt really bad for the boy because he didn't deserve to be picked on. It upset me, and I told the kids to leave him alone. I got in trouble because the bus driver told me that I should not be butting into their business, and I said, 'Well, you should be doing your job then.'

"I got in trouble for it. I got Saturday school, and I got kicked off of the bus for three days. But I didn't care about getting in trouble, because I thought that what I did was right."

By the end of her junior year in high school, Ashlea had worked her way up on the newspaper staff and had contributed several articles about school life to the local daily newspaper. During the school year, she worked at a drive-in to earn extra money, and she saved enough to attend the annual high school journalism conference in Seattle. There, she pulled in a prize for feature writing. Her journalism teacher, who, Ashlea says, was sparing with praise for students, encouraged her to become the paper's news editor for her senior year.

For the first time, Ashlea began to see college as a possibility. A representative from a private two-year college in Wyoming had talked to her journalism class about the college's journalism program, and Ashlea became excited about the possibility of attending the school.

I asked her what she saw in her future. Without the slightest hesitation, she said, "I want to be a journalist."

———

I met Ashlea's father, Gary Jackson, one cold November afternoon at a Boise coffee shop, a few hours before his shift was to start at a downtown convention center where he worked setting up rooms for events. His cell phone rang while we were talking. "That was my Ashlea," he beamed.[11]

Jackson grew up on a farm in eastern Idaho and left home at the age of sixteen to join the army because he didn't get along well with his stepfather, who was just five or six years older and had himself recently returned from Vietnam. Gary Jackson was a good student. His grade school, located in the farm country around Pocatello, consisted of a few rooms, with just a couple of kids in each grade.

"I loved school," Jackson told me. "I got to learn and I got to think. I went through physics and chemistry and everything when I was in high school. I had enough credits to graduate when I was in the eleventh grade."

But Jackson went to Vietnam instead, essentially trading places with the stepfather who had just returned from the war. He showed enough aptitude to move up to staff sergeant and was assigned to a Special Operations unit in Thailand and Cambodia. Jackson left the army in 1982. "For a while, I had a lot of post-traumatic stuff," he said, declining to describe in detail the years in Southeast Asia. "Pretty heavy stuff," he said. "I saw a lot."

After getting out, Jackson rode freight trains, living as a hobo on the streets. He found his way to the Pioneer Square district in Seattle, when it was still a pretty rough place, before urban gentrification. There, he met his wife, Patty, who had also served in the army.

"I was playing cards at a place called First Avenue Service Center. It's gone now, but I was playing cards, and I looked up and I see these beautiful legs, and then I see the rest of her, and I just fell in love with her. She fell in love with me, and here we are, twenty-one years later," Jackson said.

Gary and Patty found their way to Utah, rode a freight train to Reno, and then moved to Arkansas, where Gary found a job as a long-haul truck driver, delivering loads of wheat across the country. They ended up in Bremerton, Washington, a navy town, where Ashlea was born in 1988. Jackson drove trucks for seventeen years.

"I would leave, and nine days later I'd be back, and I might stay for four or five hours. You know, wash my clothes and get something to eat, and I'd be gone again," Jackson said. "It was pretty constant, and I was—it was something else. One week I would be in New York, the next week I would be in Washington, and the next week I would be back in New York." Eventually, Patty gave him an ultimatum, insisting that he find another job that would allow him to be around more. "I missed Ashlea's birth by five minutes," he said.

When Patty developed breast cancer, during Ashlea's fifth grade year at Whittier, Ashlea took on more of the family's burdens than any child probably should have. Until Patty's illness, school had always been Ashlea's first priority. But then came her mom's surgeries and recovery time at home. Ashlea started missing school to help out. "My mom needed someone to be there with her when my dad had to work, because he was the only one bringing in money at the time. And she needed someone there when she was really, really sick, so I would be that person," Ashlea remembered.

Ashlea became a source of stability in the family, the one who might have a chance to go to college and break out of poverty. Over the years, she became the dependable one, not just for her immediate family but also for friends in Garden City whose lives were equally troubled. Eventually, the burdens became too much for a teenager to bear.

I asked her about her depression and her suicide attempt.

"I wasn't talking about my feelings or my problems. I took on a lot of other people's problems," Ashlea explained. "I've always been the strong one in my family because my mom had cancer, my brothers were troublemakers, so I had to be there, you know. I had to be the good one, I had to be the one to help out. Well, at least, I thought so. And so I felt that for a really long time. And then last year, I just kind of got overwhelmed with everybody else's problems, and it caused a big problem for me."

————

Things fall through the cracks when a sixteen-year-old must rely mostly on herself for planning her school life. Ashlea says that her parents want the best for her. But they could provide little besides emotional support in terms of helping Ashlea actually get to college. With limited help from guidance counselors at school, who in public high schools typically have caseloads of hundreds of students, Ashlea's knowledge of the details she needed to consider when preparing for college was hit or miss, at best.

What's more, her father, Gary, had left school at the age of sixteen and her mother's highest degree was a high school diploma. There was little information they could pass on to Ashlea about college—the seemingly small things that middle-class children get from the very air they breathe.

In affluent families, at least one parent is often available to ride herd on the details of school: to ensure that the child signs up for the right classes, to advocate for the child's enrollment in accelerated classes that lead to college-track math and English, and generally to make sure that the child's interests are protected in rule-bound school systems. In working-class and low-income families, where both parents work full-time jobs with inflexible hours, that extra bit of parental support and advocacy is rarely available—not because the families don't want to help but because they don't know how to help or don't have the extra time to help.

The way students are steered into college-track mathematics is a good example. When most American students make the transition from sixth to seventh grade, schools effectively put colored tags on their backs, labeling them as remedial, regular, or accelerated, depending on standardized test performance and teacher recommendations. Only students in the accelerated category are deemed ready for algebra, which will track them into calculus by their senior year of high school. And it's calculus—Advanced Placement (AP) calculus, in particular—that selective colleges look for on high school transcripts. Well-educated parents know these things, and there's ample evidence to suggest that they advocate vigorously to get their children into accelerated math courses, exploiting whatever wiggle room there is in school policies about track placement.

Elizabeth Useem has extensively studied the relationships between students' social class status and their placement in mathematics courses in American schools. In one study of the math placement patterns in Boston public schools, Useem found that almost 60 percent of the students on the accelerated math track had fathers with doctoral degrees, and 33 percent had fathers with master's degrees. In contrast, almost 50 percent of students in remedial math classes had fathers with only a high school diploma or less. Just 5.6 percent of the students in accelerated math had fathers with a high school education only.

Useem discovered that educated mothers were typically the ones in families who knew the details of school tracking policies. Indeed, 69 percent of students in accelerated math had mothers with a high degree of knowledge about such policies. By comparison, 70 percent of students in remedial math had mothers who seemed to know little about tracking. What's more, Useem found that mothers' understanding of school tracking systems was powerfully related to their own level of education. Some 65 percent of the knowledgeable mothers had advanced degrees, and more than three-quarters were well integrated into school affairs. In contrast, Useem quotes one mother whose child was in remedial math: "I learned about my son's math placement at the Open House this fall. I was under the impression that he was in regular math. The sixth-grade teacher never told me he would be in remedial math. There was no conference, no letter. . . . I was shocked."

As Useem concludes:

> Parents with baccalaureate and graduate degrees appear to pass on their educational advantages to their children in many direct and indirect ways. They do so by being much more aware of the implications of academic choices made in schools, by being more integrated into school affairs and parent-information networks, by having a greater propensity to intervene in educational decisions that are made for their children in school, and by the greater likelihood that they will exert influence on their children over the choice of courses.

She continues, "In a number of cases studied here, it appeared to be the parents' lack of involvement, social isolation, and reluctance to intervene and influence their children's program in a more demanding direction— factors that are all highly associated with their own educational background—rather than the children's academic ability, that accounted for the children's placement in a lower level mathematics course."[12]

———

As Ashlea continued to recover from her suicide attempt, she discovered a newfound sense of purpose in school. She was going to college. She quit her job at the drive-in to give herself more time for studying. She went to a college fair at the downtown convention center where her dad worked.

I asked Ashlea whether her emphasis on the importance of school came from within her or from her parents.

"No, it is coming from me," she said. "I want to go somewhere. I do not want to be like my brothers. And my parents know that, and they are really proud of that. They are basically telling me, you know, we just want you to be happy and go as far as you can."

But for all the hopes and dreams, details slipped from her grasp. When Ashlea first took pre-algebra, she didn't do well and was forced to repeat the class during the summer before her sophomore year. She aced the summer course. Then fall came, and she was enrolled in what she thought was algebra. But halfway into the semester, Ashlea realized that she was repeating pre-algebra.

"I don't know what happened there," she told me. "I just know that, after I realized that I wasn't supposed to be in that class, it was too late."

And then there was the chemistry snafu. Ashlea took chemistry during her junior year and got a B in the course. But when her senior year started, she missed a pre-registration session at the school, and her counselor simply placed her into the same chemistry class. It didn't seem right. But her learned passivity had gotten Ashlea by in such circumstances before, and she was ready to let this one slide, too—that is, until Kathleen found out what had happened and coached Ashlea on how to talk to her counselor and firmly tell him that being assigned to the same chemistry course for two years was simply not acceptable.

———

When Gillian Brunet was growing up near Santa Monica, California, she was virtually guaranteed that such details concerning her education would not slip by her mother and father, Ann and Jim Brunet. Gillian had but one main responsibility when she was growing up: to do well in school, period. She was assured that her parents would take care of everything else.

Gillian, who is white, was halfway through her freshman year at Smith College when I spoke to her and to Jim Brunet.[13] It's not likely that she would have made it to a college like Smith had Jim Brunet not been, as he put it to me, the "anal-retentive nudge" with Gillian's school life, mapping out her school plan and tracking nearly every detail of her progress.

The notion that Gillian would go to college wasn't simply part of the air she breathed in the Brunet family. It was explicitly planted in a conversation that her father had with Gillian when she was a first grader in a Santa Monica elementary school.

Gillian had clashed with her teacher, who, as first grade teachers are prone to do, spoke to her in a "touchy-feely," condescending tone, which Gillian "absolutely loathed," Jim Brunet told me. The child was bored with school and didn't even like the stories the teacher read.

One day, after Gillian came home from school complaining about her teacher, Brunet told his daughter that some day she'd get to go to college and that it would be a lot more fun and interesting than first grade. "Gillian is, as am I and my wife, a very rationally thinking kind of person, and what Gillian had expressed very, very early was that she wasn't into touchy-feely at all, and she was one of these kids that would rather read than be read to," Brunet explained.

"I told her—and I felt almost like a biblical prophet, so it came to pass—I said, 'Honey, you know, this is kind of tough right now, but you're going to like middle school a lot more than elementary school. You're going to like high school a lot more than middle school, and you're really going to blossom and love college.' "

So began Gillian Brunet's path to Smith College.

When she was young, the Brunets couldn't afford to buy a house in Santa Monica, but they wanted Gillian to attend the high-quality Santa Monica schools. Rather than do the financially prudent thing and buy an affordable home a long commute from where Ann worked at the University of California at Los Angeles, the Brunets rented apartments near Santa Monica, a lifestyle choice that allowed the family to socialize with university professors, writers, and other professionals. And Jim Brunet made every effort to ensure that Gillian got the best teachers and the best schools that the Santa Monica public school system had to offer.

"You had to jump through all the hoops, but I made sure we did it," Brunet said. "I told Gillian that as long as she didn't screw up, she could continue."

When I spoke to Gillian just before her winter break at Smith, she remembered her beginnings in Santa Monica schools essentially the same way her father did, particularly after she was old enough to figure out what her parents had sacrificed for her schooling. But she said her parents also taught her a certain orientation toward the future that has paid off throughout her school years.

"A lot of times I was a very quick student, and I would complain that it was boring, like 'Why do I want to learn this in elementary school?' " Gillian told me. "When I was in first grade, I wondered why I should learn to read, because I couldn't read anything that was interesting to me. My parents were very patient with me and said, 'You have to do the boring stuff before you can do fun stuff.' And also that even if something wasn't interesting in and of itself, it could have interesting applications. In doing the boring stuff, I would get to more interesting stuff later on. In other words, delayed gratification. I got that really early on."

———

Jim Brunet's career has been an eclectic concoction of stints as a public relations professional, an aeronautical engineer, a U.S. Senate staffer, a science fiction writer, and, for the past several years, a real estate agent in Santa Monica. He grew up in Evanston, Illinois, and in Southern California, graduating with a degree in political science from the University of California at Santa Barbara. His father, who left the family when Jim was young, was an English professor at the University of Massachusetts in Amherst, and his stepfather was a mathematician who taught at a small college. His mother's father had committed suicide when she was young, during the Depression, forcing her to go to work and dashing her hopes of attending college.

"My mother was very bright and should have gone to college," Brunet told me. "I think she even got admitted somewhere, but there wasn't money for it. I've seen some of her artwork and some of her writing. She had great potential, and I think it's actually a crime that she didn't go to college. Her life might have been much happier if she had. Lots of unfulfilled potential, let's put it that way."

Jim met Ann at an evening writing class at UCLA. They bonded through words and books, and they passed on their love of books and reading to Gillian. Ann was a graduate of the University of Missouri's highly regarded journalism school, and she has worked in public relations at UCLA for some twenty-five years.

Ann's first gift of note to Jim was a copy of *The French Lieutenant's Woman,* in hardcover. They accumulated loads of books together; one of their requirements for an apartment was that there be enough space for their fourteen bookcases. Brunet knows this figure because he once counted them.

"Good Lord, we are some of these people that when we are looking for a place to live, looking for space to stick the bookcases is high up among the top five concerns," Brunet told me. "And as a real estate agent, which is my day job, it's a very interesting thing: the nation really does split, based on my anecdotal experience. Walk into homes, and there are homes that have books and homes that don't. It's actually fairly rare that it's in between. Either people have books or they have none."

Brunet went on, "So that's one of the things we always had, lots of books. Somebody did a watercolor for my wife. I forget what you call it, it's one of those illustrations based around the letter A—my wife's first name is Ann. Anyway, it is of a young woman sitting in a window seat reading, which in many ways captures my wife."

One evening after writing class, Ann and Jim were walking on the UCLA campus, and the love light was lit when Jim referred to T. H. White's *The Sword in the Stone.* "For some reason, I remembered the line about the gods saving the king and dragon, long may his reign drag on, and she knew it too, and I was just stunned that anybody else had known that. We shared these cultural reference points. It was one of those times when she first said, 'Uh-oh, this is somebody I could see myself marrying.' "

––––––

When Gillian was seven or eight years old, she first became aware of class distinctions in the apartment complex where the Brunets lived. Although all the families were then situated in similar economic circumstances, Gillian realized that she and her parents were different and that those differences seemed rooted in literacy.

There were, of course, the fourteen bookcases. Other families may have had books, but Gillian noticed that her parents actually read them. Watching TV was not important, and the rule in the house was that Gillian could not watch TV until her homework was done. Ann read to Gillian every night until the child was in fourth or fifth grade.

"From the time I was very small, my parents really felt reading and books were always important," Gillian said. "I know that even among my peers, that was not that common. I have always been an obsessive-compulsive reader, which most people aren't, and a lot of that was given to me by my family." She continued, "Literacy definitely made me feel separated."

When the family did watch television, Gillian realized that they watched different TV shows than other families did. "My parents didn't usually watch TV shows until after I went to bed," Gillian said. "They did watch sports and things, and everyone else did that too, and they would watch the news, but the TV was not on as often in our house. We never had the TV on during dinner, and a lot of other families did.

"When I was younger, we were probably a social class lower [than we are now], and we lived in a very middle-class area with a lot of apartment buildings. But because my parents were so literate, it always felt weird going into the other kids' houses. Class is mostly defined economically, but it is also a school of thought, and there are certain expectations. It is generally formed by economics but is not simply economic. It always felt weird, and it wasn't something that I could ask anybody about. It was just something I figured out as I got older."

She also realized that her parents' social circle reached beyond the apartment complex to include other well-read people like themselves. "My parents really did have a wider circle of friends than other people's parents that I knew," Gillian told me. "There was definitely a realization that this is our socioeconomic group, this is what we can afford, this is the level of restaurant that we go out to. It is something you are not even aware of as a small child, but it is there."

Indeed, as a Santa Monica real estate agent with close ties to UCLA, Jim Brunet figures that as much as a third of his business stems from referrals to UCLA professors and administrators looking for new homes. "I tend to do my most comfortable work with other educated people," Brunet told me. "Pretty much everybody we know and friends we socialize with have gone to college, and they have intellectually oriented jobs and careers, like professors and writers."

Having well-educated parents meant a richly literate way of life for Gillian. As the only child, Gillian went with her parents to places where children didn't normally go. Jim Brunet recalled Gillian, at age ten, being the youngest person in the audience of a Shakespeare play at the summer festival in Ashland, Oregon. Brunet described one play in particular. "I didn't know if she was tracking, and I looked over, and there were tears just rolling down her cheeks. She got it, she was engaged, she understood exactly what was happening."

Throughout Gillian's childhood, the Brunets subscribed to both the *Los Angeles Times* and the *New York Times*, and they made an effort to discuss articles with Gillian that might interest her. "While she might not always invest the time to religiously read something, the discussion was in the air around her," Brunet said.

Then there was ballet, which Gillian performed throughout her childhood. She had considered dance to be her calling since age two, when she saw her first *Nutcracker*. As her father, a baseball aficionado, put it, she became good enough to be the equivalent of a solid Double A ballplayer. Indeed, ballet would become an important consideration in Gillian's eventual choice of college.

"The whole ballet side of things is funny to me," Jim Brunet said. "I was never a jock or that sort of thing. But, I mean, I could still give you the starting lineup of the 1969 Chicago Cubs," which he then proceeded to do. "When my daughter started doing ballet, I didn't know a plié from a pipe wrench."

———

But Brunet did know his way around the Santa Monica school system. As the parent with the most flexible working hours, Brunet took on the role that many mothers in affluent households play, staying on top of the details of Gillian's school life to ensure that she took maximum advantage of opportunities in school.

Brunet understood that Gillian's transition to middle school would be critical, a realization that was reinforced by other sources of family cultural capital, particularly Gillian's aunt. As the chief financial officer at Seattle's Lakeside School—the private Seattle prep school from which Bill Gates graduated—Aunt Sylvia impressed on the Brunets the importance of Gillian getting on the accelerated track in middle school, to position her for the high school path that would lead to selective colleges.

Even before Gillian was in elementary school, Brunet began assessing her middle-school options. The family had considered sending her to a magnet middle school for gifted children in the Los Angeles district. But Brunet was keen on Lincoln Middle School in the Santa Monica district. Compared to the magnificent facilities and teaching staff at Lincoln, even the LA gifted program fell short, in Brunet's considered view. Hence, Brunet chose Gillian's elementary school, McKinley, in large part because it was among the three elementary schools that fed into Lincoln.

"I asked for McKinley because I had visited it and was comfortable," Brunet explained. "It was very diverse. My wife has a better eye than I did; she knows, for instance, that the kids weren't ethnically clumped on the playground when we visited. It was very integrated. I had scoped out the situation. Part of being a real estate agent is meeting people and talking about schools, like, 'Oh, you have kids. Where do they go to school? What is your experience there? How do you like it?' "

He went on, "So I had sort of built up this mental database about Lincoln Middle School. It was like a California Distinguished School, National Blue Ribbon School, yada, yada, yada—awards out the wazoo—and I really wanted to make sure she went to Lincoln. I mean, this was my thinking when she was four years old. I wanted her to go to Lincoln Middle School in terms of preparation for high school. So to that extent I can sometimes put the 'a' in anal-retentive."

The Brunets were not disappointed in Lincoln, which proved to be academically a good choice for Gillian, setting her up, Brunet said, "for a really good run at high school." Still, there were times when he had to intervene on Gillian's behalf.

For example, the school assigned students to one of three "cores" per grade level, clumping together their math, English, and science sequence around a core group of teachers. Brunet lobbied hard for Gillian to be assigned to the "Bronze Core."

"By all accounts, in talking to students or parents that had been there before, the Bronze Core was significantly better," Brunet said. "I mean, they always tried to balance the kids; it wasn't a case that 'one core was for dumb kids and one core was for smart kids' kind of thing. I was just looking for where the teachers were. I wasn't trying to make a major pain in the ass of myself, but it's sort of like you're on the sidelines and the ball comes rolling along, and you reach out and kick it in the direction you want it to go. So I did that."

There were various important milestones on Gillian's path to Smith, much like the father-daughter talk in first grade. Another important event came during the spring of her eighth grade year at Lincoln, when Brunet sat down with Gillian to literally map out her entire curriculum plan for her four years at Santa Monica High. And, because Ann had worked at UCLA, Brunet says he was intimately aware of the course requirements for admission to the University of California system, and those requirements served as the baseline for Gillian's four-year plan.

"We sort of sat down, Gillian and I—I don't know what Ann was doing, but I think she was probably present for most of the discussions—and we talked about what's available in high school and sort of blocked out most of her four-year schedule," Brunet said. "We knew she would take AP language, figured the math sequence, figured the history sequence. . . . In terms of college, I said, 'You need the four years of English, the four years of math; you will be going into honors geometry, and so the sequence from there is this,' and so on. We mapped it all out for her."

There would be as little as possible left to chance or logistical oversight. As I listened to Brunet describe the details of the family's plans for Gillian's high school career, I couldn't help but be impressed by their store of cultural capital—their knowledge, information, social networks, and, perhaps most important, their commitment of time that allowed them to be fully engaged in Gillian's school life, a commitment afforded by a sufficient degree of economic comfort. And I couldn't help but compare the Brunets' surplus of cultural capital to the scant resources available to Ashlea. I recalled our conversation with Gary Jackson, who had not been familiar with the term "GPA."

Listen to Brunet. His knowledge of what it takes to get his daughter into college is of a different order altogether.

"Part of it is our own experience having gone to college ourselves. Part of it also is that Ann works at UCLA. She doesn't work in admissions, but working in external relations she has to be familiar with what UC requirements are—three years of math, four preferred; the language thing. By our design, Gillian took two years of Latin, freshman and sophomore year, and three years of French beginning sophomore year, so sophomore year she doubled up on language. She is glad she did it. She is taking Latin now at college and plans to take intermediate French.

"A lot of colleges say they want four years of the same foreign language, and she did three and two, so she actually has an extra year of language, but it wasn't the same one. I still think she did the right thing; it's what she wanted to do, but it nags me that it hurt in terms of her admissions profile. And the response in my internal voice was, 'Look, she's at Smith, she's having a great time, let it go.' But the questions are there."

Brunet continued, "Taking the three years and two years of language was mapped out for her in eighth grade. We said, there are six slots a day, seven if you go for the optional A.M. period. Now you will be in band, and there really aren't that many elective choices. There was not an AP bio class that she could get into. By the time senior year came around, she had too many singletons classes and doubletons classes, where there were only one or two sections offered. Two sections of French 3, only one of band, only one of orchestra, only two of calculus. So putting together a schedule just became problematic, and she could not get the AP bio in there. That and a one-semester art elective were probably the only deviations from what we laid out as a team in eighth grade."

––––––

"I remember sometimes I wanted to kill him," Gillian told me, recalling the occasions, beginning in middle school, when her father would bring his *Barron's Guide* to family dinner outings in order to launch Gillian's college search. They would eventually develop a list of some sixty-nine colleges and universities, to be pared down over the next few years.

"There was no question of if I would go; it was where I would go," Gillian recalled. "My dad would help me with the process. He would go buy books. He would read a lot of the books on financial aid and stuff. I remember my best friend: her parents made her apply to a lot of public universities, and she really could have gone to a much better place. She ended up going to a private school, but it wasn't as good as a lot of the private schools that she could have gone to. Her parents didn't realize for a long time that she could get better aid at a better private school. My dad definitely knew that.

"We had all of those college guides. I did my share of the reading on stuff, but my dad would do a lot of the background research because I had so little time with all of my homework, et cetera. We would go out to dinner, and he would drag the big college book along. While we were waiting for the food, he would want me to read through stuff."

The engineer in Brunet thus began to transform the information he gleaned from the college guides and Web sites into a computer spreadsheet, in which he entered the SAT scores of a college's admitted class, tuition costs, financial aid information, and so on. When Gillian was in ninth grade, the Brunets took her on her first college visit. Seeing an opportunity when the family was vacationing in the Midwest, Brunet made a side trip to Northwestern, near Evanston, where he had spent his high school years.

"On the tour, they asked for a show of hands, and it was, as you expect, mainly high school seniors, maybe a few juniors," Brunet said. "She was the only freshman. She felt awkward, she felt a little bit dragged along, but this was one of those cases where we were exercising parental rights, so just go along with the program." Several more college visits would follow. By the end of the eleventh grade, she'd visited at least ten other colleges and universities, all private, on the East Coast.

Why and how were Gillian's aspirations seemingly unlimited compared, say, to Ashlea's? In Ashlea's case, her aspirations, if not her opportunities, were confined to Boise, Idaho, and, if she got lucky, perhaps a private two-year college in Wyoming.

Considerable differences in family economic circumstances, of course, explain much of the gap between Gillian and Ashlea. But there is more to it. Pierre Bourdieu captured this sense of "more" with a concept he called *habitus*. McDonough explains one's habitus as "a deeply internalized, permanent system of outlooks, experiences, and beliefs about the social world that an individual gets from his or her immediate environment. . . . Habitus is a common set of subjective perceptions held by all members of the same group or class that shapes an individual's expectations, attitudes, and aspirations."

She continues, "Those aspirations are both subjective assessments of the chances for mobility and objective probabilities. They are not rational analyses, but rather are the ways that children from different classes make sensible or reasonable choices for their own aspirations. They do so by looking at the people who surround them and observing what is considered good or appropriate across a variety of dimensions. . . . Students believe that they are entitled to a particular kind of collegiate education based on their family's habitus or class status."[14]

McDonough's interpretation of Bourdieu has the benefit of clarity, though she may overstate the permanence of one's habitus. Rather than considering it a fixed and predetermined reflection of one's social and economic conditions, Bourdieu would argue that habitus is a "system of enduring dispositions" in one's social identity.[15] The notion of habitus was the linchpin of Bourdieu's project to explain how vastly unequal social and economic conditions, particularly in advanced democracies, reproduce themselves generation after generation. In the realm of education, the disadvantaged "know their place," as it were, often failing to recognize that seemingly universal evaluation and selection methods (such as the IQ tests required for entrance to prestigious preschools or the admissions tests for elite universities) are rooted in the struggle for power, serving to legitimate the reproduction of the social order.

"Habitus thus refers to the way in which an individual's instinctive sense of what might be achieved is structured into a pattern of behaviour, forming, in Bourdieu's own words, 'an acquired system of generative schemes objectively adjusted to the particular conditions in which it is constituted,' " writes Jim Wolfreys. "The modes of behaviour, or dispositions, produced by the habitus are passed on through the generations, inculcated from an early age and socially reinforced through education and culture."[16]

———

Gillian's being "entitled" to attend a good college on the East Coast was not how Jim Brunet accounted for her decision to confine her college search to private and elite colleges and universities. Rather, Gillian's opportunity horizon was established early in the college search process, Brunet told me, with the posting of her PSAT scores in high school.

Her first try on the SAT produced a score of 1400 (on the old version of the exam)—a very good score, but not one that would allow her to play in the "big leagues," as Jim Brunet put it. The family hired a private SAT tutor for Gillian because her ballet classes conflicted with the test prep firm's scheduled sessions. With more test-taking experience and the training she got from her tutor, Gillian managed to raise her composite SAT score to 1580, a score that would surely put her in the game for elite college admissions.

Brunet, who told me he had a dim view of the SAT as a measure of academic merit, justified the extra attention the family paid to Gillian's SAT preparation this way: "Gillian needed to work mainly on test-taking mentality. Sort of like, you don't have to work the problem to get the answer," he explained. "It's a test that really doesn't measure anything other than how well you take the test. So teaching Gillian to basically be aggressive and to make informed guesses or to be able to exclude answers quickly and really concentrate on the others was probably the biggest thing. I have a very—well, moderate—dose of hypocrisy about this. I actually don't approve of test prep, but it's an arms race kind of thing: if you don't do it, you're at a disadvantage. So we went along, and we went with the flow."

Indeed, among Gillian's peers at Santa Monica High, receiving such private tutoring from sources outside school was commonplace—not simply for the SAT but for many academic classes, particularly the more challenging Advanced Placement classes. The extra tutoring expense for the SAT paid off. "She had been looking for around a 1530 to 1540," Jim Brunet explained. "That seemed to be the severe drop-off point for a lot of the top schools. Even though she probably would have gotten into Smith, Wellesley, and Barnard anyway, the test scores helped her get some fairly nice scholarships and stuff at Smith, so it wound up being worth it."[17]

After arriving at Smith, Gillian's opportunity horizon grew even wider, becoming international in scope. She decided to major in the unusual combination of government and math and was relishing the fact that her classes were taught by professors, not the graduate assistants she would have found at large research universities, even at the best of the Ivys. She was taking a political theory course taught by the department chair. Her classes were small, with never more than twenty students in each. What's more, she got the chance to work on a research project for the chair of the computer science department. She was narrowing her choices for a semester studying abroad; an intensive mathematics rotation in Budapest was at the top of the list. Another semester in D.C. working at CNN was also an intriguing possibility.

"She's looking at all sorts of different options for junior year abroad," Jim Brunet explained. "I think she's trying to figure out how she can do a semester in Washington for political science and a semester either in Budapest for math or in Oxford for government. Apparently, Budapest is the place to go for math. It's the traveling to Vienna and Prague that kind of opened her eyes up just a little bit and gave reality to what Europe was like, and in some ways gave her a taste for more."

He recalled the moment when the years of family preparation and planning for Gillian's academic future led her to an important, emotional realization. "She had been turned down at Stanford, Harvard, and Yale. Her hopes came down to Wellesley, Smith, and Barnard. We flew into Boston to revisit Smith, and when we were listening to a presentation by students about internships abroad, this one student was telling about her experience as an intern in the political unit at CNN, and Gillian was just enraptured," Brunet told me. "I could see that on her face, and I said, 'You're going to go here, aren't you, honey?' And she just nodded. She couldn't even speak. That idea of, 'Wow, an internship at CNN.' It sort of gave her like a crystal idea: 'Yeah, I can see myself doing all that. I'd like to do that kind of thing.' "

———

Gary Jackson's face still lights up at any mention of his only daughter. His hopes for Ashlea are large, but he articulates them only as that—hopes.

"Ashlea—she's my Ashlea. She's my girl, she's pretty smart, she's working hard, and she's, you know, different than my boys," Jackson said. "My boys just aren't—they're not trying, I don't know, they're not trying to excel. But Ashlea is. Ashlea is going to be my key," Jackson said to me.

"Be your what?" I asked.

"She's like a key, you know, she's going to be the first one of our family that goes to college. I'm really proud of her. When she goes to college, I'm going to miss her."

A few months later, Kathleen and I were talking to Ashlea about her college plans. She had come to dinner at our house. We were standing in the kitchen, and she couldn't wait to tell us her big news. Part of it was that she had recently taken the ACT college entrance exam and thought that she'd done pretty well on the math part. But something even more thrilling had happened.

For years, the Boys and Girls Club in Garden City had been a reliable source of summer activities for the Garden City kids, and when she got to high school, Ashlea became a volunteer for the group. She loved working with the kids and felt as passionately about helping them as she did about journalism. After all, she had been one of those kids. And now the Boys and Girls Club had just informed her that she would be the recipient of a $1,000 college scholarship.

With such good news, Ashlea's getting to college somewhere was becoming a more realistic possibility. Then she said something that made clear just how much more work there was to do. Ashlea said she might start out at Boise State University near home and then transfer to the two-year college in Wyoming for its journalism program. Kathleen corrected her, explaining how the transfer system worked: Ashlea would have to start out at the two-year college and *then* transfer to the university.

Nobody had ever told her otherwise.

———

Several months went by, and through Kathleen, I heard nothing but good news about Ashlea, and I thought that the young woman just might pull off her goal of not ending up like her brothers. She'd been excited about heading into her senior year, working as the news editor on the paper and planning for college. She was also looking forward to summer school and the chance to retake biology, learn a lot, and perhaps get a better grade.

Then one day in July, Kathleen got a call from Ashlea. She was frantic and crying. The days had turned brutally hot in Boise, and Ashlea was alone at home in the family's small apartment without air conditioning. The power company had shut off the electricity because of unpaid bills.

Two nights previously, Gary Jackson had been riding his bicycle home late at night and was pulled over by the police because he didn't have a rear reflector. Apparently, the officers found an outstanding warrant concerning some unpaid fines that were owed by his minor son, and Jackson was taken to county jail. He wouldn't get out for ten days or so, which meant that he would be unable to pick up his last paycheck and use it to pay the power bill. Ashlea's mother, still recovering from breast cancer, went to stay with a friend, leaving Ashlea to fend for herself.

Not knowing where she would sleep from night to night, Ashlea gave up on summer biology.

The latest crisis made me realize just how precarious Ashlea's hopes for college remained, despite Kathleen's occasional help and the modest scholarship fund we set up for her. With just a few untimely events at home, the Jackson family could come apart. What would happen if Gary's supervisors at work were not understanding about his legal predicament? What would happen to the family if he was fired from the job that had provided so much stability over the past few years? They'd been homeless before, and being homeless again just as Ashlea was entering her senior year could prove devastating for her. The possibility that she might have to drop out of school to earn money loomed larger than I dared think.

A week later, the unthinkable did happen. When Gary Jackson got out of jail, his steady job at the convention center was gone. His employer said he'd missed too much work. For the time being, however, the family still had a roof over their heads.

I was worried for Ashlea that summer before her senior year. I wondered how, with so much to think about at home, she could possibly cope with the details of financial aid and college applications—the sorts of details that kids like Gillian took for granted that dads like Jim would handle.

In fact, Kathleen discovered that summer that Ashlea had forgotten to follow up with an appointment to learn about test preparation for the SAT. It was then that Kathleen realized that someone in Ashlea's life needed to become far more proactive about her college planning. Her school counselors were of limited use. There was nobody else.

So Kathleen asked Ashlea, "How would you feel if you and I sat down with our calendars this fall and planned out every detail, every deadline you need to meet this year? How would you feel if I bugged you until you got it done?"

"Oh, that would be wonderful," Ashlea said.

Later, the three of us were again in our kitchen, the day after Ashlea found out about her dad going to jail. We had invited her over for dinner to keep her company, to get her out of her hot apartment, and to try to cheer her up. Ashlea's eyes brightened when she and Kathleen started telling me about their plan of action for the fall. No detail within their control would be left to chance. Those things that were beyond young Ashlea's control—well, we could only hope for the best.

————

The stories of Ashlea and Gillian illustrate the profound effect of family social class on the ability of children to succeed in school and on the futures that children envision for themselves. But, as we shall see in the following chapter, the influence of families on children's academic success doesn't stop at home. That influence goes deep into the belly of the American school system, as affluent and politically powerful families wield inordinate influence on the way that schools function.

TWO

"DO WE LOOK INTIMIDATING?"

Where family ends and school begins for families like Becky Parkinson's is a blurry line indeed. Not only do affluent families provide their children with the cultural and financial resources that enable them to succeed in school, but these same families also assert political influence over teachers, principals, and school affairs to a degree that helps to ensure that success.

Parkinson, a parent of three children, has a full-time job at Highlands Elementary. That, of course, is hardly unusual. Even the job itself, teaching math and science and leading novel-reading groups for schoolchildren, isn't uncommon.

But what is noteworthy about Becky Parkinson's job is that she does these things almost forty hours a week as a *volunteer* at her children's school. And at Highlands, located in the wealthy neighborhoods that nestle in the foothills across from the Crane Creek Country Club in Boise, Idaho, and known as the "private public school," Parkinson isn't alone. Other parents too work as full-time volunteers and view their activities with utmost seriousness.

"I consider it my job," Parkinson told me. "I view this as a commitment. When I sign up that I'll show up for math at ten-thirty every day, I show up for math at ten-thirty every day. I take it very seriously. If you need me to help with that group, I will be there to help. I don't not show up. I'm panicked if I can't make it for some reason."[1]

It's a job that Parkinson first learned in Palo Alto, California, where her husband's work as a corporate executive took the family. He had grown up in the small town of Blackfoot, Idaho, and attended college at Columbia University.

"What preschool are you at?"

That was the first question other mothers in Palo Alto would ask Becky Parkinson when they met her.

The child of a university professor, she had always been good at math and science. (Her own career path had led her, however, into banking before she married and had children.) Parkinson says she's an information junkie who sees herself first and foremost as a researcher—no matter the topic. "That's just what I do," she told me.

Parkinson applied her research skills to finding the right preschool for her eldest son, Gary. From the circle of parents she knew, Parkinson learned that the Stanford University preschool was preferred but that the waiting list was long. She kept looking and researching and discovered a small, cooperative preschool near their neighborhood. She felt at ease with the school's noncompetitive atmosphere, especially compared to other schools in the area. She became intimately involved as a parent volunteer, an experience that taught her several lessons about the nature of schools and families and the nexus between them.

"I chose it because it was small, and it was in our neighborhood, which seemed to make sense to me, and I could go there and help, because I was not actually willing to let go of my children yet," Parkinson told me. "I didn't want them to go to school at all. But I was feeling so weird not having them in a school."

Gary started school just before he turned five. Because her younger child would tag along with him, the school simply admitted them both. Parkinson tagged along as well, launching her new career as a school volunteer. "I could go whenever I wanted. I helped in the classroom, and that's when I decided the schools per se don't matter so much as the philosophy of the program—the philosophy of the teachers and parental involvement.

"My kids began to accept that I would be involved. I loved being involved. I loved seeing who their friends were. I loved seeing how they interacted, where the shortcomings were. I could see them in that environment. If I just sent them off, I would have no idea. And so that cooperative preschool kind of dictated from that point forward what schools I would choose for my kids. It had to be a school that I could be involved in."

———

I would occasionally run into Becky Parkinson at a local Starbucks. She apparently had a running date with Gary, who was then twelve. After saying hello and going back to my work, I would glance up and see the mother and son simply talking quietly over their mochas and hot chocolates.

Watching them interact, I thought about what Parkinson had told me in an earlier conversation about her evolving philosophy toward schools and education, starting with her own childhood growing up as a professor's daughter.

Socially, school had been hard for Parkinson, who was a thoughtful and reserved child. She attended public schools in Caldwell, Idaho, the home of what was then called the College of Idaho, where her dad taught physics. They had also lived in New York when her father was working on his PhD at Columbia. Whether Becky would go to college someday wasn't something her father or mother discussed or pushed on the girls. They didn't need to.

"I remember we just grew up at the college," Parkinson recalled. "I mean, we'd walk up there and hang out at the lab with our father. We hung out there after school sometimes. That's just where we were comfortable. We only lived three blocks from the school, so that's where we went. Pounded on his window and waved at him in the lab.

"We were definitely around education, but my parents did not push education. When I was a junior in high school, I was thinking about where I wanted to go to college, so I started writing down all these schools, and my mom said, 'Oh, are you going to college?' I was like, well, 'Absolutely.' She said, 'Well, I didn't want to assume.' That's how my parents were. Because my dad was an academic, he did not want to push that on us, so they actually were almost the opposite. I think they had an assumption that we would go, but refused to pressure us."

Parkinson's parents instilled in her a quiet confidence in her dealings with the world. Her school life couldn't take that away. She felt isolated from her peers and would often just watch, studying the social norms of school culture. Oddly, she thought a lot about social class and status.

"I was very shy and considered smart, so I wasn't really cool. And so I spent a lot of time dwelling on the whole class system thing," Parkinson said. "I sat in class bored and was intrigued by the way people behaved, which is what really led to my major in psychology. I was very introverted, very shy, and very reflective. At the time, I thought everybody was. I watched how people behaved and why one person was popular and others weren't, and whether it was money or whether it was something else that I didn't have."

I asked Parkinson what she came to believe after watching life at school.

"I concluded that I didn't fit in. I concluded that it was confidence, self-confidence, that caused somebody to achieve more in school. I would just watch these kids be cruel to each other, tease each other, put each other down, and then at some point realize, 'Okay, I don't want to do what it takes to be popular.' You're not respected necessarily for being smart—you're teased. You're not necessarily accepted for much of anything except the things I didn't really have. But I did become aware of that early on and [became] just kind of reconciled to it and thought, 'I'll wait till I get to college. Then I'll have fun.' "

And, more or less, it worked out exactly that way. She wound up going to the College of Idaho, where her dad taught physics, and she studied psychology. The college wasn't her first choice, but the family's economic situation at the time made the decision for her. Still, she managed to make it into a fresh and educationally exciting time.

"It was a great experience. I even think it was somewhat of a benefit to see my dad on campus. But I didn't feel like my parents were there hovering over me. I didn't feel oppressed by their presence. So it was just a regular college experience, right in my hometown. And it was completely different from my high school experience, which I hated."

———

And so I was thinking about what Parkinson had told me about growing up and going to school when I would see her talking to her oldest son in Starbucks, and I realized that she was doing for her children exactly what her parents had done for her—quietly talking to her child, slowly building up his confidence in himself and his relationships to the bigger world. I could hear echoes of her own childhood and her relationship with school.

I recalled a story she had told me about how Gary had been interested in astronomy from a very young age, an interest that Parkinson fed without hesitation when making weekly visits to Barnes and Noble with her son.

"My oldest is a very inquisitive child and was from the get-go, so when he wanted to learn about astronomy at age three, we started learning about astronomy. People at the bookstore would say he wouldn't understand it, but I got the book anyway. Then he wanted a college-level astronomy book at four years old, and I got it for him. And he just would look at the pictures and read the captions. That's been my belief all along: if they show an interest, you have to feed the interest. I think my parents did that without trying to do it. They tried to downplay the whole thing, but, really, just being in that environment, we had discussions, we talked about things, and that's what I wanted to give my kids.

"I am an information addict, and if I don't know something, I'm looking it up. I'm compulsive. My oldest is at least as compulsive as I am. And that's just what we do. That's how our house is. If we don't understand something, we get out the book. Every week we go to the bookstore and pick out books. So that's been my personal philosophy, that you don't need to wait until you're an adult to learn and to appreciate learning. That's what I've tried to instill in them."

While Parkinson's parents never pushed—and, to hear Parkinson tell it, were even quite passive in directing her educational path—she had clearly decided to exert significantly more influence over her children's school life. From the choice of schools down to the individual teachers, Parkinson exercised her influence whenever possible. Recalling her own less happy moments in school, she came to believe that reproducing in her children an orientation toward the future would make the day-to-day challenges of school seem less daunting.

"When you hit adolescence and you have no idea what the future holds, you get stuck. You're living day to day, and it doesn't seem all that rewarding. It doesn't seem that grand. I had this great anticipation about adolescence, and it was like, horrible—not only not good, it was horrible.

"So I thought that if my kids had something that they're seeing further in the future, then whatever they're going through now is just a part of the course, not the end-all and be-all. I don't know that I have any grand aspirations for them, but I think they'll do wonderful things. I believe they will, and that's just because it's always bigger, it's always greater, as you go on. That's what I want them to understand. And I think they do. They do very well in school, and all I need are teachers that don't mess with that."

———

Given the wealth of cultural and economic capital that Parkinson and her husband are able to give to their children, quite independently of schools and far more than any school would be capable of providing, Parkinson had but one basic requirement of any school: that it not interfere with the transmission of that human capital from parent to child.

"I want a school that doesn't interfere with my children's learning, that won't interfere with their natural curiosity," Parkinson explained. "I think children naturally want to learn. I think they are naturally inquisitive, and if it's not handled properly, you actually kill the desire to learn."

In order to ensure that her children's interests are protected and promoted at their schools, to make sure that the schools and teachers "don't mess" with her kids' desire to learn, Parkinson became a full-time volunteer at Highlands, where she also coordinates the other parent volunteers. As the volunteer coordinator, Parkinson tallies the hours that parents like her devote to Highlands. She said that there are at least ten parents who work daily at the school, putting in about the same hours as she does. Some five other parents work a bit less but are at the school "a lot," she said. All told, the school is endowed with 1,300 to 2,000 volunteer-hours each month from the "staff" of parent volunteers, averaging about 20,000 hours per year in total. Even that is an underestimate, Parkinson noted, because parents often forget to turn in the hours that they work at home preparing for their class time.

Parkinson described her typical work week at Highlands. Much of her job revolves around math and science, aligning with her own interests as well as with the academic strengths of her children. It also lines up with the school district's new emphasis on science teaching at the elementary level, despite insufficient resources.

And that's where parents like Parkinson come in. At this "private public school," parents are generally a very highly educated bunch. In the year 2000, 60 percent of the adults in the neighborhoods around Highlands had bachelor's degrees or higher, and about a third had graduate or professional degrees. By comparison, only 22 percent of adults in Boise had bachelor's degrees, while fewer than 10 percent had graduate or professional degrees. Almost 60 percent of Highlands-area adults were in management and professional occupations, and the median family income for Highlands neighborhoods in 2000 was more than $92,000—almost twice that for the city of Boise.[2]

Mondays are Parkinson's "day off" from the classroom, so she spends the time preparing science kits for her seven-year-old's first grade class. As part of the district's effort to emphasize science, teachers are provided with science kits intended to help the students learn science by doing it experientially. But using the commercially provided kits requires time and lots of out-of-class preparation in order to set up the science projects and experiments. And because the district's teachers often don't have time to properly use the science kits, the unpaid but generally skilled parents like Parkinson pick up the slack.

In truth, Parkinson said, she actually "delivers curriculum," as would a fully certified teacher—a fact not widely known and one that, she told me, runs contrary to the school district's policy. Delivering curriculum— teaching—falls within the domain of state-certified teachers, much as writing prescriptions is a physician's legal prerogative. But with so much skilled volunteer help readily available to fill in the teaching gaps at affluent schools like Highlands, the policy is apparently rarely enforced.

"Science is a big deal at these schools," explained Parkinson. "The school has science kits, and parents are not supposed to deliver curriculum, but the teachers don't actually use the kits because they're so cumbersome. . . . So a lot of the time the teachers just don't do them, and they just try to teach science the way that we used to learn it. By the book, or a lesson here and there."

Outside of class, preparation time alone required Parkinson to spend three hours a week or more on the science kits. Eventually, helping teachers with the preparation evolved into actually teaching the kits as well. Parkinson told me, "They've tried to get parents to do the prep. And that's how I started out. I was coming in and saying, 'Okay, I'll do the kit inventory, and I'll do the prep every week, and I'll get it set up so the lesson's ready to teach.'

"I actually ended up loving it. And so now that's what I do for my first grader. Only now, I'm doing both first grade classes, so I have forty-some kids. But I love it. . . . I can do it in detail. Part of their objective was to study motion—lifting, pushing, pulling—and so I did a unit on Newton's Laws of Motion, and first graders were 'getting' inertia. . . . I get hold of these science kits, and I'm off exploring what we can do."

When Parkinson told me this, I was startled at the scope of her teaching responsibilities as a parent volunteer. At least in terms of delivering science curriculum, I told her, "You do more than the teachers."

"And that's why they want me doing it," she answered. "But, like I said, we're not actually supposed to be doing that."

On Tuesday afternoons, Parkinson teaches her two science classes, and she occasionally goes to school on Tuesday mornings to help out in other classes as needed. On Wednesdays, she works in the school's gifted and talented program, which her two eldest children at Highlands attend. On Thursdays, Parkinson spends the entire day in her eldest son's gifted class, leading the novel-reading groups and coaching the students for upcoming math Olympiad competitions. Fridays she spends drilling the first graders on spelling and conducting social studies lessons in the school's computer labs.

Because parent involvement in the daily affairs of the school is so intense, parents carry a great deal of political clout in the school district. Occasionally, the politics highlight divisions between the haves and the have-mores, for there are few poor children at Highlands. In fact, only 2 of the 215 students enrolled at Highlands when I visited in 2005 were eligible for free or reduced-price lunches.[3] That compared to almost 50 of every 100 kids in the Boise school district who were eligible for the lunch program.[4]

When Parkinson and I spoke, Highlands was in the middle of a push by some of the parents to add a full-time school for gifted children, staffed with its own teachers and operating within the same building. At Highlands, one of every ten kids was designated as "gifted" according to standardized test results—twice the district average. Some 95 percent of Highlands' first graders started school already reading at grade level (compared to 75 percent for the entire city).[5] The battle lines over the gifted school were drawn between parents who wanted the school for their own children and those who believed that pulling out only some of the children for the new school would make those not classified as gifted—who were high achievers nevertheless—feel inferior. Animosities intensified when parents supporting the gifted school organized closed-door meetings about the school, shutting out parents who were opposed to it.

When I spoke to Highlands' recently hired principal, Sally Skinner, about the controversy, she seemed intimidated by the parents' political power, apparently unable to speak a word that might offend either side. "I mean, I am really and truly taking it one step at a time here," she said, choosing her words with care. "I don't want it to be a divisive issue. I don't want [gifted] kids to feel like they are getting something unfair for them, but I also don't want [nongifted] kids to feel like they are not as special, so it's a challenge."[6]

Parkinson knew well the reputation of the highly involved parents at Highlands. She explained, "We are right across from Crane Creek Country Club. Because the people who don't live in that neighborhood associate the school with Crane Creek, they think that it's an extension of the whole country club theme. And then we have all these parents with all this time, and they volunteer all their time, and they donate money, so we have the reputation of being the country club school. I mean, that's the reputation.

"All the parents want to be involved. It's what I was saying about the Palo Alto schools. There are a lot of very brilliant people down there. Smart, and they expect their children to do well in school. They volunteer a lot to make sure that happens. And that's the same thing here. These people have got some time, and they want to make sure that the best thing is happening for their kids. You want to have your finger on the pulse."

At one point during the brouhaha over the gifted school, Parkinson spoke privately with the district superintendent, Stan Olson. "You've got a difficult group of parents at that school," Olson told her.

"I stand there and say, 'Really?' Of course, I know that that's the reputation. He said, 'I mean, you can be an intimidating group.' I said, 'Do we look intimidating? Give me a break.' "

In truth, schools need more parents like Becky Parkinson, because they, more than any federal laws about leaving no child behind, are what hold public schools accountable for excellence. But when schools like Whittier Elementary, where Ashlea Jackson attended school across town, are judged by the same criteria as schools like Highlands, it's patently unfair to the disadvantaged children whose parents are struggling just to make ends meet. In such cases, the public must intervene with sufficient resources to balance the scales.

In the case of Becky Parkinson and Highlands Elementary, the accumulated cultural, economic, and social capital of the affluent families in the neighborhoods around the school translates into intensive parental involvement in the school's affairs, so much so that the nominally public space that was Highlands has become an extension of the private interests of the families themselves. The boundaries of school and family are blurred by the powerful influence of this "intimidating" group of parents.

But if a public school like Highlands amounts to a manifestation of private family capital, and if its supposed function of serving the general public has become subservient to the school's real purpose—the reproduction of the existing social and economic structures of Boise and environs—then how might the public sphere respond to even more powerful private interests, such as corporations, and the collection of powerful families who make up those enterprises?

Welcome to the Treasure Valley Math and Science Center.

———

It was a typical day in Angela Hemingway's biology class, where her students were in the beginning stages of work on new projects for a NASA-sponsored competition. In Hemingway's classroom at the Treasure Valley Math and Science Center (TVMSC), a public school in Boise, Idaho, the line between the laboratory work and the lessons she taught about biology was indistinguishable. Most traditional schools use textbooks and lectures, and maybe the students are lucky enough to have a laboratory experience thrown in. But here, in Hemingway's domain, all those elements blended into a whole that was constructed from the students' own interests, centered around the laboratory experience itself. From project to project, her students were intensively engaged in biology. Students built concepts and knowledge as they needed to know them in order to complete the projects—typically aimed at a math and science competition of some sort. Students used Hemingway's expert knowledge, her mini-lectures, and the textbooks as resources and tools for a larger purpose.

They also drew from the technology applications class of teacher Mike Wiedenfeld, who was in the room next door to Hemingway. Wiedenfeld and Hemingway were in constant communication, as were the center's other teachers, hand-picked for their teaching excellence from schools throughout the Boise area. At TVMSC, the teachers worked with students in grades seven through twelve who were widely regarded as the region's best and brightest in mathematics and science.

Hemingway's class was working in teams to design experiments for NASA's Hyper-G Competition for high school students, work that would span several months. Most of the experiments were intended to determine how various organisms respond to the hypergravity environment of space travel. One team wanted to investigate the effects of hypergravity on photosynthesis in algae; another wanted to look at the growth rate of vitamin-rich plants like spinach. Yet another chose to examine whether spiders spin stronger or weaker webs in hypergravity. The mood of the class was exciting, exploratory, and, as NASA engineers might say, mission-centered.

It's fun stuff. I found myself wanting to enroll in the Treasure Valley Math and Science Center and sign up for Hemingway's and Wiedenfeld's classes. It is the sort of school that Becky Parkinson wants for her own children, one that meets her first requirement of a good school: that it not interfere with her children's natural love of learning. And that's why her son Gary leaves his home school at Highlands for several hours each day to attend TVMSC.

"He can't wait to go back. He loves the learning there, and he knows the difference" between the center's approach and that taken by traditional schools, Parkinson told me.

One day, Parkinson picked up Gary from the Center, which was housed at one of the junior high schools across town. Gary was excited about school, and he wanted to tell his mom about it.

"You know, Mom, the people are different at the math and science center."

"How do you mean?"

"Well, they talk different, think different."

"The teachers or the kids?"

"Both. It's just different."

Parkinson explained to me, "The kind of conversation [at the Center] is different, and it's at a different level than he would get at other schools. More than anything, the teachers are different. He's gotten a higher level of instruction there, which he appreciates a lot. But they've probably made him a little less tolerant of being bored."

————

The Treasure Valley Math and Science Center was a nearly new public school when I first visited there in late 2004. The school is operated by the Boise school district, but it is open to students from public and private schools from throughout the region.

Holly MacLean, the school's principal, had come to Boise from Texas, where she had, ironically, worked with low-achieving, at-risk students. In Texas, she had championed ideas from scholars in Australia and China who were leaders in the "math recovery" movement, which emphasized retooling students' "number sense" from the ground up.

Some two years prior to the launch of TVMSC, a couple of high school mathematics teachers had begun talking to district officials about the need to create more challenging classes for high-achieving students who, MacLean said, were breezing through even Advanced Placement courses. MacLean told me that when those students entered college, they often lacked the study skills and discipline to succeed in the more rigorous college environment. "If we don't properly challenge our higher-end kids with enough enrichment in their courses in high school prior to hitting college, we will not be doing them a proper service," MacLean said.[7]

The idea of a high-end school for math and science spread into the corporate community. The foundation arm of a locally based Fortune 500 company, Micron Technology Corporation, one of the world's leading manufacturers of computer memory chips, became interested, as did executives at the local Hewlett-Packard facility. In the case of Micron, that interest eventually led to a $1 million grant to the math and science center. HP supplied several hundred thousand dollars' worth of computers and equipment.

But Micron's million-dollar grant allowed it to call the shots. Micron already was among Boise's sacred cows, along with a number of other companies such as Albertsons, the giant grocery chain that had also been founded in Boise. Among Micron's early investors was none other than J. R. Simplot, the Idaho potato king whose freeze-dried french fries became a staple of McDonald's. Since Micron's founding in 1978, the Simplot family and other executives of Simplot companies had left their imprint all over Micron; many served lengthy terms on the company's board of directors.

"J. R." and the Simplot family were among the secular royalty of Boise. When I first came to Boise in 1996, I saw Simplot's family home, a modern, western mansion that stood atop a perfectly manicured hill of rich green grass, which rose perhaps 500 feet overlooking the neighborhoods near the Crane Creek Country Club and Highlands Elementary. This was no ordinary hill. The foothills of the larger mountains in the Boise National Forest begin at the city's northern boundary, and Simplot's property *was* one of these massive foothills. In its natural state, Simplot's hill would have been covered with sagebrush and inhabited by quail, gophers, and foxes. At the peak of the Simplot hill protruded a flagpole a few hundred feet high, topped with an enormous American flag the size of a house. Eventually, one became accustomed to this unusual sight, a constant of the Boise skyline that one could see from almost any point in the city. But when I first saw it, and heard who J. R. Simplot was, the scene struck me as undeniably feudal: Simplot with his giant house and flag on a giant hill of green grass, overlooking the subjects far below, a constant reminder of who was who and where one stood in the Boise nation.

As Micron grew, so did Boise, transforming itself from a relatively sleepy large town in the 1980s, known mainly as a pit stop on the way to Sun Valley, to a regional economic powerhouse by 2005. According to an economic analysis prepared in early 2005 for the company by ECONorthwest, a consulting firm in Portland, Oregon, Micron had become the largest private employer both in Boise and in the state of Idaho. The report, which was coincidentally completed amid intensifying debate over the wisdom of large corporate tax breaks for the state's largest employers, enumerated the various economic benefits the company brought to the region. It pointed out, for instance, that the company and its employees paid $95.7 million in taxes that supported local schools and other government entities, an amount that exceeded by $41.9 million the costs of providing services to Micron and its employees.[8]

And so, with the largesse of Boise's largest private employer, the city's public school system, joined by the public school systems in surrounding communities, created a math and science school that would, in the words of the center's design document, train future leaders. "The world in which we live is fast paced and ever changing. It is paramount that our school systems create individuals who can adapt and solve problems in a multitude of settings." The document went on: "The intellectual development of the leaders of the future must contain elements that allow for adaptive, independent thinking. The major purpose of a TVMSC is to educate tomorrow's leaders, not only in mathematics and science, but also in independent thinking, teamwork, problem solving abilities, and ethics."[9]

In a similar vein, the promoters of the school endeavored to shroud the need for the elite academy in the public interest, relying on a number of alarming national reports regarding the deficient performance of American schoolchildren in math and science. Furthermore, many metropolitan areas, with which Boise competed for employers and jobs, were already offering elite science schools. At stake, the school's backers argued, was nothing less than the future of the Boise area economy. "To compete, the Treasure Valley must be able to offer programs that match those seen in other thriving metropolitan areas."[10]

Indeed, it was the sort of public interest argument that sold well in most communities, whose ordinary citizens wanted the best for their children and the communities they lived in.

But as I continued my conversations with principal Holly MacLean, the picture began to change.

———

"How do people find out about this school?" I asked MacLean.

"A lot of it's word of mouth," she told me. "For instance, I had a phone call this morning from a parent who was just desperate. She said that her son is a seventh grader who is just so bored, and he's in an accelerated program and has high grades but just hates school because it's so boring and basically, she was begging me to bring him in. And I had to say that we have a waiting list of sixteen children for our seventh grade program, all who have the same type of story. And it breaks my heart to have to say it—and her son can be considered for our eighth grade cohort next year—but now we're full. We're over full."

"Of the people who do know about the school, do they tend to be from the upper economic strata?" I asked MacLean.

"This program first grew out of, in part, community interest and support," she answered. "People were interested in it because they were here with high-end positions themselves, and they wanted to make sure that educational opportunities would be available for their children. Many of these people had gone to Harvard, Yale, and Stanford, and they were here for community leadership–type roles."

"Who are you talking about?" I asked MacLean.

"Top people in the corporations in this community in the Treasure Valley," she replied. "And so early on they bought into helping to shape this program because they wanted something for their own children. At the same time, they wanted to make sure it was available for other children—but really what was driving it was that they wanted it for their children, most certainly."

"Are there any names you could tell me?" I asked MacLean.

"Nope, I wouldn't do that. But it's people from Micron and Boise Cascade and HP and top companies across the city."

Given the easily dismissed rhetoric about the public interest that MacLean could have served up, I was floored that she had made these admissions to me about the *real,* private power behind the school's origin and purpose. Beyond all the "Boise at risk" arguments and the need to develop math and science talent for the national good, this public school was intended for the children of Boise's growing elite.

It was all beginning to make sense. The Boise region was indeed expanding rapidly (surprisingly enough, without the help of TVMSC graduates), as more and more engineers, corporate executives, and other professionals left larger, more expensive cities across the country to settle in Boise with their families. For many years in the postwar era, ordinary public schools had served the city's middle- and working-class families well. At least in modern times, the city had seemed relatively untouched by social class divisions. There were a few enclaves of old money, but the vast majority of schools served the middle-income families working for government, technology firms, and the local state university. But in recent years, Boise had begun to present disturbing symptoms of segregation by social class. At the same time that *Forbes* magazine was touting the city as one of the best places in the nation for business, the numbers of poor children in the schools were reaching unprecedented levels.

In 1990, just 27 percent of the city's elementary schoolchildren qualified for the federal free lunch program. But by 2004, almost 44 percent qualified. In junior high schools, the number of students living in families whose incomes were at or below the poverty level increased from 24 percent in the early 1990s to 37 percent by 2004.[11] As the numbers of low-income students in Boise grew, it became more difficult for public schools to appeal to status-conscious parents, who measured good public schools by scores on standardized achievement tests. Parents in Boise, as elsewhere, continued to base their educational choices on school test scores and the real estate values to which they equated.

Never mind that several decades of research evidence showed that schools contributed only weakly to student achievement beyond the effects of the educational, economic, and cultural capital children acquired from families themselves. For Boise's growing numbers of affluent families, who sought high-status schools filled with high-status children, the options were becoming limited at the junior high and high school levels—which was exactly the niche that TVMSC intended to fill.

If you were a scientist moving to Boise from Chicago, for example, and your child had been attending a school such as the University of Chicago Laboratory School or another elite college prep school, equivalent options in Boise were scarce. A school like TVMSC would put Boise on the travel itineraries of elite colleges and universities when they went across the country recruiting at well-regarded private and public high schools that fed students to the nation's most prestigious colleges. All the better for Boise's affluent families if such a school were publicly subsidized, costing them nothing to send their children there.

"Maybe I should be talking to somebody at Micron about this," I said to MacLean.

She answered: "The school provides a lot of opportunities for their own staff members' children. They bring people in to work at Micron. They don't want their kids . . . they're not going to compromise the educational progression of their own children. That's what's really behind some of the support. Yeah, it's to build the local economy, but also to have opportunities for their own children."

Sure, Micron was interested in funding projects that helped to build its long-run prospects in the semiconductor industry. But the direct payoffs to the company for such projects were amorphous at best. A school like TVMSC would more directly benefit the firm, which could use it as a tool to recruit engineers and executives to Boise. I spoke with Dan Spangler, a former educator, who headed up the Micron Foundation's higher education grant programs.

"We've got a few funding goals, and one of them certainly is to support programs that improve the state of the art of the semiconductor industry and improve math, science, physics, and chemistry disciplines because of their central importance to that industry," Spangler told me. "The other, of course, is to improve the quality of life in the areas where our employees live and work. Really, I think that's as big a factor as the math and science focus on this."[12]

I asked Spangler to elaborate.

"I think it became clear to us that to continue to be the type of technology leader that we have become, it's important to be able to bring the best talent that we can into the Treasure Valley," he explained. "Certainly one component of that is to make sure that the families that come along with that talent have every opportunity to excel that they would find anywhere else."

Spangler went on to tell me an anecdote involving the Boise school superintendent, Stan Olson. At one TVMSC meeting, Olson had discussed a recent recruiting coup involving two high-powered physicians who had decided to relocate to Boise. "Stan Olson was telling the story about a couple of doctors that were brought into the community, and they had mentioned that one of the primary reasons they came was because of the center and because the Valley had those options available to their families," Spangler said. "When we want to bring in top scientific and engineering talent, that's important to us as well."

———

But while TVMSC's guiding educational philosophy would be attractive to any parent or child seeking enriched opportunities to learn math and science, these publicly supported opportunities are afforded only to a select few children. Students are chosen by a selection committee, and school officials would not disclose the identities of its members. At one meeting I attended, I spoke to Joe Gordon, the school district's director of science curriculum, and asked him about the selection committee's membership. He mentioned, in an offhand manner, that a couple of parents were on the committee and that their identities were secret. *Parents?* Their identities a *secret?* I thought he was joking.

I e-mailed Gordon the next day with a few follow-up questions. "You mentioned that parents were on the committee and that their identities were a secret. Were you joking?" I asked. I heard nothing back for a few weeks. I e-mailed him again. He finally replied with a terse message informing me that two parents were indeed on the student selection committee, along with two representatives from local high-tech firms, a handful of math and science supervisors from the school district, and two university professors.[13]

Only the most precocious children, who score in the top 2 percent on the school's selected test of "aptitude," are eligible for TVMSC. While nominally open to seventh graders and up, even a fourth grader would be considered if his or her "innate" thinking ability was sufficiently well developed, Holly MacLean told me.

When I visited TVMSC, the school's main screening test was the Otis-Lennon School Ability Test, a timed, multiple-choice exam known as the OLSAT. I asked MacLean how the school had settled on that particular exam. She replied that the test tapped into "innate" thinking abilities that students hadn't acquired from school or their family environment, which supposedly leveled the playing field among students who might not have been exposed to certain material.

"We wanted to be able to identify students who had a previous disposition for that higher level of thought pattern that supports much of what happens in algebra and higher-level mathematics," MacLean explained. "So that we weren't selecting students based upon the quality of teaching that they had been exposed to but rather upon that innate ability to think on that very abstract level."

———

When schools adopt tests such as the OLSAT to make important selection decisions, and in the process label children as smart or not so smart, it's a very good idea for school officials to know how well the test results correlate to some meaningful outcome—like the quality of a student's work in Hemingway's biology class or the ability to think creatively on the hypergravity project. Test publishers are ethically obligated to publish statistical evidence on a test's validity and reliability, and they typically do so in the technical manuals they provide to schools and other users of the tests.

But when I asked TVMSC and Boise school district officials about the OLSAT's technical manuals, wondering whether I could inspect them, I was astonished to find that neither Gordon nor MacLean seemed to know what I was talking about. I first asked Gordon for the technical manuals, figuring that, as chair of the selection committee, he would have carefully reviewed the validity evidence for the test. Gordon told me he didn't have the manuals and referred me to MacLean. She sent me an information sheet pertaining to test administration, but no information from the test's publisher about its validity. She did, however, send me a link to an obscure Web site that described the OLSAT as "one of the most widely used group-administered general intelligence tests with levels for primary through high school grades. The OLSAT is employed primarily for predicting success in cognitive and school-related areas."[14]

The OLSAT is indeed widely used in American schools, particularly for admission into selective private schools and into public gifted and talented programs. According to the OLSAT's publisher, Harcourt Assessment Inc., the exam is designed to measure a student's "abstract thinking and reasoning abilities."[15] But the case for whether the test actually measures useful outcomes for school isn't entirely persuasive.

In a review of the seventh edition of the OLSAT published by the widely regarded Buros Institute, Lizanne DeStefano, a professor of psychology at the University of Illinois at Urbana-Champaign, raises several concerns about the test and its use in schools. She questions the lack of information from the publisher regarding potential misuse of the test in educational settings. DeStefano is particularly concerned about the dearth of validity information in the technical manuals she reviewed—that is, how well did the test actually predict something useful about school performance? Merely stating correlations between OLSAT scores and scores on another standardized test is insufficient. She also questions the test's utility in high school settings when students are nearing college or the end of formal schooling. "If this is true, then, what is the practical value of OLSAT?" she wonders.

But DeStefano's most withering criticism goes to the heart of the exam itself and its underlying theory that such tests quantify some overall, general human intelligence, impervious to schooling or the effects of families. "The history of the OLSAT can be traced back to a period of testing that was dominated by hierarchical theories of intelligence that devolve from a general, omnibus single intelligence," she writes. "In light of recent advances in cognitive theory, the theoretical foundations of the OLSAT should be questioned."[16] Also reviewing the seventh edition of the OLSAT for the Buros Institute was Bert A. Goldman of the University of North Carolina, who notes that "one should proceed with caution in using this instrument."[17]

———

When French psychologist Alfred Binet described the development of his IQ test for Paris schoolchildren in the early 1900s, he noted with some dismay that his test of "intelligence" was highly skewed in favor of cultured and affluent children—the sons and daughters of university professors, physicians, lawyers, and other educated professionals. Binet warned, famously, against the misuse of his intelligence scales, which he intended merely as clinical tools for diagnosing severe mental handicaps. But those warnings went unheeded when his test was imported into the United States by an eager group of early "psychometricians," including Stanford University's Lewis Terman, who would go on to transform Binet's test into the Stanford-Binet Intelligence Scale. Terman and his associates helped to spawn the new age of mental measurement in America. It was an age in which testing specialists like Terman found themselves in league with influential policy makers in business, government, and academia, including Harvard University's James Bryant Conant, all under the ideological banner of a post-aristocracy, scientifically based "meritocracy."

The brave new meritocracy, often laced with absurd elements of eugenics, held that individuals were endowed with a general human "intelligence" that could be precisely quantified by IQ tests. Going far and tragically beyond the limited use of the IQ test that Binet had originally envisioned, Terman, Conant, and their allies believed that mental aptitude testing would allow society to place the intellectual elite into positions of leadership. By the same token, such tests could be employed to place the mentally deficient into more lowly but socially necessary positions, subservient to those in leadership. The tests could also be used to identify mental "defectives," Terman argued in his 1916 book *The Measurement of Intelligence*. "It is safe to predict that in the near future intelligence tests will bring tens of thousands of these high-grade defectives under the surveillance and protection of society. This will ultimately result in curtailing the reproduction of feeblemindedness and the elimination of an enormous amount of crime, pauperism, and industrial inefficiency," Terman wrote.[18]

The Stanford-Binet test—and the ideology of meritocracy undergirding it—led to the creation of the first Scholastic Aptitude Test, which Conant championed at Harvard. It survives to this day as the SAT, the college entrance exam that millions of high school juniors take each year as a requirement for admission to the nation's elite colleges and universities.

Perhaps the most notorious early application of the ideas about intelligence and meritocracy espoused by Terman and his associates can be seen in the U.S. Army's Alpha test. During World War I, the army wanted a means of sorting new recruits according to their mental fitness for various duties, differentiating the officers from those who would serve as grunts in the trenches. Some of the era's most highly regarded academic psychologists, including Terman, Robert Yerkes, Carl Brigham, and Edward Thorndike, participated in the project, which tested almost two million recruits.

In his 1923 book, *A Study of American Intelligence,* Brigham reported the results of the army Alpha tests. According to his interpretation of the results, the most mentally gifted recruits had immigrated to America from the most "intelligent" northern European countries, including Germany, England, and Scandinavia. In contrast, more recent immigrants, such as Italians, Jews, and Poles, were labeled as mentally deficient according to their performance on the army's IQ tests. Brigham attributed the differences in test performance to innate abilities, arguing that they were determined by the amount of "nordic blood" in recruits' family histories. He completely discounted the most obvious explanation: that northern European families, who had immigrated to the United States decades earlier than most Jews, Italians, and Poles, had far more familiarity with the American language and culture reflected in the Alpha test items.[19]

Among Terman's students at Stanford was Arthur Otis, who was also heavily involved in the army testing project. Otis's key contribution in that effort was to take individually administered IQ tests such as the Stanford-Binet and transform them into pencil and paper group tests. The commercial applications of such group testing, from widespread testing of school children to the testing of army recruits, were obvious.

Otis became one of the leading figures in the early American meritocracy movement. The first IQ test that bore his name was the Otis Group Intelligence Scale, whose origins can be traced to the army's Alpha test. Otis's IQ test went through various name changes over the years, becoming the Otis-Lennon Mental Ability Test and eventually, in its most recent iteration, the Otis-Lennon School Ability Test—the very same OLSAT that the Treasure Valley Math and Science Center came to use for its primary selection tool.

As much as test publishers—and school officials who use the tests—

disassociate exams like the OLSAT from words like "IQ" and "intelligence," OLSAT is the proverbial walking, talking, and quacking duck. For it closely resembles the IQ tests that preceded it, erected on the same pseudoscientific assumptions about human intelligence perpetuated by Terman and his early disciples. And while officials at the TVMSC might well disavow any ideological linkage between themselves and Arthur Otis or Lewis Terman, they might be surprised to learn that they share far more with the past than they might want to believe. When school officials speak of using mental tests to identify children who have "innate ability to think on that very abstract level," as Holly MacLean put it, they might consider this passage in the *Encyclopedia of Human Intelligence,* edited by Yale's Robert J. Sternberg:

> In the 1920s and 1930s, some proponents of intelligence tests thought of them as measures of innate ability. Individuals and groups who scored low on the tests supposedly had not only less proficiency on specific skills but less underlying ability. Although testing psychologists and other experts generally abandoned this point of view, the general public has persisted in the belief that IQ tests by whatever name measure innate abilities and resist influence from formal education and other learning experiences. By that line of reasoning, a person with low IQ test scores is unfortunate inasmuch as no emphasis on study and critical analysis has much value. Testing experts, however, do not hold this discouraging view today.

"In fact," the passage continues, "studies have shown that the degree of a person's exposure to the language and content of a test of intelligence is an important factor in determining the meaningfulness and appropriateness of the results of that test."[20]

————

There are some curious things about schools created by elites for the children of elites. It is curious when those schools are financed with public money and operated by public officials. It is particularly curious when such schools are created with the added patina of glorified rhetoric about staying economically competitive and the horrid state of math and science performance of American schoolchildren. Because the school system employs the OLSAT to legitimate TVMSC and its students with the various labels of precociousness—gifted, brilliant, bright—these children are endowed with a certain inalienable right that children in ordinary schools are not given.

And that is the right not to be bored.

According to the contract that the Micron Foundation signed with the school district—a contract that allows Micron to have a significant voice in student selection and faculty hiring—the school is required to offer curriculum and pedagogy that go beyond the Advanced Placement classes provided by area schools. "Grantee will maintain a sufficiently rigorous curriculum so that students at all levels remain academically stimulated," the contract specifies.[21]

Micron's desire to go beyond AP courses is understandable. Even AP classes, which had in recent years become the standard for college preparatory "rigor" in many American high schools, had developed a certain cookie-cutter quality, as teaching and learning were increasingly geared toward passing the College Board's AP exams. This, in effect, created a default curriculum that eliminated the possibility of exploring biology, history, or physics in great depth. The standardized AP curriculum also eliminated opportunities for applying academic knowledge in interesting, meaningful, and creative ways.

Devotion to compelling and engaging *applications* is in fact the sine qua non of the Treasure Valley Math and Science Center. It is the principal component of the educational experience that companies such as Micron and HP, and the families who run such companies, demand that the school provide their children.

Mike Wiedenfeld explained to me the pedagogical differences between TVMSC and the traditional schools at which he'd taught for many years.[22] For example, his students take field trips to the Boise River to gather data at different points along the river in order to study its water quality. Science becomes something to touch and smell, as students forage through the brush and weeds of the river banks to physically insert sensors into the cold river. The data itself takes on a tactile quality, as the precious indicators of the river's health, and each student then plugs results into models that lead to greater analytical insights. Understanding is built literally from the river up. The computational nature of the problem becomes incidental to a deeper understanding of the big picture—the environmental health of a living, breathing river.

Too often, traditional schools turn naturally inquisitive children into clerical number crunchers. Science becomes a boring abstraction of the natural world. The students, preoccupied with the computational aspects of the exercise, lose sight of the big picture and why they are even studying science.

"In a traditional setting, the students would most likely get some made-up set of data that comes out of some book that has nothing to do with anything they're working on in their world. And they would sit there and grunt their way through this stuff," Wiedenfeld explained. "Here, we went to the river and got a bunch of data. I had nine different groups, and we had the data collected in two different ways with electronic sensors, some with dissolved oxygen and some from chemical tests. We had different numbers of dissolved oxygen readings and chlorophora sample readings and nitrates. So they had to get all that information into one spreadsheet. Then they had to average all the nitrate data, average all the chlorophora data, fill everything down and sum everything up to get a final water quality value. To me, that's a much richer way to learn than doing it from some goofy set of data that comes out of some Microsoft applications document.

"If I compare this to my experiences at a traditional high school, it is trying to make sure that kids see a connection between the classes and the sort of the world they live in." Wiedenfeld gave me an analogy. "So often in school, it's 'Run two little tiny matchbox cars into each other and try to analyze that.' Here, we say, 'Let's analyze a real automobile accident.' It's sort of placing it into a context for them and giving them a reason for learning. The other aspect is to allow them to have some sort of say in what they're interested in looking at."

But it's an approach that runs contrary to the standards movement and the federal No Child Left Behind law, which have forced teachers at most public schools to be much more focused on test results. In ordinary schools, taking the time to help students learn by doing, combining field trips, lectures, and books into an enriching experience that excites young learners in real-world applications, has taken a back seat to teaching superficial facts and formulas necessary to pass the tests.

"That's what we're really fighting right now with the standards movement," Wiedenfeld explained. "I mean, if you were to take this hypergravity biology competition and drop it into a regular biology course, I think it becomes pretty difficult to find time for pulling things together and seeing the cross connections and curricular connections. What brought me here was a philosophy of trial and error in doing those types of projects."

Finding time to do math and science in depth is a fight that neither Wiedenfeld nor his students have to face at TVMSC. The projects are occasionally "grueling," but never boring. According to the school's philosophy, if the price for such enrichment and engagement is a few pages of missed material from a textbook that might represent an item or two on a state achievement test, then it is a price well worth paying.

In short, the teachers and students at TVMSC have been given the gift of time. Time for teachers to collaborate. Time for students and teachers to really investigate a project and pursue it to a satisfying conclusion. Time that traditional public schools serving the general public are not afforded. And even as experts in math and science education bemoan the shortcomings of math and science teaching in traditional schools, particularly the lack of depth and conceptual understanding, state and federal policy makers are exacerbating these shortcomings with short-sighted public policies. In the era of No Child Left Behind and other state accountability mandates, ordinary schools and teachers are under immense pressure to cover "standards" and teach to the tests that cover those standards. Allowing students to sign up for NASA projects and make field trips to the river are considered luxurious sideshows.

Because TVMSC is not a self-contained "school" per se, but a "center" that imports its students for large blocks of time each day from their respective home schools, TVMSC isn't required to file accountability reports in order to meet the test score targets set by state and federal authorities. Neither is it required to report the demographic statistics of its student body, including its enrollment of ethnic and racial minorities or the numbers of economically disadvantaged students, as public schools are required to do. Although I asked school officials to provide more precise data on the demographic characteristics of TVMSC students, my requests were refused.

———

Micron's corporate largesse and the pressure exerted by the influential families who want TVMSC for their children has given the center's students and teachers the ability to educate the way *all* schools might hope to educate.

Some might argue that schools such as Highlands Elementary and the Treasure Valley Math and Science Center in Boise represent somewhat extreme examples of how the private interests of affluent families are swaying public institutions in an effort to ensure the success of their children—even at the expense of children from less privileged families. In Boise, a relatively conservative city in a largely Republican state, I observed little public resistance to these arrangements. The following two chapters, however, move to the opposite end of the political spectrum: Berkeley, California, where students, parents, teachers, and administrators are engaged in a sometimes heated battle over the soul of the public schools in an age of growing gaps between haves and have-nots.

PART 2

STRUGGLE FOR THE SOUL
OF PUBLIC SCHOOLS

THREE

BERKELEY HIGH AND THE POLITICS
OF EXCLUSION

As I walked back to my hotel through downtown Berkeley on a gloriously sunny February day, I took in the sights of this vibrant, politically progressive, and diverse city. In certain respects, Berkeley is not remotely like the rest of America, and the people who live there are clearly proud of that separateness and difference. Politics and culture, especially, are what set Berkeley apart from the mainstream. Tucked up next to the Oakland Hills on one side and the San Francisco Bay on the other side, being in Berkeley feels a bit like being on an island. It's an island full of smart, articulate, and culturally aware people, including professionals, intellectuals, and political activists as well as professors and students from the University of California.

And if you don't believe me on that score, simply ask a Berkeley resident. More so than in many places, Berkeley people seem keenly aware of their separateness, aware that others view them as different. They are both wary of outsiders and proud that outsiders want to observe their special town in all its quirkiness. As I talked to people there, several commented to me that I wasn't the first author or filmmaker to come to observe Berkeley High, and that people here were quite used to the attention, thank you very much.

And yet for all its political and cultural separateness, for all its reputation as a bastion of liberal values, it was Berkeley's economics, as well as the politics of class and race, that attracted me to the city and its only public high school, Berkeley High. While Berkeley's liberal reputation was the facade that outsiders saw, the questions of economics, class, and race seemed to me more fundamental to the real Berkeley, making the place and its high school a lot more like the rest of America than many residents might want to believe.

Indeed, the city's liberalism is probably irrelevant when it comes to the class struggles that lurk just beneath the surface in Berkeley. Unlike schools in homogenous demographic enclaves with little variation in race or class, at Berkeley High the sons and daughters of rich, middle-class, and poor families—white, black, Asian, Hispanic, and multiracial— commingle, at least in principle, if not in actual fact. That's why Berkeley High looks a lot more like the rest of America than most urban and suburban schools, and why Berkeley High is a microcosm of the struggle over educational equity and excellence that is transpiring across the nation. In effect, it is a struggle for the soul of American public schools.

———

When Hasmig Minassian teaches a freshman seminar on race and ethnicity at Berkeley High School, she asks students to stand silently in response to several prompts. "Stand if you consider yourself upper class." Nobody moves. "Stand if you consider yourself lower class." Again, nobody moves. "Stand if you consider yourself middle class." Virtually the entire class rises.

"No one wants to be rich, no one wants to be poor," Minassian told me. "And I look at them and tell them, 'There's no way that all you guys are in the middle class.' I'm talking to kids with mansions on the hill and the kids who have nothing, and all put themselves in the middle class. I think they know way more than they're willing to admit about social class. They'll happily admit what race they are. . . . But when it comes to social class, you can't have too much and you can't have not enough."[1]

Minassian continued, "What's funny is that kids won't tell you what social class they're in, but they will be real quick to tell you where everybody else is. They see the divide. They see what happens when these kids turn sixteen or seventeen years old—who gets the new cars and who doesn't, who's riding the bus, who's getting dropped off, whose parents always show up on field trips because they have a stay-at-home mom versus ones who are never around. They get it. They see it."

Even more than race, social class may be a taboo subject for students at Berkeley High. But the class divide is abundantly evident all around them.

Consider one neighborhood that feeds the high school, an area surrounding John Muir Elementary School near the toney Claremont Hotel. There, in the hills above the University of California campus, 84 percent of residents have earned at least a bachelor's degree, and more than half hold graduate or professional degrees. The median family income is about $150,000 a year, with two-thirds of families earning at least $100,000 per year. More than 12 percent of the families in the neighborhood of John Muir Elementary own homes worth $1 million or more. The poverty rate is less than 5 percent, and the child poverty rate is zero. Almost 90 percent of the neighborhood is white.[2]

Across town from John Muir sits another neighborhood that feeds the high school. It is in the flatlands, near Rosa Parks Elementary. This neighborhood is considerably less prosperous and more racially mixed than the John Muir neighborhood. In contrast to the exceedingly well educated parents near John Muir, only about 35 percent of those in the Rosa Parks neighborhood have earned a bachelor's degree or higher. The median family income is about $44,000, and almost 60 percent of families earn less than $50,000 a year. Near Rosa Parks, about 19 percent of individuals are poor, as are more than one in four children. Racially, the neighborhood is truly diverse, with relatively equal percentages of whites, blacks, and Hispanics, in addition to sizable numbers of multiracial individuals and families.[3]

Certain trends that characterize Berkeley High reflect these statistics. One is that affluent whites often opt out of Berkeley public schools until their children reach high school. The attraction, for these parents, is Berkeley High itself. The school offers dozens of Advanced Placement classes in everything from Latin to computer programming, as well as a variety of sports and other extracurricular activities. I am told that well-to-do whites view the school as an attractive alternative to most private high schools in the area.

Berkeley High is something of a regional school, drawing students from the surrounding communities of Oakland, Richmond, and Emeryville, whose populations contain significantly more black families and far fewer upper-middle-class families than Berkeley itself. But while disadvantaged students of color see Berkeley High as a better alternative than their neighborhood schools in Oakland or Richmond, middle-class black parents have considered it a potentially dangerous place for their children academically, because black children at the school have been negatively affected by a culture of low achievement and low expectations. This has especially been the case for those students who flounder in the traditional, comprehensive part of the high school.

Indeed, students at Berkeley High have very divergent academic experiences and outcomes, and the fault lines split neatly along the divisions of race and class. Among African American and Hispanic students at the school, just 20 and 25 percent, respectively, were at least proficient on a state English exam in 2004, whereas almost 80 percent of whites were proficient. In the comprehensive section of the school, 75 percent of African Americans got a D or an F during one semester, compared to only 20 percent of white students. Sixty-five percent of Hispanic students got a D or an F during the semester.[4]

At the same time, Berkeley High's white students, often the sons and daughters of university professors and other highly educated professionals, are among the highest achievers in the state and the nation, with average scores of 817 on California's Academic Performance Index, compared to black, Hispanic, and economically disadvantaged students at the school, who all averaged about 540 in 2004. An API score of about 800 is considered the mark of high-performing schools and students in California.[5]

Advanced Placement courses, which have become the ticket to high GPAs in the race to pile up credentials for college applications—and which have also become the new standard by which colleges evaluate an applicant's college-worthiness—are dominated by white students at Berkeley High. Although only 37 percent of the students at the school are white, 66 percent of the AP enrollees are white students. African Americans, at almost 30 percent of the student body but only 5 percent of the AP enrollees, are the least well represented of all ethnic groups in AP classes. The affluent white students who fill up Berkeley High's AP offerings are among the highest-performing students in the nation on the AP exams. On the Latin exam, for instance, Berkeley High students averaged 4.48 out of 5, compared to a national average of less than 3. In physics, Berkeley High students averaged 4.38, compared to nationwide scores of 3.3.[6]

Hence, Berkeley High is hardly just one school. Its layers could be peeled into separate schools within the school, each serving a distinctly different clientele of students and their parents. These layers clearly correspond to class divisions. Because class and race are closely related at Berkeley High, the layers also reflect racial divides.

The layer that initially brought me to Berkeley was the one known as "Academic Choice," which had become a symbol of the class divide at the high school. A relatively new program of study, reportedly more academically rigorous than the rest of the school, Academic Choice was geared to high achievers preparing for college, who more often than not were the children of well-off professionals. Academic Choice was taught, various people told me, by many of the school's best and most experienced teachers. At the time of my visit, Academic Choice was considered an unofficial program within the "big school," which was the comprehensive part of the high school that was not parceled out into the two self-contained "small schools," each adhering to an academic theme.

In response to parental demand over the five years since its beginning, the Academic Choice program had grown from just a few dozen students to include some 450 students by the end of 2003. The program and the parents behind it were a force to be reckoned with.

———

I got kicked off the Berkeley High School campus one afternoon in February of 2005. As a former newspaper journalist, I had covered almost everything a reporter can cover: the police, defense contractors, public utilities, high-tech companies, banks, the economy, and nuclear power plant operators. But getting kicked off the Berkeley High campus, by the principal himself, was the first—and the only—time I've been forced out of any building or any event in my role as a researcher, reporter, author, or investigator. It was becoming increasingly clear that some public schools, even in this age of public accountability, had public images to protect. And they were becoming as aggressive as any Fortune 500 company in taking whatever steps they deemed necessary to spin and shape their public images.

It was of course humbling and a bit embarrassing to get kicked off a high school campus at the rebellious age of fifty-one. But what made this particularly strange was that I had just finished an interview with Jim Slemp, the Berkeley High principal, a few moments earlier. I was waiting in the hallway in one of the school's instructional buildings for my next appointment, with a teacher. I'd been on campus the entire morning, visiting classes and talking to teachers. In fact, I first met Slemp in the hallway that morning while Rick Ayers, a teacher, was giving me a tour of a few classes. Slemp and I exchanged pleasantries and took note of our planned meeting later that morning.

I had been planning the trip to Berkeley for several months, talking to teachers and parents by phone and setting up several appointments with various individuals, including Slemp. I was grateful and excited about the meeting with him. To understand the Academic Choice controversy, it seemed necessary to talk to Slemp, who'd been at the center of an abrupt reduction in Academic Choice courses, resulting in nearly 36 percent fewer students, during the fall of 2004.[7] Academic Choice parents and students were outraged, and the sleeping giant of the program's mostly white, affluent parents, until then relatively unorganized, had awoken.

During the interview, Slemp was hesitant to say much of any substance. That was partly understandable in light of the apparent difficulty of his new job as principal of Berkeley High. I'd heard that few people wanted the job, which required balancing the various competing political factions at the school, ranging from the wealthier families living in the Oakland Hills above Berkeley—by and large the Academic Choice parents—to those who lived in the poorer, racially mixed flatlands between Berkeley and the Bay. Slemp told me that Berkeley High had been through six principals in five years.[8]

A former school administrator from Eugene, Oregon, Slemp said he wanted to be at an urban high school, and Berkeley fit the bill. I had been told by at least one well-connected parent that Slemp was particularly ambitious and wanted to become a major player in a national urban high school reform movement. And yet parents and teachers had complained that he was impossible to pin down on questions of policy and the direction in which he wanted to lead Berkeley High.

I asked Slemp what to me seemed a softball question, after sensing that he wasn't going to be especially responsive or expansive.

"What is the American high school becoming, and how is it different than it was a generation ago?" I inquired.

"I'd have to think more about that," he answered.

"You've never thought about that?" I asked.

"Yes, but I don't feel comfortable answering that question."

I wondered why he'd even agreed to the interview in the first place.

I left Slemp's office and headed toward my next interview, with an Academic Choice teacher, David Bye. I was waiting in the hallway when Slemp walked by and saw me. He looked surprised and asked what I was doing there. I thought it was an odd question, given that we had just spoken a few minutes earlier. I told him that I had arranged interviews with several teachers.

"I'm sorry, you can't do that," Slemp abruptly said, informing me that all interview requests had to go through the district's central office. He then asked me to leave. Slemp is a very tall, physically imposing guy. I left. I tried to call David Bye and left him a message that, according to Slemp, I couldn't speak to him without permission. I was in a state of mild shock at the principal's strong-arm tactics, and it still wasn't entirely clear to me why he didn't want me there. I knew that Academic Choice was a hot-button topic at Berkeley High. Had I made Slemp, who was clearly a politically careful guy, uncomfortable with my questions?

———

"Most of my friends think my husband and I are crazy to send our son to Berkeley High," said Karen Hemphill, an African American parent who works as an assistant manager for the nearby city of Emeryville. Hemphill grew up in a Maryland suburb of Washington, D.C., graduated from Brown University, and came to UC Berkeley for graduate school; her husband, an astronomer, worked as a quantum electronics engineer at UC Berkeley.[9]

"You will hear story after story after story after story of black students who in middle school were getting As and Bs, and then by their sophomore or junior year at Berkeley High are getting Cs and Ds, and their parents are pulling their hair out," Hemphill told me.

"And, interestingly enough, the percentage of white students at Berkeley High is higher than the percentage of white students districtwide. There is a phenomenon in Berkeley of parents sending their children to private school through eighth grade, and then they come back and send them to Berkeley High because of the caliber of education they'll be able to receive. Not to mention the music and the largest athletic program west of the Mississippi. I think the jazz band is always in the top three in the country. The amount of resources is just unbelievable at Berkeley High. It's far more than at any private high school in the area. So you have this phenomenon of white middle classes coming back to Berkeley High. On the other hand, you have a flight of black middle-class families."

Hemphill decided to run for the school board in Berkeley in 2004. She did so, she said, from a sense of obligation. Her child, who had just started at Berkeley High when I spoke with her, had gone though Berkeley elementary and middle schools and had done well. But there were still times when teachers or counselors made certain assumptions about his academic inclinations and aspirations, and those of his family, because he was black.

There was the time, for instance, in middle school, when Hemphill and her husband decided to meet their son's teacher in a particular class in which he was doing very well—earning an A, in fact. "So we go and sit down, and this young white teacher looks at us, looks at me, and he reaches up with his hand and says with all sincerity, 'Did it ever occur to you that your son could be college material?' I thought I was going to have to restrain my husband.

"And I joked and I said, 'No, actually, in our house we never talk about going to college.' And he said, 'Well, you know, you should.' He didn't realize I was joking. He didn't get the joke. And it made me realize, this is a student who was getting As, but the teacher thought that his parents would not have a clue that perhaps college was an option. What were his thoughts about the students who were getting Cs and Ds in his class?"

As a well-educated, upper-middle-class black woman, Hemphill describes herself as straddling two worlds. Based on the family's educational and professional backgrounds, their social class makes them similar to Berkeley's upper-middle-class whites. But race remains a powerful influence for her. She told me that she felt responsible to other African Americans who weren't as well off as she and her husband were—particularly the kids from less fortunate black families who were getting those Cs and Ds and Fs.

"I ran for school board because I thought of myself as a bridge between two communities," Hemphill explained. "Because of my husband's and my educational backgrounds, we're sort of closer to one side of the fence, so to speak. But in terms of dealing with race and dealing with that aspect of the public school experience, we're also close to the experiences of people who don't have the education that we do as middle-class blacks."

On the Berkeley Unified School District's Web site, one can find an uncommonly sophisticated discussion of the theories of a prominent French sociologist and the influences of family social class on a child's educational opportunities. But despite such outward concern for class and race differences, Hemphill argued, the district and the current board were not doing enough for disadvantaged students, nor were they addressing in a focused way the unsettling gaps in educational outcomes between advantaged and disadvantaged children.

"Up until this last political campaign, when it was kind of continually brought in front of the school board, they never have addressed the achievement gap that exists in Berkeley," she explained. "And, in fact, even to talk about issues of race and class was something that . . . well, the words couldn't come out of their mouths, I would say."

———

From Hemphill's perspective, the most important idea to come before the Berkeley School Board in recent years for resolving the disquieting achievement gap between the haves and have-nots at Berkeley High was a proposal to essentially break up the school into several "small schools"—an idea inspired by the small schools movement unfolding across the nation. But she believes that the school board dropped the ball when it nixed the initial proposal offered by the advocates of small schools. After a period of study and a new recommendation from the superintendent's office, the board eventually approved a compromise plan that limited small schools to no more than half of the entire school's enrollment. When I visited in early 2005, two small schools had been officially approved, one called Communication Arts and Sciences, and the other known as the Community Partnerships Academy.

According to Hemphill, this political compromise meant, in effect, that just half of Berkeley High "had a plan" for closing the achievement gap. But for the remainder of the big school, where so many disadvantaged students fell though the cracks, there still was no plan.

That is, there was no overarching plan for the big school until Academic Choice came into being. But even then, Academic Choice involved only a fraction of the students; more accurately, it wasn't a program for the big school at all. Rather, it was an informal collection of teachers and classes geared toward a select group of high-achieving students who wanted an enriched curriculum but also wanted to remain part of the big school so that they could access its great range of AP courses instead of being limited to the offerings of the self-contained small schools. Instead of a program to close the achievement gap between advantaged and disadvantaged students at Berkeley High, Academic Choice appeared to be a different animal altogether. Indeed, though few at Berkeley High would put it in such terms, from my perspective as an outsider, Academic Choice seemed conceived to accomplish exactly the opposite, by providing the educational haves at Berkeley High with an even more enriched educational opportunity, and by doing so in an exclusive enclave quite apart from their peers in the rest of the big school.

The origins of Academic Choice are somewhat murky. Hemphill told me that its roots could be traced to something called "Teacher Choice," a system in which high-performing students, who happened to be mostly white, sought out particular teachers in a sort of self-selecting—and self-segregating—process. On the Academic Choice Web site—which was, interestingly enough, not part of the official Berkeley High School Web site, but instead was run independently by Academic Choice parents with the cooperation and input of the program's teachers—an official history of the program claimed that it had been inspired by the head of the

African American Studies department, Robert McKnight.[10] But whenever I raised the subject of Academic Choice with parents or with other teachers, McKnight was not the name that usually came up. Talk to Doug Powers, I was invariably told. If you want to learn about the origins of Academic Choice, Powers is your guy.

When I found Powers in his classroom between classes, he was meeting with an Academic Choice parent about promoting the program to middle-schoolers coming to Berkeley High as freshmen. It so happened that Academic Choice was in great flux at the time of my visit. Its supporters, including a number of teachers and parents, were scrambling to develop a formal proposal to the school board that would make it an official "program" at the big school. But that status would require Academic Choice to comply with the same diversity requirements as Berkeley High's small schools—that is, according to district policy, its racial and socioeconomic composition would have to reflect the diversity of the high school generally. Academic Choice parents were debating the merits of going this route, but there seemed little choice if they wanted to save the program—and save it from its reputation as an enclave of white, upper-class students.

After Powers and other teachers conceived of Academic Choice in 2001, it quickly developed into something not unlike the defunct Teacher Choice program. As an off-the-books program at the school, public knowledge of it was limited to word of mouth. Certain highly regarded teachers, such as Powers, developed what were supposed to be more academically rigorous courses than those found in the typical big school or small school classroom, geared to well-prepared students who wanted the challenge of a college prep experience. The unofficial program grew rapidly to several hundred students, as middle-class parents and students sought out the Academic Choice courses.

Its creators had been careful to keep Academic Choice out of the small school category, because that label would have required them to abide by the district enrollment standards that were intended to prevent the small schools from becoming racially unbalanced. But applying those standards to Academic Choice classes, in the view of some parents and teachers, would hamper attempts to make Academic Choice an elite alternative. Academic Choice, as the name implied, was nominally open to any student who wanted in. But that nod toward egalitarianism notwithstanding, the program, by all accounts, evolved with an enrollment of mostly white students, who at Berkeley High often came from relatively privileged backgrounds. It was impossible to get demographic information about Academic Choice from school administrators, but Hemphill told me that during the course of her campaign for the school board, she obtained figures showing that white students made up 65 percent of the program, although only 37 percent of Berkeley High's students were white.

This is how one leading Academic Choice parent, Jessica Seaton, described the evolution of the program:

> The administration at [Berkeley High School] did nothing to actively encourage or discourage the growth of the program, but information on enrolling students in the program, its requirements and limitations, was not formally disseminated by the administration to parents or counselors. As the program grew minority families and their students were increasingly marginalized; those few minority students that enrolled in the program found themselves racially isolated in the classroom and accused of "selling out" by their friends. Last fall the Academic Choice program had become so popular that it began to compete with the small school programs for motivated and involved students. Supporters of small school programs at [Berkeley High School] increasingly began to feel that Academic Choice was an exclusive club of primarily white, well educated, and affluent students.[11]

Nancy Feinstein is an organizational consultant who has had a long involvement with Berkeley High as a parent and former teacher at the school. When we spoke, her daughter was attending Berkeley High, and she has a son who taught there. She has worked with the district on a pro bono basis for the past ten years, most recently regarding the small school initiative. She explained to me how Academic Choice managed to maintain its exclusivity despite being nominally open to any student.[12]

"Oh, it's really quite clear it's the proper students who apply. I mean, the reputation is that these are the hardest classes, and this is who signs up for the hardest classes. It's just known to be a program for the white and Asian kids. Part of it is that African American kids, for example, . . . want to be in a social situation with other African American kids, so it's a very segregated situation. And it's hard to break segregated situations for any number of reasons.

"In Berkeley High, academically, the white and Asian kids rule; and, socially, the African American kids rule. And so Academic Choice became the turf for the highest-achieving academic kids, while the turf for the general social culture in the school is much more controlled by the African American kids."

In terms of its power as a political force, more than one person with whom I spoke referred to Academic Choice as a sleeping giant or as the new nine-hundred-pound gorilla at Berkeley High. After Slemp's administration unexpectedly scuttled a number of Academic Choice courses in the fall of 2004, a move that Academic Choice parents believed was a cave-in to outside community pressure, these parents flexed their collective political muscle. A Web site devoted to the program was launched, as was an active electronic discussion list. Nearly four hundred Academic Choice parents converged on a meeting of Berkeley High's School Site Council and managed to get all their candidates elected to the powerful body, essentially taking over the parental positions on the council.[13]

Jessica Seaton, an architect, was among its political leaders. "Actually, it was a little terrifying for the rest of the school community because the response was overwhelming," Seaton told me. "We frightened everybody. Everyone is suddenly aware that Academic Choice had the potential to be a powerful political participant in discussions at Berkeley High, which were very polarized. On the one hand, we accomplished our goal; but on the other hand, we polarized the situation further, I think, by frightening people."[14]

———

After my initial chat with Powers a few weeks earlier on the phone, I anticipated finding a bookish intellectual when we met in person. Instead, Powers struck a youthful, athletic, and clean-cut presence, looking like a former college tennis player or golfer. But when he started to talk, it soon became evident that he is something of a force of nature, whose intellectual interests span history, economics, political science, and Shakespeare. He told me that he had "a couple of master's degrees" and had completed the coursework for a few PhDs as well but had seen no particular reason to complete the doctorates. Besides his teaching and his work building a Buddhist university in Northern California, Powers is a former U.S. State Department official who worked with refugees. He seemed as comfortable talking about Marx as about conventional macroeconomics.[15]

Powers skipped out on a faculty meeting to speak with me, and he steered me to the corner of his classroom, out of sight from the door so that he could escape notice from teachers and administrators passing by in the hallway. As he described his work in creating and sustaining Academic Choice at Berkeley High, it became clear that a variety of different motivations, not always consistent, drove the program, depending on whom you talked to.

For his part, Powers expressed a disdain for the small schools movement at Berkeley High, which had been given an extra boost from the Bill and Melinda Gates Foundation with a grant of more than $1 million. In Powers's view, those who would break up large, comprehensive high schools into small schools didn't understand the value of traditional high schools, which were able to exploit economies of scale and offer a tremendous number of courses and subjects to students.

As I understood his argument, Berkeley High's small schools were more about a recent crop of left-leaning college graduates delivering ideological points of view to students and less about actual content—the hard knowledge that high schools were responsible for delivering. "This school, being an actual functional high school, is, for a lot of kids, delivering a pretty high level of academic knowledge, which I don't feel like most people even understand," Powers asserted. "I think there's a huge confusion among most people in education. There is an actual knowledge base of what kids should know at the end of high school, and I think that Gates doesn't understand it at all."

It became evident to me during our conversation that Powers viewed Academic Choice as part of a larger culture war taking place in education and that he saw Academic Choice as Berkeley High's way of upholding academic rigor in the face of an onslaught of deconstructionism and mediocrity. The small schools at Berkeley High, Powers believed, were asking students to critique the edifice of Western values and modern institutions without first giving them the intellectual standards and tools necessary to do so. He reminded me that he had led the charge several years earlier to abolish tracking in the ninth grade—creating heterogeneous classes in terms of student skills—and that he remained a strong advocate of mixing student skill levels within classrooms.

"I disagree with tracking," Powers told me. "During the battle for heterogeneity, we promised we'd keep the same level of [academic] outcomes. Well, in ten years, that same level of outcomes completely disappeared, and what happened instead was an incredible dumbing down of the curriculum to meet this middle that doesn't even exist. It got to such a point that in a lot of classes there was no writing, there was almost no reading, and students would watch movies all day. The bar that had been there before disappeared over that ten years, and something very different came from what was intended. And it finally reached a level of mediocrity across the board.

"Now the new teachers that have come in the last twelve years have come up in an educational system and methodologies that are related to that mediocrity. They're invested in the styles of teaching that have a lot to do with that mediocrity. I could get half the history teachers in this school to admit in a private personal conversation that they believe that the knowledge base of economics or the knowledge base of U.S. history is a patriarchal, capitalistic construct that's oppressing them and the world. And if they can teach the kids how that's oppressing them, then they've done their job here.

"There's zero accountability at the small schools," Powers continued. "Right now, talking about holding them accountable still would be very difficult because there's no construct to hold them accountable that's at a high enough level. And I think by having Academic Choice as the nine-hundred-pound gorilla in the room, it's now forced everybody to have to start talking about it and thinking about it."

How then does something like Academic Choice address the equally important questions of educational equity? How might it close the achievement gap between educational haves and have-nots, or is that not what Academic Choice is about? Powers told me that by the time kids get to Berkeley High, the achievement gap between racial groups, between advantaged and disadvantaged students, is too intractable a problem to realistically solve. Besides, it was the wrong question to ask, he insisted.

"The problem is that it starts from kindergarten and continues on through the twelfth grade. There's no way that gap between people's skills by the time they reach the ninth grade can be closed very much from ninth to twelfth grade. So we're trying to eliminate the achievement gap? That's just a politically correct term, and it's totally bullshit. I mean, we've been talking about that for thirty years, and we'll talk about it for another thirty years. But it's totally ridiculous. It has no reality to it at all. In fact, if we actually taught kids at their potential right now, the gap would probably grow. If we really made kids in the tenth grade work to the potential of the skills they started with, absolutely work at their absolute potential for all kids, it's not at all clear that the gap would close at all. So the gap is a red herring used politically for all kinds of stuff."

I asked Powers, "If you believe that, then what are you doing here?"

"We are not here primarily to close the gap," he answered. "We're here primarily to teach all kids to their potential. We should get four years of growth or more for every kid here. That's what we're here for. If we're not doing that, we're not being successful. Now, how do we do that? Once you've changed the question, we might be able to get an answer. If we don't change the question, we'll never get an answer, because if we're only talking about changing the gap, it's no problem. Just don't teach a damn thing to the top half. Give everybody an A. I don't think the gap is what we're here for. What we're here for is to teach all kids to their highest potential. If we can close the gap in the process, then more power to us."

Beyond Powers's argument that Academic Choice represents Berkeley High's attempt to draw the proverbial line in the sand against academic mediocrity, there is a *realpolitik* aspect to this nine-hundred-pound gorilla. The suddenly recognized political clout of the Academic Choice parents makes it forcefully clear that their interests will be well represented at the school. But what exactly are their interests?

The Academic Choice program, parent Dibsy Matcha told me, boils down to just that, choice. It is "an approach to education of saying there's a certain group of kids feeling like they want to be challenged academically and that they will thrive in that environment, and maybe more kids will thrive in that environment."[16]

"The kids know what's going on," Matcha argued. "While we're all pretending this kind of facade of maybe equality or political correctness, the kids know what's going on. They'll tell you who's sliding through and what classes are stimulating them and what classes are a complete loss. Some of them will be choosing those classes, and some of them won't."

But there is another, more subtle aspect to the Academic Choice phenomenon. By "choosing" the Academic Choice designation and its self-labeled "rigor," the parents, teachers, and students are in essence speaking in a certain code. As in all good marketing, the connotations of the Academic Choice label speaks volumes. The label conveys a certain exclusive environment in which the right students, exposed to the right teachers, will position themselves properly in the competition for selective colleges. There is "rigor," whatever that really means, and if you aren't sure what it means, it doesn't ultimately matter, because the label itself conveys sufficient reality. Once legitimized at Berkeley High as the "choice" for students seeking "rigor," Academic Choice also conveys the impression that "rigor" isn't to be found elsewhere at Berkeley High.

———

In the following chapter, we continue this story of the struggle for the soul of Berkeley High. As we'll see, other options besides Academic

Choice, such as the small schools, might well have been equally rigorous in their own right. Still, their promotion of critical thought, creativity, and deep analysis by itself wasn't sufficient to put those alternatives on a par with Academic Choice in the minds of parents for whom the right label was as important as anything else.

"DO I MAKE THE KIDS SMART OR GET THEM INTO COLLEGE?"

Several questions were in play at Berkeley High for which there weren't clear-cut answers, let alone a consensus among the school's different factions. Was Berkeley High's primary job to serve individual interests, or should individual interests be secondary to public interests? Are public high schools simply taxpayer-subsidized arenas for a collection of private interests? Was Berkeley High a gathering place for several schools within a school, in which students were sorted—and sorted themselves—along racial, class, and ethnic lines? Was "academic rigor" code for legitimizing more invidious ways of sorting by race and class?

At Berkeley High, fundamental questions of pedagogy were imbued with the influence of class, racial, and power hierarchies. For the Academic Choice community, the most valued pedagogy—at the top of the academic pyramid, they believed—was the pedagogy of the middle- and upper-middle class. It was based on a teacher-centered model that delivered what Doug Powers called an "actual knowledge base," which he and others believed prepared students for competitive college admissions.

Powers, an Academic Choice teacher, believed that the pedagogy of the small schools was more about leftist ideology than about academically rigorous knowledge, and he argued that this approach inevitably led to a level of mediocrity that was bad for *all* students, regardless of their race or class. Powers, age fifty-nine, told me that he was part of a cohort of several older teachers at Berkeley High who were in a position to institutionalize Academic Choice and the traditional values it stood for before they retired.

"When we leave, there will be a joyous party," he predicted, describing his adversaries in the small schools. "There's not going to be any grieving, I can guarantee that. We've been a real thorn to them, but if we're not able to get this institutionalized in the next two years, it'll be like a sand castle very close to the tide. Academic Choice is a way to kind of focus that and give people the opportunity, and the community, to choose to maintain that element at Berkeley High or not."[1]

For Powers and others who believed those things, Berkeley's small schools occupied a niche a few rungs below Academic Choice in the academic hierarchy, where rigor was nonexistent and students were cheated by a culture of low expectations. But, I would discover, it was too easy to place Berkeley's small schools in such a simplistic box. Although their academic approaches flew in the face of tradition—particularly those traditions perpetuated by college admissions offices—maybe Powers was dead wrong. And maybe Karen Hemphill was right when she argued that the small schools were the last best hope, not just for the least advantaged kids at Berkeley High, but for the high achievers as well.

———

Nina Robinson is the mother of Ellen Cushing, a student in Communication Arts and Sciences (CAS), one of the small schools at Berkeley High. Robinson is also a college admissions policy expert at the University of California, who worked on admissions issues during a tumultuous period in the UC system. She understands well the pull of Academic Choice for upper-middle-class parents, who see it as a means to properly "package" students for admission to competitive colleges. Indeed, her firsthand knowledge of what selective colleges and universities like to see on high school transcripts has so colored Robinson's perspective that she has concerns about Ellen's desire to remain in CAS, despite her delight at the educational experience Ellen is having in the small school.

As it turned out, there was another very large gorilla at Berkeley High, and it wasn't Academic Choice. Rather, it was the College Board's Advanced Placement program, which had come to virtually define college preparatory academics for many students at Berkeley High, as it has at countless high schools across the country. Colleges and universities place so much stock in Advanced Placement courses that they give precedence to students with piles of "AP" designations on their transcripts, despite the gross inequities in the availability of such courses, which are frequently not offered in schools that serve racial minorities or poor students. High schools, too, award extra grade points for AP courses, and students and parents are engaged in a race to accumulate grade point averages well in excess of the quaintly "perfect" 4.0.

But for many of the teachers, parents, and students I spoke with at Berkeley High who were involved in the small schools, this academic competition that revolves around AP classes was not their first priority. Time not spent in CAS in order to take AP classes in the big school, for instance, was time away from a community of students and teachers who had learned to know and care about each other over four years as they worked on interesting projects together. In addition to the conflict in values between AP classes and CAS, there were scheduling conflicts. Ellen couldn't do both. Either she was committed to CAS, or she wasn't.

And yet, if Ellen spent most of her time in CAS, it could mean that she wasn't grooming herself properly for competitive college admissions. That was Nina Robinson's dilemma.[2] "I have very mixed feelings," Robinson admitted. "I love CAS; it's a wonderful community. There's a real sense of commitment, and it does what it's supposed to do. When you go to a parent meeting, you walk into the room, and you feel like you know the people there. You feel like you're engaged in a common enterprise.

"It is genuinely diverse, although the kids constantly whine that it's not diverse enough, and they complain that there are many horrible inequities even within CAS. Their concern and the ways they talk about it just warms my heart, because it's a model for the rest of the world. There's an achievement gap within CAS, too, which anybody who knows anything about education could predict, and the students and the teachers take that stuff on. They have a sense of outrage.

"On the other hand, I'm disappointed that, given the way CAS and Berkeley High are structured, it is not easy for kids to compile the kinds of résumés that they need in order to be admitted to the most competitive colleges and universities. Particularly in California, because we have this very dominant college preparation track and a college preparation process that is really uniform across the state. As that has become more and more competitive, it's become more and more important that students have access to honors or AP courses in the tenth and eleventh grades. It is very important because they affect the kids' GPAs. Even as a CAS student, if you take an AP class in your senior year [after the college admission cycle], you get credit for taking an AP class, but you don't have the opportunity to develop the astronomical GPAs. So for the kids in CAS, the highest GPA they can earn, if they take the most rigorous courses available and get As in everything, is around a 4.14. That's below the median GPA at four of our UC campuses.

"These are great students, but they are not packaged appropriately. And so you have to hope that campus admissions systems will capture them for other reasons—capture them because they write brilliant essays or because they submit fantastic videos to a local film festival for teenagers, where half of the films are from CAS kids."

Ellen Cushing had just taken the SAT when I spoke with her during her junior year.[3] "It was hard," she acknowledged, but she felt confident that she'd done well, based on her practice tests and her score on the PSAT. By all appearances, Ellen was the sort of student who would naturally gravitate to Academic Choice. She came from an academically oriented family, with a mother who held a prestigious job at the University of California and was intimately familiar with the world of competitive college admissions. Many of Ellen's friends were in Academic Choice, as were most of the students on staff at the school paper, *The Jacket,* where she was a reporter.

Ellen had started out in the big school but didn't like it. She thought some of her classes were academically challenging, but she didn't like many of the teachers. "Berkeley High is a huge school, and it's so easy to get lost in the shuffle. I wanted a community," she told me. She decided to opt out of the big school and try CAS instead.

Unlike her mother, Ellen has no mixed feelings about that decision. She bristles, in fact, when she hears people say that Academic Choice is all about academics, that Berkeley High's small schools are not academically rigorous, or that she won't be ready for a good college after CAS.

"Well, I get that a lot. There's a big perception at Berkeley High of CAS being a slacker school. I hear it all the time, and it really hurts me because it implies that the reason I chose to be in CAS is because I didn't want to work hard. I'm working very hard. I take two AP classes this year, I do a lot of extracurriculars. My CAS classes are a lot of work. But it's true that in CAS I have less access to AP classes, and that's the main— that's one of the biggest things that colleges look for. In CAS, I can't take AP U.S. history. I can't take AP science. It's just part of the curriculum that I can't take."

Nevertheless, Ellen told me that's okay with her, because in her view AP courses aren't all they're cracked up to be. She mentioned the AP U.S. history class at Berkeley High as a good example of a course that was *less* intellectually challenging than the history she learned in CAS.

"In AP U.S. history, you are being taught to get a 5 on the AP test. You are taught the things that are on the AP test, and there's no room for any-thing else. But in CAS U.S. history, and in all of my CAS classes, we focus much more on analysis and critical thinking instead of just having facts and dates thrown at us and having to regurgitate them every two weeks for a test. That's not what it is in CAS. I think it is so much better, be-cause I feel like I'm learning much more, and I'm thinking much more. My thought process has grown so much in CAS.

"My history teacher's name is Mr. Pratt. He does say, 'You guys need to know what year the Spanish-American War was,' but that's not the most important thing. It's much more important that you're able to think critically about what caused the Spanish-American War and whether the U.S. options were just, and what were the ramifications on foreign pol-icy, and all of that stuff."

One day, I visited Bill Pratt's history class, where the students were doing a unit on the Great Depression, as were a number of other classes within CAS that week. The shades were drawn, and Pratt was showing the students a 1933 black-and-white photograph by Dorothea Lange, "White Angel Bread Line," shot in San Francisco. I noticed the consid-erable ethnic and racial diversity in the class of more than thirty students; white students like Ellen were in the minority. I noticed, too, that the stu-dents seemed polite and focused, allowing Pratt to conduct the lesson without interruption. When he asked for students' reactions to the fa-mous photograph of the grizzled man in the worn hat leaning on a makeshift fence at the bread line, many displayed what I thought were considerable powers of observation and insight.[4]

"What do you notice about this photograph?" Pratt asked the class.

"People from different social classes coming together. Because they're all just hungry," said one student.

"Let's shift to the composition of the picture," Pratt said. "What do you see?"

A student answered, "It's dingy and gray. It's very dark. His hands, the cup, the fence. There are no unimportant details."

"They're all very powerful things here," Pratt said. "Is this guy giv-ing up or does he have some fight left?"

"He looks tired and worn out," said a student, and another one added, "He's sad, but he can't give up."

It was the beginning of a new term for Jessica Quindel, a math teacher in Berkeley High's CAS school, when I visited in January 2005. I listened

as she reminded her class of tenth graders about the importance of homework and study habits. She also told them that she was there to help
them become "active learners" and that working on "hard problems,"
without easy answers, was the way to actively learn mathematics.[5]

"You can even do your homework every night and still not understand what's going on," she stressed. "It's important to do your homework, but also to understand it every step of the way. That is what makes
you strong mathematicians—not just getting it done. You have to actually understand it. You have to be active in your education. Otherwise
you won't learn it.

"Some of you say it makes you think hard. Well, that's a good thing!
I know a lot of you want me to come around and say, 'that's right' or
'that's wrong.' But that doesn't help you learn. Just remember that I'm
not trying to be mean when I don't tell you if you have the right answer.
I'm just trying to get you to think harder, because thinking is really important. Sometimes when you have a hard problem, it makes you think
hard, and that's going to prepare you for college, for the workplace, and
beyond. Thinking about a new problem is very difficult and very challenging and makes you think at higher levels. That's working that part
of your brain you might not use much."

"Okay, the problem of the week," she began. The class then launched
into examining a math problem, which they worked on in small groups
while Quindel traveled the room, watching and offering feedback. The
class contained fifteen or twenty black students, six whites, four Hispanics, and one Asian. Some of the small groups seemed to segregate by
race, but others were well mixed. Their problem was to calculate how
many cookies they could bake, iced or plain, given constraints on baking space, amounts of cookie dough and icing, and preparation time.

As Quindel promised, it was a hard problem, and she provided the
students with no particular facts or formulas that would allow them to
simply plug in numbers and crank out a solution. Instead, different
groups approached the problem in different ways. Quindel's goal was to
let the students discover the mathematical relationships and formulas on
their own.

The class is part of the Interactive Math Program (IMP), which
Berkeley High has offered for several years. IMP has become central to
the teaching of math in CAS, replacing the traditional sequence of
courses in geometry, algebra and pre-calculus. Quindel told me that the
IMP courses have had great success at CAS, and she pointed to studies
showing that on the math SAT, IMP students do as well as or better than

students in more traditional math courses. The reason, she asserted, is that IMP addresses the "mile wide, inch deep" problem of math education in American schools, one of the chief reasons U.S. high school students are relatively weak in math compared to their peers in Asia and Europe.[6]

"We go into much greater depth in certain concepts," Quindel explained. "And we also work a great deal on problem solving through the week, the problems that are really hard and difficult for anyone, even myself, to solve. And so when the students in IMP see a problem they've never encountered before, they can think through it and try to solve it."

But then something interesting happened with the IMP program at Berkeley High, as pedagogy became intertwined with the politics and stereotypes of class and race. According to Quindel, "there was a big backlash against IMP in the late '90s." IMP proved so successful with disadvantaged students and students of color, teaching math to kids who had not done well in the subject in the past, that it got a reputation among white, middle-class parents as being "dummy math," even though the program proved equally advantageous to the white kids. "The white parents basically said, 'Oh, students of color are successful— that must not be for my kid,' " Quindel said. In short, if the pedagogy wasn't the traditional sort advocated by the mathematical conservatives, particularly college mathematics professors, and if it produced results with disadvantaged students, then the new approach to math must be "less rigorous." Quindel explained the difference between IMP and traditional pedagogy, speaking from her experience as a math major at UC Berkeley. She recalled that she had limited success with the traditional approaches that were based on having students "reproduce" content delivered by the teacher instead of having them think through problems and in the process discover the concepts on their own.

"I wasn't super successful in college because it was so traditional," she told me. "I didn't learn that much; I didn't get a single A in any of my courses. I got all Bs and Cs, which meant I tried hard, but I didn't really totally grasp any single concept.

"In traditional courses, they don't let you discover it on your own at all. You do like forty practice problems, and the answers are in the back of the book. That was the structure of most of my textbooks, and most people's textbooks. But people don't really learn that way. And that's one of the reasons I liked IMP so much. I didn't feel that I learned in that traditional way. Sure, I felt like I could reproduce [the material]. I was one of those students who could reproduce it if a teacher was asking me to.

Show me an example, and I could do it—but that didn't mean I was really thinking deeply."

Having students discover math concepts by working through hard problems was not the only aspect of the IMP approach in Quindel's class that diverged from the individually centered competition of traditional classrooms. In addition, her teaching stressed the importance of the community itself. Like most teachers, Quindel was engaged in a delicate dance between the needs of each individual and those of the group as a whole. But in this classroom, there was an important difference: built into the IMP approach was the proposition that each student was individually better off if his or her peers were also better off.

"The math is more engaging if the students work in groups," said Quindel. "They can talk to their peers, and they don't have to feel that the teacher is watching every step. They can ask questions. Part of the class is developing a community where you can feel comfortable asking questions." She pointed to a spot in the now-empty room.

"You know, in the group right here, for example, three of them knew exactly what was going on. The other one had a lot on her page but really was confused. I said, 'Okay, let's stop. Let's not move on until Holly understands, because it's not good for just some people to understand.' We stop and make sure everybody understands. One of the things that's really important to me is not leaving anybody behind."

———

Early in 2005, the Berkeley school board approved a proposal submitted by Academic Choice parents and teachers that made this alternative an official program within the big school, on the condition that its enrollment reflect the socioeconomic and racial composition of the entire high school. The proposal also included language calling for extra academic support for students in the program, anticipating the enrollment of more disadvantaged students who in the past would not have met the profile of the typical Academic Choice student.

Some Academic Choice parents were not happy with the concessions, arguing that, since the program was subject to individual "choice," then the chips ought to fall where they may in terms of its racial and socioeconomic diversity. There was also the potential for bitterness among parents whose children might not be allowed into the program because of the new diversity requirements. In an open letter to the newly elected Academic Choice members of the School Site Council, one parent wrote:

In fulfilling your campaign promise to support the Academic Choice program at Berkeley High, please bear in mind there is no good argument for racial balance, or skin-color diversity, to be a requirement for the program to continue. . . . To say that it must be demographically balanced in any way would be the same as saying that Berkeley High must reflect the demographic makeup of the City of Berkeley in order to remain open. That would be, of course, not only impossible but absurd, because Berkeley High is required by law to admit all eligible students who apply. The same is true for Academic Choice. Further, one might as well require every school club and sports team to reflect skin-deep diversity—as opposed to, for example, the kind of diversity reflected in the ability to hit a baseball versus an aptitude for pitching it.[7]

Indeed, the fundamental differences in the opposing philosophies held by the Academic Choice adherents and the small school advocates couldn't be easily erased by administrative modifications to the program. Berkeley High's experience with Academic Choice was emblematic of the schism working its way through all American public education, reflecting fundamentally different philosophies about what a public school is and whose interests it serves. For Quindel, not leaving anyone behind was just as important as allowing each student to reach his or her full potential—the primary purpose of public schools, according to Academic Choice teacher Doug Powers. In fact, Quindel might even argue that no student could reach his or her full potential when others were left behind.

To the extent that Powers had come to be a sort of Academic Choice guru, his chief adversary in the small schools was Rick Ayers, a rumpled former Berkeley restaurant chef and a Vietnam-era antiwar activist from Chicago, who had turned to teaching in middle age. Just as Powers's name always came up in discussions of Academic Choice, Ayers struck me as the unofficial senior spokesperson for the small school movement at Berkeley High.

Ayers had been teaching there for ten years when I spoke with him. He had helped to start CAS in his third year of teaching at Berkeley High, when he was among a handful of teachers who were frustrated by the large size of the big school and the absence of community among teachers, students, and parents. They were rebelling against the "factory model" of schooling and pedagogy that seemed inherent to comprehensive high schools.[8]

Ayers generally divides the world of students into two kinds: the kids who have learned the "culture of endurance" that the factory model of schooling demands; and those, often from disadvantaged backgrounds, who rebel against the middle-class norms of the comprehensive American high school. But as a teacher in a public school, Ayers insisted, he could not pick and choose which students he would teach. His job was to figure out how to engage both kinds of students—and do so in a single classroom.

"I do think there are fundamentally different philosophical approaches between me, for instance, and someone like Doug Powers, on the purpose of public education," Ayers told me. "Public education is a place where everyone goes to school, and our purpose is to train future citizens. It's not that we need to make them the future physicians of America or make them future English teachers of America. But we need to make them readers, and we need to make them citizens. And so when it comes time to vote, they've read the damn paper, and they can pick apart a manipulative ad on TV. This is a civic responsibility of public education. And we have to educate the reluctant kids, the disruptive kids, the more difficult kids. That's why we get paid the big bucks.

"The other position I've heard, particularly from some Academic Choice teachers sometimes when their guard is down, is that they'll say, 'I don't care about race. I don't even want know the person's race. All I'm concerned about is a kid who wants to learn. I'll put out if he wants to learn. If he doesn't, well, then, fuck him, because I don't have time for them.' "

Academic Choice, Ayers believed, *was* thinly disguised code for class and racial segregation at Berkeley High, as affluent whites determined that they could form an alliance of equals, geared to their high-performing children, that would in effect keep blacks out. At the same time—and I heard this from several people—the affluent parents could claim on college application forms that their children were attending a "diverse" urban high school, which was said to play well with selective college admissions officers.

I asked Ayers, "So you think that under the surface there's something else going on besides academics?"

"Oh, there's vicious racism in this community," he answered, explaining that the city of Berkeley itself was becoming increasingly isolated and homogenous by race and class as the result of economics and housing prices that were driving out lower-income people. Many of Berkeley's "former '60s radicals," as he put it, had become closet racists with their rising affluence, trying to keep outsiders out and remake Berkeley schools into suburban-style schools that served only elites.

For Ayers, stratifying schools into factions, with high-achieving, motivated students in one part of the school, set off from other students, was antithetical to the very notion of public schools. "It divides the school, because it says we're going to get all the really sharp cracker kids over here, and then we're going to get those disruptive, confused kids out of our way, and then we can really do some high-end stuff.

"The other thing is," he added, "there's a lot of patting themselves on the back about what a fabulously high level of rigor and accountability and standards we have in this class or that class, and it's the biggest Emperor in No Clothes. A lot of these elite teachers sit on their ass and kind of philosophize and blow about what Freud said and what Camus said, and the kids' jaws are hanging down, but the teachers are not really doing their work. They're not actually reading essays carefully and showing students how to write a good essay, because they think these are the brilliant kids anyway. These are the kids whose parents are professors, the kids who are already going to good colleges. We could hardly screw it up."

While the Academic Choice community believed that its curriculum and the AP classes were the gold standard of academic quality at Berkeley High, the best way to prepare students for good colleges, Ayers countered—in a similar vein as Nina Robinson's observation about proper "packaging" of students for college—that such pedagogy was more of a stylistic response to the demands of middle- and upper-middle-class parents that their children attend brand-name colleges than a substantive effort at genuinely making kids smart.

In other words, Ayers might well have agreed with Powers that the purpose of schools is to allow students to reach their highest potential; but he countered that the Academic Choice orientation not only shortchanged disadvantaged students but also gave the best-prepared ones the false illusion of academic quality. "Do I make the kids smart or get them into college?" Ayers asked. "Because sometimes it's not the same thing."

He continued, "I get annoyed sometimes when the people who recruit all the 'AP-grade' sorts of kids say, 'This is where the standards are being upheld.' It's trickle-down academics to think that really high-end stuff in that group will help everyone. Just look at the big school. It's dividing the really marginalized and drifting kids from this little cohort of a mostly white part of the school that so many of the teachers love. I don't think it serves those kids well either, because they are the ones who learn the skill of endurance, but they're not getting a strong education."

Ayers echoed Ellen Cushing's feelings about the approach of the AP classes. One of the school's best AP biology teachers, a friend of Ayers, once told him that the curriculum suffered because it tried to teach far too many topics, none in sufficient depth to allow students to really understand concepts. "And so instead of understanding biological concepts deeply, you're doing wind sprints and doing little memorization things," Ayers explained. "This is what I mean by an endurance test, which is especially difficult to expect for a lot of working-class kids."

He told me about his own high-achieving daughter, who had been in the big school and was required to write a paper on the larger-than-life blues singer Bessie Smith. "She was an A student in the big school, and she got what is referred to as the lazy A. She got all kinds of As and didn't have to do a damn thing. She did a paper on Bessie Smith, and when she's all done, she got an A and was so happy, and I said, 'So, did you ever listen to her?' And she said, 'I never had to listen to her; I never had to listen to a thing.' She just got the damn paper done."

Colleges, Ayers argued, bear much of the blame for the pedagogical conflicts. The question of making kids smart versus properly packaging students for college wouldn't exist if colleges didn't use Advanced Placement courses as important gatekeepers. To be sure, colleges are rationing scarce enrollment space, he acknowledged, but he believes that they've promoted wrongheaded pedagogy that harms both the students who adapt to the "culture of endurance" as well as those who are alienated by it. Colleges have also promoted individual competitiveness over the value of community. "My wife's a college counselor at Berkeley High," he noted, "and the colleges literally say, 'Show me how you distinguish yourself; show me how you beat down the other kids. I don't want to see that you just did all these great things with all your peers. How did you beat 'em? This is America.'"

Nor does Ayers spare the competitive culture of affluent parents. "I think if the colleges said tomorrow, 'We will base a third of our admissions decisions on how well you play recorder music,' there would be recorder music studios popping up all over the country. The parents aren't as concerned about the damn content as they're concerned about the right bumper sticker on their cars." As a result of the conflict between Berkeley High's small school advocates and those who wanted to maintain the privileged position of the Advanced Placement curriculum, district officials decided to limit the small schools to no more than 50 percent of the whole school. But, like Karen Hemphill, the African American parent who ran for school board, Ayers believed that limiting the small schools was potentially disastrous for the kids in the big school who weren't among the AP elite.

"The fear is that if we have that many cool small schools, then you'd have, on the one hand, a default large school of kids who just couldn't figure out how to sign up, and on the other hand, another elite school within the big school. But it's happening anyway. We have an elite AP end of the large school and a sort of marginalized end of the school."

The other aspect of the political compromise to limit the small schools was perhaps the even deeper fear that affluent families, who had opted for private schools during elementary and middle school years and had come back to public schools for Berkeley High, might stay away if the high school didn't meet their needs. Without Berkeley High's affluent families, according to this view, the school would degrade into just another urban high school. As Ayers said, "Do you make Berkeley High work by making it like every other boring suburban school that has a bunch of white academic kids, or are you going to make it live up to the incredible diversity of Berkeley?"

———

The story of Berkeley High presents a messy case indeed. Various factions were pulling the school in far different directions, and those with seemingly polar-opposite philosophies about public education were all contending that they had the best interest of disadvantaged kids at heart—though in practice it didn't always appear that way to me. One of the compelling aspects of this conflict is that, ideologically, the large majority of Berkeley residents see themselves as political liberals who espouse the rhetoric of equal opportunity for disadvantaged students. But it is increasingly true not only in Berkeley but across the country that economics, self-interest, and the willingness of public schools to bend to the will of influential parents often trump political ideology.

FIVE

PUBLIC SCHOOLS, PRIVATE PRIVILEGE

As Americans, we like to think that our public school system can be a great equalizer, able to overcome social and economic disparities, not an institution that may in fact reproduce and justify existing inequalities.

But by reinforcing the advantages conferred by the abundant human capital that affluent parents provide their children at home, many public schools have effectively put themselves in the business of widening the school performance gaps between the rich and the not-rich, of reproducing the class barriers that exist in the larger society, not lessening them.

Indeed, as the twenty-first century unfolds in cities and towns across America, from liberal Berkeley to more conservative Boise, well-to-do families are engaged in a heated, yet loosely cooperative competition to give their children an edge in the race to elite colleges, pressing their schools to carve out havens of privilege for their high-performing children within the public school system.

A balkanization of these public spaces we once called public schools is taking shape, as middle- and upper-middle-class parents cajole schools to create gifted and talented programs, accelerated classes, magnet schools, and pullout programs, groups set apart from children in the "regular" and "remedial" schools and classrooms. Those students in the latter categories are almost invariably poor, working class, or people of color.

Under the guise of "choice," "academic rigor," and similarly veiled code words, school officials are bowing to a growing sense of entitlement on the part of wealthier parents, who are both highly vocal and politically savvy. From an early age, children are labeled, categorized, and slotted as never before into various academic tracks, schools, and programs. Often, the slotting depends on how well children perform on standardized tests, which reflect the existing social and economic order. And some parents are, in effect, demanding that things stay this way.

American elites vigorously promote and defend their positions in the high-stakes game of educational opportunity for their children. From tracking policies that largely benefit white and upper-middle-class kids in public schools to strategies for admission to prestigious private colleges, the privileged and well-educated inhabit an information-rich web of connections and access, in which they and their appointed agents can work closely with schools to perpetuate their advantages.

The education system shunts culturally and economically disadvantaged kids into classes whose principal mission is to drill into their heads whatever "content" is necessary to pass some state-mandated standardized test and meet federally imposed targets for "Annual Yearly Progress," so that schools, fearing the consequences of No Child Left Behind sanctions, might stay out of what educators call "AYP Jail." Meanwhile, as we saw with the Treasure Valley Math and Science Center in Boise and the Academic Choice program in Berkeley, upper-middle-class parents pressure schools to create challenging, interesting, and enriched learning environments exclusively for their children, staffed by the best and most experienced teachers.

Affluent parents—dare I say politically liberal, too—like to talk about making these special programs more ethnically and economically diverse. In defense of Berkeley High, there were many teachers and even parents who argued forcefully for the values of educational equity for disadvantaged children. These teachers and parents resisted efforts to make high-quality education the exclusive domain of the children of elites. Still, I would later discover that, after the Academic Choice program was required to conform to the same diversity policies as the rest of the school, principal Jim Slemp had proposed creating an International Baccalaureate program at the school. If the effort proved successful, Berkeley High's big school would then consist of two parts: a new and expanded version of Academic Choice and the new International Baccalaureate program. Of course, IB would officially be open to all interested students who made it through the selection lottery. But one can easily envision that the proposed program would fulfill the role once played by Academic Choice, providing a self-selecting means for Berkeley's elite parents, students, and teachers to segregate themselves from the rest of the big school. Hence, after reshuffling the deck chairs, Berkeley High would be faced with the same problems of educational segregation: Academic Choice would serve as a reservation for the same disadvantaged students who had been neglected in the old big school, and the IB program would become the new choice for the well-off and well-educated families who "deserve" something better.

The likely persistence of such inequalities at Berkeley High is in fact just what the social reproduction theories of Bourdieu and others would predict. For example, sociologists Adrian Raftery and Michael Hout have proposed a theory they call "maximally maintained inequality" to account for evidence that an expansion of educational opportunity in twentieth-century Ireland did not diminish class barriers.[1] The theory suggests that dominant groups, even under the guise of such reforms as extending Academic Choice to all students at Berkeley High, will strive to differentiate themselves from groups of lesser status as the latter continue to gain in educational participation. Hence, if the coin of the realm for some parents at Berkeley High is prestige, social standing, and admission to elite colleges, then it's not the achievement of educational credentials per se that matters as much as achievement relative to others—and a new International Baccalaureate credential at Berkeley High would quite nicely meet the demands of elites to maintain the existing levels of inequality. Only time will tell whether the more populist sentiments reflected in the views of Rick Ayers and other advocates of Berkeley High's small schools might challenge such an outcome.

At the Treasure Valley Math and Science Center in Boise, I saw virtually no public resistance to a school created by elites—with the financial assistance of a major locally based corporation—predominately for their own children. Any talk of diversity was easily sacrificed on the altar of high real estate values, impressive standardized test scores, and Boise's entree into the world of elite college admissions. If Boise school officials had been concerned about equal opportunity, they could have revised the admissions policy at the math and science center to include some sort of class-based affirmative action, acknowledging that children from disadvantaged families who might have promise in math and science rarely test as well as their peers from advantaged families. Alternatively, they could have provided equivalent learning opportunities to students at all schools, not just the privileged few.

But neither Boise nor Berkeley is an isolated case of private interests overtaking the public realm in American schools. In her 2004 book *Dividing Classes: How the Middle Class Negotiates and Rationalizes*

School Advantage, Ellen A. Brantlinger describes how highly educated professionals in "Hillsdale," a pseudonym for a university town in the Midwest, manipulated public schools to serve their best interests, at the expense of working-class or poor families. Of the affluent mothers Brantlinger talked to, all were white, 90 percent were professionals, and 55 percent had themselves attended private schools. Some 70 percent had master's degrees or higher, and 75 percent were also spouses of professors at the university. Many considered themselves politically liberal, with progressive beliefs about education.[2] But when Brantlinger posed tough questions to them about the nature and extent of their class advantages and whether, for instance, the city's highly stratified schools ought to be economically integrated and their curriculums detracked, many of the mothers became visibly irritated and unsettled. They denied that they had any particular advantages and blamed the working-class and poor students and their families for not measuring up.

Indeed, these well-to-do parents had the legitimacy and power not only to label their own children as success stories but to label others as failures. They called their own children "people with ambition," "the stars," "super-motivated kids," and ones with "superior intelligence"; the low-income students were the "low-ability children," "kids who aren't smart," and "angry, at-risk kids." In Hillsdale, educated professionals favored progressive education for their own children, but offered little resistance when schools imposed regimented, drill-and-kill educational methods on children of lower social rank.

———

What, then, *is* the purpose of public schools in a democratic society? The question has become hotly contested terrain in the America of George W. Bush.

The evolving model of schools in the public domain, particularly those that serve wealthier families, holds that schools are stage sets designed for the maximization of private interests within the school and that it is the school's responsibility to serve those private interests to the exclusion of public interests. Although it might be in the public interest, for example, to raise educational achievement and expand opportunities for the most disadvantaged students relative to the privileged ones, schools and school systems, fueled by a new era of federal intervention in their operation, seem instead to be adopting a plethora of strategies that, intentional or not, produce exactly the opposite outcome.

To the extent that some families pass along ample reserves of private human capital to their children, the "market value" of such children rises for status-conscious schools seeking to position themselves in an increasingly competitive marketplace for education. Public schools seek ways to look and act like private schools in order to appeal to status-seeking parents. School administrators and the teaching staff become tantamount to the appointed agents of the parents who exercise the most political influence on the school's affairs.

For many schools, equality of educational opportunity has become a secondary consideration, at best, in the privatization of the public school mission. American schools, as they were designed and funded—with their funding principally a function of property values in the neighborhoods in which they were located—are decidedly inefficient at alleviating the vast differences in human capital accumulation between rich families and poor ones. Indeed, the contributions of schools themselves pale in comparison to the influences of a child's family background—parents' education, income, cultural resources, and other components of social class—in accounting for the educational achievements and outcomes of individual children.

This was a lesson that the Coleman Report taught four decades ago. It has been a lesson reiterated in the research literature ever since.

"We have argued that schools have rather modest effects on the degree of cognitive and noncognitive inequality among adults," sociologist Christopher Jencks writes in his book *Inequality: A Reassessment of the Effect of Family and Schooling in America.* "Most people find this argument difficult to accept. Highly educated people differ from uneducated people in many important ways, and most people assume that schools must cause many of these differences."

Jencks continues, "We have argued, in other words, that schools serve primarily as selection and certification agencies, whose job is to measure and label people, and only secondarily as socialization agencies, whose job is to change people. This implies that schools serve primarily to legitimize inequality, not to create it."[3]

Yet these lessons have been largely ignored by the most recent generation of American policy makers. Instead of a policy agenda driven by findings that continue to confirm the centrality of family poverty, parental education levels, and other factors related to one's social class, Americans got *A Nation at Risk*—that "other" government report that celebrated its twentieth anniversary in 2003. This report firmly entrenched the notion among state and federal policy makers—conservatives and liberals alike, from the first President Bush through the second—that targeting schools and penalizing the ones that didn't perform up to par on standardized tests would be better for American education than helping families and individuals improve their social and economic conditions.[4]

For families who lacked stores of human capital to pass along to their children, the public realm, embodied by the public education system, represented virtually the only hope for such children to have a relatively equal opportunity to succeed. And, to be sure, government spending on schools that served poor children was sizable, working through the Elementary and Secondary Education Act, a Great Society–era program designed to funnel federal money to low-income schools.

But in 2001, with the passage of George W. Bush's No Child Left Behind (NCLB) Act, the government created a revolutionary new compact with the beneficiaries of Title 1 funds, based on still unproved and even radical theories of educational accountability. Under this law, states receiving the federal funds were to make 100 percent of their students "proficient" on standardized tests in language and math by the year 2014 or face a multitude of possible federal sanctions, some of which could ultimately lead to a school's closure and seizure by the state.

The new compact sounded plausible in theory, but in practice it has led to a wide variety of punishing consequences for children attending low-income schools. In Boise, Idaho, as elsewhere, schools in wealthy neighborhoods, such as Highlands Elementary, begin the NCLB race with proficiency levels far exceeding the government's intermediate test score targets. Such schools have immense latitude to pursue stimulating and enriching opportunities for both teaching and learning that are not solely aimed at drilling students for tests. Highly educated parents in these schools, such as Becky Parkinson, recoil at the notion that schools would teach their children simply what they must know for a state-mandated test. She and other parents in her position want a far deeper and more intellectually enriched experience for their children, and they have the resources to help make it happen. But in schools like Whittier Elementary, children begin school far below the federally mandated targets, which means that the school must make up far more ground in the same amount of time with students who present far greater challenges. These low-income schools are under immense pressure to aim instruction at improving test scores, in order to avoid facing closure by state education regulators.

In short, American schools and educational policy are structured to enhance the opportunities of culturally, economically, and politically powerful constituencies, at the expense of families who lack this human capital. But the special feature of this concentration of private power in the public realm, as it functions in democratic capitalism, is its sublime nature and its widely perceived legitimacy.

These are not new concerns. In his 1973 essay "Cultural Reproduction and Social Reproduction," Pierre Bourdieu describes the preservation of power among elites through the education system:

> Indeed, among all the solutions put forward throughout history to the problem of the transmission of power and privileges, there surely does not exist one that is better concealed, and therefore better adapted to societies which tend to refuse the most patent forms of hereditary transmission of power and privileges, than the solution which the education system provides by contributing to the reproduction of the structure of class relations and by concealing, by an apparently neutral attitude, the fact that it fills this function.[5]

There is little evidence that these fundamental relationships, exposed by Bourdieu and others, have changed in noticeable ways. That schools would *not* tamper with the arrangements of power and privilege existing in the larger society—this is precisely what Bourdieu predicted, and it has come to pass with a vengeance in American schools.

"Although these strong links between class status, school structures, and student outcomes are well known, social class is still ignored or treated as if it were relatively unimportant to schooling," Ellen Brantlinger explains. "Regardless of evidence to the contrary, because schools are thought to reward capacities rather than social standing, they are believed to be meritocracies in which students have equal chances to succeed."[6]

The tracking and sorting function of American schools typifies the obfuscations of social class. In fact, the clinical nature of the term "tracking" obscures its very purpose, which is to divide schoolchildren on the basis of the school's determination of "merit," an equally blurry term that most often translates as a child's performance on a standardized test of "achievement" or an IQ test. Thus, under the guise of social scientific credibility, schools are able, with widely perceived legitimacy, to allocate power and privilege to the already privileged and powerful.

Indeed, as Elizabeth Useem observes in her studies of mathematics tracking in Boston, the lion's share of "merit" that justified a child's placement into high-track math courses—which in turn placed the child into the pool of eligibles for later admission to elite colleges—was found among the most culturally well-endowed children from affluent and highly educated families. The parents' intimate knowledge of and experience with school sorting and tracking systems allowed them to exploit the rules to their personal advantage.[7]

In 1985, Jeannie Oakes published *Keeping Track,* a landmark study of how tracking works in American schools. In an interview several years later, Oakes noted that her study raised general awareness of tracking, particularly the educational and emotional damage inflicted on low-track children. But she acknowledged that the practice remains a prevalent fixture of the school system. She estimated that 80 percent of high schools and 60 percent of elementary schools engage in some variation of tracking, which she simply defines as "educators making some rather global judgments about how smart students are."[8]

Children internalize these judgments of themselves as being as high, middle, and low, as being smart or not so smart. The entire culture of public schools is organized around this value-laden process of labeling and sorting, with schools like Whittier Elementary at the bottom of the heap, with its abundance of "slow" and "remedial" children, and schools like the Treasure Valley Math and Science Center, created as a magnet for the region's crème de la crème, the most "gifted" of the gifted, at the top of all academic tracks.

By the late twentieth century, tracking in American schools had become more concealed than in previous decades, often obscured by a more egalitarian-sounding rhetoric among educators for whom books like *Keeping Track* may have been required reading in graduate school. But in recent years, scholars have observed a distinction between the formal tracking and classification schemes in times past and the more subtle forms of tracking that have nevertheless continued to sort children harshly by class and by race.

In one study of these trends, published in the *American Journal of Education* in 2004, Ronald Heck, Carol Price, and Scott Thomas used mathematical network analysis of an urban comprehensive high school in Hawaii to uncover seven dominant patterns of course-taking among students. It so happened that the resulting patterns differentiated students quite sharply by social class and race.

For example, Track 1, as they defined it, consisted predominately of students who took regular world history, low English in ninth grade, low English in eleventh, math applications, geometry, marine science, low physical science, physical education, "self and society," food science, and food service. This group, 30 percent of the school, was mostly made up of the native Hawaiian, working-class students who would follow their own parents into low-paying jobs in the food service and tourist industries in Hawaii.

Track 2 students, however, were those whose course-taking patterns included honors world history, honors U.S. history, honors English in ninth and tenth grades, geometry, third-year algebra, trigonometry, precalculus, biology, chemistry, physics, Japanese, and band. In the social culture of Hawaii, these students, 8 percent of the school, were mostly affluent and often Japanese.

The social traits of students in the observed tracks were starkly different. A fifth of Track 1 students were poor, while there was no measurable poverty among those in Track 2. Just 1.8 percent of Track 1 students later attended four-year colleges, compared to 95.5 percent of those in Track 2. Some 84 percent of Track 1 students attended community colleges, while only 4.5 percent of Track 2 students did so.

As the authors remark:

> For Hawaiians, this finding is discouraging because social and cultural policies in Hawaii over time have resulted in their prolonged social marginalization through reduced access to education. . . . This marginalization unfolds educationally over a period of years through selective course differentiation and leads to a greater likelihood of not completing high school at the end of four years. Overrepresentation in the lowest academic profiles also leads to diminished access to higher education and decreased likelihood of graduating from a four-year university. This suggested to us that the school "curricular structure" (i.e., with Hawaiian, Samoan, and low-SES students, many of whom were Hawaiian, confined to the lowest two academic profiles) tended to reproduce the cultural capital of the surrounding community. Because of Hawaiians' status as an indigenous group that was involuntarily colonized, this continued social reproduction represents a pressing challenge for achieving social justice in education.[9]

Samuel R. Lucas and Mark Berends, writing in *Sociology of Education* in 2002, note that, prior to the 1970s, so-called de jure tracking was commonplace, as students were assigned to formal tracks that they rarely crossed during their high school years. That practice has been replaced in recent decades with what these researchers call de facto tracking, as similarly situated students share the same courses and course-taking patterns. "Students appear still to be tracked; however, the mechanisms of tracking may be much more subtle than in the past," the authors explain. "The differentiated curriculum is still the dominant form of pedagogical organization in secondary schools in the United States."

Lucas and Berends examined 975 public and private high schools in a government database known as High School and Beyond and regressed the number of eleventh grade students sharing courses and levels on various socioeconomic variables. Even after controlling for student achievement, they found that de facto tracking in public schools increased as the racial and socioeconomic diversity of the student body increased—lending further support to the notion that public schools have, in a very literal sense, been co-opted in the primary service of dominant groups. Interestingly, that wasn't the case for private schools: in those schools, de facto tracking was strongly related to students' achievement, not to their race or social class.

While acknowledging that their study cannot directly explain the mechanisms behind these findings, Lucas and Berends suggest, plausibly, that dominant economic and racial groups engage in aggressive political action within public schools to ensure that their children are effectively segregated by curriculum—similar to the sorts of political moves of affluent parents at Berkeley High and in Boise. Lucas and Berends conclude, "Whether this story is apt or not, the motivation for focusing intently on the politics of tracking does seem deepened by our analysis."[10]

———

The most common defense of tracking is that it results in educationally "appropriate" learning opportunities for students who have widely different academic abilities and skills. In short, the story goes, tracking by ability is good for both low-performing and high-performing students because the groups are matched with content and pedagogy that are suited to their needs.

But a variety of research evidence suggests that this is a myth. At best, tracking amounts to a zero-sum game: gains in academic achievement among the high-track students are offset by losses among the low-track students. What's more, the academic gains at the high end follow from high-end teaching and learning opportunities that rarely exist for students relegated to the lower tracks.

Sociologist Adam Gamoran, who has studied these relationships for many years, sums up his research this way: "I conclude that grouping and tracking rarely add to overall achievement in a school, but they often contribute to inequality. This finding is most consistent for high school tracking, but it is not uncommon in other forms and at other levels. Typically, it means that high-track students are gaining and low-track students are falling farther behind."[11]

What accounts for this? In one study, Gamoran showed that high-track students in American high schools achieve more in school simply because they have more opportunities to learn: they learn more because they are taught more.

Examining a sample of twenty thousand students from the High School and Beyond database, Gamoran found that the effects of students' socioeconomic status (SES) on achievement disappeared once he controlled for the effects of tracking on achievement. And the effects of tracking on student achievement were large—larger, in fact, than the differences in achievement between staying in school and dropping out of school.

"Thus, high SES students achieve more because they have more advantaged school experiences," Gamoran explains. "They are less likely to drop out, more likely to be found in the college track, and more likely to take advanced academic courses. When these experiences are held constant, SES has little effect on achievement."[12]

This is not good news. Extensive tracking in public schools extends the sphere of influence of high-status families well beyond the boundaries of family life and into the public realm of the education system. There would be nothing wrong with that if this expansion of private interests into the public realm didn't occur at the expense of low-status children. Schools place disadvantaged children into tracks in which the *placement itself* results in less academic achievement compared to those in the privileged tracks.

Hence, schools themselves, acting in the interests of economically and socially dominant groups, exacerbate the achievement gaps that already exist among children from the first day of kindergarten as a result of the disparities in cultural and economic resources between rich families and poor families. The unfortunate outcome of such politics and power in the public education system is an artificial restriction of the flow of talent. Certainly this is bad for the individual children who are excluded from the enriched learning opportunities that schools offer their more privileged constituencies. What may be worse, however, is the collective damage that this restriction of potential talent has on the nation as a whole.

Commenting on her findings concerning tracking policies in suburban Boston, Elizabeth Useem told an annual meeting of the American Educational Research Association:

> The evidence from this study of twenty-six public school districts in the Boston area shows that many of the systems, including some where students come from highly educated homes, adopt very restrictive placement

practices in the middle grades which artificially restricts the flow of students into accelerated mathematics leading to twelfth grade calculus. . . . For policy makers, the results of this study suggest that if the proportion of students trained in advanced mathematics is to increase and to include students from a wider range of social class and racial backgrounds, then middle and high school tracking and curricular policies must undergo substantial alteration. The exclusive and elitist character of course assignment policies in many school districts virtually guarantees that the pool of mathematically capable students leaving high school will continue to be both underrepresentative in composition and insufficient in size.[13]

There's perhaps no better illustration of the collective costs of this elitism than the mediocre performance of U.S. students in mathematics and science over the past several years, compared to their peers in other countries. In 2003, mathematics achievement among American eighth graders placed them in a peer group that included the Slovak Republic, Malaysia, and Latvia, according to the *Trends in International Mathematics and Science Study,* one of a series of studies known as TIMMS. Although the American eighth graders were about average among the forty-five nations in the latest survey, their mathematics performance put them significantly below their peers in Asian and European countries of similar economic circumstances, such as Singapore, Japan, Korea, and the Netherlands. The nations that the American eighth graders bested included such Third World countries as South Africa, Turkey, Jordan, and Botswana.[14]

But the meager average performance of U.S. students obscured the significant differences among students in different social classes. The American average on TIMMS in 1995, for instance, was 500 in mathematics, placing U.S. students in the lower tier of math performance internationally. But American students whose parents did not graduate from high school averaged 463, which was about the average of students in Cyprus. American students with college-educated parents averaged 535, which put them among the world's best—in the same league as average students in France and Austria—but still well below the average student performance in Japan (605) or Singapore (643).

"Some groups of U.S. eighth graders are literally among the best in the world," researchers at the U.S. Department of Education concluded. "Other groups of U.S. eighth graders perform so poorly in mathematics and science that they stand among the lowest scoring of the TIMMS nations. What has not been established is whether population group membership *per se* is responsible. It is not necessarily the case, for example, that students from poor families do less well because they are poor."[15]

If family poverty itself isn't necessarily to blame, what is? Since the 1995 TIMMS survey, various analysts have examined the role of schools themselves—including the heavy tracking of American mathematics education compared to other countries—to account for the mediocre performance of American students. In math, fully 80 percent of American schools surveyed in 1995 reported that students were tracked into different curricula. But the opposite was true for science: just 20 percent of schools said that their science teaching was tracked. Interestingly, American students have tended to perform far better on average in science than in math in the international comparisons. In science, the American eighth grade students in 2004 ranked in the same tier as their peers in the Netherlands, Sweden, and Australia and were not far behind the world's best students in Japan, Hong Kong, and Korea.[16]

As a correlate to the intensive tracking of math for American eighth graders, U.S. schools are also heavily engaged in teaching remedial math for some students while offering math enrichment programs for others, variously consisting of pullout programs, magnet schools, gifted and talented programs, and other forms of differentiation based on the schools' determination of students' intellectual abilities. In contrast, it's rare for American schools to place students into "dummy science" classes set apart from enriched science classes. Science is science for most American eighth graders—just as math is math for some of the highest-performing nations in the various TIMMS surveys since 1995, such as Japan and Korea. In those countries, tracking students into ability levels is alien to the educational philosophy of the schools and to the overall national culture.

"As far as inborn ability goes, I can't say that it isn't there, but I say that it doesn't matter," one Japanese teacher told U.S. Department of Education researchers Harold W. Stevenson and Roberta Nerison-Low in a follow-up study to the 1995 TIMMS report, comparing the teaching practices of Germany, Japan, and the United States. The teacher continued, "Regardless of whether you have ability, if you persevere, you can get a good outcome." Another Japanese teacher remarked to the researchers: "If I use instructional grouping, those who are placed in a slow group would feel very ashamed. When I think of how they feel, dividing them has a more negative than positive effect."[17]

Indeed, ability tracking is prohibited in Japanese schools through middle school, which means that all math and science students are exposed to the same curriculum, the same educational enrichment, and the same opportunities to learn. Teachers downplay the importance of "intelligence" and "natural ability," adopting the egalitarian view that all students are capable of learning science or mathematics, education that depends "on the slow and steady accumulation of knowledge and skills," Stevenson and Nerison-Low explain.[18]

The American educators' perspective on these matters is quite different—as is the American students' relative performance in math and science. The underlying philosophy of the Treasure Valley Math and Science Center, for example, is that only children who meet highly selective, standardized definitions of intelligence, as measured by an aptitude test, are chosen for the public school's in-depth, project-oriented approach to learning math and science. As the school's principal explained to me, such children are endowed with the higher-order abstract thinking abilities that will enable them to become future leaders in fields that are based on math and science.

This abiding belief in "ability," that some children are naturally more suited to the study of advanced academic content, just as some individuals are more suited to excel in athletics, is among the most fundamental educational precepts of American culture. And, as Ellen Brantlinger discovered in her interviews with affluent mothers of children in the public schools of Hillsdale, Stevenson and Nerison-Low found that the belief that natural talent is necessary for academic success is far more common in wealthy American families than in poor ones. This American ideology about the importance of innate ability is at the root of the American schools' approach to tracking, which is decidedly more elitist than the Japanese approach. Ability tracking in American schools begins as early as kindergarten, with the imposition of school "readiness" tests, and continues through the elementary years with pullout programs, gifted and talented classes, and remedial classes for "slow" learners. By middle school and high school, tracking becomes integral to the American education system's structure and function.[19]

But the proverbial proof is in the pudding. American ideology about merit is thumped by Japanese pragmatism when it comes to actual performance in math and science—a fact not lost on Stevenson and Nerison-Low. "It should be pointed out," the U.S. Department of Education researchers note carefully, "that in the Third International Mathematics and Science Study the scores of the eighth-grade students in both science and mathematics in the United States . . . were significantly below those of students in Japan. The degree to which these differences are a result of the society's responses to individual differences in academic ability is a matter for further consideration."[20]

That further analysis came in 2001, in a report prepared for the U.S. Department of Education by Daniel Koretz, Daniel McCaffrey, and Thomas Sullivan at the Rand Institute. Conventional wisdom had held that American students' math and science performance was far more variable than that of their peers in other countries. America was a big country, with lots of diversity, and would naturally produce more highly skewed differences in performance than smaller, more homogenous nations. Or so it was widely believed.

In setting out to investigate that question, Koretz and his colleagues unearthed some intriguing sources of the variation in performance in America compared to Korea and Japan. Korea ranked second only to Singapore in eighth grade math performance on the TIMMS repeat in 1999, and Japan's eighth graders were also among the world's best. Quite remarkably, both Korea and Japan had very high levels of variability among students, but the variability occurred *within* math and science classrooms. This meant that teachers in both countries were encountering a wide range of student skills and abilities but were nevertheless teaching to very high performance levels overall. In the United States, the opposite pattern appeared: the lion's share of variability in eighth graders' performance took place *between* classrooms. This reflected the highly stratified nature of the American classrooms, where teachers taught relatively homogenous groups of students—a system that worked well for some elites, but produced decidedly lackluster results for the nation as a whole.[21]

American schools, then, are burdened with an impossible contradiction, which undermines the growing political rhetoric at the beginning of the new century about creating "world-class" schools. Such a goal is necessary for the nation's future economic well-being, but it will remain nothing more than pie in the sky until this contradiction is openly confronted. Schools cannot, on the one hand, serve as handmaidens to elites, carving out sanctuaries of privilege for children of the affluent within the boundaries of the public sphere, and at the same time fulfill the nation's future needs for mathematical and scientific talent and literacy. America's schools, and the state and federal policies supporting them, are doing a very good job of nurturing the talent of its most privileged children. But the nation as a whole continues to pay a steep price.

———

Like a prevailing wind that rarely changes direction, the signs of political and economic power often go unnoticed: from the public's perspective, that's just the way things work. Nowhere are the prevailing winds more constant than in American higher education. While in recent years the public has paid a lot of attention to race-based affirmative action in college and university admissions, a far more potent kind of affirmative action takes place day in and day out, largely out of plain sight and certainly not in the crosshairs of those who criticize racial preferences in college admissions. Call it affirmative action for the rich—the informal system of institutional arrangements and economic imperatives that provides great rewards to the children of affluence and privilege but shutters the gates to those who have grown up without such privilege. Part 3 addresses these issues, beginning with chapter 6, which argues that American higher education continues to be plagued with class barriers, despite our progress on several other fronts of educational inequality.

PART 3

AFFIRMATIVE ACTION FOR THE RICH

SIX

CLASS MATTERS

In the past few decades, the controversies over affirmative action in higher education have preoccupied America's debates about equal educational opportunity. This battle led to feverish public and media attention in the summer of 2003, when the U.S. Supreme Court finally entered the affirmative action fray for the first time in a quarter century. In *Grutter v. Bollinger*, a case involving the University of Michigan's law school, the Court in a 5–4 vote upheld the use of affirmative action in the school's admissions policy. Justice Sandra Day O'Connor's majority opinion largely turned on the question of the educational benefits of having a diverse student body at the law school. That was an important educational goal, O'Connor argued, because the University of Michigan law school, like similar elite programs across the country, served as a training ground for the nation's future leaders.[1]

But in a separate opinion involving the University of Michigan's undergraduate college, *Gratz v. Bollinger*, the Court in a 6–3 vote struck down that institution's admissions system, arguing that its affirmative action plan placed too much emphasis on race. In a subsequent interview with the *Chronicle of Higher Education*, the University of Michigan president, Mary Sue Coleman, announced that the university would create a new undergraduate admissions system in response to the *Gratz* ruling that "continues our commitment to a richly diverse student body."[2]

But even as Coleman was talking expansively about diversity, the university's commitment to diversity was, in practice, rather narrow. In fact, around the time Coleman made that statement, only 12.6 percent of Michigan's undergraduate students were eligible for Pell Grants, the federal aid program for students from families with low and modest incomes. In contrast, about 31 percent of undergraduates at all public universities were eligible for the low-income grants. Although Michigan is one of the nation's most prestigious public universities, its limited commitment to social class diversity put it on a par with highly selective private universities.[3]

The virtual silence of educational leaders on the question of social class inequities at their institutions has been particularly curious in light of the critical trends in higher education over the past thirty or forty years. During that time, not only has social class been a generally more intractable problem of equal educational opportunity than gender or race, but America's higher education system has also become more dangerously stratified by social class.

After the Second World War, the higher education system expanded rapidly, fueled first by the GI Bill, then later by the Baby Boom generation, and, perhaps most important, by the political will among national leaders to open up educational opportunities to segments of American society which had been excluded in the past. Given the growing political strength of previously disenfranchised groups, particularly women and minorities, and their demands to level the educational playing field, national leaders had little choice. Since 1970, the nation has experienced a staggering transformation in the opportunity structure for women and, to a lesser extent, for minorities as well.

But the opportunity gaps between advantaged and disadvantaged social classes in the United States have *not* lessened over the past thirty years. In fact—though one might not know it, given the nation's focus on the affirmative action remedy—disparities between social classes have significantly worsened on several dimensions of educational opportunity. From reading achievement in high school to enrollment in graduate and professional schools, educational inequalities along gender, racial, and ethnic lines have significantly diminished. At the same time, educational gaps have widened between students of affluent backgrounds and those of low and modest economic means.

To the extent that educational inequities remain between American minority groups and Caucasians, many—though certainly not all—of these disparities are rooted in persistent inequalities of social class: family income; parental education level; and other social, cultural, and economic circumstances that shape children's lives. All these we may sum up as features of one's social class background.[4]

For example, in terms of high school achievement, social class disparities continue to surpass those of gender and race, according to national statistics compiled by the U.S. Department of Education. In 1972, young women achieved slightly less than males in reading. That gap was eliminated by 1982. By 1992, girls' reading achievement surpassed that of boys. Over the same two decades, though reading and math achievement gaps hardly disappeared, both African Americans and Hispanics steadily improved relative to whites.[5]

Despite these improvements along gender and racial lines, school achievement gaps between rich students and poor ones—already sizable—worsened between 1972 and 1992. Even among those high school seniors who tested at the highest levels of academic achievement, the gaps by social class are far more pronounced than those by gender and race. If we look at students who scored in the highest quartile of academic achievement, for instance (see appendix A, figure A-1), equal percentages of girls and boys were performing at this level. Whites tested in the highest quartile at about four times the rate of blacks (32 percent versus 8 percent). But students from the highest socioeconomic group scored in the highest quartile at almost eight times the rate of students from the lowest socioeconomic group (50 percent versus 6.5 percent).[6]

A similar pattern holds when we look at the number of high school seniors enrolled in an academic track curriculum that prepared them for college (see appendix A, figure A-2). In 1972, fewer girls than boys were on the academic track; but by 1992, the percentage of girls surpassed that of boys. Blacks and Hispanics also showed significant improvement during the twenty-year period. But while the lower socioeconomic groups improved slightly on this measure, their disadvantage compared to their more affluent peers far exceeded the gender and racial gaps. In fact, in 1992, fully 63 percent of students in the highest socioeconomic group were enrolled in the academic track—35 percentage points more than the lowest socioeconomic group. In contrast, whites and blacks, who had been 16 percentage points apart in 1972, differed by only 7 percentage points in academic track enrollment by 1992.[7]

———

For all the fury over former Harvard president Lawrence Summers's off-the-cuff conjectures in early 2005 regarding the supposed inferior performance of women in the upper reaches of academic science,[8] it may be only a matter of time before Summers is simply proved wrong by the sheer force of history. Among the most significant changes in the landscape of educational opportunity over the past thirty years has been the democratization of a "college-going culture" for previously underrepresented groups, particularly women.

In the 1970s, Mary Tyler Moore was a novelty on the television screen, playing a young professional woman trying to bust into the world of male-dominated broadcasting. A decade later, Candice Bergen's Murphy Brown ran the newsroom. By the close of the twentieth century, the same Candice Bergen was playing the power broker, a senior partner in a powerful Boston law firm, calling the shots from behind the scenes in *Boston Legal.* And that's just TV, though the cultural symbolism remains profound. In real life, women were managing Fortune 500 companies, running the U.S. State Department, and legitimately contending for the office of president of the United States. All of which required, at a minimum, a bachelor's degree—and by the 1990s, women were significantly more likely than men to expect to earn a bachelor's degree and to take the necessary steps to do so.

What's more, in terms of who expected to go to college and who actually applied to college, the differences between whites and most minorities declined to negligible quantities. For example, when high school seniors in 1992 were asked about their expectation of graduating from college, the white-black gap had shrunk to just 3 percentage points, and the white-Hispanic difference had declined to 9 percentage points. However, the expectations gap along class lines dwarfed these modest differences by race. Indeed, a 50-point expectations gap existed between seniors from the highest and lowest socioeconomic groups, and a 26-point difference remained between the highest and the middle social classes.[9]

If one doesn't apply to college, one naturally can't go to college. In 1992, 45 percent of high school seniors from the lowest social class group submitted at least one college application. That compared to 58 percent from the middle socioeconomic group and 79 percent from the highest group. On average, 60 percent of seniors submitted at least one college application. Even among seniors who scored in the highest quartile on achievement tests, who would presumably be college-bound, the differences among the social classes are astonishing. Indeed, 34 percent of students from the lowest social class with high test scores filed no college applications, compared with just 8 percent of seniors from the highest social class. In contrast, the difference between whites and blacks on this dimension had become almost trivial (see appendix A, figure A-3).[10]

Furthermore, the social class inequities in educational attainment have largely proven much more difficult to remedy than the gender or racial gaps (see figure 1). For example, on average, 26 percent of students surveyed as eighth graders in 1988 had earned a bachelor's degree by the year 2000. Males earned BAs at slightly less than the average rate, and females at slightly more than average. The gaps between whites and blacks and between whites and Hispanics in the attainment of bachelor's degrees were significant, at 14 percentage points and 16 percentage points, respectively. But consider the social class differences. Fifty percent of eighth graders whose parents had gone to college earned BAs, compared to only 11 percent of those whose parents were not college-educated—a gap of 39 points. The chasm between eighth graders from the highest social class and the lowest was a staggering 44 percentage points (see appendix A, figure A-4).[11]

Even once students begin college, the racial and gender gaps in attaining bachelor's degrees are far less than the differences along class lines. According to the National Center on Education Statistics, which surveyed beginning college students in 1989–1990 and followed up four years later, about 27 percent of white students completed their BA degrees within four years, compared to about 17 percent and 18 percent of black and Hispanic students, respectively (see appendix A, figure A-5). However, 41 percent of affluent college students completed their degrees in four years, compared to just 6 percent of low-income students.[12]

The unfortunate fact of the matter is this: a wealthy low-achiever in America has a significantly greater chance of attending a four-year university than a highly accomplished student from a lower-income family. According to U.S. Department of Education data, for instance, 77 percent of students from the highest socioeconomic quartile who score in the lowest quartile on high school achievement tests go to college. In contrast, 63 percent of students from the lowest socioeconomic quartile who score in the highest quartile on achievement tests attend college.[13]

None of this is to suggest, however, that class and race can be separated or that racial equality of educational opportunity is a done deal in American higher education. The fact is that class and race continue to overlap to an astonishing degree in American society, a fact that bears heavily on who gets a college education in this country. According to the U.S. Census Bureau, the median income of white families with college-

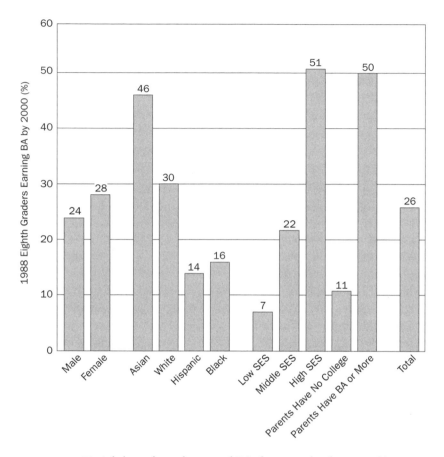

Figure 1. 1988 eighth graders who earned BAs by 2000, by demographic group. Source: U.S. Department of Education, National Center for Education Statistics, *Coming of Age in the 1990s: The Eighth-Grade Class of 1988, 12 Years Later,* by Steven J. Ingels, T. R. Curtin, Phillip Kaufman, Martha Naomi Alt, Xianglei Chen, and Jeffrey A. Owings, NCES 2002–321 (Washington, D.C.: U.S. Government Printing Office, 2002).

age children in 2003, at $62,900, was approaching twice the $36,700 income of a black family.[14]

As we've seen in earlier chapters, such differences in income and wealth, reinforced by differences in cultural and social capital between rich and poor families, produce staggering inequalities in children's educational aspirations and achievement. Because too many minority children grow up in families that bear the brunt of low-paying jobs and high levels of unemployment, the odds are stacked heavily against their graduating from high school, being admitted to a university, finding the money to pay for college, and then, finally, graduating with a bachelor's degree. Indeed, underrepresented minorities made up 26 percent of high school graduates in 2001, and yet they constituted just 10.8 percent of the enrollments at the fifty flagship state universities.[15]

Consider, for example, the persistently slow progress of black males in American higher education. The glacial pace of their progress is especially pronounced at the nation's flagship public universities, according to a 2006 report by the Joint Center for Political and Economic Studies, a Washington, D.C., think tank. In its analysis of federal education data, the center found that, while college-age black males made up almost 8 percent of the U.S. population, they constituted just 2.8 percent of undergraduate enrollments at the fifty flagship state universities. Shaun R. Harper, a researcher at Pennsylvania State University's Center for the Study of Higher Education and author of the report, told the *Chronicle of Higher Education,* "Given all of the institutional rhetoric regarding access to equity, multiculturalism, and social justice, I just see next to no evidence of those espoused values being enacted on behalf of black male undergraduates."[16]

———

I had a conversation with an independent college counselor who advises students from elite private high schools who are working on their college applications. When I mentioned the word "stratification" to describe the opportunity structure of American higher education, he responded with what I have found to be a common objection: "Well, when you say 'stratified,' people complain about something being elitist, and everything in our society has an element of elitism to it," he told me. "It is very easy for anyone in the United States who wants to get a college education to get one—and to get one at a reasonably inexpensive price. Community colleges are open to anyone for the first two years. They are open admission, and they are relatively cheap. And there are state universities, and there are local private schools that pretty much accept almost everyone who applies. We have an enormous spectrum from which to choose, which doesn't exist in any other country."[17]

Indeed, America's vaunted system of higher education is an institution worthy of immense pride for many people. Between 1965 and 2003, the number of colleges and universities grew by 92 percent. Public community colleges alone ballooned 171 percent during that period. These open-access institutions enrolled 17 percent of all college and university students in 1965; four decades later, they enrolled almost 40 percent of all students in higher education. The number of four-year colleges and universities also increased, growing 51 percent for private institutions, and 55 percent for public ones.[18]

The American higher education system resembles a pyramid, consisting of a relatively few highly desirable and selective institutions at the top, a sizable number of moderately selective institutions in the middle, and a far larger number of nonselective community colleges at the base. It's the sheer size and variety of colleges and universities that observers often point to when they suggest that American higher education is a relatively free, open, and egalitarian enterprise. But the massive expansion of the system, especially at the bottom of the pyramid, along with America's apparently flexible system of individual consumer choice among a myriad of public and private institutions, has masked the tightening rigidity of the system as a whole along class lines.

It seems hard to fathom, given our generally optimistic views of educational opportunity, but the chance of getting a bachelor's degree by age twenty-four has improved *only for those who come from families in the upper half of the nation's income distribution.* In 1970, about 6 percent of high school graduates from families in the lowest income quartile obtained a bachelor's degree by their twenty-fourth birthday. This statistic essentially flatlined in subsequent decades: in 2002, it remained at just 6 percent (see figure 2). The number of students from lower-middle-class families (in the lower middle income quartile) who attained their BAs also stagnated during this period. In contrast, students from upper-middle-income families (in the upper middle income quartile) saw their prospects for earning a BA nearly double, from 14.9 percent to 26.8 percent. Prospects for those from the highest-income families improved from 40 percent to more than 50 percent.[19]

Perhaps the most glaring aspect of this stratification is the growing concentration of poor and working-class people at the bottom of the educational pyramid, in community colleges and, increasingly, in proprietary schools (colleges that primarily serve older students who return to college later in life, such as the University of Phoenix). In 2002, community colleges, which at that time enrolled more than 43 percent of all undergraduates in the country, also housed almost 40 percent of all recipients of Pell Grants.[20] In contrast, four-year colleges and universities have become more exclusive domains for America's middle and upper-middle classes. In the early 1970s, public four-year institutions enrolled 40 percent of all Pell Grant students; but by 2001, this figure had dropped to

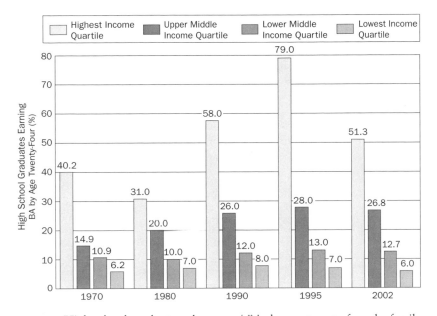

Figure 2. High school graduates who earned BAs by age twenty-four, by family income, 1970 to 2002. Source: Thomas Mortenson, "Bachelor's Degree Attainment by Age 24 by Income Quartile, 1970–2002," *Postsecondary Education Opportunity* 143 (May 2004): 1.

31 percent. Private four-year institutions enrolled 22 percent of Pell Grant students in the early 1970s but only about 13 percent a quarter century later. By 2002, proprietary institutions served a larger share of low-income students than private four-year colleges and universities.

"What is emerging is a postsecondary education opportunity system based on economic class in the United States," says education policy analyst Thomas Mortenson. "Students born into low-income families face a narrowing set of postsecondary choices. They are increasingly concentrated in community colleges, while students from more affluent family backgrounds are concentrated in four-year public and private colleges and universities."[21]

Community colleges represent a particular contradiction, in terms of creating meaningful educational opportunity for disadvantaged groups. Admirably, such two-year colleges have, by definition, greatly expanded access at the bottom of the pyramid; and those students who do obtain associate degrees or transfer to four-year institutions to earn bachelor's degrees are better off than they would be without community colleges.

What remains controversial, however, is whether community colleges have made a sufficient difference for a sufficient number of people. The vast majority of community college students, some 63 percent, would *like* to earn at least a bachelor's degree. But relatively few actually do so. In fact, of students who started at a community college in 1995, who expected to transfer to a four-year college eventually, just 23 percent had earned a bachelor's degree six years later.[22]

What's more, the chances of community college students transferring to a four-year university—often their ticket into the middle class— largely depend on the social class from which they come. Of students who expected to earn at least a bachelor's degree in 1995, just 21 percent from both the bottom and the lower-middle socioeconomic classes actually transferred to a four-year institution. In contrast, 36 percent of the upper-middle-class quartile and 49 percent of the top socioeconomic quartile transferred to a four-year college or university.[23]

The contradictions of the community college movement are hardly new concerns. In fact, the democratization of American higher education after the Second World War, as it changed from an institution exclusive to elites to one nominally open to the masses, has appeared to follow a familiar pattern. Consider the public high school as an American institution. Prior to the period when education was expanded to the masses, as Martin Trow has observed, a high school diploma was an elite educational credential. But even as the American high school opened its doors early in the last century, it also became more stratified and segmented, as separate curricular tracks were created to differentiate the college-bound from the vocationally bound.[24] Similarly, educational opportunities expanded with the massive growth of community colleges. But so did stratification of the entire higher education system. The growing rigidity of the dividing lines between sectors within the system raises serious doubt that simply enlarging the system of higher education has fundamentally diminished social class inequalities.

Indeed, an increasingly vivid line is dividing American higher education. On one side are those trained at intellectually elite academic centers, professional schools, and selective undergraduate programs, who are part and parcel of the fabric of the American leadership establishment that Justice O'Connor envisioned. On the other side are individuals trained to serve the interests of a leadership class. Which side of this growing divide a young person inhabits can mean that he or she is exposed to quite disparate notions about what it means to be educated, how knowledge is defined, and whose knowledge even matters. For all the hopes and dreams of the community college movement, its existence may ultimately be counterproductive in terms of a genuine attack on inequality. The institutions, in effect, permit the creation of a separate system of postsecondary education for the poor, recent immigrants, and children of the working class, who receive training and credentials for jobs that serve the dominant leadership class. Separate and unequal systems of higher education—one for the rich, the other for the not-rich—would not exist but for the deeply stratified nature of the social and economic structure in the larger society.

As Jerome Karabel, a UC Berkeley sociologist, writes in an article that first appeared in the *Harvard Educational Review*:

> Despite the idealism and vigor of the community college movement, there has been a sharp contradiction between official rhetoric and social reality. Hailed as the "democratizers of higher education," community colleges are, in reality, a vital component of the class-based tracking system. The modal junior college student, though aspiring to a four-year diploma upon entrance, receives neither an associate nor a bachelor's degree. The likelihood of his persisting in higher education is negatively influenced by attending a community college. Since a disproportionate number of community-college students are of working-class origins, low-status students are most likely to attend those institutions, which increases the likelihood that they will drop out of college. Having increased access to higher education, community colleges are notably unsuccessful in retaining their students and in reducing class differentials in educational opportunity.[25]

———

It hardly takes a Supreme Court opinion to note that a great deal of America's cultural and intellectual attention is given not to community colleges but rather to the opposite end of the educational pyramid: the relatively few elite colleges and universities that close their doors to the vast majority of those who seek admission. It is primarily at such highly selective institutions that questions of racial preferences come into play, because most other American colleges and universities continue to admit most students who apply.

Because highly selective institutions are so few in number, observers sometimes wonder why, as a society, we should be so preoccupied with them as a policy matter. As an example, in January 2005, I gave a presentation about class and higher education to an audience of college admission and financial aid officials, many of them from elite universities. I tried to challenge them to broaden their notions of diversity. Afterward, a senior official from the College Board, which had sponsored the event at a toney resort hotel in Bal Harbour, Florida, said privately to me, "You're aiming too high." Her clear implication was that I was focusing too much on the pinnacle of the higher education pyramid.

The College Board official was right—but only to a point. Who goes to college, as a general concern, is fundamental in a society that so vigorously promotes individual economic achievements based on one's educational credentials. For a young woman like Ashlea Jackson, whom we met in chapter 1, attending and graduating from a college of any variety would be a monumental achievement given the obstacles she has faced growing up.

But Justice O'Connor was exactly right. America's elite institutions do represent the training grounds for the nation's future leaders—and thus for any nation that purports to uphold egalitarian and democratic values, it matters who is educated at these institutions. It matters that the University of Michigan law school and schools like it be diverse in many ways, not only racially and ethnically diverse. To the extent that these colleges and universities educate the individuals who will lead in government, education, and commerce, it matters fundamentally that access to these schools is guided by the principles of equal opportunity, open to individuals from all walks of life. It matters that these training grounds are not merely playgrounds for the children of privilege.

Notwithstanding the importance of these principles, America's record of upholding them is indeed bleak. Despite the overall growth of the higher education sector—indeed, perhaps because of that expansion—American higher education by the 1990s had become even more rigidly divided by social class than it had been thirty years earlier. By the last decade of the twentieth century, a mere 3 percent of the freshmen enrolled at the nation's 146 most selective institutions came from the lowest socioeconomic quartile, according to a 2004 study by the Century Foundation (see figure 3). But almost 75 percent of the freshmen at these widely respected and influential universities came from the highest socioeconomic quartile.[26]

To be sure, access to the best universities in the United States has also been highly skewed by race and ethnicity, as blacks and Hispanics each accounted for only 6 percent of the freshmen at the same universities. But access to such colleges and universities remains even more distorted by one's social class. Consider the seminal defense of affirmative action in college admissions, *The Shape of the River*, by William Bowen and Derek Bok. The authors report that students from affluent families, both

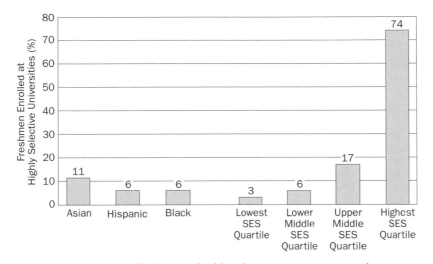

Figure 3. Freshmen enrolled at 146 highly selective U.S. universities, by race and socioeconomic status, 1995. Note: Selective universities are defined here as those whose freshman class has a median SAT score of at least 1240. Source: Anthony P. Carnevale and Stephen J. Rose, "Socioeconomic Status, Race/Ethnicity, and Selective College Admissions," in *America's Untapped Resource: Low-Income Students in Higher Education,* ed. Richard D. Kahlenberg (New York: Century Foundation Press, 2004), p. 106.

white and black, dominated enrollments at twenty-eight highly selective colleges and universities. Fully 98 percent of the white students at these colleges came from social class backgrounds that ranged from middle class to upper class, as did 86 percent of the black students.[27]

What's more, evidence suggests that access to the nation's most desirable colleges and universities has over time become more powerfully influenced by family background factors and relatively less so by the meritocratic factors that these institutions have long labored under the illusion of upholding. In one of the more definitive proofs in recent years of the growing class stratification in higher education, Alexander W. Astin and Leticia Oseguera analyzed enrollment patterns at institutions of varying degrees of selectivity between 1971 and 2000, looking specifically at students' family backgrounds.

Astin and Oseguera found something quite startling. Consider first the students at highly selective colleges whose parents both had at least bachelor's degrees. In the relatively egalitarian days of 1971, this group, whose parents were highly educated, made up 28 percent of the entering class (see figure 4). By 1990, they made up 50 percent; and by 2000, students with highly educated parents were more than 61 percent of the freshmen at highly selective institutions. Also during that thirty-year period, the enrollment of students whose parents had not gone to college declined from 25 percent of the freshmen to just 9 percent. Students whose parents had a medium level of educational attainment (one parent with a BA) constituted almost 47 percent of the freshman class at these selective universities in 1971, but by 2000, their representation had declined to about 30 percent.[28]

Of course, part of the growing dominance of freshmen with highly educated parents at selective colleges is a result of a generally more educated society over the past thirty years. But even accounting for this sort of educational inflation, Astin and Osegueva determined that students from affluent, highly educated families had a far greater chance of attending an elite college than students of more modest social and economic backgrounds. "This analysis of three decades of data from national samples of entering college freshmen shows substantial socioeconomic inequalities in who gains access to the most selective colleges and universities in the United States," the authors conclude. "Further, these inequities have increased during recent decades, despite the expansion of remedial efforts such as student financial aid, affirmative action, and outreach programs."[29]

The advantages that accrue to students who attend selective colleges are not merely symbolic. "The economic benefits of attending a selective college are clear," write Anthony P. Carnevale and Stephen J. Rose in the Century Foundation's 2004 book *America's Untapped Resource: Low-Income Students in Higher Education.* Compared to those who attend less selective institutions, students who go to selective colleges graduate at significantly higher rates, have a greater chance of attending graduate or professional schools, and are likely to earn significantly more money. Indeed, Carnevale and Rose cite several recent studies suggesting that attending a top university compared to a middling one boosts one's earnings roughly 10 to 20 percent. The economic payoffs are also evident when one considers the differing amounts that colleges spend on students in the form of student subsidies, which can show up vividly in the quality and quantity of resources devoted to teaching and learning, as well as in cultural and recreational activities. In fact, annual student subsidies at wealthy private institutions can be several times greater than those at less selective public institutions, ranging as high as $24,000 per student and as low as $2,000, according to Carnevale and Rose.[30]

What accounts for the growing class stratification of American higher

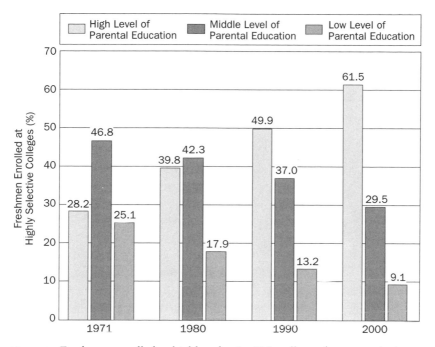

Figure 4. Freshmen enrolled at highly selective U.S. colleges, by parental education level, 1971 to 2000. Note: Selective colleges are defined here as those whose freshman class has a median SAT score of at least 1200. Source: Alexander W. Astin and Leticia Osegueva, "The Declining Equity of American Higher Education," *Review of Higher Education* 27, no. 3 (2004): 321–341.

education? One possibility is that differences in educational attainment among social classes or any demographic group are largely the impartial result of the American "meritocracy" working as it should. Is the meritocracy machine, then, simply grinding away, impervious to the winners and losers?

Astin and Osegueva suggest otherwise. They examined the changing relationship over time between academic factors such as test scores, a student's family background, and the student's chances of enrolling in a highly selective college. Between 1990 and 2000, they found that the correlation between the SAT or ACT admissions tests and the chances of enrollment remained stable, that high school grades declined in importance, and that both parental income and parental education increased in importance.[31] Their results suggest that academic factors became relatively less important in the 1990s and that nonacademic factors associated with social class—parental income, educational levels, and the cultural capital that students inherit from birth—became relatively more powerful influences on one's chances of going to an elite university.

Astin and Osegueva's results are by no means isolated. Other researchers have reached similar conclusions while examining distinctly different sources of data. For example, Jeffrey Owings, Timothy Madigan, and Bruce Daniel at the U.S. Department of Education found that students from upper socioeconomic brackets enrolled in the top fifty national universities, the so-called Tier 1 schools as defined by *U.S. News and World Report,* at three times the rate of students from low socioeconomic backgrounds (see appendix A, figure A-6).[32]

In fact, many if not all of the factors that correlate with getting into the Tier 1 schools can be traced directly to one's place in the socioeconomic hierarchy—the material and cultural circumstances into which a child is born and which shape his or her childhood. SAT scores, for instance, are powerfully correlated with the wealth and education levels of parents. A school's Advanced Placement class offerings are related to the "college-going culture" of the school and the demands made by parents for these courses, not to mention a school's financial ability to offer them. The extensive tracking in U.S. schools according to advanced, regular, and remedial courses, particularly in math, bears heavily on opportunities to take courses such as high school calculus. Being on the right math track, which leads to calculus, is powerfully related to a student's race and the social class of his or her parents.

In an analysis of the U.S. Department of Education's High School and Beyond database, a longitudinal survey of thirty thousand high school seniors from the class of 1980, James C. Hearn isolated the relative effects of academic merit versus social and economic background. How much does each factor explain whether a high school graduate finds his or her way to the top or bottom of the higher education pyramid? Hearn found that nonacademic factors explained as much as one-half of the differences among high school graduates in the selectivity of colleges they attended:

> When one considers the evidence . . . that influential academic characteristics, such as educational expectations, seem to be shaped in significant ways by social origins by way of socialization, tracking, teachers' attitudes, unequal schools, and so forth . . . any purely meritocratic interpretation of the dominant effects of academic characteristics in the present analysis is called into question. The most stubborn barriers to meritocracy seem to be those

that are directly and indirectly based in [socioeconomic status], rather than those that are based in race, ethnicity, or gender.[33]

In a 2002 update and replication of Hearn's study, David Karen, a sociologist at Bryn Mawr College, reported that one's social background—particularly one's father's education—proved to be just as powerful as academic merit in predicting the selectivity of the college one attended. "This finding suggests that for a cohort of students who were in high school a full quarter century after the Higher Education Act of 1965, which was designed to equalize opportunities for higher education, where one goes to college continues to be dependent on one's circumstances of birth," Karen writes.[34] Furthermore, the relative strength of social class as a predictor appears to have substantially increased. When Karen compared the relative power of academic merit and social background factors for 1980 graduates versus 1992 graduates, he found that the effects of the father's education and parental income actually *doubled* in power between the two cohorts.

In fact, the probability of attending a four-year college shoots up from 37 percent to 60 percent when we compare students from lower socio-economic backgrounds to those from higher socioeconomic backgrounds—even when we control for all other explanations, including academic merit and college costs. That is, if we take two otherwise identical students who differ only in their social origins, the student with affluent, well-educated parents has a 23 percent greater chance of attending a four-year institution than the poorer student, as David T. Ellwood and Thomas J. Kane discovered in their 2000 National Educational Longitudinal Study research analyzing a cohort of 1992 high school graduates (see appendix A, figure A-7). "We find no support for the conclusion that academic preparation accounts for all of the difference in college going," they argue. "Moreover, we think the real issue is the finding that college-going rates among young people with identical high school records and test scores differ greatly depending on the combination of parental income and education."[35]

This isn't to suggest that academic merit, at least as determined by test scores and grades, makes little difference. Ellwood and Kane's research suggests that merit so defined remains central to a student's chances of going to college. Indeed, the chances of attending a four-year institution increase from 29 percent to 74 percent when we compare a student with modest grades and test scores to one with high grades and scores. "The single most powerful determinant of college-going remains high school achievement," Ellwood and Kane write. "Anything we do to reduce the achievement gaps that are present by high school will do a great deal to equalize the enrollments of students from various backgrounds. But that effort is gargantuan indeed, and major successes remain rare."[36]

––––––

In a nation in which 40 percent of adults believe that they currently are at the top of the social and economic pyramid, or will someday rise to that position, regardless of their circumstances of birth or how they grew up, the notion that a student's social class origins remain important to his or her educational prospects can be hard to collectively rationalize. So we invent various stories that we like to tell ourselves, to make us feel that the world is working as it should.

I spoke with David Karen, the Bryn Mawr sociologist who has studied educational opportunities in the American class structure for several decades. As someone who also teaches at a highly selective college, Karen has as good a sense as anyone for how members of the upper and middle classes rationalize their fortunate outcomes in the system.

"I basically think their concerns are how the system works for their group. And as far as they're concerned, if you're not in their group, most likely it's because you screwed up in some way," Karen told me.[37] "Because they know how hard they worked in order to get where they are. If you're an upper-middle-class kid who's applying to the top colleges, all you know is that you have been busting your butt from day one, as far back as you can remember. You've been doing all these extracurricular activities; you've worked really hard in school, staying up late. You've worked hard for what you've gotten. And anybody had that opportunity."

"Anybody?" I asked him.

"Anybody. Anybody had that opportunity. That's your perception of where you are, and indeed when they look around at their friends in school, that's their perception. You know—they outworked the other kids, and that's why they're eighth in their school and the other kids are behind them. Because they've gone through this crucible of the college admissions process, that totally reinforces the sense that their hard work and their outcome are totally connected."

I asked Karen: "Do you think that the kids you teach at your school have a sense of awareness of their privileges relative to kids that don't have anywhere near their advantages?"

"You mean the ones that don't take my class?" he answered, only slightly joking. "Well, you know, there's tremendous variation in how self-reflective kids are about their social locations. In sociology, we're constantly talking about the social structure and race differences and class differences and gender differences, et cetera, et cetera, so you know, I hope, I *hope* we do a better job than with kids who avoid us. Kids who avoid us miss that. I think there is a tendency of the small contingent of working-class kids who do go to elite colleges—my sense is that they are disproportionately more likely to go to places like sociology. But, yeah, you know, it's amazing how unreflective students can be."

"If one isn't admitted to a selective college and happens to come from a disadvantaged background, do you think that the more advantaged kid would say, 'Well, he or she just didn't work hard enough'?" I asked.

"I think there is a sense that, yeah, there might be financial considerations. But in terms of simply getting in, people think that there's some luck involved. Because at their fancy schools, there's always one kid that they thought would get into X place but didn't. So there's the sense that there's some degree of uncertainty about the process, because otherwise, why have the anxiety? And that's what the whole system lives on," Karen explained. "Anxiety."

He continued, "Basically, I think there's a whole set of reasons that the upper-class kids would say why the lower-class kids don't go to the top colleges. They'd say, 'Well, they didn't work hard enough, they're not smart enough, they didn't have enough money. Oh, I'm sorry, they weren't ambitious enough.' Low down would be the opportunity aspect."

————

While social class dominates the opportunity structure of American higher education, we will see in the following two chapters that colleges and universities often behave as if economic disadvantage has little place at the table of equal opportunity. We'll discover that colleges and universities, while often talking the talk of equal opportunity, frequently act in ruthless ways to maintain their rankings in a higher education marketplace driven by status, prestige, and other values that reward the rich and punish the poor.

SEVEN

PART CHURCH, PART CAR DEALER

The unfortunate irony of our collective dismissal of class questions in public debates about educational equity is that class is the grand organizing principle of American education. Class, and where one fits into the class structure, *defines* the American education system. Social class—measured by parents' education, their cultural and financial resources, and their occupational status—is fundamental to a student's chances of even considering going to college, and it is fundamental to the kind of college a student can hope to attend. To paraphrase Albert Einstein's famous portrait of the universe, God does not play dice with the opportunity structure in America.

Still, there's a common view that an individual's success in this opportunity structure is often a matter of luck. For example, Pulitzer Prize–winning author Louis Menand lamented in a *New Yorker* essay a few years ago that admission to elite American colleges had become a crap shoot, an unpredictable game, despite the best efforts of parents and their kids to beat the odds. Meritocracy, he argued, was a "canard."[1] As a descriptor of the workings of American higher education, meritocracy may be a canard, but not because one's chances in the game amount to a game of dice. An individual's opportunity to even play the game is preordained long before an application reaches the admissions office. Access to the game is determined by an elaborate, self-perpetuating arrangement of social and economic privilege that systematically grants advantages to affluent, well-educated families, while systematically shutting the gates of opportunity to those without such advantages. But our meritocratic, yet egalitarian, ideal of American higher education persists, a fiction useful to the wealthy and educated classes that are largely its beneficiaries.

Just as elites harbor the conceit that their unlimited opportunities are well deserved, nonelites tend to believe that their disadvantages should not be attributed to their social and economic circumstances, but rather to something else, something more sinister. Scapegoats are invented. Consider a young woman named Cathy, daughter of a police officer and a secretary, as described in Patricia M. McDonough's book *Choosing Colleges: How Social Class and Schools Structure Opportunity.* Although she was a good student at a Catholic girls' high school, Cathy assumed that the University of California campuses weren't a possibility for her because minority students, aided by affirmative action programs, were taking her place.[2]

But the most remarkable aspect of the admissions game is its widely perceived *normality.* It is normal life, the logic goes, therefore it must be legitimate. But in fact, the consequences of the affirmative action programs that have engendered so much controversy and public scrutiny over the years are almost undetectable compared to the effects of a far more powerful and subtle kind of affirmative action, one that most Americans don't blink an eye at.

Cathy may well believe she didn't have a chance of getting into top universities like the University of California because of racial preferences in admission (which actually were designated as illegal in California, owing to university and state initiatives). But she and countless other Americans do not readily acknowledge the most important kind of "affirmative action" taking place every day in American society, which defines American higher education to its very core. It's the elephant in the room that nobody acknowledges. And, in recent decades, this elephant has gotten even bigger and more dangerous, to the point that no sensible person who claims even a scintilla of fondness for such ideals as fairness, equal opportunity, and democratic values can continue to ignore it.

———

Tom Mortenson is one who refuses to ignore.

When I spoke to him, he had just concluded a meeting with important officials at the University of Iowa, in his home state, trying to get them to listen to his concerns about the university's plan to raise admissions standards for undergraduates. In the age of *U.S. News and World Report*'s annual rankings of America's "best" colleges, Mortenson had seen the same story unfold time and again. Colleges and universities, public and private, were engaged in a highly competitive race, doing whatever it took to beat out their peer institutions in what have become the most hated—and most cherished—rankings in the higher education industry.

In pursuit of status and high rankings, colleges were embarking on extravagant marketing strategies in an effort to boost applications from the most desirable student customers—preferably those with high SAT or ACT scores who were also at the top of their high school classes, students who would bring academic prestige to the institution. All institutions, it seemed, were competing for the same high-scoring students. Increasingly, these most desirable students came from relatively privileged backgrounds, with families who had provided them with good schools, high-performing peers, and the best college preparation money could buy.

Colleges were beefing up "development" staffs to raise endowment funds for "merit" scholarships, in order to entice those same high-performing students to their universities, regardless of whether the students actually needed the money for college. The tactical maneuvers to boost institutional prestige were limited only by the imaginations of inventive marketers and "enrollment managers." Acceptance rates were to be minimized, and "yield rates" were to be maximized. The latter were among the more obtuse measurements in the college rankings game, referring to the percentage of students admitted who actually enrolled, supposedly an indicator of the university's desirability and prestige. But most important of all, the colleges sought to increase their overall academic "reputation" among college and university presidents, admissions officials, and provosts. This nebulous quality was higher education's beauty contest, and it carried the most weight in the *U.S. News* rankings. The most direct route to success in the beauty contest was to become far more picky about who got admitted, and the surest way to accomplish that was to continue to raise the average SAT score of the admitted class.

At the same time, however, educational institutions were trying to maintain a delicate balance between the competitive demands of the race for prestige and their historical mission to serve some larger public good. American colleges and universities have long been seen as stalwarts in the nation's battles for justice, equal educational opportunity, and civil rights. They have been on the front lines of the affirmative action wars. In the interests of maintaining some semblance of diversity, universities fought vigorously for the right to take race and gender into account in their admissions decisions. But how much of this concern for diversity was just rhetoric?

To put it bluntly, Mortenson was getting pissed off. As a higher education analyst who has long published a newsletter called *Postsecondary Education Opportunity,* a monthly statistical tract on the condition of equal educational opportunity that has virtually become required reading among higher education leaders, journalists, and analysts, Mortenson could no longer contain his contempt for recent developments among American colleges and universities. With each new issue of his newsletter, his voice kept rising louder, hoping that his readers would listen and that the nation might confront the worsening inequities in educational opportunity. At a time when a college education was becoming the definitive marker dividing America's haves and have-nots, colleges themselves were failing the tests of equal opportunity. For all their rhetoric about diversity, the universities were turning their backs on children born into working-class and lower-income families. In their endless pursuit of prestige and *U.S. News* rankings, the universities were talking the talk of Martin Luther King Jr., but they were acting like freshly minted MBAs.

"I'm old, I'm angry, I'm frustrated, and I don't see much reason to hold things back any more," Mortenson told me.[3]

At age sixty-two, and nearing retirement, Mortenson described for me his thirty-five-year journey, a journey about educational justice that began in earnest after he left the Peace Corps in 1970. He had worked as a volunteer in Colombia, after college in the late 1960s. "I learned a great deal about a country that did not take care of its poor," Mortenson recalled of his Peace Corps years. "And, in fact, exploited its poor."

At his Minneapolis high school, Mortenson had taken an American Studies course, in which his teacher, Miss Bergeron, gave her students a quarter-long assignment to write up their family histories. That assignment turned into a lifelong project for Mortenson that deeply influenced his life's work. By finding the roots of his own family, he discovered for himself what America meant in relation to the class structures of the Old Europe of his ancestors.

After college and the Peace Corps, Mortenson made his first trip to Europe, in 1975, to try to understand why his ancestors left. He explained, "Most of my ancestors came to this country between about 1840 and 1880. The first place I visited was Sweden, where my great-grandparents left in 1880, and I was surprised to find that my ancestors lived in the shadow of a castle. When I went to East Germany, I found that my ancestors had lived in the shadow of a castle there. And I found this pattern as I went around to the five places that my ancestors came from. Four of them lived in the shadows of castles. And one was a draft dodger. My Prussian ancestors were bailing out of Prussia in the 1860s when Bismarck was marching up and down Europe and fighting all sorts of wars.

"What I came to understand is that my ancestors left Europe because there was no opportunity for them. They were basically all poor peasant farmers. And there was land available in the United States, and so they came here to exploit the opportunities. They farmed here, and they did really quite well. This is up in rural Minnesota. And even though my great-grandfather signed his name with an 'X' when he left Sweden in 1880, his first-born son, my grandfather, got a grade-school education. I know from the letters that survived that he was very proud of being a literate person. And he married a dynamic Prussian woman who wanted to send all three of her boys to college. Now, this is back around 1910 and 1920.

"When the oldest boy got up to college age, they sold their house and store in rural Minnesota and moved down to Minneapolis. They bought a house a half a block from the Minneapolis campus at the University of Minnesota, and they put all three boys through the University of Minnesota. So my father got a college education, and I've got a master's degree. I've got a daughter who, when her husband's career settles down, is probably going to go back and get a PhD. In every respect, the opportunities that were available in this country and were not available to my ancestors in Europe brought us to where we're at. Then it was land, the availability of land, that brought people here. That was the meaning of opportunity in the latter part of the 1800s and early 1900s."

In the early 1970s, the American economy began to shed the last vestiges of the industrial revolution and the nation's dependency on land, natural resources, and manufacturing for its economic vitality. In his newsletter, Mortenson makes constant references to what he calls the "Human Capital Economy," the now widely received notion that, increasingly, the value of labor derives less from what a worker can make, move, or dig and more from what the worker knows and the sorts of information over which he or she has command—in other words, cognitive skills that formal education creates and nurtures. Since the early 1970s, this economic reformation "has brutally redistributed," as Mortenson puts it, wealth and income from the less educated laboring classes to the professional classes with college educations and advanced degrees.

Indeed, income statistics from the U.S. Census Bureau underscore this brutal and familiar reality. Between 1967 and 1992, families headed by a parent without a high school diploma saw their real incomes *decline* an average of 14 percent. Incomes of families headed by a high school graduate inched up just 1.2 percent, while the incomes of those headed by a college graduate shot up more than 30 percent. Heads of households with advanced degrees saw their real incomes surge 42 percent. In 2002, a family headed by a high school graduate averaged $53,000 a year. When the head of the house had some college, family income went up to $65,000, while a bachelor's degree increased it to $95,000. And when the head of the household had a professional degree, family income averaged $157,000—fully three times the income of families headed by an individual without any college.[4]

"Since 1973, a college education has been the requisite credential for access to the middle class," Mortenson said. "Basically, I think that is the American experience. So the question of who gets higher education really defines, in my view, what America is all about. And given my ancestral origins, from peasant farmers in a European system that really didn't give a damn about poor people, it seems to me that the core of the American experience is who gets a higher education. And it's not just immigrants I'm talking about. I'm talking about everybody who is born into lower-income families or poverty. If we believe that the American experience is for everyone, then the question has to be, how do we design public policy to make that happen?"

Recently, Mortenson told me, he had begun to take aim at colleges and universities themselves as key gatekeepers in the American opportunity structure. Because of the lack of public information, it's difficult for outside observers to determine the distribution of family incomes of students at American universities. But Mortenson and other analysts do pay a lot of attention to one widely available indicator, which is the number of undergraduates at a given university who are eligible for federal Pell Grants, which are designed for lower-income students. Not coincidentally, as universities strive to compete in the prestige-driven marketplace governed by the *U.S. News* rankings, there is often an inverse correlation between a university's commitment to lower-income students and its performance in the ranking game.

As an example, Mortenson described for me his somewhat unpleasant meeting with the Iowa officials. "I had a very intense meeting at the University of Iowa. I was beating up on them over the fact that they are increasing their enrollment of Iowa residents without Pell Grants, and they're greatly increasing their enrollment of nonresidents, while they're cutting their enrollment of low-income Iowans," he explained. "And these are people that publicly profess to be committed to diversity. So I'm challenging the integrity and values of people who are professing one thing, but their institution's bottom line says they are doing the opposite."

Make no mistake, for all its progressive and idealistic rhetoric, higher education has become a fully branded big business in America, stocked with higher education's equivalent of blue chips, penny stocks, and start-ups. While the abundance of higher education institutions in the United States is extraordinary, the industry is highly stratified, and the economic disparities between rich schools and poor ones are sufficient to place some elite colleges, their students, and their faculty a world apart from those of more common means.

Although public and nonprofit private institutions don't maximize "profits" per se, they do compete fiercely for institutional prestige and endeavor to maximize their endowments—which represent the residual of their particular sort of revenues, less costs. That "profit," as it were, enables an institution to add to its stores of prestige and to further enhance its endowment, a vicious or virtuous circle, depending on whether you happen to be Harvard University, with an endowment in 2005 exceeding $25 billion—the largest of its kind on the globe—or Georgia Perimeter College, with an endowment of $440.[5]

Although higher education is big business, the economics of the industry are peculiar indeed. As Gordon C. Winston, a leading higher education economist at Williams College, observes, one of the most striking aspects of the "firms" in this industry is that they lose money on every unit they sell. Students at traditional public and not-for-profit private schools never pay the full cost of going to college. Never. Elite private institutions subsidize students through their often enormous endowments, while public institutions have historically subsidized students from state tax revenues.

Winston notes that it is the size of the student subsidies—from the salaries paid to professors, to the size of the student recreation center, to the collegiate "feel" of an institution conveyed by its ivy-covered walls and well-manicured lawns—that separates the elite institutions from "Wal-Mart U." So, for example, Winston estimates that cut-rate private colleges in 1995–1996 provided an average student subsidy of about $3,000, so that the net price to students was 71 percent of the full cost of educating them. At the other extreme, elite private institutions provided student subsidies of nearly $24,000, and students therefore paid only 28 percent of the actual education costs.

"Larger student subsidies give more and better maintained buildings, better faculty, neater lawns, a better stocked library, more and more imaginative academic programs, more extensive student services, better food. . . . And all this at a net tuition not much higher than that charged by the austere low-subsidy college down the road," Winston explains. "To compound all this, since students find high-subsidy schools attractive and queue up to get into them, larger subsidies bring more selectivity and higher-quality peers," at least as measured by SAT scores, he notes. "Economically, a college is part church and part car dealer and can only be understood that way."[6]

Other economists have taken a somewhat different tack to reach similar conclusions. We can think of colleges and universities as falling into one of two very different camps, Dominic J. Brewer, Susan M. Gates, and Charles A. Goldman argue in their study *In Pursuit of Prestige,* about the higher education industry. Based on interviews with two hundred administrators, students, and faculty at twenty-six institutions throughout the country, the authors identified a number of institutions that were focused on seeking "prestige," while others were more keen on building their "reputation."

Prestige-seekers were consumed with the world of the *U.S. News and World Report* ranking scheme, which is dominated by prestige-oriented measures. This is how Brewer and his colleagues describe the prestige-seekers:

> Identification of the "best providers" may be based purely on the opinion of the customer, or may also be based on the insights of the producers themselves or industry experts. On the basis of this information . . . customers develop images of the features of good service providers. Certain characteristics of a college or university become associated with good providers even though these characteristics are not directly related to the quality of the output. For example, it may be observed that good schools tend to have sports teams and impressive buildings with ivy covered walls. A rule of thumb is developed that suggests that a high quality, broad education can be obtained at institutions that have sports teams and ivy covered walls.

Prestige-seeking colleges, the authors found, developed their images "by 'looking right,' " rather than directly meeting the primary demands of customers. As a result, such institutions "tend to become very forward looking—focused on acquiring the trappings of the most prestigious institutions in the industry."[7]

Prestige-seekers were obsessed with rankings, with data of any type that compared their institution with its competitors. Prestige was a zero-sum game, because one institution's gain in the prestige game meant another's decline. As a consequence, investments that made any significant dent in one's prestige ratings were costly. These investments in prestige took the form of recruiting the right kinds of student customers, valued according to their SAT or ACT scores; investing heavily in research and capacity for obtaining federal research grants; and building up their profiles in collegiate sports, primarily NCAA football and basketball.

The reputation-oriented colleges that Brewer and his colleagues examined were a different beast altogether. They were uninterested in prestige and had no desire to compete with other universities on such terms. Indeed, the difference between reputation-based institutions and prestige-seeking ones was a bit like the difference between image and substance. "Quality" for prestige-seekers bordered on the abstract— "becoming a world-class university" or "to become a university of hemispheric importance." These were the sorts of slogans found in the strategic plans of the prestige-seekers. Reputation-based colleges, in contrast, were far more concrete about their objectives because they wanted to serve their students and the communities in which they operated. Hence, they measured their performance on that basis: How much did students learn at the institution? What kinds of jobs were they prepared to do after graduation? How satisfied were alumni of the college? Was the local community satisfied with the college's contributions to families, employees, and other local institutions? "These institutions are focused on meeting the identifiable demands of customers," the economists explain. "Because reputation is built by successfully meeting customer demands at a reasonable price, as opposed to meeting the . . . expectations of internal groups, [reputation-based] institutions tend to be student-centered, dynamic, and responsive to the changing needs of society."[8]

Among the most vivid distinctions between the two types of colleges, the economists discovered, was their attitude toward students. Prestige-seekers valued students for the amount of prestige that the students bring to the institution at the point of admission—long before the colleges have a chance to teach them anything. High school grades and test scores are the measures of this value. For reputation-based colleges, which tended to be far less selective in their admissions practices than the prestige-seekers, such a perspective on students would have been nonsensical. As Brewer and his co-authors explain:

> We identified a strong distinction between the strategies pursued by [reputation-based] institutions, on the one hand, and [prestige-seeking] institutions on the other. The primary reason is that, whereas [reputation-based] insti-

tutions are focused on building their reputations by meeting the needs of students, [prestige-seekers] are focused on improving the selectivity of the admissions process and only secondarily on actually meeting the needs of the students. . . . Because [reputation-based] institutions are not trying to build prestige, they derive little benefit from the attributes of the student, per se. Because these institutions do not engage in highly selective admissions processes, students do not benefit simply from the fact that they were admitted to the institution. Instead, in order to provide benefit to the student, the institution must actually provide a service, generate knowledge, teach the student a skill, or provide the student with consumption benefits.[9]

Many colleges no doubt see their main job as creating programs to best serve their students and help them learn what they need to succeed after they graduate. But the prevailing zeitgeist of higher education in twenty-first-century America is centered around the status game, with *U.S. News and World Report* as its self-appointed arbiter and game master. Though Brewer and his colleagues didn't identify the schools they studied, nor did they estimate whether the growth of prestige-seeking schools was in fact outpacing that of reputation-based ones, a variety of other evidence suggests that more and more institutions are choosing to play the prestige game—and that they do so at the expense of their obligation to serve the greater public good.

Except for private, for-profit institutions such as the University of Phoenix, colleges and universities can't legally earn profits, but they can try to boost their prestige ratings. In truth, they're in the business of "prestige management." But for obvious reasons, they won't publicly admit to that coarser side of their nature. Instead, the industry has invented innocuous terms for these enterprises, and the latest buzz phrase encompassing the prestige-driven nature of higher education is "enrollment management."

Universities have always had enrollments, and they've always "managed" them, most basically by deciding who is admitted to the freshman class. But the enterprise has become considerably more complicated in recent years as the industry has become more competitive, more prestige-driven, and more fluid, as students and colleges play an elaborate matching game, each player continually jockeying for the best position possible. Students want admission to the most prestigious universities possible, given their financial resources, grades, and SAT scores. Universities want to maximize revenues and build their endowments, but that objective is limited by their short-run need to spend scholarship money on the right sorts of students with the right profile of grades, extracurriculars, and SAT scores, which the universities believe will lead to long-run prestige and financial gain.

Enrollment management in higher education is similar to what happens in other industries such as health care and finance, where customers or patients come with both potential risk and reward for the firms. Health insurance companies want to manage their enrollees by making sure that the enterprises don't have too many old or sick patients who are likely to run up health care costs that exceed what they pay in premiums. Managed-care firms in health care engage in elaborate "utilization review" schemes to ensure that doctors don't spend too much money treating patients. Financial institutions lend money to businesses and consumers after evaluating their risk of default. Banks want to market to customers who maintain healthy balances and don't use too many banking services.

Higher education's version of this risk-reward calculus is enrollment management, and colleges and universities have borrowed elaborate and highly sophisticated marketing techniques from other industries to ensure that they enroll sufficient numbers of the "right" kinds of students. Just 1 percent of public and private four-year universities were *not* doing formal enrollment management in one recent national survey, and more than eight of ten institutions had designated a senior-level administrator in charge of enrollment planning, often reporting directly to the president of the university. Undergraduate admissions was the main job of enrollment planners, including all the recruiting, marketing, and publication activities. But increasingly, the admissions and financial aid functions were being melded at the universities, and enrollment managers were in charge of both.[10]

A glimpse of the sophistication with which enrollment management has transformed higher education, using data-mining, predictive statistical modeling, and other marketing techniques borrowed from the for-profit sector, can be seen in the part of the enrollment management industry that consults with colleges and universities. One firm, Education Systems Inc., pushes the notion of "strategic" enrollment management and challenges universities somewhat bluntly:

> Will the size of the incoming class be more than last year or less? Will the incoming class bring "better" students that will allow the institution to increase their average ACT or SAT score? These and many more enrollment

challenges are complex problems to solve. Historically, many institutions and their leaders thought it sufficient to open their doors and students would fill their classrooms. . . . In this competitive environment, Education Systems provides colleges, universities and community colleges software solutions that will give them a competitive advantage in today's crowded higher education market.[11]

Finding the right kinds of student customers and their families begins with recruiting, and that begins with enrollment managers identifying prospects who are likely to fit the university's admissions and financial profile. In this brave new world of "strategic admissions" and "financial aid leveraging," the unassuming students and their families are swimming with sharks. When a high school junior takes a standardized test for admission or scholarships, or fills out some career or college "interest" form under the supervision of counselors and teachers at the local school, or looks for possible colleges on some Web site offering "free" college counseling, that student is in fact providing colleges and universities with personal data that shapes from the get-go whether that college has even the remotest intention of ever granting admission or providing financial aid.

Consider, for example, a tax-exempt organization called the National Research Center for College and University Admissions (NRCCUA), based in Lee's Summit, Missouri. This somewhat obscure organization has been gathering data on millions of individual students, under the auspices of the twenty thousand public and private high schools that have granted the company permission to collect the data, for some three decades. Over the past several years, the company has used this data, gathered from some 5.5 million students each year, to develop proprietary enrollment management products for the higher education industry. The firm charges students and their schools nothing, but its clients (about a thousand colleges and universities) are willing to pay for the company's impressive assortment of marketing tools.

One product, College Choices—Who's Who Edition, identifies students with B averages who've been nominated by a "qualified" adult to be among the Who's Who of American high school students. But only certain colleges are qualified to receive the data: they must be classified as "selective" or "most selective" according to the *U.S. News and World Report* rankings. There is also an honors edition of the product, which enables the firm's clients to target some 220,000 students—at their home addresses. Another of the company's products, E-Match, is especially interesting. Because colleges and universities cull individualized data on students from a variety of sources, no single information source offers a complete profile of a given student. E-Match allows the colleges to fill in the data gaps on students. The company supplies colleges with a student's birth date, home address, e-mail address, GPA, high school, intended major, participation in a college-prep track in high school, ethnicity, and extracurricular interests.[12]

Any time students take a college admission exam, they are knowingly—and perhaps unknowingly—supplying key marketing data to the testing companies, which in turn sell that personal data to colleges and universities trying to target the right students for admission and financial aid. The College Board, the tax-exempt company that owns the SAT, and ACT Inc., another tax-exempt company that produces the ACT Assessment, are the two biggest players in this area of enrollment management. Indeed, these testing companies combine information gleaned from the students directly on the day of the exam, including their test scores, with a variety of other demographic data gathered from sources such as the U.S. Census Bureau to create highly detailed profiles of the socioeconomic status of their potential customers, including their ability to pay for college and the likelihood that they will enroll in college. The College Board, ACT Inc., or any other data-mining enterprise can determine approximately how much money students' parents and their neighbors earn, the size and value of their homes, whether they own homes or rent them, the occupational status of family members, the educational attainment of parents, and how many cars they drive.

Take, for example, the College Board's Enrollment Planning Service. The company informs potential higher education clients that EPS

> is the marketing software that pinpoints the schools and geomarkets where your best prospects are most likely to be found. With the click of a mouse, EPS provides you with comprehensive reports on your markets, your position in those markets, and your competition. Focus your valuable time and resources on the right prospects. EPS is the most effective way to find the students you need to reach. . . . With EPS, you can pinpoint your most promising states, geomarkets, counties, zip codes, and high schools, assess your competition, and calculate your market share. EPS provides you with accurate, up-to-date information on college-bound students, including . . . addresses, phone numbers . . . college-going rates, instate and out-of-state mobility rates, academic interests, average family income, religion, Advanced Placement Program information, SAT score averages, and more.[13]

Besides the testing companies and NRCCUA, other firms see the enrollment management wave as integral to their business plans. The

Princeton Review, for instance, is widely known in the test-prep business for coaching students for all manner of standardized admissions tests. According to Princeton Review's public filings with federal securities regulators, the company is hoping to exploit its brand name, garnered in the test-prep industry, in order to sell marketing information to colleges about potential student customers. The company does so via its Web site, princetonreview.com, taking advantage of personal data supplied by students and their families who are looking for information about colleges and standardized tests. Princeton Review turns around and sells that information to colleges.

And it's all based on "trust." A billion dollars' worth of trust. Says the company: "We have been evolving the business model of that website for over a decade. Our test prep business and content give us access to, and the trust of, students early in the college and graduate school admissions process. At the same time, we believe post-secondary schools spend over a billion dollars each year marketing to these students, and we are positioned to be the category leader as those funds are increasingly spent online." The company's Admissions Services Division nearly doubled in size between 2001 and 2004.[14]

I trolled princetonreview.com to see how the company is trying to tap that billion-dollar enrollment management market. The site essentially plays matchmaker. To the enrollment managers at universities, the company says: "By looking at how students use our site—what schools they visit and what majors they are considering, for example—and analyzing their answers to the questions in our searches, we learn a lot about our visitors. We use this information to give them a better experience. When a student's behavior and academic profile indicate that your school might be a good match, we promote your school to that student. You tell us which characteristics you're looking for in a student, and we'll work to find those kinds of students for you."[15]

But first, the company must hook individual students, and it does so by offering a nominally cost-free, Internet-based service it calls Counselor-O-Matic, which promises students that it will find the colleges and universities for which they are best suited. All one must do is plug in the numbers and answer the brightly worded questions. So I played the game, inventing a persona that would be highly desirable for any prestige-driven institution, with very high grades, high SAT scores, and no financial need. I typed in the requested information as required: GPA (3.9); class rank (top 5 percent); SAT scores (750–790 on each of the verbal, math, and writing sections); preferences of college location (any); my

academic track (college-prep); extracurricular activities (literature, poetry, and golf); my ZIP code (very important for data-mining from outside sources); my ethnicity (white); my gender (male); my parents' ties to
particular colleges (I provided my alma mater); my religious preferences
(none); whether I wanted to commute to college or live on campus (I
want to party!); class-size preferences (small!); and whether I would need
financial aid (my parents are rich!).

The Princeton Review site asked me for these and many other details,
which captured not simply my personal preferences but also a fairly complete picture of my persona's socioeconomic class—information most
useful to college enrollment managers in search of the right students.
When I got through about fifteen or twenty minutes of this inquiry, the
site then asked me to supply my mailing address and my parents' income
and told me that I would not be able to see my results without providing this information. Counselor-O-Matic then told me:

> Hey, Peter! You've completed Counselor-O-Matic and signed up to let
> schools contact you based on the information you've entered. Nice work!
> See the data you're sharing with schools. Or, update your contact informa-
> tion. Here are the schools fitting your needs, organized by your likelihood
> of getting in (Good Matches, Reaches, and Safeties). The "percent fit"
> within each category indicates how closely the school matches your prefer-
> ences. *Note: Schools with a shaded background are Counselor-O-Matic
> sponsors.*[16]

My "good matches" included an 81 percent match with Carnegie Mellon University, and 75 percent with Bucknell University, Duke University, and Lafayette College. I also looked good to Georgetown, Oberlin,
University of Miami, Notre Dame, and other nice-looking colleges, all
with matches of 68 percent. Washington University in St. Louis was
pretty good at 62 percent, and I got a 56 percent fit with Harvard, Tufts,
California Institute of Technology, and so on. I was pleased. The brand
name schools seemed to like me. So I sat back and waited for my
Counselor-O-Matic experience to pay off, waiting for the recruiters from
Harvard, Tufts, and Carnegie Mellon to roll in.

One day, I came down with a sort of buyer's remorse. I logged on to
the Princeton Review site to take a look at my profile. As detailed as the
previous information had been, the site enticed me to disclose even more
personal information, with an online college application program called
Embark. The Embark site contained my financial, educational, and application profile (which, I noticed, was *not* Internet-secure) and told me
that if I provided the requested information, I would avoid the "aggra-

vation" of filling in a different online application form each time I applied to a college. Hassle-free. The Embark application, in addition to the standard academic and extracurricular profile, asked me for highly detailed information about my parents, including their occupations, where they went to college, what degrees they had obtained, and so on. The site also asked about my siblings, including where they went to college. What's more, if I wanted to supply information about my financial background, I could receive "offers" from the "financial institutions" that worked with Princeton Review.[17]

At this point, I became sufficiently alarmed with the potential for intrusion into my privacy that I read the site's privacy statement. You'd need to be a privacy lawyer to completely understand it. But I read enough to determine that, at the point where I had agreed, early on in the process, to allow my information to be shared with colleges that might be interested in me, I was essentially screwed. But when I read that the site employed "Clear Gifs," or "web bugs" the size of a period on my screen that permitted Princeton Review advertisers to track my movements on the Internet, my little game of Counselor-O-Matic was beginning to look more sinister. I was indeed playing with fire.[18]

––––––

Colleges and universities targeting the right customers and persuading them to file an application are just the first steps of the prestige-driven enrollment management process. Colleges itching to rise in the rankings by becoming more selective can't reject students if those students haven't applied. And once admitted, the proportion of students who go on to actually enroll, the yield rate, is another prestige boost. Targeting the right customers, with the help of Princeton Review, the College Board, ACT Inc., and the rest generates a pool of potential applicants who live in the most desirable "geomarkets," who have the right profile of grades and SAT scores and extracurricular interests, and who also have the right parents and the financial means to pay for college.

But a college can't build prestige by admitting only a lot of rich kids with modest SAT scores. In fact, the test scores are paramount, despite assertions made by some apologists in higher education that the admissions process at highly selective colleges isn't driven by SAT numbers and that test scores are simply one aspect of the application file. Examine any list of American colleges ranked by their degree of selectivity and similar measures that have come to dominate the ubiquitous rankings of "best colleges," and you will find that these rankings correlate almost perfectly to the colleges' average SAT scores. With the help of *U.S. News and World Report* and other self-appointed arbiters of educational excellence, higher education has become a deeply branded market, and average SAT scores have become perhaps the single most important market signal by which consumers rate and distinguish various brands.

The upshot is that gatekeeping tests such as the SAT are an important linchpin in a system dominated by social class, sustaining a highly stratified system of higher education. Being affluent or born to parents with advanced degrees certainly doesn't guarantee a fine performance on the SAT and other admissions tests, but the odds are very, very good. Consider the relationship between SAT I scores (math and verbal) and the education levels of parents. A college-bound senior in 2005 whose parents had only high school diplomas could expect, on average, to score 181 points below the SAT score of a student whose parents had advanced degrees. And that gap is larger today than it was in the past: in 1996, for example, that SAT score gap was 165 points.[19]

Money also matters, affording some students the best teachers, the most enriching schools, motivated peers, and a whole host of cultural and social resources that help children excel in school and perform well on standardized tests. In 2005, students with family incomes of more than $100,000 outscored students from families earning $40,000 to $50,000 by some 123 points on the SAT I. That gap has also increased in the last decade, rising from 113 points in 1996.[20]

How, then, to entice high-scoring students from a highly desirable "geomarket"—say, the students at New Trier High School, from a wealthy suburb of Chicago—who have a multitude of attractive higher education options? If you're an enrollment manager at an up-and-coming university whose job performance is evaluated on whether your college rises in the rankings, how do you "kick ass," as one leading university enrollment manager referred to his job in an interview published in the *Atlantic Monthly*?[21] How do you convince those New Trier students to choose you over Northwestern or Tufts or Emory, for example?

Well, you could buy them.

That is exactly what scores of colleges and universities have been doing over the past several years in order to survive the *U.S. News* arms race. As is the nature of an arms race, failure to expend the resources necessary simply to stay in the same place in the rankings would mean that you lose ground to your competition. They'll eat your lunch, as that same aggressive enrollment manager told the *Atlantic*.

"In an arms race, there's a lot of action, a lot of spending, a lot of worry, but, if it's a successful arms race, nothing much changes," writes Gordon Winston, describing the state of the higher education market. "It's the purest case of Alice and the Red Queen who had to run very fast, indeed, just to stay in one place. The essence of an arms race is position—how a country stands relative to others. So it's not what the country does that matters, but what it does relative to what everybody else does. No single country, alone, can safely quit the race even when all countries, together, would be better off if everyone did; unilateral disarmament—sweetness and cooperation—will swiftly be punished by loss of position."[22]

This is the car dealer side of the higher education business, with a vengeance. In order to persuade those high-scoring New Trier students to enroll in your up-and-coming college, you bribe them—and you do so by giving them merit scholarships; or you charge these highly desirable students lower tuition than you charge less desirable students; or you do both. You do it in exchange for the prestige such students provide to your institution. No matter that those New Trier students are sufficiently wealthy that they don't need your merit scholarships or your tuition discounts.

As a result of this arms race for rankings, and as a consequence of the inexorable relationship between SAT scores and parental wealth and education, colleges and universities have been spending a lot more merit-based scholarship and tuition dollars on the very students who *don't* need the money for college—at the expense of those students who can't afford college without need-based financial aid.

For example, in the mid-1990s, institutions gave students with family incomes of $100,000 and more an average of $1,359, which was less than 40 percent of the aid they gave to students from families earning $20,000 a year or less. Five years later, the aid given to students from the most affluent families equaled 82 percent of the total aid provided to the lowest-income students. This was a result of less need-based aid plus the staggering growth of merit scholarships and tuition discounting for wealthier students. For instance, students from families of modest incomes, earning $20,000 to $39,999, saw their institutional aid increase 21 percent at public universities during that five-year period. But students from families earning at least $100,000 saw their institutional aid shoot up 159 percent. At four-year private institutions, the story was similar, as aid to wealthy students surged 145 percent compared to just 15 percent for lower-income students.[23]

Besides buying a prestigious class with merit aid and steep tuition discounts off the sticker price, enrollment managers have various other tricks that help students who don't need the help and hurt those who do. For example, early admissions programs have long been used by selective private institutions in creating "proper" freshman classes, but they've become more common at public universities as well. In their recent book *The Early Admissions Game: Joining the Elite,* Christopher Avery and Richard Zeckhauser, both on the faculty of Harvard's John F. Kennedy School of Government, and Andrew Fairbanks, a former admissions dean at Wesleyan, offer a disturbing indictment of the early admissions game. The authors document the significant advantages accorded to those applicants who choose early admission, often because they possess the right family and school connections. Indeed, the authors show that the lion's share of the benefits of early admissions programs go to those applicants with insider information, involving a cozy alliance of privileged students, their guidance counselors at private prep schools, and college admissions officers at prestigious colleges.[24]

Well-heeled students, most of whom attend prep schools or certain public high schools that are part of the informal network of "feeder schools" to top colleges, are the early admissions winners. Because accepted students are obligated to enroll at the colleges to which they apply early, lower-income students cannot consider or negotiate their financial aid packages and therefore rarely consider submitting an early application. Wealthy students, for whom financial aid isn't a deal breaker, face no such dilemma.

Why does applying early matter for one's prospects of being accepted at the top colleges? Early application programs, along with other special categories of admissions, have become so dominant at highly selective colleges that they have virtually crowded out those who go through the front door, as it were, those who apply with the masses during the regular admissions cycle. Consider one recent admissions season at Princeton, cited in *The Early Admissions Game:* of some twelve thousand applications, two thousand students were admitted, and almost one-third of those were admitted early.[25]

Differences between admission rates for early applicants at top colleges and rates for regular applicants are substantial. In one recent year at Princeton, for example, 41 percent of the early applicants were admitted, compared to less than 8 percent of the regular applicants. At Harvard, 21 percent of the early applicants got in, compared to just 5 percent of the other applicants. All told, Avery, Fairbanks, and Zeckhauser determined, the admissions advantage accorded the early decision applicants they studied was the equivalent of nearly 200 extra points on the SAT I.[26]

The often-cited claims that differences in academic credentials explain the gaps in admission rates between front-door and side-door applicants is a canard, the authors found. Even after holding SAT scores constant, admission rates for the early applicants dwarfed those for the unfortunate students who waited for the regular cycle. At Yale, for example, early applicants with SAT scores of 1410–1450 were admitted at the same rate as regular applicants with SAT scores 100 points higher. For those scoring in the 1510–1550 range, 75 percent of early applicants were admitted to Yale, compared to just 19 percent of the regular applicants. "The evidence indicates that if you want to attend an Ivy League college, MIT or Stanford, then you should apply early," Avery and his co-authors tell us. "As one Harvard student explained in an interview, 'That's just how you apply to Harvard.'"[27]

Fundamental to this game that largely benefits affluent families is the nature of the information one has about early admissions programs and elite college admissions generally—public versus not public information, who has access to expertise, and who does not. The authors describe elaborate, back-channel "slotting" operations, far from public view, in which highly connected and expert counselors at the feeder schools work closely with admissions officials to place students at prestigious institutions. As one student told the researchers, "My counselor has a good relationship with the Harvard admissions office. He handpicks people for admission and tells Harvard who to admit."[28]

In fact, a student's knowledge of early admissions and likelihood of applying early are directly correlated to his or her social class background. Avery, Fairbanks, and Zeckhauser studied early applications by ZIP codes and found high concentrations of early applicants in high-income neighborhoods. While 90 percent of students at private high schools had a "good understanding" of early admissions programs, only 77 percent of those at public schools, even at schools where most students go on to college, had such knowledge. At public high schools where relatively few attend college, just 52 percent understood the early admissions process and its advantages.[29]

Rarely do colleges concede in public that early applicants are advantaged in the admissions process. But it's no accident that the colleges are so coy about the information they give the public, the authors explain. "Any acknowledgment of favoritism for early applicants—a wealthy and well-connected group—would play poorly with many constituencies. . . .

Perhaps colleges believe that the most desirable group of applicants—better-connected students who tend to be full-payers from leading feeder schools—will be able to ferret out the information that early applicants are favored, and that others [are] not. Then a garbled message, but one decipherable with hints or considerable experience, may be the preferred message to disseminate."[30]

Why are early admissions programs so popular with enrollment managers? That a large percentage of early applicants are potentially full-payers is surely one reason. Too, having a substantial portion of an entering class fill up early helps universities manage the risks of the admissions process, particularly the problem of accepted students who might not enroll without the binding commitment that early decision programs require. But the prestige arms race is also a factor. Because students admitted early will almost surely enroll, admitting a high percentage of the freshman class through early admissions ensures a higher yield rate. And then there's the sucker factor. A surefire method to make your college more selective is to juice up applications from those middle-of-the-road students who have a small chance of success. Most likely, these are the least well informed students of modest economic circumstances who don't have insider information on how to play the early admissions angles. These are the suckers who knock on the front door, the ones who are most likely to find rejection. But, for kick-ass enrollment managers, bumping up your applications, rejections, and yield rates over those of your arch-competitors just might get you a promotion.

Clearly, the pressures to retain early admissions in this competitive marketplace are great. This is why the decisions of some prominent universities in the latter part of 2006 to stop early admissions struck observers as bold. In September 2006, Harvard showed its cards, becoming the first elite institution to announce an end to its early admissions program. In this arms race for top students, it was undoubtedly necessary for a school with the stature of Harvard to make the first move in order to provoke any competitor to follow its lead. Indeed, just a week later, Princeton did exactly that. And then came the University of Virginia, becoming the first elite public institution to quit practicing early admissions. All three universities stated that their driving motivation was the unfairness of the practice for students from modest economic backgrounds.

Unfortunately, these moves by a select few top-tier schools aren't likely to provoke widespread reform. Neither Harvard, Princeton, nor the University of Virginia had much to lose; they'll continue to dominate in their respective markets with or without early admissions. As market leaders, these three universities know that high percentages of admitted students will enroll, so early admissions probably had only a small effect on the composition of their freshman classes. But most institutions are not Harvard or Princeton or the University of Virginia. As matters stand, without significant reform of the entire system, the vast majority of colleges that are not at the pinnacle of the educational pyramid will abolish their early admissions programs at their own peril.

"Harvard moves and Princeton follows. Princeton moves and Harvard follows," Robert J. Massa, vice president for enrollment and college relations at Dickinson College, told *Inside Higher Ed*. "These institutions, as is pretty clear, can make these decisions with relatively no risk."[31]

———

As an acknowledgment of the growing class divide in American higher education, Harvard's decision to abolish early admissions may in the end produce little more than symbolic value, because the problem goes so much deeper than most educational leaders seem willing to delve. As Tom Mortenson noticed in his home state of Iowa, in the race to boost their *U.S. News* rankings and to market themselves to an increasingly narrow range of students, colleges and universities are systematically turning their backs on disadvantaged and working-class students—even as these institutions espouse the rhetoric of expanding campus diversity.

Recent admissions trends at colleges and universities underscore the degree to which American higher education is engaged in a sort of affirmative action for the rich. Colleges and universities have become considerably more selective over the past several years, admitting decreasing percentages of those who apply, which means that students who lack the advantages of well-educated parents, the best teachers and schools, and the help of experts who know how the college admissions game is played are systematically disadvantaged in the admissions process. As mentioned earlier, the average SAT score of the freshman class is widely considered the gold standard for admissions selectivity. Between 1986 and 2003, the number of colleges and universities classified as "highly selective," those with average SAT scores of 1220–1380, increased by 21 percent; and the number of "selective" schools, those with SAT scores averaging 1030–1220, rose by 30 percent. In contrast, the number of institutions with "liberal" admissions policies, whose SAT scores averaged 870–990, fell by 20 percent; while colleges with "open" admissions dropped 33 percent.[32] Remarkably, this overall increase in selectivity, which inherently biases the schools to target relatively affluent students, occurred in part during a period when the pool of high school graduates was shrinking. Only since 2000 has the size of the pool begun to surpass what it was in 1988.[33]

What's more, even as college admissions officials take pains to point out that scores on such gatekeeping tests as the SAT and ACT are just one piece of an applicant's admissions dossier—a claim that is belied by the great institutional emphasis that prestige-conscious colleges place on average test scores—the weight that admissions offices give to *individual* test scores has also increased enormously in recent years. According to a periodic survey of admissions practices by the National Association for College Admission Counseling (NACAC), 43 percent of colleges gave test scores a weight of "considerable importance" in admissions decisions in 1994. But ten years later, 60 percent of colleges weighed admissions tests that highly.[34] Another prominent survey of college admissions trends sliced the numbers differently to reach similar conclusions. In 1979, 64 percent of public universities "routinely considered" test scores "in reaching an overall judgment regarding admissibility," according to the survey published by the Association of Institutional Research (AIR). But by 2000, 71 percent of public institutions used admissions tests this way, placing them on a par with private universities on this dimension.[35]

Meanwhile, college admissions offices have always highly valued high school grades in college prep courses—83 percent of colleges gave such grades a weight of "considerable importance" in 1994. But that importance has shown indications of slipping. In 2002, according to NACAC, 76 percent of colleges rated such grades so highly, although the figure crept back to 80 percent two years later.[36] According to the AIR survey, 43 percent of colleges rated an applicant's overall high school grades as the "single most important" admissions factor in 1979; but by 2000, only 21 percent did so.[37]

In addition to test scores and high school grades, colleges weigh other aspects of the admissions portfolio in ways that indicate a clear pattern of systemic bias in favor of students from affluent families. This trend is especially true of elite private institutions. For example, the NACAC survey found that almost 26 percent of private colleges and universities in 2004 valued recommendations from high school counselors as having "considerable importance" in the admissions decision, while less than 4 percent of public institutions had the same view.[38] That's a significant statistic in light of how the availability and quality of college counseling in American high schools stratifies along social class lines.

Consider Jacques Steinberg's recent book *The Gatekeepers*, a chronicle of the college admissions process at one highly selective institution, Wesleyan University. On one side of the admissions game, the author, a *New York Times* reporter, focused on a college counselor at Harvard-Westlake, a Los Angeles prep school that is among the nation's top feeder schools to elite colleges and universities. On the other side of the process, Steinberg profiled an admissions officer at Wesleyan. One remarkable aspect of Steinberg's account is the old friendship between the counselor and the admissions officer, going back to their undergraduate days at Stanford. While that friendship could not, of course, determine Wesleyan's admissions decisions, the close relationship established a channel of communication between Wesleyan and Harvard-Westlake that was not available to ordinary students with ordinary high school counselors. Further, elite university culture had been part of the Harvard-Westlake counselor's life from undergraduate days through graduate school. She was an expert in the field, with intimate knowledge of how competitive college admissions worked. She was among a handful of college counselors at Harvard-Westlake who were each accountable to a small cadre of students and their families.[39]

Under the circumstances, the counselor's precisely targeted letters of recommendation for her Harvard-Westlake fledglings carried a great deal of weight, not only at Wesleyan but at other elite universities as well. Sure, this was no "old boys club" from the days when counselors at Andover or Exeter handpicked young men to fulfill their birthrights at Harvard, Yale, or Princeton. Rather, this was the new and improved version of that world, where "meritocracy" trumps all, right?

Think again. Steinberg's portrait of the close ties between a college counselor at one elite high school and a senior admissions officer at one elite university isn't that unusual. In a 2002 survey of the elaborate dance between elite prep schools and the admissions offices at Harvard, Yale, and Princeton, *Worth* magazine concludes: "We learned that a college feeder system is alive and well in America." That report also included the comments of some admissions officials themselves. Lloyd Peterson, a former senior admissions officer at Yale, told the magazine, "'Is there still clearly a pipeline from the top schools in the country to some of the top colleges?' The answer is yes."[40]

With their enormous resources devoted to college admissions, including the meticulous "packaging" of each student; with personnel from top to bottom assigned to manage the college-admission process; and with the careful cultivation of personal relationships with key individuals at elite colleges, the Harvard-Westlakes and their kind are nothing if not highly specialized enterprises whose principal mission is to place students into America's best universities. The *Worth* report includes some astonishing revelations:

> Private school students often have access to admissions officers during the review process. Matt Upton, a graduate of the Lawrenceville School (No. 39 on our list) in Lawrenceville, New Jersey, who attended the University of Pennsylvania and is now a graduate student at Berkeley, says that Amherst admissions officers came to his school to critique students' essays before they were sent. The senior admissions officer at Harvard spoke to students at Roxbury Latin last year, says Henry Seton, a recent graduate who will attend Harvard this fall. "It's an established tradition at my school that if you're a smart kid, you go to Harvard," Seton says. "The dean of Harvard College is our head trustee."[41]

In contrast, the ability of counselors at ordinary American high schools to help their students navigate the college admissions process amounts to criminal neglect by policy makers. In an era when public schools, particularly those that serve high concentrations of poor and minority students, are under fire to raise test scores simply to stay out of the clutches of federal regulators enforcing the No Child Left Behind law, college counseling is seen as expendable, as a last priority.

"A third of American counselors are in high-poverty public high schools, the schools that enroll the vast majority of low-income students and students of color, the schools that enroll a significant proportion of the 12.8 million high school students today," David A. Hawkins and Jessica Lautz conclude in the NACAC report. "Some of these schools have student-to-counselor ratios of 500 to 1, some 5000 to 1, and some multitrack, year-round schools in urban areas have no counselors available for certain tracks of students." When student-counselor ratios exceed 500 to 1, the authors point out, counselors are limited to an hour per year or less that they can spend with each student on college counseling.[42]

Hence, there is one path to college and beyond for children born to the right parents, a path that is paved with gold by colleges themselves; and there is another, more rocky path for ordinary kids. With increasing rarity, that path for working-class and lower-income children can even lead to higher education. But the public-private schism in this respect is profound. In 2004, fully 95 percent of students at nonparochial private schools attended a four-year college or university. This contrasts with barely one-half of students at public high schools. When high schools had student-counselor ratios of less than 100 to 1, about 85 percent of students attended four-year colleges. But when those ratios exceeded 500 to 1, which is about the average for an American public high school, college attendance fell to 59 percent.[43]

In addition to merit scholarships, early admissions, greater selectivity, and the rise of enrollment management, other long-established habits of the higher education industry illustrate the deeply entrenched bias against disadvantaged students. As we've seen, the size of institutional endowments is enormously important for prestige-seeking universities, because they can leverage those funds to pay for more "merit" scholarships that enable them to enroll the "right" students and build even more institutional prestige. To encourage donations to their endowments, colleges and universities have long granted special admissions privileges to the sons and daughters of alumni, allowing the institutions to more easily cultivate relationships with affluent parents—and their resulting donations. Alumni donations are big business for universities, accounting for about a third of the $25.6 billion in total gifts to universities in 2004–2005, rivaling the giving from private foundations and far surpassing the amount given by corporations. The so-called legacy preference in admissions is powerful indeed. In their study of admissions practices at several elite universities, William Bowen, Martin Kurzweil, and Eugene Tobin found that, on average, candidates with a 50 percent chance of being admitted saw their odds jump up to 70 percent if they were a legacy candidate.[44]

While legacy admissions are common, a more recent spin-off of the practice is less widely known. Some universities have discovered that they can raise money for endowments by granting an admissions preference to the sons or daughters of rich people, alumni or not, who are likely to give money to the university. Investigating this practice of "development admits" for the *Wall Street Journal,* Daniel Golden describes how Duke University, in particular, was bending its admissions standards in order to enroll the children of wealthy people whom it would recruit as potential donors.[45] Duke denied that there was any "quid pro quo," but Golden suggests that Duke is an "under-endowed" university compared to its very rich competitors such as Harvard and Princeton and so had aggressively linked its admissions decisions and developmental efforts. Whereas a decade earlier Duke had admitted just 20 or so wealthy and well-connected students this way, recently the university has opened its highly selective gates to as many as 125 students a year whose family connections could lead to big gifts to Duke.

It's impossible to know exactly how widespread this practice is, but other prestige-seeking universities have undoubtedly taken note of Duke's success at targeting wealthy parents. In 2004–2005, parents gave the university some $11 million, or 4 percent of the $275.8 million it raised from all sources.[46] "I understand why universities leverage parent contacts to enrich themselves," Marilee Jones, dean of admissions at MIT, told Golden. "If somebody's offering them a check, why not take it? But I honestly think it's out of control."[47]

———

Perhaps the most troubling implication of these trends is that American higher education is hardly the open and meritocratic system that we commonly believe it is. Rather, it is a system that is deeply segregated by social class—the very thing we don't like to talk about. And because it's divided by class, it's also increasingly segregated by race and ethnicity. As we saw in the previous chapter, lower-income students are increasingly not going to college at all or are being funneled into the community college system. Although community colleges provide the postsecondary destination of last resort for many disadvantaged Americans, students who attend these schools with the hope of eventually completing a bachelor's degree have but a small chance of actually doing so. At the other side of the class divide, private four-year colleges and universities have become bastions of privilege in America. At highly selective private colleges and universities, the average family income of freshmen averaged almost $120,000 in 2002, more than twice the average family income of about $50,000 for freshmen at community colleges and nonselective four-year colleges.[48]

Nearing retirement, Tom Mortenson says that in the few years he has remaining to work, he'll keep pounding on colleges and universities, harassing school presidents, and raising hell in his newsletter. He'll continue trying to convince policy makers and the general public to confront the increasing and untenable levels of stratification of educational opportunity in the United States, an ominous trend that, he believes, threatens the very existence of an American middle class.

"When I look at our gains in baccalaureate attainment in the United States in the most recent data, compared to 1970, nearly all of the gains have gone to the students who were born into the top half of the family income distribution," he reminded me. "And I really wanted to believe, and I think in the seventies there was good reason to believe, that we were making progress on equalizing educational opportunities. Since 1980, my data show—and I'm now coming to understand from the academic work of others—virtually everything we've done since 1980 has made access to the middle class worse or more unequal."

For the past few years, Mortenson has targeted institutions themselves, and especially their admissions and financial aid policies, as prime contributors to this growing stratification. Like Fortune 500 corporations that have become more responsive to quarterly profits and stock prices than to customers, communities, and employees, Mortenson sees colleges and universities acting myopically in terms of the public interest, responding instead to the narrow, short-term monied interests as capitalism demands.

"They're tax-exempt social institutions, in many cases being operated as for-profit businesses," he told me. "The reason our public organizations get tax-exempt status is because they are serving the public interest."

Mortenson is naming names. He names Harvard, with its accumulated "profits" of $25 billion, the richest university in America and among the most powerful tax-exempt institutions in the world, as perhaps the most notorious offender against the tax-exempt principle. "It seems to me that Harvard is the most successful for-profit but tax-exempt higher education business in the country, and maybe the world," Mortenson explained. "It's not clear to me that they need to be tax-exempt to remain the kind of for-profit business that they are."

He continued, "I'm more than willing to sit down and listen to a good argument from Harvard about why I'm misinterpreting and misunderstanding what they're doing. But as an outsider, as far as I can tell, it seems to be the case that they do nothing at all to expand higher educational participation in the country. The kids that they serve are kids that are going to go to college and go to excellent colleges anyhow. If they were to close down tomorrow, every one of those kids would be at a fine college someplace else in the country."

Harvard is Harvard. But what particularly grates for Mortenson is the behavior of public universities. "Where I get particularly bent out of shape is when I see these institutions, like all three of our public universities in Iowa, increasing their enrollment of non–Pell Grant recipients and cutting their enrollment of Pell Grant recipients," Mortenson said. "These are public institutions, and while they're just turning away from serving low-income kids, they find the resources to go out and recruit a lot of nonresidents because they're really quite profitable. And they do add some ethnic diversity to the academic environment on campus. But in the case of the University of Iowa, most of these kids tend to be rich white kids from the white-collar counties of Chicago.

"These people honestly believe they're committed to diversity, they talk the talk—but the enrollment numbers don't back them up. They're considering raising admissions standards at the University of Iowa, which contradicts what they profess they believe in. A shrinking share of kids in our three public universities are low-income kids, but a growing share of the kids in the K-12 pipeline are lower-income. You can't tell me that they're addressing the needs of Iowa by turning away from serving low-income kids. I don't accept that argument.

"So, in a really naïve way, I really think we are all better off when we're all better off. And we're not all better off if only some of us are better off. I'm going through a really agonizing sort of realization about the work that I've done for the last thirty-five years. We are reverting back to exactly the kind of Europe that my ancestors fled, where, if you are born poor, you don't have a chance. You won't starve, but life won't be a very pleasant experience, and you certainly won't be able to engage in the full range of opportunities that surround you. You'll sit there as an outsider; you'll be isolated from it. My ancestors had the balls to bail out of Europe and get away from that godawful place. I think we're replicating that cycle of history in the United States now. And I fight it in every way I can. And, frankly, I'm losing badly on all fronts. There's a lot of work to do, and I don't have a lot of time left. I'm going to get bolder and braver and sassier than I was when I was younger and had to cover my ass. I don't have to cover my ass anymore."

———

In the following chapter, we'll examine the split personalities of a handful of colleges and universities where the rhetoric of inclusion and equal opportunity is clashing with their perceived need to rise in the U.S. News rankings. We'll also see how, in some cases, that contradiction is laying waste to their historical social compact to serve the public good.

EIGHT

A SOCIAL COMPACT BROKEN

The inequities of social class, which permeate and largely define the American education system, remain a cancerous lesion that policy makers and university presidents themselves have long ignored. Educational leaders seem to believe that if they pay sufficient attention to ethnic and racial diversity in higher education—and use race-based affirmative action as the means to achieve that diversity—then their institutional and collective obligations to the public trust are fulfilled.

When industrialist Andrew Carnegie founded the Carnegie Technical Schools in 1900, he did so as a gesture to the public good, to help the sons and daughters of the steel workers and coal miners in the Pittsburgh region get a higher education.[1] Carnegie himself might well have appreciated the irony in Carnegie Mellon University's recent impressive efforts to improve its *U.S. News and World Report* rankings at the same time it slashed its percentage of lower-income students.

In the *U.S. News* 1990 rankings of "best" colleges, the average SAT score of Carnegie Mellon's entering freshmen was 1225. In the magazine's 2005 survey, the university's average score shot up to 1385. The university also dramatically lowered its acceptance rate, from 64 percent to just 42 percent. In 1990, some 20 percent of Carnegie Mellon's undergraduates were Pell Grant (lower-income) students, ranking the school 128th among Pennsylvania's 183 colleges and universities on that measure. By 2002, while the university was gaming the prestige rankings, its percentage of students receiving Pell Grants had declined by half, to about 10 percent. But other universities were also gaming the system, and Carnegie Mellon's actual ranking among its peers remained unchanged between 1990 and 2005.[2]

The university has acknowledged the hazards of competing with other institutions that have greater brand recognition for a limited number of similar students. In becoming more selective, Carnegie Mellon's yield rate slipped, because the sorts of advantaged students it was vying for saw it as a second choice, behind the likes of MIT, Harvard, Cornell, and Johns Hopkins. "While student quality standards have improved (as measured by SAT scores) primarily through increasing the application pool, the potential decline in the high-quality applicant market poses a threat to the university," noted a 1998 self-study report.[3]

Carnegie Mellon is just one example of how colleges and universities, facing the competitive pressures of an increasingly cutthroat higher education marketplace, are finding it in their best interest to reward affluence in their admissions and financial aid decisions—and to do so under the legitimating guises of meritocracy and diversity. In fact, an emerging body of research suggests a profoundly negative relationship between the degree to which institutions attempt to buy prestige with merit scholarships and their enrollment of lower-income students.

For example, in a study published by the National Bureau of Economic Research, Ronald G. Ehrenberg, Liang Zhang, and Jared M. Levin found that every National Merit Scholarship (NMS) that a selective university awards displaces *four* Pell Grant recipients at those institutions. Commenting on this trend, the authors conclude:

> While our research has focused only on NMS awards, it highlights the trade off that may exist more broadly between using institutional grant aid to craft a more selective student body than would otherwise occur. . . . If selective institutions, especially public ones, are committed to serving students from all socioeconomic backgrounds, these institutions must track the share of their students that receive Pell Grants and focus on socioeconomic diversity as well as on student selectivity as goals. Absent concerted efforts by these institutions to increase the representation of students from lower and lower middle income families in their student ranks, current inequalities in the distribution of students attending these institutions by family income . . . are likely to persist or worsen over time.[4]

Consider, too, the University of Wisconsin at Madison, that state's flagship institution, as another illustration of the inverse relationship between a university's commitment to prestige and its commitment to the economic diversity of its students. Over the past decade, Wisconsin has dramatically increased its selectivity by admitting significantly more students with very high SAT scores and far fewer students with modest test scores—scores that unfailingly sort students by class and race.

Between 1992 and 2004, the average SAT score of entering freshmen at Wisconsin rose from a modest 1180 to 1260, which placed it in the ranks of other selective colleges and universities. In 1995, the university admitted 366 freshmen with SAT scores between 900 and 1120. Nine years later, it admitted just 225 students with those modest scores. During the same period, the number of freshmen admitted with very high SAT scores (1350 to 1600) grew from 322 to 418. (In these same years, mean SAT I scores for the nation went up slightly, from 1001 to 1026.)[5] As the price of greater selectivity, however, the university cut deeply into its percentage of lower-income students. In 2002, Wisconsin enrolled 1,360 *fewer* Pell Grant students than it had ten years earlier, with Pell Grant recipients declining from 16.4 percent of undergraduate enrollment to 11.7 percent.[6]

The University of Wisconsin at Madison clearly takes pride in its *U.S. News* rankings and the prestige associated with enrolling more students with higher SAT scores. But one would be hard-pressed to find any evidence that enrolling more students who are not from middle- and upper-middle-class backgrounds is a major institutional priority. To be sure, as evidenced in a cornucopia of recent strategic planning documents, the university has championed the values of diversity, particularly the need to enroll more students of color. But keeping track of its economic diversity rarely figures into the overt measures that the university uses to monitor its progress.

That job is left to rabble-rousers like Tom Mortenson.

In his newsletter, *Postsecondary Education Opportunity,* which in many respects is the antithesis of the *U.S. News and World Report* ranking system of "best colleges," Mortenson has developed a ranking system of his own that grades universities on their performance in enrolling lower-income students, as measured by their Pell Grant numbers.

In terms of their overall enrollment of Pell Grant students, the best fifty national universities as defined by *U.S. News*—often private universities with enormous endowments, and often flagship public institutions—have a dismal record indeed. There are exceptions: among the top fifty, those with the best records at enrolling lower-income students include several in the University of California system, such as UCLA, with more than 35 percent of its undergraduates receiving Pell Grants in 2002; UCLA was followed by UC Berkeley, with 32 percent. Those figures are about twice the national average for that year in the *U.S. News* top fifty.

At the bottom of Mortenson's list, we find those at the very top of the *U.S. News* list, schools that are also the top tier of universities in terms of their accumulated "profits"—their massive institutional endowments. Harvard University, always among the top two or three national universities and possessing a record endowment, occupied the basement of Mortenson's rankings, as its Pell Grant students were just 6.8 percent of undergraduates in 2002. Harvard was followed by Wake Forest (7 percent), Princeton (7.4 percent), the College of William and Mary (8 percent), Washington University in St. Louis (8 percent), and Notre Dame (8 percent). Mortenson has also calculated the Pell Grant enrollment deficits of the *U.S. News* top fifty—how many lower-income students these institutions would need to add in order to bring them up to the average in their states. In 2001–2002, the University of Florida had a deficit of more than 4,000 Pell Grant students. Penn State had a shortfall of 3,500. The University of Wisconsin at Madison was short 2,500, Harvard came up 1,300 students short, and Carnegie Mellon had a deficit of almost 1,000 students.[7]

The worst public university in Mortenson's ranking system was the University of Virginia, with only 8 percent of its undergraduates eligible for Pell Grants in 2002. At the other extreme, lower-income students made up almost 50 percent of undergraduate enrollment at the University of New Mexico in Albuquerque that year. Among the *U.S. News* top fifty national universities, only UC Berkeley and the University of Washington exceeded the national average (21 percent) of flagship state universities in their percentage of lower-income students in 2002.[8]

Overall, the recent record of flagship public institutions is particularly troubling in light of their historical mission to serve all segments of the public. Many of these premier institutions, including some land-grant universities, are choosing to cut their enrollment of lower-income students in favor of students from more affluent backgrounds. While the University of Wisconsin at Madison cut 28 percent, in absolute terms, from its Pell Grant numbers between 1992 and 2001, the University of Illinois at Urbana-Champaign dropped 15 percent, Pennsylvania State University at University Park cut 8.5 percent, and the University of Michigan at Ann Arbor cut its Pell Grant numbers by almost 48 percent.[9]

Michigan represents a particularly interesting case, as a premier public institution that has been in the forefront of the affirmative action battle in higher education. Between 1992 and 2002, when Michigan was slashing its Pell Grant enrollment in half, affecting almost three thousand students, the university was championing the values of diversity and leading a legal fight for affirmative action at public universities that went all the way to the U.S. Supreme Court. At the beginning of the 1990s, Michigan's enrollment of lower-income students ranked near the middle of the state's 131 colleges and universities; but by 2002, the university ranked almost dead last in the state on this measure. In 1992, almost a third of the university's undergraduates were lower-income students. As of 2002, Michigan's enrollment of Pell Grant students stood at about 13 percent of undergraduates. That was the fourth worst record in the nation among the state flagships, ahead of only Virginia, Delaware, and Wisconsin.[10]

But, in terms of prestige, Michigan's performance has been impressive. In the 1996 *U.S. News* rankings, Michigan reported that freshmen had an average SAT score of 1180; that 65 percent of students had been in the top 10 percent of their high school class; and that its freshmen acceptance rate was 68 percent. The university ranked twenty-fourth overall among the top fifty. By the fall of 2004, entering freshmen had SAT scores averaging 1305; 90 percent of Michigan undergraduates had been in the top 10 percent of their high schools; and the freshmen acceptance rate had been cut to 62 percent.[11]

Detailed trends in the SAT scores of entering freshmen vividly highlight Michigan's big tilt toward students from affluent backgrounds. In the fall of 1998, for instance, 29 percent of entering freshmen had SAT math scores in the top range, 700 to 800. By fall of 2004, fully 40 percent had such scores. Students with SAT verbal scores in that range went from 15 percent of entering freshmen to 20 percent. The opposite trend held for students with modest SAT scores, who more often tend to be minorities and those from less affluent backgrounds. In 1998, 33 percent of freshmen had verbal scores of 500–599, declining to 26 percent four years later. Freshmen with modest math scores dropped from 19 percent to 13 percent.[12]

At the same time that Michigan was becoming increasingly selective and cutting its Pell Grant numbers, university president Mary Sue Coleman was touting the university's commitment to diversity, including its commitment to economic diversity. "The University of Michigan has become the face of diversity in higher education because of our successful U.S. Supreme Court fight to defend affirmative action and the use of race in admissions," she said in an October 2005 speech. "It is a role we welcome and continually seek to improve. . . . We must pay attention to race. We must pay attention to ethnicity. We must pay attention to socioeconomic class. If we look away, the future is bleak."[13]

But are Michigan and other universities of its kind really paying attention to economic disadvantage? Pell Grant percentages are an admittedly rough indicator of the degree to which universities target economic disadvantage in their admissions decisions, and on that score the performance of many institutions is clearly poor. Are more precise indicators available? In fact, enrollment managers at major universities have very good information on the demographic profiles of their customers; like any well-run business, they know who their customers are. But the demographic information these institutions publicly report on a routine basis is scant and woefully general. Michigan, for example, routinely reports enrollments by legal residence, by ethnicity and race, by gender, by major, even by age. It does not report enrollments by the economic status of its students.[14]

Thus, observers like Mortenson, who are far less sanguine than university presidents like Mary Sue Coleman regarding higher education's genuine commitment to lower-income students, must search for other types of public information to hold the schools accountable. Besides Pell Grant enrollment, Mortenson has examined the degree to which individual universities participate in federal TRIO programs, a handful of initiatives born of Lyndon Johnson's Great Society era aimed at helping disadvantaged students not only learn about college and prepare for it but also succeed in college once there. TRIO programs serve lower-income students and also those who would be the first in their families to attend college.

On this measure, too, Michigan's record is bleak. Across the country at colleges large and small, public and private, there are about 2,617 TRIO programs serving 859,228 low-income and "first-generation" students. In fact, Michigan was among two dozen of the best names in higher education, at the top of the *U.S. News* pyramid, which had *no TRIO programs whatsoever on their campuses*. These included Brown, Cal Tech, Carnegie Mellon, William and Mary, Virginia, Cornell, Dartmouth, Duke, Emory, Georgetown, Georgia Tech, Harvard, Johns Hopkins, Lehigh, NYU, Northwestern, Princeton, Rensselaer, Rice, Tufts, Vanderbilt, Wake Forest, Yale, and Yeshiva University. Without any TRIO presence, it's no accident that many of these universities also have such a poor record in enrolling students eligible for Pell Grants. Nor is it accidental that the only two flagship public universities among the *U.S. News* top fifty that had Pell Grant enrollments above the national average—UC Berkeley and the University of Washington—also had eleven TRIO programs between them. "This is a record of staggering failure to share the environment of America's best 50 national universities with students from the bottom half of the family income distribution," Mortenson says. "It is a record of shame and disgrace."[15]

The recruiting behavior of universities is yet another indicator of their genuine commitment to economic disadvantage. We've seen the elaborate enrollment management systems that universities have installed to target, recruit, and enroll the "right" sorts of students who make the universities look attractive in the *U.S. News* beauty contest. In my interviews and in my research for this book, I frequently encountered the belief that economic disadvantage is a big selling point for lower-income students in the admissions process, particularly at elite universities trying to create socioeconomic diversity. But to what extent are lower-income students included among the groups that universities go out of their way to recruit?

Among four-year public institutions in 2000, the single most heavily recruited group consisted of "academically talented" students—invariably those students with high test scores from generally affluent circumstances, according to a survey by a consortium including the College Board, ACT Inc., and Educational Testing Service. Some 76 percent of colleges actively recruited such students. The next most heavily recruited were athletes, targeted by 66 percent of colleges, followed by ethnic minorities, who were recruited by 65 percent. Except for the children of alumni and relatives, recruited by 27 percent, lower-income students were at the bottom of the institutional recruiting priorities, with 37 percent of colleges claiming them as a targeted group. Indeed, international students were a higher recruiting priority than disadvantaged students in the survey. Recruiting priorities at private four-year institutions were similar: only 24 percent of the private schools targeted lower-income students.[16]

And then there's the question of universities putting their money where their mouths are in terms of financial aid offered to students. In 2000, 76 percent of public four-year universities offered aid to "academically talented" students—the so-called merit scholarships discussed in the previous chapter. Nearly 60 percent gave aid to athletes, and 47 percent offered financial help to underrepresented minorities. Just 34 percent of public universities provided aid based on economic disadvantage. Among the private schools, the story was the same, as only 27 percent gave financial aid based on economic disadvantage.[17]

More evidence suggests that when elite universities talk about diversity by social class, it is often more rhetoric than reality. As a corollary to their demonstrated recruitment and financial aid priorities, the admission advantages provided to selected groups also show higher education's aversion to confronting the lack of social class diversity on their campuses.

In January 2005, at a College Board event in Bal Harbour, Florida, Eugene Tobin of the Mellon Foundation reported findings from a remarkable statistical study of admissions practices at nineteen of America's most prized colleges and universities, all having highly selective admissions systems. That Mellon Foundation study would become the basis for a book, *Equity and Excellence in American Higher Education*, which Tobin, a former university president himself, co-authored with William Bowen and Martin Kurzweil. Tobin told the gathering of senior officers in the admissions and financial aid offices of many highly regarded colleges what they probably already knew. But outsiders to that world might find the results somewhat startling.

Recruited athletes were the most prized group in these elite universities' admissions offices, receiving a net admission advantage worth 30.2 percentage points, when other factors were held constant. Underrepresented minorities were the next most important group, receiving an admission boost worth 28 percentage points. Legacy applicants were accorded a 20-point advantage, as were applicants who applied under an early admissions program. In sharp contrast, students from families in the bottom quartile of family incomes were actually *disadvantaged* in the admissions process, having an admission "drag," as it were, amounting to minus 1 percentage point. First-generation college students also fared poorly compared to the most favored groups, with an admission advantage worth just 4.1 points.[18]

———

But playing the *U.S. News* rankings game is like bargaining with the devil. If you aren't already at Harvard, Princeton, or Yale but would one day like to be mentioned on the same list of brand-name schools as those institutions, you must engage in the prestige arms race. But once you become involved in this race, however dim your hopes of significantly advancing in the long run, opting out is not an option if you're a university president or an enrollment manager who wants to keep his or her job. Scores of universities, public and private, have joined the race; and increasing numbers of regionally focused institutions, not wanting to be left behind, are "going national," making their own Faustian bargains. These are the "wannabes," colleges and universities striving to climb the rankings and build their prestige.

But they are signing up for what may be an economically untenable position in the long run. In order to pay for the hefty tuition discounts and merit scholarships that help to attract the right students, or to pay for the most attractive faculty who bring in the big bucks from federal research grants, or to pay outlandish salaries to winning Division I football coaches, universities *must* build empires. They must embark on multibillion-dollar campaigns to erect newer and more impressive buildings and state-of-the-art facilities. They must continually appeal to wealthy donors, alumni, and corporations in an endless fundraising campaign to sustain their empire building.

"There's no one among public universities who's not saying it," Mark G. Yudof, chancellor of the University of Texas system, told Michael Arnone of the *Chronicle of Higher Education.* "It's a mantra. They're all a variation of 'We're No. 1.' " Arnone continued, "Ambition and arithmetic, though, are bound to collide because the number of aspiring institutions far exceeds the slots at the top of any ranking. No matter how hard they try, 100 universities can't squeeze into the top 20."[19]

The economic calculus for public institutions becomes all the more complicated as states' support for higher education continues to shrink dramatically, forced by a slow but steady abandonment of the principle that higher education is a public good, for which the public must bear the greater burden of support. Guided by that social compact, American higher education was shaped by great waves of democratization over the past century, from the 1862 Morrill Act, which created the first generation of public land-grant universities, to the GI Bill after the Second World War and the Higher Education Act of Lyndon Johnson's Great Society. That latter era was the historical peak of public commitment to higher education for the masses, and countless Baby Boomers, myself included, were its beneficiaries. I was able to attend a flagship public institution in the 1970s, at a reasonable cost, because the lion's share of my education was financed by the state's taxpayers. Working summer jobs and taking out a small low-interest loan from the federal government, I was able to finance the unsubsidized part of my undergraduate education basically on my own.

But since around 1980, the states' disinvestment in higher education has been massive. At the end of the 1970s, state governments invested almost $100 billion in higher education. By 2005, that investment had declined to $63 billion. Between 1976 and 2001, states jacked up tuition at public institutions by $9 billion, while slashing public appropriations for higher education by $16 billion. In many states, the public commitment to higher education has been decimated. In Colorado, for instance, the state cut public higher education investment by 70 percent between 1971 and 2005, twice the national average. Colorado spent almost $14 per $1,000 in personal income on higher education in the early 1970s, but that investment is now down to less than $4. In 2005, Colorado's public investment in higher education was half the average for all states.[20]

This trend has left the public institutions little choice but to become quasi-private, relying on tuition hikes and corporate donors for their revenues. Indeed, some of the public universities with the worst recent records on Pell Grant enrollment are encountering some of the greatest pressure to privatize in the wake of dwindling state support.

At the University of Wisconsin at Madison, the state contributed just 19 percent of the school's total budget in 2005, down from about 30 percent ten years earlier. As a result, the university has shifted the cost burden onto individual students in the form of tuition hikes. During that ten-year period, tuition and fees for state residents shot up 107 percent, from $2,800 to almost $6,000. Families have increasingly become reliant on loans, the form of financing that most discourages lower-income students from attending college. In fact, loans for UW undergraduates, at some $142 million in one recent year, dwarfed the value of grants and scholarships, at $65 million. In those ten years, student debt at graduation increased almost 40 percent. In a recently published brochure titled *Points of Pride, Causes for Concern,* the university acknowledged the danger of this privatization wave for its larger mission to serve the public good: "Without an increase in need-based financial aid, we risk putting the cost of a UW-Madison education out of reach for some of our citizens."[21]

At the same time, however, the university was amping up merit scholarships—money that often goes to students who don't need it. These included the Wisconsin Academic Excellence Scholarships, for which some 1,300 students received more than $3 million in 2001. That same year, the university provided need-based grants to just 866 students, worth $1.8 million.[22]

Penn State University, whose flagship campus at University Park has cut its Pell Grant enrollment, is also undergoing a de facto privatization. Its president, Graham B. Spanier, has been vocal in his condemnation of the trend. "Penn State has the dubious distinction of having had our revenue lines cross two decades ago," he told the faculty senate in 2004. In 1984, tuition and fee revenue replaced state funding as the largest source of money for the university. In 2003–2004, tuition and fees made up 69 percent of the university's teaching budget, while just 25 percent came from the state. Only 12 percent of Penn State's total budget came from state taxes when Spanier made that speech, and he expected that figure to soon slip to below 10 percent. "As states continue to back away from providing sufficient educational funding to their public universities, those same institutions continue to turn to other sources of funds—most notably tuition—to absorb the burden, thus shifting costs for higher education from the taxpayer to students and their families," Spanier said. "This trend troubles those of us who believe higher education is a public good, not just a private benefit."[23]

In Virginia, it is no coincidence that the state's flagship, the University of Virginia, receives just 8 percent of its funding from the state—a decline from almost 30 percent in the late 1980s. Among public universities, UVA enrolls the lowest percentage of undergraduates receiving Pell Grants. For all practical purposes, UVA is a public university in name only, and university officials have not been shy about proclaiming this brave new reality. "We're committed to becoming the first privately funded public university," Robert D. Sweeney, UVA's senior vice president for development and public affairs, told the *Chronicle of Higher Education* after the university announced a $3 billion campaign to raise money from private donors, the largest ever by a public university.[24]

"This is not how Virginia's founders intended things to work," UVA president John T. Casteen III said in support of legislation to rewrite UVA's charter in order to cut the remaining bureaucratic ties to a state government that no longer supports public higher education. Just as Andrew Carnegie in Pittsburgh would be shocked at the elitist institution his working-class vision had become, Virginia's own Thomas Jefferson, the father of the public university ideal as we know it, would be astonished to witness what has become of Virginia's public universities. Casteen continued, "Just how far Virginia has tumbled in its support for the most basic public services . . . baffles persons who remember the days of our 'education governors' and master plans for improving higher education."[25]

––––––––

The resources to build the empires are not unlimited, and for every Carnegie Mellon, University of Southern California, or Washington

University in St. Louis, there are the likes of Boise State University, whose new mantra calls for it to be the next "metropolitan research university of distinction," or a Washington State University, which has embarked on a new mission to become "World Class. Face to Face."

In the case of Washington State, a land-grant university in eastern Washington that has historically operated in the shadow of the University of Washington in Seattle, the pitch is familiar. The university's first goal is to "offer the best undergraduate experience in a research university" and to "attract, recruit, and retain a diverse high quality student body" by implementing "recruitment and admissions strategies that reach and serve high ability students from high schools and community colleges." Within the overall plan, the University Relations office writes that its job is to "establish the university's brand position for world-class quality and challenging hands-on involvement," increase WSU's enrollment of "high-performing students," and "enhance WSU's reputation as one of the nation's premier research universities among influencers and business and opinion leaders."[26]

How to achieve these grand plans? Again, elements of the WSU formula are familiar, and the university's strategic planning documents suggest that it will challenge the University of Washington on its home turf, along the populous Puget Sound corridor, where the lion's share of the state's most desirable students live. Whether or not the students need money for college—that will be of no concern. WSU will buy them with tuition waivers and "Regents Scholarships," reserved for "high ability" students with an SAT score of 1200 or better.[27]

In his 2004 State of the University Address, WSU president V. Lane Rawlins suggested that the university would resort to minimum entrance requirements, based on an index of high school grades and SAT scores, to "improve the quality" of the freshman class, so that average SAT scores of entering freshmen would equal or exceed those of students at WSU's peers within three years. In the same breath, he said that Regents Scholarships would be strategically deployed to achieve this goal. In numerous PowerPoint presentations to the larger public and to the university community, Rawlins has displayed charts and graphs meant to show how WSU has lagged well behind its peer institutions in terms of SAT averages.[28]

The guiding assumption, of course, is that such a test score gap is a very bad thing for WSU and the "world-class" university it must become. What Rawlins has never pointed out in these presentations is that WSU's Pell Grant numbers weren't bad. In fact, its Pell Grant enrollment increased from 22 percent of undergraduates in 1992 to 26 percent in 2002. Its performance on that measure was about average in the Pac 10 athletic conference, where WSU competes with UCLA and UC Berkeley, which have quite high percentages of Pell Grant students compared with other major research universities.[29]

"Five years ago, we committed ourselves to taking control of our destiny in decisions on size and quality of our entering freshman classes," Rawlins told the university community in 2005. "A look at the profile of this year's new freshman class confirms that we continue making meaningful progress toward this goal." Indeed, the MBA side of Rawlins pointed out, high school GPAs were up, and SAT scores of entering freshmen were up 20 points from the previous year. "At the same time," the Martin Luther King Jr. side of Rawlins said, "the diversity of our new freshman class continues to increase. Preliminary estimates show that students of color make up 15 percent of the freshman class, as compared to 14.5 percent of new freshmen in fall 2004 and 13.7 percent in fall 2003."[30]

Perhaps, in refashioning WSU, Rawlins is trying to implement a far different model for a public university than what evolved under his tenure at the University of Memphis. A UC Berkeley–trained economist and a native of Idaho, Rawlins served as president of the University of Memphis from 1991 through 2000. The college was created in 1912 as the West Tennessee State Normal School, its blue and gray colors a symbol of a reunited country after the Civil War. The institution then became West Tennessee State Teachers College in 1925, Memphis State College in 1941, and Memphis State University in 1957, admitting its first black students two years later. Under Rawlins's tenure, it became the University of Memphis in 1994.[31]

But while many universities were becoming more selective during the 1990s, Memphis was doing the opposite. The average SAT score of entering freshmen dropped from 1086 to 1045, hardly significant in terms of actual academic performance in University of Memphis classrooms, but quite significant in the world of *U.S. News,* university presidents, and the university regents to whom presidents must answer. But despite this slip in the prestige race, the university was doing good things for real people. Between 1992 and 2001, Memphis added more than a thousand undergraduates to its Pell Grant ranks, increasing the percentage of lower-income students from 26 percent to 33 percent. At the same time, the university was becoming far more racially diverse. The number of black students went from about a quarter of the freshman class to more than a third. The percentage of Hispanic students doubled. As the number of white freshmen fell from 67 percent to 60 percent of undergraduates, the university became less white and more representative of the racial diversity of the Memphis region under Rawlins's watch.[32]

For WSU, however, the writing is indelibly on the wall. If it continues trying to close the gap between itself and its peers on the prestige rating scales that it deems so important to its image and future survival, its social class diversity will devolve. WSU's efforts to sustain a measure of ethnic diversity is indeed worthy, and with sufficient merit scholarships to cherry-pick minority students with the highest test scores, WSU might get lucky on that score. But implicit in the university's strategic plan to "improve student quality" is that serving students from modest economic circumstances will not be a high priority for WSU.

Implicit in the entire culture of the prestige game is that serving students of modest means isn't worthy of a great research university. Perhaps, as a land-grant university serving the less populated and less prosperous regions of Washington, WSU had for years been engaged in worthwhile work for society, creating opportunities at a major research university for lower-income students that they wouldn't have elsewhere. But because that contribution is not highly valued in the larger society, which takes its marching orders on educational quality from a weekly news magazine, WSU seems willing to abandon that legacy on the altar of prestige.

———

The elitist wave overtaking much of public higher education shows up in various other unseemly ways besides admissions and financial aid policies, though the underlying rationale is cut from the same cloth as the prestige-driven university. For a slightly different angle, simply look inside a college football stadium at a Big Ten university, where the public university's uncomfortable relationship with class becomes live theater on fall Saturdays. As Big Ten football programs have become like profit-maximizing corporations, they are unabashedly allocating the real estate of their football stadiums to the highest bidders, belying the egalitarian foundations of their public institutions. I don't mean to keep picking on the University of Michigan, but it's again a prime example of how elitist values have consumed the missions of public institutions that were founded on populist ideals.

In Michigan's case, the university was founded in 1817, one of the nation's first public universities, "primarily to serve the working class," says James J. Duderstadt, who was president of the university from 1988 to 1996. But according to the *New York Times,* the University of Michigan is building private luxury boxes at Michigan Stadium, licensing the rights to these preferred seats for $500 a pop.[33] The notion of elite seats for the privileged few doesn't sit well with Duderstadt and other critics of the stadium plan, who believe that Michigan Stadium has always been a common meeting place for fans of all social classes. "For 125 years now—whether at Regents Field, Ferry Field or in Michigan Stadium— the Maize-and-Blue faithful have stood together, shivered together, cheered together and won together, side by side," argues the nonprofit group Save the Big House, which has organized against the Michigan plan. "Private luxury boxes represent the very antithesis of that tradition, dividing Michigan fans by income and undermining the unity, excitement and camaraderie that Michigan fans of all ages and backgrounds share as they experience the game together."[34]

For yet another glimpse at how elitist values are corrupting public higher education, look to the proverbial backrooms where the deals are cut among power brokers. Consider the executive compensation scandal that unfolded in 2005 in the University of California system. The *San Francisco Chronicle* discovered that university officials had been engaged in secret executive compensation deals, routinely granting special salary exceptions to highly paid administrators in order to pay them even more money, supposedly in order to compete for highly qualified talent in the higher education marketplace. A university task force investigating the backroom deals condemned the practice as a violation of the university's public trust. The scandal quite rightly raised the hackles of the press, the public, and the state's legislators.

But less widely acknowledged was the underlying cause of the compensation scandal. Public institutions like the University of California have in recent years been trying to serve at least two incompatible masters: their historical obligation to the public trust, and their perceived need, amid a climate of declining public resources, to build prestigious empires in order to compete with enormously wealthy private institutions. California's public officials might have been indignant at the behavior of UC administrators, but in a sense they helped create the scandal that was merely symptomatic of the privatization cancer consuming public higher education. When state governors and legislators tell public universities to raise tuition, to do more with less, to maximize private sources of revenue, and generally to act less like public institutions and more like profit-maximizing businesses, those same officials ought not be alarmed when university officials employ the tactics of capitalism in the way they pay top executives.

In fact, the UC compensation scandal isn't really about building more efficient protocols and communications systems between policy makers and the university. The scandal suggests that there should be a profound reexamination of the nature and purpose of the public university and a reestablishment of its core values. Indignant as the public might be with the University of California's lack of public accountability, it's time that the public itself revisits and reasserts what values it holds dear in its public universities and decides whether compelling them to behave more like private institutions is really in the public's best interest.

––––––

Unfortunately, affirmative action for the rich doesn't end with status-driven admissions and financial aid practices at colleges and universities. In the following chapter, part 3 concludes with an examination of how state and federal governments are also shirking a historical commitment to equal educational opportunity by providing college financial aid to students who don't need it, at the expense of those who do.

NINE

GOVERNMENT GIFTS TO THE RICH

It is the responsibility of the community, at the local, state
and national levels, to guarantee that financial barriers do not
prevent any able and otherwise qualified young person from
receiving the opportunity for higher education. There must be
developed in this country the widespread realization that
money expended for education is the wisest and soundest of
investments in the national interest. The democratic community
cannot tolerate a society based upon education for the
well to do alone. If college opportunities are restricted to
those in the higher income brackets, the way is open to the
creation and perpetuation of a class society which has no
place in the American way of life.

President's Commission on Higher Education, 1947

[The Higher Education Act of 1965] means that a high
school senior anywhere in this great land of ours can apply to any
college or any university in any of the 50 States and not be
turned away because his family is poor.

**President Lyndon B. Johnson, on signing the Higher
Education Act, 1965**

No qualified student who wants to go to college should be
barred by lack of money. That has long been a great American
goal; I propose that we achieve it now.

**President Richard M. Nixon, Special Message to the
Congress on Higher Education, 1970**

Aged eighteen and a recent high school graduate, Katelyn Ware ought to have the world at her feet. With her love of learning, her good grades, and her fondness for Shakespeare, going to college would seem to be the natural next step for Bonnie Butler's youngest child.

But Katelyn saw what happened to Jordan Ware, her older brother, and she saw what happened to Erin Ware, her older sister. Erin, who is twenty-eight, was the first in the immediate family to go to college. After attending a local community college and then graduating a few years ago with a four-year degree from the University of Massachusetts at Dartmouth in graphic design, she faces an education debt of $30,000. Erin is trying to repay her loans by working two jobs. Her day job is at AlphaGraphics, a copying and graphic design franchise, which pays her about $11 an hour. She bartends one evening a week to help pay back the loans and make ends meet.

Then came Bonnie's son, Jordan, who, at age twenty-two, is $40,000 in debt after completing a two-year degree at a prestigious culinary institute in New York. Cooking is his passion, but Jordan now confides to Bonnie that he has doubts about his decision to go into such debt. "Oh, he regrets very much the debt that he has," Bonnie Butler told me. "He feels like he will never be free of this because there's just no way that he can realistically pay this back."[1]

And so, in this working-class family that cannot afford to pay much, if anything, to help its children with college costs, Katelyn Ware is well aware of the financial risks that going to college would pose for her. "Katelyn is very, very bright academically," Bonnie said. "She's the brightest of all my children, academically. She loves Shakespeare, and she could be a teacher very easily with the potential she has. . . . But she's also seen her brother and sister struggle. If the finances were secure for her, I don't think she would hesitate about college. She's scared to death of the debt."

Katelyn was born into a Vermont family with a mother, Bonnie, who had escaped the life of welfare in which she herself had grown up, and a father with a high school education, who worked as a machinist. Throughout Bonnie's divorce and her remarriage after four years as a single mom, she was able to build a decent life for her children. Bonnie taught herself computers while serving as the tax collector in her town, an elected position she held for twelve years. That skill would lead to her current job, as the computer specialist at a local law firm in Wallingford.

"My children actually had a much more secure and stable upbringing than I did," Bonnie told me. "However, in building that life for them, I have literally had no financial extras. . . . But, you know, I worked very hard to make sure the kids had a good, standard upbringing."

As for planning for her children's college education, there were more immediate needs, such as recovering financially from the divorce and forming a stable household with her new husband, who had two younger children of his own. "Well, I can honestly say that we did little or no planning for college because we were planning for life," Bonnie said. "We were establishing some security and buying a home."

But Bonnie Butler did have the foresight to sign up Erin, and then Katelyn, with the Upward Bound program at their high school, a federal program for lower-income students and students whose parents did not go to college. Erin participated in Upward Bound for a year, and Katelyn for four years. The program gave the children at least some of the things that Bonnie could not give them. Mostly, Upward Bound exposed Erin and Katelyn to a college-going culture: the girls made visits to colleges, learned tips for taking the SAT, and received information about financial aid. "Upward Bound had knowledge and could give them things that I definitely could not," Bonnie explained. "You know, I hadn't gone to college. I had really focused on the family, and I just didn't have that experience."

———

But what neither Upward Bound nor Bonnie Butler could provide her children was money for college. Katelyn was not an academic all-star at her Wallingford, Vermont, high school, where she earned a GPA of 3.0. Admissions offices from prestige-seeking colleges and universities were not clamoring at her door. With Katelyn's modest SAT scores of about 1000, there would be no "merit" scholarships or tuition discounts in her future. Those perks were far more likely to go to children from the best high schools and those with affluent parents who could afford college even without extra help from the schools. As for financial assistance based on actual need, that sort of aid was *so* last century. Increasingly, need-based aid made little business sense for colleges and universities seeking to attract the right student customers who would help the institutions rise in the prestige rankings.

And what made matters even worse for kids like Katelyn were the state and federal governments themselves. Instead of upholding a financial safety net for lower-income kids who wanted to attend college, and rather than reaffirming the bedrock societal value that no one in America should be denied a higher education for lack of money—a value established by presidents from Truman through Nixon—state and federal governments in recent years have been reworking the college financial aid system in ways that would be unrecognizable to Harry Truman, Richard Nixon, or Lyndon Johnson.

For politicians and policy makers, it would seem, helping the economically disadvantaged pay for college didn't pay the political bills. For, just as colleges and universities were creating admissions and financial aid schemes that excluded lower-income students, state and federal policy makers were enacting measures that were systematically aiding the fortunes of the wealthy and politically powerful upper-middle and upper classes and damaging the prospects of higher education for children born into less privileged lives.

———

The federal government, which contributed $82 billion in 2004, accounting for 74 percent of the nation's college financial aid system,[2] has more than sufficient financial capacity to help lower-income students like Katelyn feel confident about going to college. However, that has not been the result. To understand why, we need to look at the essential, indisputable facts of the government's neglect:

> *The eroding Pell Grant program.* The essential premise of the Basic
> Educational Opportunity Grant program, which was based on
> need, was that higher education was so fundamental to the
> American enterprise that the federal government would step in to
> provide college funds that families couldn't afford. Four years
> after the program came into being in 1972, the maximum award
> covered almost 90 percent of the cost of a lower-income student
> attending a public four-year university. It paid almost 40 percent
> of the full cost of going to a private university. And the Pell
> Grants do go to students who need the money for college: some
> 90 percent of Pell recipients come from families earning less than
> $40,000 a year.[3]
>   Although the total size of the program has grown over time,
> the purchasing power of the grants has been on a downward
> slide since the mid-1970s. In 1980, when the program was re-
> named in honor of Senator Claiborne Pell, the Rhode Island De-
> mocrat who sponsored the original legislation, a Pell Grant paid
> 35 percent of public university costs. As of 2004, the grant cov-
> ered just 23 percent of attendance costs at public universities and
> 9 percent of the average costs at private colleges and universities.[4]
> *The rise of the debt-based financial aid system.* As the federal gov-
> ernment allowed the Pell Grant program, the cornerstone of the

college finance system, to erode, it fueled a meteoric expansion of both public and private lending, a system of college financing that most discourages lower-income students like Katelyn Ware from attending college.

The rapidly expanding federal loan programs were not those based on need. For example, while total Pell Grant dollars increased 76 percent in the ten years ending in 2004, unsubsidized Stafford loans increased by 795 percent. Education loans by private lenders increased by 692 percent. By 2004, loans made up nearly 70 percent of all federal financial aid. In contrast, Pell Grants were just 15 percent of federal aid.[5]

For policy makers who argue that education is a private good that ought to be privately financed, the massive shift from grants to loans surely fits within their ideological blinders. However, if the nation's goal is to increase college enrollment and educational attainment for the sake of national economic productivity, this transformation of the financial aid system fails not just the test of basic economics but also the test of equity.

"The shift of individual student aid from grants to loans over the last decade has probably benefited largely students from middle and upper middle income families at public colleges and universities, mostly in the form of unsubsidized loans," conclude Michael S. McPherson, an economist and president of the Spencer Foundation, and Morton Owen Schapiro, also an economist and president of Williams College. "Although these students no doubt welcome such support, there is little evidence that it is essential to their attending college. Yet federal grants targeted to students from lower income families do influence college enrollments of this group. Therefore, the recent redistribution of federal dollars appears to be going in the wrong direction, both from the standpoint of social equity and of efficiency in promoting college enrollment."[6]

Education tax breaks. In the Taxpayer Relief Act of 1997, President Bill Clinton argued that the federal government could nurture more investment in education, and help out the economy, by providing tuition tax credits to families.

If only he had left such a legacy. Instead, this monumental shift in federal financial aid policy would become Bill Clinton's version of trickle-down economics. According to most analysts, changing the tax code has had little effect on the nation's total investment in higher education because the lion's share of the tax breaks has gone to relatively affluent families who would have sent their kids to college even without the tax credit. In order to have a real impact on college attendance, federal subsidies would have to lower the college costs for lower-income families, for whom such costs constitute a relatively high percentage of family income.

As the creator of the education tax breaks, Clinton "argued consistently that the country needed to invest more in education and training to boost economic growth, expand opportunity, and reduce income disparities," notes financial aid expert Lawrence E. Gladieux. "But tuition tax breaks are not an effective means to achieve these worthy objectives. They are one way to cut taxes, but not a sound strategy for lifting the country's net investment in education or eliminating discrepancies in opportunity."[7]

But it may be too late to roll back these tax subsidies. Because the politically popular tax breaks are embedded in the U.S. tax code, they are unlikely to be unhinged any time soon, because it would, literally, require an act of Congress. That alone sets the tuition tax credits apart from the Pell Grant program, for example, which is subject to annual budgetary reviews.

The upshot is that federal policy itself has widened the educational opportunity gap between haves and have-nots by creating, growing, and entrenching programs that are not based on actual need. Combined, unsubsidized Stafford loans, federal loans to parents, and education incentives built into the federal tax code—none of which are based on need—made up 45 percent of all federal student financial aid in 2004. Consider that in 1986 only about 14 percent of federal aid was not need-based.[8]

What accounts for the federal government's shifting emphasis? One explanation is brute politics. Once institutionalized in federal policy, the need-based ethic has now been supplanted by the Machiavellian calculation that affluent voters are politically more profitable to politicians and policy makers than poor voters or those from the working class, who participate less frequently in the political process.

In addition, a sea change in ideology has occurred within the U.S. Department of Education itself, the agency that administers the federal aid programs and conducts research that informs policy. Since the late 1990s, this shift in perspective has resulted in the government downplaying the role of finance in closing college access gaps. In fact, a series of analyses by the National Center for Education Statistics has argued that finances are just one of several factors that account for depressed college-completion rates among poor and working-class kids. When lower-income students are sufficiently prepared academically and take all the requisite steps in planning for college—including filling out college applications and financial aid forms, and taking college entrance exams—the access gaps all but disappear, NCES has claimed.[9]

But in the past few years, some scholars, such as Edward P. St. John of the University of Michigan, have called into doubt NCES dogma about the importance of academic preparation. After reanalyzing the differences in college-going rates between rich kids and poor ones and correcting NCES's statistical errors, researchers have discovered that the NCES conclusions about preparation were deeply flawed. Essentially, these researchers suggest, NCES's findings about the role of preparation are based on an overly simplistic, static view of the world.

Why are children from low-income and working-class families less academically prepared than their more affluent peers? We've seen how families and the cultural, social, and economic capital they pass on to their children play important roles in students' success in school and their ability to plan for college. How, for instance, would a child such as Gillian Brunet, whom we met in chapter 1, have fared in school if she had grown up thinking that going to college (let alone one like Smith) was out of the question because of her family's finances? How might Katelyn Ware have behaved differently in high school had she known that finances would not discourage her from going to college?

Indeed, lower-income students often behave differently than affluent children, making different decisions about academics, college planning, and life, precisely because they lack confidence in their financial outlook. If kids like Katelyn were confident that they would be able to afford college, then they would work harder in school, take more college prep courses, sign up for college admissions tests, and fill out college applications—all that stuff that colleges "expect them to do," as the NCES contends.

"There are sound reasons to argue that raising educational standards may have enabled more high school graduates to enroll in college, but the academic preparation rationale does not explain the new inequality," writes St. John, one of the leading challengers to the NCES.[10]

In order to control for academic preparation and isolate the real impact of finances, one must compare students from different economic backgrounds who meet the NCES definition of "college-qualified." According to NCES, one becomes college-qualified by taking tests, filling out applications, and having the minimum scores, grades, and courses that colleges want.

On the path that leads thirteen-year-old eighth graders to eventual graduation from a four-year university, they encounter various social, economic, and academic filters along the way. Some make it through the filters and others do not. Consider two groups of eighth graders identified in 1992. Both groups were college-qualified by the time they graduated from high school. In one national study, based on NCES's own data, these students were divided only by differences in finances. At high school graduation, the cohort of low-income students faced an unmet financial need of $3,800 to pay for college, while the cohort of high-income students faced an unmet need of just $400.

Along the college-access pipeline, the gaps between *equally prepared* low-income and high-income students showed up early and continued to widen along the way (see figure 5). And at the end of the pipeline, the differences in outcomes between the two cohorts of students, both equally qualified for college, who had begun the journey together in eighth grade, were stark indeed. Fully 62 percent of the high-income students completed a bachelor's degree, compared to 21 percent of the college-qualified low-income students.[11]

In other words, about half of the *well-prepared* low-income students did not enroll in a four-year college, and almost a quarter attended no college at all. According to the Advisory Committee on Student Financial Assistance, which advises Congress on financial aid policy, that deficit adds up to hundreds of thousands of lower-income students who don't go to college—not because of lack of preparation or how many college degrees their parents have, but solely because of money.

"Most Americans believe that all students have the opportunity to earn a college degree through hard work in high school and college," the Advisory Committee's 2002 report, *Empty Promises: The Myth of College Access in America,* concludes. "Over this decade, 4.4 million . . . high school graduates will not attend four-year colleges and 2 million will attend no college at all. For these students, the promise of a college education is an empty one. For the nation, the loss of human capital will exact a serious economic and social toll for much of this century."[12]

The debate about the importance of finances versus preparation is not idle chatter among academics. Clearly, the academic preparation dogma has infused educational policy in George W. Bush's administration, fueling an unprecedented effort at the federal level to reform the

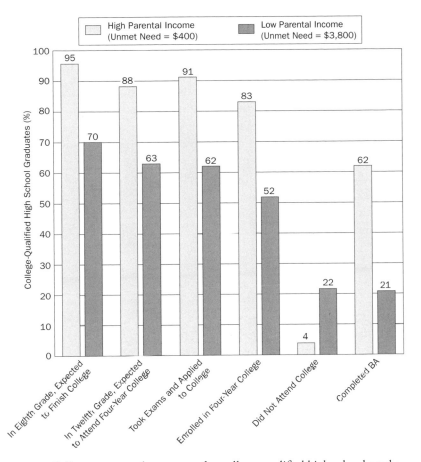

Figure 5. College access and outcomes for college-qualified high school graduates, by parental income. Source: U.S. Congress, Advisory Committee on Student Financial Assistance, *Empty Promises: The Myth of College Access in America* (Washington, D.C., 2002), p. 22, www.ed.gov/about/bdscomm/list/acsfa/emptypromises.pdf (accessed February 17, 2006).

nation's K-12 school system, with heavy emphasis on standardized testing and accountability as the main policy levers. The federal No Child Left Behind Act, passed in 2001, which requires public schools to make yearly progress on standardized tests in order to receive federal funds, is perhaps the clearest illustration of the hegemony of the preparation rationale being pushed by the federal government. The cruel joke on lower-income students is that no amount of academic preparation, taking tests, or filling out college applications can overcome the lack of financial support, unless the students happen to be academic all-stars, whom universities heavily recruit for the sake of their own financial self-interest.

———

We've already seen how states have made a historical retreat in their public support of higher education in recent years, compelling many public universities to behave like quasi-private institutions. And we've seen how many of the best public universities have been jacking up tuition and generally turning their backs on lower-income students in favor of the "right" sorts of students, who can help them compete for prestigious rankings.

Compounding the retrenchment of both schools and the federal government from need-based aid, "merit" has been all the rage for the states in deciding which families deserve money for college. While many Americans believe that academic merit ought to be rewarded, such scholarships have nevertheless been a curious expenditure of limited state money: because eligibility for the programs is not based on family income, the money most often goes to students from families who don't need aid in order to send their children to college. In essence, then, many of these state scholarship programs are subsidies from the state to relatively affluent taxpayers, offered under the legitimating guise of academic merit. To be sure, at 74 percent of all state aid in 2004, need-based aid remained the largest portion of state grant programs. This figure has declined, however, from 87 percent of all state financial aid just ten years earlier. During that same ten-year period, grants not based on need doubled, from 13 percent of state aid to 26 percent.[13]

The states' relatively sudden turn from need to merit as the basis of giving money to students for college can be traced to 1993, when Georgia governor Zell Miller, a conservative Democrat, created that state's so-called HOPE Scholarship program, to be funded from a state lottery. Ten years later, several states had followed Georgia's lead. Besides Georgia's $430 million program, the nation's largest, states that devoted the most dollars to merit programs in 2004 included Florida's $237 million, South Carolina's $184 million, Louisiana's $110 million, and Michigan's $70 million.[14] To put this trend in context, the dozen or so states that had created merit-based scholarship programs, with no consideration of need, gave nearly $900 million in such aid in 2001. That was fully three times the amount of money *these same states* gave to lower-income students with demonstrated need.[15]

Indeed, the expansion of the merit programs between 1994 and 2004 in some states was astonishing. Georgia's funding went up 1,239 percent. Indiana's surged 25,000 percent, as did New Mexico's. Mississippi's shot up 3,600 percent. All told, merit-based grants increased five-fold for all states, dwarfing the growth in need-based financial aid.[16]

As the first and largest of these programs, Georgia's HOPE Scholarships deserve special attention. The program's stated purpose was, and is, "Helping Outstanding Pupils Educationally," by providing money for college based on student academic performance and increasing college-going rates in the state. HOPE was a first for a state-funded scholarship program in that it was not means-tested. In terms of its actual effects, however, HOPE seemed to be aimed at helping the middle and upper-middle classes. According to studies by the Civil Rights Project at Harvard University, HOPE has largely been a gift to white students from relatively affluent families. Susan Dynarski of Harvard's Kennedy School estimates that HOPE has increased college enrollment of students from families earning more than $50,000 by 11 percent while having no measurable effect on the enrollment of students from lower-income families. And, although HOPE has bumped up enrollment of white students at Georgia universities by 12 percent, the program has not improved access for the state's black students, who are disproportionately from lower-income families.[17]

HOPE is cruelly ironic. While Georgia's lower-income students have seen little benefit from the program, they and their families do pay more than their fair share for the scholarships that go mostly to well-to-do whites. Why? As is commonly the case for state lotteries, the poor and the working class play Georgia's lottery significantly more often than middle-class and upper-class whites, Christopher Cornwell and David B. Mustard found in their report for the Civil Rights Project.[18]

But Georgia's colleges and universities aren't complaining. While HOPE has done little to expand access to the state's more selective universities for lower-income students, those universities have improved their position in the higher education marketplace as a result of the program. Encouraged by HOPE, affluent students have increasingly chosen schools such as the University of Georgia and Georgia Tech instead of going out of state for college. With higher enrollments of such students, HOPE has, indirectly, boosted these Georgia universities in the prestige rankings. Because these wealthier students from the state's better high schools have chosen Georgia and Georgia Tech, the SAT score averages of those institutions got a substantial boost. That, in turn, has helped those universities to become even more selective, further enhancing their competitive position in the *U.S. News* rankings. Inevitably, greater selectivity further restricts access for black and lower-income students. Writing in the Civil Rights Project's report, Cornwell and Mustard explain: "Thus, HOPE may exacerbate student sorting by ability and race (to the extent black test scores lag behind those of whites), leading Georgia colleges to become increasingly stratified along these lines."[19]

To be fair, the HOPE Scholarships and similar state merit-aid programs are pointed in the right direction, in that they appear to attack the financial barriers to college that may well supersede the preparation barriers. But with their glaring absence of a family income cap for eligibility, these state merit programs fail to target needy students. States eager to promote merit scholarships might target lower-income families with qualified merit programs aimed at the best-prepared needy students. That would actually have a real effect on a state's college enrollment rates. The finding that much of the merit funds, as the programs are currently conceived, do not go to lower-income students suggests that preparation barriers remain a serious concern. But if the lack of academic preparation among lower-income students is driven by their very lack of hope for completing a college degree without a mountain of debt, then the state merit programs are too little and too late.

———

Indeed, it's only when you add up the total effect of the institutional, state, and federal trends in financial aid that the system's pervasive tilt toward the affluent becomes painfully obvious. The totality of the effects can be summed up by looking at unmet need for various income groups and how it has changed over time. Unmet need is the difference between the amount of money families are expected to contribute to their children's college costs (according to federal formulas), less the "net price" of college attendance. Net price is figured by deducting scholarships, grants, loans, tuition discounts, and other subsidies from tuition, fees, and living costs.

For example, even at public community colleges, where college costs are the lowest, students from the lowest parental income group faced unmet need of $2,500 in 1989, and it increased to $4,500 ten years later (see figure 6), in constant dollars. At public four-year institutions, the students from the poorest families encountered unmet need of $2,900 in 1989, which rose to $3,800 by the year 1999 (see figure 7). Unmet need for lower-middle-income students at public universities also increased substantially during that period. With numbers like those, it's little won-

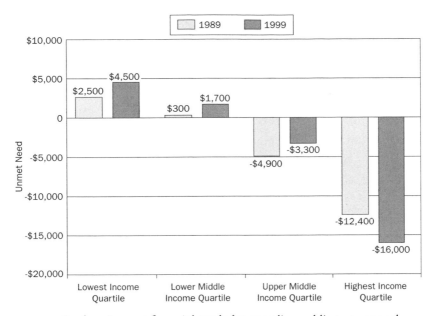

Figure 6. Students' unmet financial needs for attending public two-year colleges, by parental income quartile, 1989 and 1999. Source: U.S. Department of Education, National Center for Education Statistics, *Paying for College: Changes between 1990 and 2000 for Full-Time Dependent Undergraduates,* NCES 2004–075 (Washington, D.C.: U.S. Government Printing Office, 2004), pp. 32–33, http://nces.ed.gov/pubsearch/pubsinfo.asp?pubid=2004075 (accessed September 2006).

der that bright kids like Katelyn Ware might plan to do something with their lives other than go to college.

But then look at the numbers for students from the upper middle and highest income quartiles. Their unmet need was actually negative at community colleges and public universities, meaning that, including financial assistance from their families, they were receiving more in financial aid to attend college than it was costing them. More startling, even at private four-year institutions, the richest students and families received more total financial assistance than they paid in college costs (see figure 8).[20]

If those unmet need statistics aren't scandalous enough, consider how the net price of college attendance, after deducting scholarships and such, compares to family income at various points on the economic spectrum. Even at community colleges, net prices for students in the lowest income group amounted to 32 percent of family income in the year 2000;

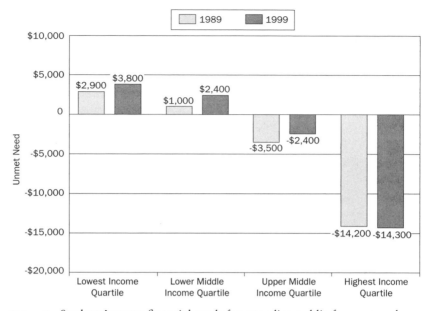

Figure 7. Students' unmet financial needs for attending public four-year colleges, by parental income quartile, 1989 and 1999. Source: U.S. Department of Education, National Center for Education Statistics, *Paying for College: Changes between 1990 and 2000 for Full-Time Dependent Undergraduates,* NCES 2004–075 (Washington, D.C.: U.S. Government Printing Office, 2004), http://nces.ed.gov/pubsearch/pubsinfo.asp?pubid=2004075 (accessed September 2006).

for students in the lower-middle income quartile, the net costs were almost 20 percent of family income. At public four-year institutions, net college costs were 42 percent of family income for low-income families and 25 percent for families in the lower-middle quartile. In contrast, net costs for students from families in the highest income quartile were just 10 percent of family income.[21]

Such a calculation vividly shows how much families have to sacrifice to send their children to college. For families like Bonnie Butler's, who would need to devote 20 or 30 percent of their income to pay for Katelyn's costs not covered by any other sources, what should they do? Not pay the mortgage? Forget the utility bills? Cut back on groceries? For affluent families, however, who face net college costs of just 10 percent of their income, the family sacrifices amount to far less: a new car every four years instead of every two, or limiting the family ski vacation to a resort in the home state instead of the annual ski week at Vail.

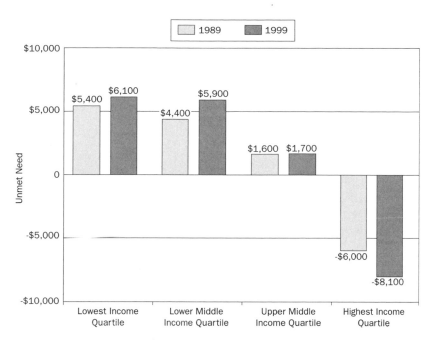

Figure 8. Students' unmet financial needs for attending private four-year colleges, by parental income quartile, 1989 and 1999. Source: U.S. Department of Education, National Center for Education Statistics, *Paying for College: Changes between 1990 and 2000 for Full-Time Dependent Undergraduates,* NCES 2004–075 (Washington, D.C.: U.S. Government Printing Office, 2004), http://nces.ed.gov/pubsearch/pubsinfo.asp?pubid=2004075 (accessed September 2006).

In the course of my research, I met one such family in the Palm Beach area of south Florida. I bring up their circumstances with some reluctance, because I do not want to bring any embarrassment to them. The parents are kind and well-meaning and simply want the best that they can afford for their two children. I do not want to identify them, and my purpose for telling their story is simply to illustrate the vast differences between the financial burden they face in paying for college and the burden faced by families like Bonnie Butler's. I interviewed their son Michael, who was in the midst of applying to colleges, as well as his mother, Laura, and visited the family in their spacious home in a gated community in Palm Beach Gardens. Laura is a non-practicing attorney, and Michael's father is a medical specialist.[22]

During our conversations, I learned that Michael had attended various private and public schools in the area. He finally settled on a private high school that permitted him to attend classes exclusively with private tutors for each of his courses, costing the family some $60,000 a year. I learned about his many sessions with SAT tutors and the extra help he received from a private college counselor. I learned about the details of his various trips with Laura to colleges across the eastern seaboard, all private ones, including Brown, Dartmouth, Cornell, Boston University, and many others. I learned that Michael was especially interested in sports and broadcasting. I learned that he had applied early decision to the University of Miami, which in recent years has become far more selective by investing heavily in merit scholarships and aggressively recruiting students from all over the world. By applying early decision, Michael and his family apparently weren't too concerned about the financial aid, if any, that he might be offered if he was accepted.

One evening, chatting around the family's kitchen table, I learned how much the University of Miami would cost. We were actually talking about the growing inequities in access to a college education, and the family members, whose politics struck me as on the liberal side, seemed genuinely bothered by the inequities. I mentioned that I had interviewed families making less than $30,000 a year who were hopeful that their children might go to college. Michael's younger brother, who was about ten or twelve, and the family's math whiz, quickly made the calculation: "That's the tuition at the University of Miami," he blurted out. There was an uncomfortable silence.

Michael's early-decision application to the University of Miami was successful. With his undergraduate attendance costs in 2005–2006 approaching $42,000 a year to live on campus, Michael told me later that the university had come through with merit scholarships amounting to 50 percent of the cost and that the state of Florida had also provided him with significant merit aid.

––––––

The relative sacrifices that comfortable families have to make to send children to college compared to what low-income and working-class families must sacrifice make the government's academic preparation argument seem like a cruel joke, a house of cards that crumbles under close scrutiny.

But, based on a story that Bonnie Butler told me, I began to wonder just how much policy makers and the affluent classes they represent really do get it. I found Bonnie through an article published by a local Vermont newspaper about the growing debt burdens on Vermont families who were sending children to college. After that article, Bonnie said she felt an odd coldness from her boss, an attorney at the law firm in which she worked. She had great respect for him, and he often encouraged her to speak up, which made his coldness seem especially odd.

"I felt a chill for two or three weeks," Bonnie explained. "My perception was that not only had I not paid for my children's education, I had publicized it, and he certainly was not impressed. I think that it never entered the realm of his life that he might not be able to pay for his children's education and support them through that education. I don't think there was ever a speck of concern."

Bonnie admitted that she was embarrassed that she couldn't afford to pay her children's college costs, just as her boss might have been not only embarrassed for her but also uncomfortable with the now-obvious class divide between them, brought into sharp focus by Bonnie's confessions in the article.

"After that first article, I was torn between feeling pride for speaking out and embarrassment as well, because I couldn't pay for my kids' education and because I now have children who are in debt," she told me.

That she encouraged her children to go to college despite the financial burdens has left Bonnie with lingering questions. "Did I let them get in debt? Did I encourage them to get in debt?"

"So it feels sort of like a failure on your part?" I asked Bonnie.

"Oh, yes, it does."

She went on, "And it's not that I feel that every child should be 'given' their education. But I feel like all children should have a fundamental— I'm not sure 'right' is the correct word—but every child should have an opportunity for funding of their core college classes. I don't think any child should be excluded from college or from higher education because of money. And I guess mine weren't, but the end result is the debt."

————

Thus far, we've explored the American education system's persistent inequalities along class lines. We've seen how differences in the cultural and economic resources of families create seemingly unlimited opportunities for some children and far more restricted chances for children from poor and modest family backgrounds. And we've seen how schools, colleges, and governments often reinforce and even exacerbate those inequalities with institutional arrangements that further enhance the opportunities of the privileged among us. Now, in part 4, we'll investigate what some schools, colleges, and universities are doing to address these inequities. We begin with the story of one urban high school in Oceanside, California, and a teacher named Dayle Mazzarella.

PART 4

EXPERIMENTS IN GATECRASHING AND THE BACKLASH OF THE ELITES

TEN

A DANGEROUS MAN

Dayle Mazzarella is crashing the exclusive party that American higher education has become. Google his name, and you'll find references to his coaching prowess: he spent decades coaching high school track and wrestling in Oceanside, California. But being a coaching legend in Southern California isn't what makes him a gatecrasher. It's because he's an educator, because of the students he educates, and how he goes about doing it at Oceanside High School, north of San Diego.

Oftentimes, the American education system serves as a handmaiden to affluent society, re-creating the cultural norms of dominant social classes and expecting all students to succeed according to those rules. Using the educational tools that society widely deems legitimate, objective, and fair, schools ensure that children habituated to the language and norms of dominant society are handsomely rewarded with good grades, high test scores, and admission to elite colleges and universities. Middle-class teaching methods, testing, tracking, and other sorting systems distinguish the children of affluence as gifted, talented, and meritorious, thus deserving the most challenging and enriched learning environments, under the guidance of the best teachers. These same methods often label lower-class children as academically deficient misfits who are in need of remediation in order to fill even the most basic societal needs.

Dayle Mazzarella is a dangerous man for such a system, in part because he has expropriated one of the tools of social class segregation in schools, the Advanced Placement program run by the College Board, and proved that its coursework could be opened up to students whom educators had long believed were not academically ready for college-level work.

Mazzarella became a dangerous man the day that his boss, the school principal, observed him teaching a P.E. class. This was in the 1980s at El Camino High, Oceanside High's sister school, where Mazzarella had taught and coached for many years. Similar to Oceanside High, El Camino was economically and socially diverse, with significant numbers of lower-income Latinos, African Americans, and whites. El Camino also enrolled a number of more well-to-do suburban kids.

As Mazzarella recalls it, his teaching that day was abysmal, prompting his boss to comment, "Mazz, if you taught the way you coached, you might be okay." Mazzarella explained, "Man, that hurt me bad. I started to think about what he said, and then I realized what he meant. I coached with a lot of passion, with a lot of direction, very mentally, very slowly, and with a goal in mind. It certainly shook me up, and I started doing a better job. I started reading about research and learning theory and why people learn the way they do. About the same time, I started teaching my first AP classes, and I thought, 'There has got to be a different paradigm here for education than the one we are using.' "[1]

During his years at El Camino High in the late 1980s, a central tenet of the system Mazzarella encountered was that the college-level Advanced Placement courses were supposed to be selective, taken only by the school's best and brightest, as determined by past performance in coursework and on standardized tests. When the best and brightest invariably turned out to be relatively well-off suburban kids, Mazzarella the coach, who had grown up on an Indian reservation in Arizona, set out to prove that the system was deeply flawed, propped up by myths about the ability of "unprepared" students from less privileged backgrounds.

He took his boss's words to heart. If he really wanted to teach like he coached, then his first move would be to tear down the AP gates.

"I was a coach for years," Mazzarella told me. "You take whatever walks in the room, and you have two choices. You can make excuses about it and complain about not having any talent, or that the middle school guys don't have a program; or you can start figuring out how to win. I had kids when they were freshmen, and I'm thinking, 'There is no way this kid can even make the freshman team.' And by the time they were seniors, they were winning championships. I coached fifty-four teams, and in the years that I coached, I never had a losing season, not once in fifty-four tries, and we had some pretty miserable individuals."

He continued, "If you can get them to believe in themselves and give them some fundamental skills and don't cover too much, people can be amazingly effective. It is just a little bit at a time. You don't get in a hurry. You teach fundamentals, and you have a good attitude. The kids who wrestled for me who were really gifted won state championships. The kids who were just average athletes won conference championships. The guys who were horrible athletes got fourth, but even a horrible athlete can beat a really good athlete if they are properly trained. We shouldn't be predetermining who has skill, ability, and talent and who doesn't. That is none of our business. That is up to the kids."

In the academic realm, Mazzarella realized that El Camino was losing a vast amount of talent by excluding kids from AP classes who teachers and administrators had long believed were unprepared for rigorous academic work. But with his experience as a coach, and taking all comers who wanted to try, Mazzarella realized that teachers were only half right. In the context of the middle-class teaching methods that most teachers themselves had been exposed to from childhood through college, disadvantaged kids were indeed unprepared to succeed in AP classes *as they were commonly taught.*

But that didn't mean disadvantaged students were intellectually incapable. What it did mean was that the teaching methods most teachers employed were rooted in a middle-class mindset, an unstated but always present paradigm. The paradigm of Advanced Placement, honors, and other high-track high school courses assumed that students came to school already possessing certain levels of cultural literacy—ways of speaking, thinking, and acting and even modes of being, acquired from well-educated parents and nurtured in culturally and economically comfortable families.

Mazzarella tossed out those assumptions and reengineered the entire approach to teaching kids who had gotten to high school with limited exposure to upper-middle-class social norms. These were kids whose parents had no experience with higher education or with the professional world to which a college degree might lead, let alone any understanding of how an Advanced Placement class differed from any other high school class. Even more shocking to such parents was that their children would have to pay an extra $80 for the privilege of taking and passing an AP test to earn the college credit. Having cultural horizons that rarely extended beyond what they were exposed to in popular culture or, in geographic terms, beyond a few square miles from the places they lived, such students and their parents rightly wondered, What was the point?

Meanwhile, teachers accustomed to middle-class culture and middle-class expectations taught middle-class children who seemed to learn the advanced material easily. Because teachers in those environments had success with such students, the educators assumed that their teaching was as good as it could be. When lower-class children inevitably failed in advanced classes, that reinforced teachers' beliefs that their methods were sound but that disadvantaged students weren't ready for the work. And, because their teaching methods were working for some kids, the fault always lay elsewhere—with parents who "didn't care about education," with middle schools, or somewhere in a litany of other explanations. It wasn't that the teachers weren't trying hard or didn't care about reaching disadvantaged kids, Mazzarella found. They simply lacked the right tools for the job.

"That culture of low expectations does not happen because people are inherently nonbelievers in kids," Mazzarella explained. "What happens is a teacher comes to a school like El Camino or Oceanside High, all full of vim and vigor, and they go into class and teach the way they were taught to teach by middle-class teachers, and it doesn't work. I mean, the bottom line is kids here don't respond in the same way a lot of the kids at Torrey Pines High would respond," he said, referring to a high-performing school serving a wealthy neighborhood.

He went on, "We don't have parents who told their kids all the time about going to college. For many of these kids, it's a whole different kind of mindset. So the teachers get into these classes, they work at it, the kids don't really respond, they don't do very well. And the teachers feel sorry for the kids because they think, 'Oh, man, this is just too hard. The kids can't do it.' They are looking at all these kids getting Fs, so they lower their expectations, and they say, 'Look, what we have to do is get even more basic here.' So it's a vicious cycle."

Consider for a moment the high school that Mazzarella mentioned, Torrey Pines High, and the contours of its college-going culture. Many affluent and well-educated families pay a premium for housing in order to send their children to Torrey Pines. And the parents of these students are certainly well educated: in 2004–2005, almost six of ten had graduate or professional degrees, 29 percent had only bachelor's degrees, and just 5 percent had a high school education or less. Only 6 percent of students at Torrey Pines were considered low-income, qualifying for free or reduced-price lunches (see table 1).[2]

By way of contrast, there is Oceanside High, where Mazzarella went to work in 2003. Oceanside's demographics are just the reverse: 4 per-

TABLE 1. CHARACTERISTICS OF STUDENTS AT THREE CALIFORNIA HIGH SCHOOLS, 2004–2005

	Torrey Pines	El Camino High	Oceanside High
Parents lack high school diploma	3%	14%	29%
Parents graduated from high school	2%	20%	22%
Parents have some college	9%	34%	31%
Parents graduated from college	29%	23%	14%
Parents have graduate degrees	57%	11%	4%
Low income	6%	30%	58%
Academic Performance Index (API)	821	737	659
Advanced Placement scores of 3 or higher	1,787	586	34
Total AP test-takers	1,122	541	462

SOURCE: California Department of Education, "School Demographic Characteristics: 2004–05 Academic Performance Index (API) Growth Report," http://data1.cde.ca.gov/dataquest/, report generated by author, December 2005.

NOTE: Totals may exceed 100% because of rounding.

cent of parents in 2004–2005 had graduate or professional degrees, and almost 60 percent of students came from low-income families. More than half of Oceanside's parents had only a high school education or less. El Camino High, Mazzarella's former school, resides more in the center of the socioeconomic spectrum, with decidedly working-class demographics: a third of El Camino parents had at least some college, and almost a quarter had graduated from college. Some 30 percent of students qualified for free or reduced-priced lunches.[3]

As one would expect, the three schools are blessed or burdened with high test scores or modest test scores, depending on the surrounding cultural and economic wealth—or lack of it—that feeds the schools. In California, the gross measure of relative academic prowess among schools can be found in a number called the Academic Performance Index, compiled mostly from the results of various standardized tests. On a scale of 200 to 1000, 800 is the sort of magic number that allows a school to be considered high-performing. In 2004–2005, the API for Torrey Pines was 821, El Camino High's API was 737, and Oceanside's was 659.[4]

On Advanced Placement tests, Torrey Pines parents have little to complain about. In the most recent year of data, some 1,100 test-takers, taking one or more AP exams, produced 1,787 AP scores of 3 or higher. (Using a scale of 1 to 5, an AP score of 3 is generally required to earn college credit.) At El Camino High, 541 test-takers produced 586 scores of 3 or greater. But at Oceanside, 462 test-takers produced just 34 such scores.[5]

Not surprisingly, Torrey Pines graduates go to four-year colleges and universities at high rates. In a given year, the school sends 140 to 150 graduates to University of California campuses alone, and a slightly smaller number to California State University campuses. El Camino High has gained significantly in recent years as a feeder to the University of California, one important indicator of a blossoming college-going culture. It has also improved its placements at CSU. Still, in 2004, the school sent just 31 graduates to UC, a fraction of what Torrey Pines sent, even though the schools were about the same size. For its part, Oceanside High's college-going trends had been in a downward spiral for several years, the reverse of its sister school, El Camino. In 2000, Oceanside sent 16 students to the University of California, 20 to CSU, and more than 400 to community colleges.[6] In the fall of 2003, according to one report, Oceanside High sent a total of 27 students to four-year colleges—and none to the UC system.[7]

The problem wasn't just that Oceanside High's graduates were not going to four-year colleges and universities. The school was battling for its very survival, and its fate had reached a crisis point in 2003. Facing state and federal mandates under No Child Left Behind that required it to improve or else, Oceanside was already engaged in a major effort to raise test scores. Under the former principal, the school had paid hefty fees to outside consultants, including a $1 million contract for a popular program known as America's Choice, operated by the National Center on Education and the Economy, a nonprofit organization well known in the standards and testing movement. The firm specialized in raising school test scores and advising schools on how to stay out of the clutches of the No Child Left Behind law.

Often, however, such consultants focused on short-term fixes that didn't solve deeply entrenched, chronic problems in a school's culture. That proved to be the case at Oceanside as well. Coming up on its hundred-year anniversary, Oceanside High's performance did not improve with the quick fixes. Its situation was doubly embarrassing for the community's namesake high school, given that its younger sister high school, El Camino, was acquiring accolades from state and federal officials for its record of improvement, in no small measure a result of Mazzarella's efforts.

The final nail in the coffin of the old Oceanside High School came when district officials converged on the school with a team of experts, including teachers and administrators from throughout the district. They compiled a scathing report on the school, which eventually leaked out to the local media. The High Priority Schools (HPS) report, as it was called, indicted Oceanside on numerous counts, including an obsession with athletics, a dysfunctional administration, and an entrenched culture of low expectations among students, teachers, and staff.

"They came through and ripped the school," remembered Oceanside principal Kimo Marquardt, who had been running the school for a short while before the HPS report. He'd had success turning around an elementary school in the district and had been brought to Oceanside High to do the same there. "I unfortunately inherited a team that was dysfunctional. And not only was the team dysfunctional, the school was highly dysfunctional," Marquardt told me. "It did not have a clear vision of what the school culture should look like, or anything else—and, quite frankly, neither did I. I was just trying to survive and trying to figure out what was going on with this place."[8]

The immediate impact of the HPS report was to send the teachers and staff into depression and denial. Teachers had long been bitter that district officials and the community compared Oceanside's performance to El Camino's. When El Camino was formed in 1976, the district boundaries were rigged so that the upstart school served the wealthier neighborhoods east of Interstate 5, while Oceanside continued to serve the more racially diverse and economically depressed neighborhoods near the school, which stood near the railroad tracks just blocks from the Pacific Ocean.

"We went through the pain, the anger, and the stages of denial," Marquardt recalled. "We wanted to blame the superintendent and blame the parents. Even for myself, I thought, 'Well, if we just change the boundaries and bring all the nice white kids [from the more affluent suburbs], it will change our scores.' "

Marquardt recalled a meeting he had with the district's testing director, who showed him statistics indicating that Oceanside's ninth graders entered the school doing almost as well on standardized tests as El Camino's freshmen. But while El Camino's ninth graders continued to improve during their high school years, Oceanside's ninth grade cohorts floundered. What's more, the attrition was horrible. By the time a freshman class of six hundred kids reached the twelfth grade, more than three hundred had dropped out.

"By then, looking at the data and looking at the brutal facts, I realized we had significant attitude problems, and we had to go through a major culture reform here," Marquardt said. This was some one and a half years after the HPS report, in February 2005. "I know we couldn't be where we are today without having had that wake-up call. Without hearing that, 'You guys are terrible,' and the whole thing getting out in public, and having the staff upset about it. It caused us to rethink how we do business here. It caused us to look at those facts and say something is wrong. We can't keep blaming the parents, we can't keep blaming the second language, we can't keep blaming the color. It made us look at what we can control internally and see that we can make a difference in these kids."

———

Nearing the end of his coaching and teaching careers at El Camino, Dayle Mazzarella seemed to have little left to prove. At El Camino, he had shown that Advanced Placement classes could be detracked, opened up to far more students in order to tap into raw talent that had gone unrecognized in the past. But, after the HPS report, when Oceanside district superintendent Ken Noonan picked him to spearhead the reform of Oceanside High, Mazzarella saw the opportunity to go far beyond what he had been able to accomplish at El Camino. His success there was limited to his own AP government and AP U.S. history classes and those of a handful of other teachers who adopted his methods; he says that he never got the full support of El Camino's principal to push reform through the entire school.

At Oceanside, Mazzarella's official position would be special assistant to Kimo Marquardt, in charge of staff professional development. But, in truth, Mazzarella would become the glue that held the Oceanside experiment together. At Oceanside, Mazzarella would have his chance to prove that an entire high school could be detracked and its culture rebuilt from the bottom up.

When I spoke to Mazzarella, eighteen months into the Oceanside experiment, he told me time and time again that school reform as generally practiced in the United States over the past several years, embodied in policies such as No Child Left Behind, was bound to fail—and would fail disadvantaged students in particular. As we spoke in his cramped office at Oceanside, brimming with files and work in progress, I noted on his desk a quotation saying, in effect, that efforts by the states and the federal government to push high-stakes testing on disadvantaged students would actually increase the achievement gap between them and advantaged students. What disadvantaged students needed wasn't more pressure to perform, but an emotional attachment to the school as a gateway to their future life.

As the prevailing paradigm for school improvement has played out in the United States, high-stakes pressure has produced failure—and with failure has come remediation, an approach that invariably leads schools into a vicious circle of more pressure and more remediation and more failure. Indeed, that was the loop in which Oceanside High had been trapped when the HPS report came out. Mazzarella maintained that the education system's focus on remediation hasn't worked and won't work because it does nothing to solve the real problems that schools like Oceanside face. Why weren't the vast majority of kids from Oceanside High signing up for the PSAT exam or filling out financial aid applications or trying their hand at an Advanced Placement course? Why, really, had *no* Oceanside graduates been admitted to the University of California system in 2003?

The essential shortcoming of schools like Oceanside, and the reason for the ineffectiveness of the high-stakes testing movement as a tool for supposedly closing the achievement gap between rich and poor, has been the inability to provide disadvantaged kids with a *reason* for wanting to succeed in school. It was a failure of school culture and a failure of imagination that no amount of testing and spending money on remediation could fix.

Too, the obsession of educators and policy makers with closing the achievement gap was unrealistic and misplaced. In Mazzarella's experience as a teacher, the culturally advantaged children who started the race well ahead of disadvantaged students were apt to learn even faster with better teaching, because they already had the literacy tools and experience to take advantage of it.

"The gap isn't an intellectual gap so much as it is an attitudinal gap, in my view," Mazzarella explained to me. "Middle-class children know what it is to challenge themselves. They know what it is to sacrifice for the future. That is primarily what we have to do. That is where we have to close the gap. If we close that gap, the rest of the gap I don't care about. The rest of the gap is going to take care of itself."

————

When Mazzarella was growing up, his family lived on Indian reservations in Arizona, where his father worked as a social researcher. His mother, of American Indian heritage, grew up in a sod hut in the Wind River mountains of Wyoming. As a young man, his father had set out on an adventure to Wyoming, where he met his soon-to-be wife at the University of Wyoming. In Arizona, the family lived in conditions of relative poverty, in the same slums as their Indian neighbors. Mazzarella saw firsthand how fatalism affected young Indians, and he saw the same fatalism on the faces of his students at Oceanside.

"Why would our kids at Oceanside High put up with algebra? They don't understand that. There is no link between it and their lives," Mazzarella argued. "A middle-class kid puts up with it just based on faith. Their parents have told them it is important enough times that they believe it. They don't really understand the link, and they couldn't explain it to you. They just do it, and they go home and somebody beats them on the head until they get it done. They get their allowance taken away if they come home with a D.

"With our kids, who cares? Their parents didn't graduate from college. They are running a gardening truck. It is not that they don't care about their kids' future—they just don't see the future. So that is what we have to do. We have to get our kids to see the future in a different way and link it to school. It is about 'What do you see the future to be? What do you dream about?'

"Our kids don't dream. Middle-class and upper-class white kids, they dream. They dream about going to the Caribbean. They dream about going to Harvard. Hell, these kids, they don't dream about anything. . . . Their parents haven't had a vacation since they were born. Their idea of vacation is being able to go out on a Saturday afternoon, pop a beer, and watch a football game. That is it. I guarantee you we have kids who live in Oceanside who have never been to the beach. They have never walked down the street. Their society and their culture are not about exploration. Their culture isn't about dreams. Their culture is about survival."

He went on, "The problem with a school like this is, kids need to be resocialized. That is the bottom line, and if you don't resocialize them, then you are not going to get anywhere. You can forget about test scores, forget about all of that stuff. You need to resocialize the kids, and the way you resocialize them is that you provide for them what a middle-class household would provide anyway, which are the aspirations for a good career. That means they will put up with algebra even when they don't understand why they are doing it. If we are going to close that gap, we have to change the way people think about their potential and their future. Academic skills are just part of it."

And so when district superintendent Ken Noonan offered Mazzarella the chance to go to Oceanside, Mazzarella knew that this was the opportunity to bring together the ideas he had been working on since the early 1990s at El Camino High. In broad terms, the job before him was huge, but brutally simple: nothing less than creating a college-bound culture from scratch. If that could happen, in three or four years, Mazzarella brashly told me, Oceanside High's academic performance would make it competitive with the best schools in San Diego County. I asked him how he could be so confident of that outcome.

"Because the way education is, most schools run on two out of eight cylinders. They are relatively successful despite the fact that they are crappy, not because they are good," he asserted. "They do horrible things that make no sense from an educational point of view."

———

With Kimo Marquardt's backing, Mazzarella became the nerve center through which the school's cultural transformation would take place. While the underlying philosophy of the Oceanside experiment was simple, the practical details of making it work involved a complexity that I can't do justice to in these pages. In my conversations with dozens of teachers, students, and administrators, I asked over and over, Who or what is the glue that holds this experiment together?

In almost every case, people told me that Mazzarella was that glue. But, invariably, they would also cite additional features of the new culture, which led me to believe that each element was necessary even though by itself it might not have had much impact on the school culture. Combined, however, the elements added up to something greater than the sum of the parts, and when the parts of that culture were moving in harmony, the whole became a living organism—a *school*, a fully functional and vital school.

It became clear to me that this experiment was creating a set of new institutional markers that grew from a rich collaboration of a new administrative team, a teaching staff that slowly bought into the changes, and the students who were learning new ways of thinking about school. In fact, when I asked Mazzarella the "glue" question, he unhesitatingly told me, "Students do better when we all work together. Collaboration works."

And there were no secrets here. After the chilly reception I had received from Berkeley High's principal, Jim Slemp, earlier that same month, I was pleasantly surprised when I first contacted Marquardt about Oceanside. This was a story he and his staff clearly wanted to tell. I soon got a reply from Mazzarella himself, who, after initially briefing me on the phone before my visit, mailed me a very large box of materials, with a computer CD containing the complete history, including all documents, memos, and other details of the Oceanside experiment.

What was the formula? Clearly, giving kids the chance to sign up for once-closed AP classes, which were now open enrollment courses, and detracking virtually the entire curriculum, were the most basic elements of the Oceanside experiment. Teachers encouraged students by pointing out all the reasons why they *should* take the most challenging classes possible instead of barring them from difficult classes with all the traditional reasons why they shouldn't sign up.

But opening enrollment was also controversial, raising doubts and suspicions with the teaching staff. Soon after Mazzarella was picked to come to Oceanside, teachers handed Kimo Marquardt a petition saying that they didn't want Mazzarella at their school. The school's more affluent parents, whose children occupied the honors classes, also had to be persuaded that detracking the school would not "dumb down" the academic experience by lowering standards in order to accommodate the bottom students.

But Mazzarella came armed with some very persuasive data. He provided, for example, a comparison of performance on the AP U.S. history test between the tracked courses at Oceanside High and the open enrollment classes at El Camino (see appendix B, table B-1). El Camino's enrollment in AP U.S. history, at 139 students, was more than double Oceanside's enrollment in the same course. Conventional wisdom held that enrolling far more students in the AP classes would produce fewer good AP scores and higher percentages of failing ones. In fact, just the opposite happened. At Oceanside, only 17 percent of AP U.S. history students scored a 3 or higher on the AP test, qualifying for college credit. But more than 50 percent of El Camino's students got at least a 3, despite Oceanside's more restrictive enrollment policies.[9]

And, Mazzarella pointed out, the differences were not because El Camino had a surfeit of superstar teachers. Three different teachers at El Camino were responsible for producing those results, indicating that a *system* of instruction was largely responsible. Indeed, that system, which was part and parcel of the open enrollment philosophy, also engendered considerable dissension from the Oceanside staff when Mazzarella proposed it.

Called the "binder system," it consisted of a series of course binders shared by all instructors of a given subject. Each binder contained a detailed teaching plan that reflected the shared wisdom of the teaching staff. Thus, the teaching methods used by the best teachers in a given situation were always available to the entire staff teaching that subject. This collective approach produced a certain amount of standardization. Always, instructors teaching the same subject at different times gave quizzes, tests, and homework assignments on the same day.

Instinctively, Oceanside's teachers were hostile to the binder system because it challenged a number of sacred cows of the teaching profession. At the most basic level, it challenged the American ethic of individualism, that teachers, in particular, ought to be left alone to exercise their professional judgment. By spreading out the expertise of the best teachers, the binder system seemed to take from individually gifted and experienced teachers in order to give to the individually weaker or less experienced ones. As part of the Mazzarella coup at Oceanside, Marquardt pushed out several teachers and staff who were unwilling to accede to the shared demands of the binders.

Indeed, few teachers were even talking to Mazzarella in the early days of the new Oceanside. Among the few who were was Rob Driscoll, the chair of the English department. Driscoll had come to Oceanside from Clairemont High in San Diego (the same school, he told me, that had inspired Cameron Crowe's Fast Times at Ridgemont High), where he was involved in establishing a program called Advancement Via Individual Determination, simply known as AVID, the path-breaking creation of a Clairemont High teacher named Mary Catherine Swanson. Once a solidly white and middle-class school, Clairemont's demographics had changed in the 1980s under court-ordered desegregation. The school's more affluent half split off to form a new high school, leaving teachers like Swanson with many more lower-income students in their classes, whose families had no experience with higher education. Designed to provide the cultural literacy and exposure to higher education that disadvantaged students could not acquire from home, the AVID idea spread. Driscoll started out as an AVID tutor and helped write the program's first handbook.

When you talk to teachers like Driscoll, you realize just how complicated teaching is, particularly teaching in an open environment with a wide mixture of students coming to class with different skill levels. Driscoll's teaching language is laced with such terms such as "anchoring," "scaffolding," and "spiraling"—all techniques that turn out to be necessary when teaching kids who lack the cultural literacy skills that most middle-class schools simply assume in their students, literacy that wealthier and better-educated families seem to effortlessly reproduce on their own.

When I met with Driscoll, Mazzarella joined us as we chatted in an empty classroom. As an English major who later went into teaching, Driscoll described for me the sacred cows of teaching English that the binder system and its more focused instruction forced him to abandon.

Sacred cow number one was the teaching of entire novels or poems in ninth grade, and using each novel to demonstrate whole lists of concepts that the students were supposed to know according to the state standards, such as metaphor, simile, and analogy. With each successive novel, story, or poem, the teacher would throw out the same dozens of concepts, a scattershot approach that resulted in a lot of "coverage," but, in the case of Oceanside's students, not much learning. Under the binder system that Mazzarella proposed, a teacher would keep the class focused on just one story or poem, mining the same piece for as many weeks as it took to slowly and systematically introduce new concepts, one at a time.

"I remember when Dayle came over one early morning and said, 'What do you think about doing a binder situation in English and throwing out the novels?' And my initial emotional reaction was 'Hell, no!'" Driscoll told me. "It was before a meeting of department heads. And it was only about a half hour later, I couldn't tell you the actual process, but essentially I thought, 'What the hell? We have tried all of these other things, and it hasn't worked.' I went to the meeting and quoted the title of a book that I have never read, but I love the title: *Sacred Cows Make the Best Burgers*. Essentially, he was asking to kill a sacred cow."[10]

Mazzarella joined in. "Rob was hesitant, but he was the only person, literally, the only person on this campus who I talked to the first six weeks. We recognized that the statistics didn't bear out that they were being successful. I mean, there were blatant statistics that said whatever they were doing wasn't working. Even though Rob and I had disagreements about particulars, especially early on, Rob was the only person here who was really looking at that data and saying, 'Hey, look, man, this is not working.'"

Related to no longer teaching whole novels, another sacred cow Driscoll abandoned was the notion of "sustained silent reading," a common practice in high school English classes whereby teachers require students to read an assigned novel or story for twenty minutes. Mazzarella noted that sustained silent reading worked moderately well in schools accustomed to teaching high-achieving students, who were adept at assimilating ideas and information. But at schools like Oceanside, many students foundered because they didn't learn in the "holistic" ways that such reading presumed. In education circles, holistic learning generally refers to the integration of mind, body and spirit in the learning process—treating the learner as a "whole" person, as it were. But that wasn't exactly how Mazzarella meant it. Rather, he equated the term with the ability to process and synthesize large chunks of information, and generalize from it—a skill, he says, that is learned in middle-class homes and schools—as opposed to learning that occurs with discrete bits of information processed in careful steps, as directed by the teacher. In the former type of instruction, the teacher is more a passive guide, showing the active learner the path and allowing the learner to take it from there.

"A lot of kids are bright and curious, and they've learned to learn holistically just by virtue of their own intrinsic values and intelligence," Mazzarella explained. "Most kids do not learn holistically. Study after study suggests that holistic learning doesn't really take place except with the brighter and more motivated kids. We have a bunch of really, really bright and fascinating kinds of people teaching English who want to teach English the way they learned, which was fun, engaging, and rewarding. And they just miss the point that three-quarters of the kids don't learn that way, that they don't have the basic skills or motivations to learn that way."

"Do you agree with that?" I asked Driscoll, as we both listened to Mazzarella.

"Absolutely," he said. "For instance, we have a poetry unit coming up. The traditional thing in the past was you would start off the unit and tell the class, 'Here are all the terms that you are going to learn during this unit,' and give them two pages of terms and concepts. So we'd start the story or whatever and go, 'Oh, look at the simile here, and look at the metaphor there, and look at how the meter and rhythm are being used to emphasize the meaning that the poet has communicated.'"

He added, "That sacred cow is dead and buried. Actually, it has been chewed on a little bit, too."

Driscoll elaborated on how he went about the lessons under the binder system. "Say we've just read Edgar Allan Poe. You have this great poem or story filled with all kinds of examples of these literary terms that you want to teach. Let's just keep going back to that story. Just getting through a Poe story and understanding its meaning is challenging enough. Once they have that reward of finishing the story, why not reward them some more and go back to the story, and use it as a mine, and mine it for everything it's got?"

With that sort of scaffolding, looping, and spiraling, Driscoll says he covers less material but in far more depth, hence addressing one of the most plaguing concerns with American education: that standards-obsessed schools present a lot of material but leave students with only a superficial understanding. Throughout the Oceanside experiment, both Driscoll and Mazzarella immersed themselves in cognitive theories of how people learn. When teachers covered a more limited amount of content but delved into it more deeply, they maintained, high school students more readily became engaged in the material and learned it more effectively.

"People don't learn by having eighteen similar kinds of things thrown around at the same time," Mazzarella contended. "Only your very brightest person can differentiate any of that. The rest of the people are just totally lost. When you are all done, they still know nothing. What we have done is taken learning theory and applied it to actual teaching. There are a lot of people in education now who pay lip service to that, but there is not much of that actually taking place in education. They talk about learning theory and research-based education, but, honestly, I don't see it. I don't see it anywhere. I don't see it in any other school I have been at. They just don't do it because it takes too much patience, and we are not patient. We want kids to know what we know right now."

Guided by the binders and more directed and focused instruction, the new Oceanside produced teaching and learning far more efficiently than the comparatively sloppy approach of the old school. Indeed, Mazzarella's approach was not unlike that of Billy Beane's fabled data-driven methods at the Oakland As that challenged Major League Baseball's paradigm for identifying talent, as chronicled in Michael Lewis's *Moneyball: The Art of Winning an Unfair Game.*[11] In the case of the Oakland As, Beane broke through to the heart of the matter: What sorts of baseball skills really did produce winning teams—one player's ability to hit home runs or another's uncanny ability to get on base? Which sacred cows had to be abandoned? In the case of Oceanside, Mazzarella wondered, which inefficient teaching habits, accumulated over generations in American schools, had to be let go?

In most American schools, Mazzarella told me, teachers will throw out, say, one hundred concepts for students to master. Year in and year out, the students, particularly those who lack cultural literacy skills acquired from their families, fail to master even a fraction of the same one hundred concepts. By the time these students reach high school, they are seriously at risk of dropping out, failing a state exit exam, or worse. Again, it goes back to the American tendency to cover a set amount of material versus patiently teaching it, allowing students to make slow and methodical steps. It's teaching smart versus teaching dumb, insisted Mazzarella. Describing the process for me, he unconsciously slipped into his experience as a coach.

"Typically, in America, we teach concepts one through three the first week, and a student makes one hundred errors. I come to practice the next day and try to fix one hundred errors. The next week, my student still makes one hundred errors. If instead I ask, 'What are the four most fundamental errors my team made?' and I correct them, and those four help me correct two others, then my team only makes ninety-four errors. If by the end of the year my team only gets eighty errors, and your team is still making one hundred errors, I am going to beat you. You are just spinning your wheels doing nothing. Even if you beat me to start with, I am going to beat you, even though my team still makes eighty errors.

"That is what we have been doing in education. We are just spinning our wheels. For example, the fourth grade English standard in California is to write an entire essay. So, in fourth grade, we teach them all seventy things that go into an essay. And then the poor fifth grade teacher goes, 'God, these kids don't know anything. I am going to have to teach it again.' So they teach all seventy things again. The same kids that were screwed up are still screwed up. Every year, you might add two or three more kids who the light finally comes on for. Any ninth grade teacher will tell you that most of their kids don't know how to write an essay. Why is that? There is a standard in fourth grade. So they have fourth through eighth grade to learn the standard, and 90 percent of those kids still do not understand it."

Alternatively, Mazzarella proposed, learning how to write an essay to meet a supposed fourth grade standard that most kids might actually learn by ninth grade needed to begin in third grade. Teachers would begin with simple sentences that led slowly to more complex elements of the essay, one fully developed concept at a time. "By the time the kid gets to ninth grade, the kid would know that a paragraph is supposed to have an indented first sentence. They would know where commas belong and where colons belong. They would know what a verb, an adverb, and an adjective are. They would be way better off if we taught one-fifth of the standards in fourth grade, and by ninth grade they know it."

After being initially recalcitrant about breaking with so many sacred cows of teaching, Driscoll became as confident as Mazzarella that the binder system would permit Oceanside's ninth graders to blossom and compete academically with some of the better schools in the county. "This stuff is going to be hard-wired into them by the end of the tenth grade year," Driscoll told me. "In two years, we will be able to create what should have been done in the previous eight years, from first grade through eighth grade."

————

At the new Oceanside, the binder system and untracked classes went hand in glove. In fact, I was told that Oceanside had tried to detrack classes in the past, eradicating "honors" distinctions by labeling essentially all classes as college preparatory, with limited success. Binders were essential to detracking. When teachers and students in all sections of the same course were, literally, on the same page, a meaningful sort of synergy resulted, enhancing the notion of the school as a community in which everybody was working toward the same ends.

For example, accelerated classes like Advanced Placement that mixed less proficient students with more proficient ones amplified the need for extra academic support and tutoring. Because all students in a given class were at the same place in the binder, the support and tutoring opportunities flourished at Oceanside, both formally with sessions after class at school and informally as kids got together with neighbors after school.

"Three years ago, if anybody had told me that you could get high school kids to voluntarily stay after school for tutoring, I'd have said, 'Yeah, probably a few,'" Oceanside's assistant principal, Robert Mueller, wrote to the staff in a December 2004 memo titled "Not in My Wildest Dreams" (which he also sent to district superintendent Ken Noonan).

> What I really would have been thinking was, "Yeah, probably a few nerdy misfits." So today, when I was headed out to a meeting at 2:30 p.m. (ten minutes after school ended), my eye was immediately drawn to a group of 75 students crowded in front of a classroom. My mind raced through the possibilities. . . . Is there a fight somewhere in the middle of the crowd? Could detention really have 75 kids in it? Why do they look so eager to get in? Is someone giving away pizza?

I approached a group of students and asked what they were waiting for, secretly hoping . . . p-i-z-z-a. "World history tutoring," they replied. Just then Ms. Morales opened her door. Bodies surged toward the opening. It looked like a rock concert. There weren't enough seats. Kids lined the walls. . . . The shock was almost too much. No pizza, and over 100 kids voluntarily staying after school for tutoring.[12]

Mueller, who, I was told, played an essential role as the nuts-and-bolts, make-things-happen administrator in the new leadership team brought in for the Oceanside revival, penned another memo to the staff in January 2005, which he also cc'd to Noonan. Calling this memo "You Can Lead a Horse to Water . . . ," Mueller noted that on the previous *Sunday,* 74 biology students, 62 AP English students, and 153 world history students attended tutoring sessions held by Oceanside teachers. Weekly totals for tutoring outside of class were approaching 900 students. "That's not a typo," Mueller wrote.[13]

When I spoke to Mueller, he told me that such support was essential for Oceanside's disadvantaged students to succeed in the more rigorous classes. "The synergy that the binder system creates is incredible, but if you start to take pieces away, the whole thing can crumble pretty quickly," he explained. "Without tutoring, low-income kids wouldn't get it. They wouldn't be able to succeed."[14]

Along with open enrollment, binders, and tutoring, the other essential piece of the Oceanside experiment was to create a new kind of grading system, a radical departure from the grading scales that most middle-class schools, teachers, and students were accustomed to. Mazzarella maintained that unless grading systems were transformed, all efforts to open enrollment in advanced classes would fail. The challenge was to fairly reward high-performing students while not discouraging the underachieving students before they had a chance to find their sea legs in the more rigorous classes, gain confidence, and continue to learn until they were in a position to take the AP exam. In many other attempts to detrack advanced classes, Mazzarella noted, schools either eased standards, which hurt the high-achieving kids, or flunked all the kids at the bottom, creating a need for the sorts of remedial programs that rarely remediated.

"So we've developed a very nontraditional grading system that basically keeps the standard high at the top but stretches the bottom considerably," Mazzarella told me. "Our D is a big band. Traditionally, 60 percent is passing. But a kid with 50 percent knows a lot of stuff—and he's getting an F along with the kid that knows just 10 percent? What about the kid with 59 percent? He's still getting an F?"

What happened with Oceanside's geometry classes the prior year drove home the importance of the new grading scales. Indeed, in some respects, the whole Oceanside experiment rested on the success of detracking the math curriculum, which math teachers at Oceanside and many other schools believed was the great exception to the notion of mixing students by skill levels. Mueller called the math teachers a "priesthood" in this respect. But Mazzarella would have none of it, and he pushed math department chair David Kalt to adopt the binders, the tutoring, the new grading scales—the whole program.

"Where we really ran into trouble was with our math department," Robert Mueller said. "Math believes that math is different. Math believes that every set of skills is a fundamental set of skills, and you can't master the next step without mastering the step that comes before it. For a while, we were buying it that maybe math *was* different. We hadn't really committed ourselves to the notion that it wasn't, that instruction was instruction. But Dayle never doubted it."

Kalt was sold when he saw the remarkable happen with the geometry experiment. With open enrollment, his teachers began to encourage kids who might have gotten Ds in algebra to continue immediately into geometry, understanding that many students would continue to improve their skills as the semester progressed. The notion of improvement was deeply embedded in the new grading scales, rewarding students who started slowly—and would likely have flunked under the old grading scales—but showed improvement by the end of the course. Hence, hundreds more algebra students than in the past were going directly to geometry, including dozens who would have been held back in the past for remediation. In fact, geometry enrollment doubled to more than a thousand students between 2003 and 2004. But even with vastly more numbers of "unqualified" students, the grade distribution of geometry students receiving As, Bs, and Ds remained roughly the same. The percentage of Cs went up significantly, while the proportion of F grades dropped by half (see appendix B, table B-2).[15]

I asked Kalt about the opposition to detracking that he and Mazzarella encountered in the math department. "Oh, there has been a good amount of resistance," he acknowledged. "Some teachers are just in the process of saying, 'No, I don't believe in these changes,' and so are looking into transferring. Others are at the end of their careers, and they are going to retire. But the majority of our department right now is pretty much actively involved in saying, 'You know what, this is working.' "[16]

Other signs of the birth of a college-going culture at Oceanside were abundant. For example, in 1997, the school's enrollment in Advanced Placement courses was 282 students. In 2003, with remnants of the old culture still prevalent, the AP enrollment was 543. The following year, after detracking, 856 Oceanside students were taking Advanced Placement courses.[17] And consider these statistics. In 2002, only 96 Oceanside students took the PSAT exam; by 2004, that number had grown to 1,600. Among Oceanside students taking the California High School Exit Exam, 32 percent and 47 percent, respectively, passed the math and language portions of the test in 2001–2002; two years later, the pass rates had risen to 76 percent and 73 percent (see appendix A, figure A-8).[18]

More students were taking the SAT as well, and higher percentages of students of all ethnic backgrounds were scoring at least 1000. In 2004–2005, 168 students took the SAT, *double* the number from the previous year (see figure 9). And 13 percent of those test-takers scored 1000 points or higher, versus 8.5 percent the prior year. In recent years, no African American student at Oceanside had scored 1000 or higher on the SAT—but in 2004–2005, 10 percent of African Americans who took the test did so (see figure 10).[19]

Consider, too, what happened with Oceanside's AP politics course. While improved SAT participation and performance were clearly beneficial for the school's college-going culture, Mazzarella shared data with me indicating that SAT scores for Oceanside students were hardly the be-all and end-all of how they actually performed on college-level work. When AP politics students even took the SAT (perhaps only a third had done so in the data I saw), the SAT verbal scores rarely exceeded 500, and many did not exceed even 400. And yet many of these low-SAT students were qualifying for college credit by earning at least a 3 on the AP politics exam (see table 2).

For example, a student we'll call "Christa" passed the AP exam with a 3, earned a B in the AP politics course, held a GPA of 3.09, but scored a feeble 370 on the SAT I verbal test. "Lawrence" didn't even take the SAT, had a GPA of only 2.21, but passed the AP politics exam. What's more, he got only a D+ in U.S. history, which would have kept him out of AP politics under the old, more selective rules of AP access at Oceanside. "Juanita," who scored just 460 on the SAT verbal section, passed the AP test, earned a B– in the course, and held down a 3.27 GPA. This

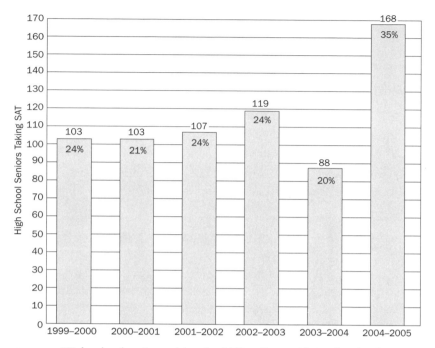

Figure 9. High school seniors taking the SAT at Oceanside High School, 1999–2000 to 2004–2005. Source: California Department of Education, "High School SAT/ACT/AP Test Results," http://data1.cde.ca.gov/dataquest, report generated by author, December 2005.

suggests that Mazzarella's methods were doing exactly what he had predicted: taking heretofore "unprepared" students, as measured by the SAT exam, and yet getting them to succeed in college-level courses.[20]

But the improvements in academics per se were just part of Mazzarella's vision for building a college-going culture from the ground up at Oceanside. How did a school go from fewer than 100 students taking the PSAT to 1,600 taking the test in a matter of months? The answer went back to Mazzarella's contention that for students at a school like Oceanside to have any real chance of attending a four-year college, the high school itself must supply the cultural and social capital that low-income students could not acquire from their families. At bottom, the school must give the students a *reason* for wanting to excel in academics by making the connections that led from school to the bigger world. That meant doing what the AVID program did in other schools—but instead of providing one class a day for a relatively small number of students, Oceanside was spreading AVID-esque practices to such an extent

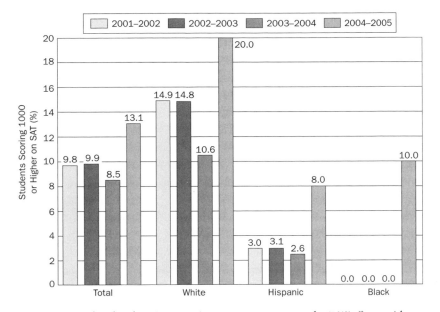

Figure 10. High school seniors scoring 1000 or more on the SAT, Oceanside High School, by race, 2001–2002 to 2004–2005. Source: California Department of Education, "High School SAT/ACT/AP Test Results," http://data1 .cde.ca.gov/dataquest, report generated by author, December 2005.

that the school itself was being transformed into something like one very large AVID program.

"Fundamentally, what we are doing is AVID-izing the entire school," Mazzarella explained. "School is pretty irrelevant for most kids. . . . Almost 50 percent of our kids are English-language learners; another 10 or 15 percent are special education students. Only 8 percent of our kids have parents with a four-year college degree, so you are talking about a super socialization problem."

He added, "If you want to make school relevant to kids and actually convince them it has something to do with the rest of their life, you are going to have to do things other than just show up and teach a lesson in math." Hence, a class in AP economics or geometry at Oceanside High was far more than sines, cosines, or the theory of competitive markets. Ninth graders began their Oceanside careers the first day of algebra class, for example, learning how to use a time planner. The school would overcome dozens of similar, nonacademic obstacles that kids from Oceanside encountered because few other entities existed to do so. Even federal

TABLE 2. PERFORMANCE OF OCEANSIDE HIGH SCHOOL
AP POLITICS STUDENTS, 2004

Student[a]	AP Politics Course Grade	AP Politics Exam Score	SAT Score (verbal section)	GPA	U.S. History Course Grade
Aaron	B-	2	370	3.87	B-
Brian	C-	3	510	2.80	C+
Christa	B	3	370	3.09	A
Diego	A	4	550	3.95	A
Fawn	B-	4	480	2.52	B
Greg	C+	3	490	3.65	C+
Hanna	B	4	490	2.58	B
Inez	C-	3	—	2.37	D
James	C-	3	—	2.44	C-
Juanita	B-	3	460	3.27	C
Julia	B-	2	390	3.83	A-
Kara	A-	4	—	2.78	B
Lawrence	C-	3	—	2.21	D+

SOURCE: Dayle Mazzarella, Oceanside High School, "Oceanside High AP Politics, 2003–04," unpublished data provided to author.
[a] These are pseudonyms for actual students.

TRIO programs, for instance, that were designed to accomplish similar ends, had nowhere near the reach into students' lives that the school itself did.

For example, most Oceanside parents had no more education than a high school diploma, and many spoke no English. Leaving families on their own to fill out a federal application for college financial aid, the so-called FAFSA form, often meant that the form was rarely completed. So the school's teachers took on that task as part of their course curriculum, making specific homework assignments for students to retrieve family financial data and allowing the students to complete the forms during class.

"The FAFSA application for financial aid is seven pages long," Mazzarella said. "It is unbelievably detailed, and those kids and their parents just look at it and wonder, 'What's the point?'" He continued, "I think the biggest problem that low socioeconomic schools have is they use the successful schools as a model of what to do. That is a model that does not apply to us. Our kids do not have direction. Taking thirty hours of classroom time at Torrey Pines High teaching kids how to fill out a University of California application would be a waste of time. We don't have anybody going to UC, and we wonder why. Here, it is not a waste of time."

He reminded me of a student I had spoken to earlier who had been accepted to the University of California. "She has already been admitted to UC, and her parents don't even speak English. Can you imagine her without any help from the school? Taking home an eighteen-page application in English and having her parents help her fill it out, or a financial aid application that requires all of the economic knowledge of the family, W2 forms, and everything else? It is not going to happen. It is never going to happen here. That girl would not be going to college. It just flat simple won't happen."

———

In the two years since the Oceanside experiment began, Sophia, a senior, had already taken *ten* AP classes. Her parents had come to the United States from Mexico when she was six, and she herself remained undocumented, along with her parents. The second oldest, Sophia had seven brothers and sisters. She hoped to attend Cal State San Marcos and study law enforcement, believing that the prevalence of job opportunities in the field would give her the best chance of remaining in the United States.

Simply trying to inform her parents about her basic academic progress in high school was challenging. Then trying to explain the difference between an AP class and a normal class, and why AP classes would help her for college, was overwhelming. She told me that most of her Latino classmates experienced the same cultural gaps between school and home.

"Our parents don't understand our grades. But we tell them that A is good and F is bad," Sophia said. "F is like you just failed a class, and they understand that. It is pretty hard trying to let them know the grade and how we are doing in school. They don't really know about AP classes. They just think they are hard. I tell them AP is a little bit more challenging, and AP will get you ready for college. They are proud of you once you tell them what is going on and get them informed."[21]

As Sophia told me her story, I was reminded of the sacrifices children like her must make to take academically intensive courses like Advanced Placement, let alone ten of them. Unlike upper-middle-class children for whom school is often their only responsibility, going to school for Sophia was just part of what her parents expected of her at home.

Sophia's school day began with her 6 A.M. ROTC class, and she played soccer after school. "Then I go home, have something to eat, help my mom around the kitchen, clean or help take care of kids or whatever, and then I am up very late at night," Sophia explained. "I clean the kids and house, and then I go and do my homework. I just don't get a lot of sleep, because right now I am taking four AP classes, so I have a lot of homework for all of them. I am up until two or three in the morning. It is a lot of work."

Without Oceanside's teachers constantly pushing her and planning activities and assignments both in and out of class that help her plan for college—like signing up for the SAT, taking SAT prep classes, or filling out college applications—the tasks probably wouldn't get done, Sophia acknowledged. For most Latino students at the school, she told me, students could not turn to their parents for help on the college-planning tasks.

"The school is like our inspiration. The teachers are the ones that push us to college. I remember my dad said to me, 'Oh, what do you need college for?' I tell him I need it for law enforcement and that college will bring more money. I am trying to show my parents that by going to college, I will have more opportunities, even though I am not a legal resident here. A lot of the Hispanics have to show their parents what the school is providing for us."

I asked Sophia to explain the difference between the old Oceanside and the new one.

"They are pushing more," she said. "A lot of the time, the students are not well informed on how to get into an AP class, how to do honors, graduate with honors, a lot of things, and this year we are becoming more organized about it. When you have nobody pushing you, then you don't do it. A lot of students that didn't have a teacher or parent pushing them to do the SATs or apply for college got left behind. They just didn't do it."

———

When Robert Mueller was growing up, his family had a backyard pool. It was small enough that when he and his brothers and sisters were in the pool, his dad would create a whirlpool with his arms and hands, making it easier for the kids to swim around. "We would try to do it, and we couldn't do it," Mueller told me. "He would get in the pool and do it because he was so much bigger."

In many respects, the Oceanside experiment has been like his dad creating the currents in the pool, said Mueller. In Oceanside's past, most kids stood around in the still waters or flopped around at the pool's edges, and there was no prevailing current to help kids start swimming with purpose, and in the same direction.

"The majority of kids were basically just putting in their time. Then you had a handful of kids swimming furiously around the edge of the pool, but they were doing it on their own and not benefiting from a current one way or another," he explained. "Everything that we have done has basically been a movement to get more kids swimming around the pool. It is like putting jets in the pool. We are creating the current that gets kids moving.

"If you get enough kids that are focused on UC entrance and meeting those high standards, kids that fall short of that still are meeting the Cal State requirements. And if you get enough of those kids moving around, and they start to create a wake, that pulls the next set of kids into the community colleges. That movement draws in more and more kids that may never have thought about college before to the point where, any given week, we can have between five hundred and nine hundred kids come in voluntarily for tutoring after school or on Sundays. We have Sundays that have had over two hundred kids show up for tutoring. That is how you change the culture of the school. You can only do it by getting kids moving in the same direction."

With so many jets in the Oceanside pool, including the binders, the detracked curriculum, the tutoring sessions, the new grading system, and the new leadership team, a promising future for Oceanside's college-going culture seemed assured.

But schools like Oceanside encounter formidable demographic and social forces, and it's unlikely that a school by itself can effectively counter those forces over the long run without enlightened public policy and adequate resources from the public. When politicians give rewards for blue ribbon schools, the schools that have overcome their socioeconomic destiny, the politicians would do well to understand that many such schools succeed *despite* public policies, not because of those policies.

The reason why laws like No Child Left Behind are destined to fail, and the reason kids in schools like Oceanside do get left behind, is that such reform amounts to a technical solution to cultural, economic, and social problems. Effective government policy would help schools like Oceanside provide the foundations of a college-going culture that disadvantaged families do not have the resources to establish on their own. As Mazzarella knew in his bones from more than thirty years of teaching and coaching, schools can't fix the academic side of education without also answering the most fundamental questions that parents and their children ask themselves: What's the point? What are schools for? How can schools help me?

For all Mazzarella's beliefs that schools can effectively supply the necessary cultural resources for disadvantaged kids, and for all the signs of a true cultural transformation at Oceanside, the school remains a work in progress and continues to struggle against the demographic tides, which intensifies the pressure for achievement. For instance, in 1999–2000, 45 percent of Oceanside's students were from low-income families, eligible for free lunches (see appendix A, figure A-9). By 2004–2005, almost 60 percent of its students were poor. In 1999–2000, 47 percent of its students were Hispanic; five years later, nearly six of ten students were Hispanic, including many English-language learners and immigrants.[22] Institutionalizing Oceanside's new cultural habits in the face of formidable demographic forces depends on many fragile sources of support. Just as impatient investors in public companies demand immediate performance in company earnings and stock prices, any slippage in Oceanside's Academic Performance Index or a failure to meet No Child Left Behind test score targets might well dampen support from district officials, resulting in yet another shakeup of school leadership. Vocal middle-class parents and teachers could press the school to abandon the open enrollment experiment.

And then there is the Mazzarella factor itself. It was hard for me to imagine the inspiration that he brought to Oceanside being duplicated after he was gone. As we were chatting informally one afternoon in his office, he told me that teaching occupied his mind night and day. It was just something that brought him pleasure. Among his hobbies was rock climbing, and he thought about teaching even on the rocks. I remarked to him that I couldn't imagine the amount of hours and labor it must have taken to create the massive binder system, for all the dozens of classes.

"It is mind-boggling," he admitted. "My wife and I, we are going to go to our tax guy tomorrow. This year is the least amount of money that I have spent on this project the last four years. I spent ninety thousand dollars one summer because the district didn't want to do this, because they didn't believe it would work. I laugh when I read about these baseball players that give fifty thousand to their school. My wife and I have donated two hundred thousand of our own money in the last six years to the development of these binders and teacher training and so on. It is not something that I tell everybody, but it happens to be the truth."

That may sound like a lot of money, and for an individual to give such a sum to a public school is significant. But compared to what schools spend on private test-prep consultants and other programs aimed solely at boosting test scores, a few hundred thousand dollars to change the fundamental culture of a school is a drop in the bucket—especially when that school is attempting to fill the cultural capital deficits of disadvantaged students. When I asked Mazzarella why he did it, he answered that it was his mission to prove the naysayers wrong, to show that an entire school could be resocialized despite the powerful forces of social class destiny constantly tugging the school in the opposite direction. Sure, he could show that ordinary kids from disadvantaged homes could thrive in honors and advanced classes, but he and other teachers had already demonstrated that. He wanted to prove that it could be done not merely for a class here and there but throughout the school, sustained and institutionalized by a new school culture.

Above all, he wanted to prove that the changes at Oceanside weren't dependent on him alone, but it was clear that they wouldn't have happened here without Mazzarella. While some middle-aged men would think nothing of spending $10,000 a week on a golfing trip to Scotland, Mazzarella said, he'd prefer to spend his money on education.

I asked Mazzarella why teaching and education were so important to him, since he had no children of his own.

"My family just taught me that this pursuit of material shit isn't going to get you anywhere," he replied. "Your real obligation in life is to think about people."

When he was forty, he said, his mother, father, grandfather, and first wife all died within a space of twelve months. He was at the bedside for all of them except his grandfather. In each case, as his loved ones were dying, they told him of their regrets in life, and they all talked about missed opportunities for human connections.

"I don't remember anybody talking about things that they hadn't bought, jobs they never got. Everything we talked about, almost 100 percent of the conversation was about missed opportunities with people," he recalled. "That is what those people talked about. Uniformly, across the board. 'I wish I would have made up with aunt so-and-so. I wish I could go back and see so-and-so I loved before he died.'

"That was a powerful experience for me. You sit there and watch people dying, and they are not talking about who got their inheritance or the car they didn't buy, or the house or the bankruptcy. They are not talking about any of that. It was human regrets. That was powerful, unbelievably powerful. I realized, 'Hey you know what, who cares? In the end, we are all going to be dirt anyway. While you are here, you might as well feel good about what you are doing.' Not that I don't have fun, not that I don't go climbing or fly fishing or whatever. I feel good about watching other people feel good. That is what makes me feel good."

————

As Dayle Mazzarella saw clearly, many students come from families who have little or no experience with higher education, and such students simply won't get on a path toward college unless schools themselves step in and show them the way. But colleges and universities also bear some responsibility for helping to even the odds. While we saw in previous chapters that the dominant trend in American higher education in recent years is toward a more elitist system, some institutions are bravely going against this tide. These colleges and universities acknowledge that fundamental inequities pervade the education system, providing students from various social classes with vastly different opportunities to go to college. These institutions are helping to level the playing field by creating admissions systems with far more comprehensive perspectives on academic merit that give disadvantaged students a chance to show their stuff. In the following chapter, we'll get to know some of those institutions and a few of the disadvantaged students they took a chance on.

ELEVEN

THE GATECRASHERS

All things considered, it's a small revolution.

In previous chapters, we've seen how our American ideal of equal opportunity in obtaining a quality education has increasingly become just hollow rhetoric. Colleges and universities, as well as government agencies, have made deliberate choices in recent years to enhance opportunities for children born into socially and economically privileged lives. Those same choices have limited the opportunities for children born without such privileges. Despite all the talk about equal access that progressive leaders of higher education often espouse, they operate the levers of America's inequality engine, a machine that systematically reproduces social class inequalities.

And so it *is* a revolution of sorts when major universities decide to push back against some of the powerful and entrenched forces that have helped to create these inequalities. A few of America's best public universities are trying to find fairer, more complete, and even more accurate ways of measuring merit. Some institutions are striving to go beyond cultural habits as well as the historical accidents that effectively placed SAT scores and God on the same stone tablet.

For instance, in the aftermath of the famous *Hopwood v. Texas* case, in which a federal appeals court banned the use of affirmative action at public universities in Texas and a few other states, the Texas legislature in 1997 passed the groundbreaking Top 10 Percent law. Known as HB 588, the law demanded that any Texas student graduating in the top 10 percent of his or her high school class be granted automatic admission to Texas's public universities—regardless of SAT scores.

Over the years since the law's passage, the University of Texas at Austin has conducted annual evaluations of the law's effects on academic standards and the demographic makeup of the university. And, year in and year out, those studies have shown that students admitted under the Top 10 Percent law do enter the university with average SAT scores significantly below the average scores of peers who were not in the top 10 percent of their high schools but were admitted on the basis of high SAT scores. And yet the top 10 percenters perform as well or better in university classrooms than peers entering UT Austin with SAT scores hundreds of points higher.

For example, consider the UT freshmen who entered the university in 2003 with SAT scores of 1000–1090 and who were among the top 10 percent in high school. These students earned an average freshman GPA of 2.90. Their academic performance was equivalent to freshmen who entered the university with SAT scores of about 100 points higher but who had not been in the top 10 percent in high school (see appendix B, table B-3).[1] In other words, the Top 10 Percent law has not harmed academic quality at the university but has actually enhanced it, by bringing in higher percentages of students who excel in what undergraduate education is all about: actual performance in university math, science, languages, and other subjects.

The Texas law also expanded access for students from many of the state's high schools that had not sent graduates to the flagship campus in the past. In just a three-year period, the number of high schools across the state that fed graduates to UT-Austin surged by almost 30 percent. Top 10 percent graduates from inner-city areas of Dallas–Fort Worth, Houston, and San Antonio, in addition to more lower-income white students from rural parts of the state, seized this new opportunity to do well in school and go to the state's best public university, regardless of test scores.

"The key to greater access lies in the fact that the 'top ten percent' law assures the very best of each high school admission to the state university of their choice," David Montejano, a sociologist and historian at UT-Austin, wrote in his evaluation of the demographic impact of the Top 10 Percent law. "Because high schools generally reflect local communities and environments, this is also the key to creating a diverse student body that roughly reflects the make up of the State." He went on, "As should be clear by now, this diversity is more than a matter of race: the new high school senders clearly point to a diversity of region, economic class and social background. In essence, HB 588 is helping the University of Texas at Austin achieve its motto, 'We're Texas.' "[2]

But war looms. Some critics of the Top 10 Percent law would prefer to revert to an older manifestation of that motto. As reported in the *Chronicle of Higher Education,* a growing number of critics have assailed HB 588 because it has allowed students with lower SAT scores, who often tend to be students from lower-income families, to "crowd out" those with higher test scores, particularly students from high-performing schools in the affluent suburbs of Dallas, San Antonio, and Houston, which traditionally send large numbers of students to UT-Austin.[3] Indeed, in 2004, 66 percent of entering freshmen had graduated in the top 10 percent of their high schools.

Actual academic performance apparently wasn't sufficient for the critics leading the backlash against HB 588. The class-rank plan, its critics contended, was leading to an erosion of academic standards because the ten percenters, though they did better in the classroom, *scored less well on the SAT*—an admissions test that's designed *only* to predict how well students will actually perform in the classroom. One of the leading proponents of this dubious reasoning was state senator Jeff Wentworth, who introduced a bill to eliminate HB 588. "There is great concern expressed to me by alumni about the dumbing down of the University of Texas," he told the *Chronicle.*[4]

I should probably add that Wentworth's "crowding out" theory—for him, proven by complaints he gathered from alumni—hasn't panned out empirically. Marta Tienda and Sunny Niu of the Office of Population Research at Princeton University investigated that very question as part of a wide-ranging study of the Texas law and concluded the following: "Our research findings help set the record straight. Despite the recent calls to rescind HB 588 on the basis of anecdotal accounts suggesting that the best and brightest are being squeezed out of Texas public institutions, empirical evidence from a representative survey of Texas high-school seniors indicates otherwise. In fact, our examination . . . reveals that, if anything, students who leave the state do so by choice, not because they were denied admission to a preferred Texas institution."[5]

To be sure, the Texas law has also had its detractors on the left, who argue that such "percentage plans" depend on geographic segregation by race and class in order to open college opportunities for minorities and disadvantaged students. To the extent that the Texas law has permitted geographically diverse schools a greater opportunity to send their better students to Texas's best public universities, then the law potentially boosts racial and economic diversity at the university. "The biggest impact of the new law has been on diversification by geography," said Tienda, quoted in a Ford Foundation report. "Everybody has been focusing on race, but this is really about boosting opportunity in Texas."[6]

But it's also becoming clear that such percentage plans are not a replacement for racially sensitive admissions when racial and ethnic diversity is considered an important policy goal, in addition to diversity by social class. Often, that is because white students still make up the lion's share of lower-income students. As Tienda and her co-authors concluded in a January 2003 study, *by itself, the top ten percent policy is NOT an alternative to race sensitive admissions;* rather, it is a merit-based admission plan that emphasizes high school academic achievement in the admission decision while de-emphasizing standardized achievement tests for top ranked students. In the absence of financial support to needy students coupled with a vigorous outreach program to high schools populated by minority and economically disadvantaged students, the top ten percent policy will not diversify campuses of selective universities."[7]

———

The key phrase in that quote from Tienda is that the Texas law is "a merit-based admission plan." But, as Texas senator Jeff Wentworth exemplifies, the critics on the right don't see it that way. The widespread impression these critics convey is that HB 588 is a sham, allowing "unqualified" students to gain admission to Texas's most prestigious public university. The backlash against such admissions reform brings together an unlikely but potent coalition. For the conservative foes of affirmative action, admissions reforms like the one in Texas are thinly disguised attempts by universities to play the race card. And for the upper-middle-class parents and alumni who complain about their high-scoring kids not getting into the college of their choice, the reforms represent a challenge to an entitlement. For both constituencies, the evolving views about merit represent an unprecedented attack on academic standards. They believe selection methods that put their faith in test scores have been objective and fair, while not always perfect. To degrade the role of test scores in the admissions process, they contend, is an invitation to mushy standards and subjectivity, which is patently unfair to the students with superior test scores, whom they consider to be clearly more qualified.

This case against admissions reforms at our best universities, myopic as it is, reflects the prevailing zeitgeist about merit. And that's the problem. The backlash is tapping into an entrenched ideology about merit that goes back to the invention of the IQ test and the SAT itself. As a direct descendant of intelligence tests developed at the turn of the last century, the first Scholastic Aptitude Test purportedly allowed society's intellectual cream to rise and be identified for selection to the best colleges. It so happened then—and continues to happen today—that most members of the academic elite selected on this self-serving basis emerge from affluent and highly educated families. In the days of Lewis Terman and Carl Brigham, early American mental testers who paved the way for widespread use of IQ and aptitude tests (described in chapter 2), that era's recent immigrants, including Italians, Jews, and Poles, were labeled feeble-minded idiots because they performed poorly on "scientific" IQ tests.

Now, in these slightly more polite times, their counterparts in poor urban neighborhoods and the rough edges of suburbia are being told that they "don't have any business going to Berkeley."

———

The opening volley in the West Coast version of this emerging backlash erupted over a new undergraduate admissions process at the University of California.

John Moores, then chair of the UC Board of Regents and the wealthy owner of the San Diego Padres, authored a lengthy "confidential" report (with the help of a UCLA graduate student) that was leaked to the *Los Angeles Times*. In the report, Moores singled out UC Berkeley, though it's not entirely clear why, given that other UC campuses had also adopted the new admissions process and were almost as selective as Berkeley. Moores and his graduate student wrote that nearly four hundred students admitted to UC Berkeley in 2002—of the more than ten thousand students admitted to the campus that year—had scored less than 1000 on the SAT I, the College Board's widely used test of math and verbal skills that is supposed to predict college success. As the *Los Angeles Times* put it, an SAT score of 1000, about average nationwide, was "far below" the 1337 average SAT I score for those admitted to UC Berkeley that year.[8]

"It is outrageous," Moores said. "They don't have any business going to Berkeley."[9]

What was worse, according to Moores, Berkeley had rejected hundreds of applicants with very high SAT scores of 1400 and above. Claiming that he had completed the report after hearing many complaints from "parents" about Berkeley's new admissions policy, Moores was described in the *Los Angeles Times* as being "shocked" by these findings. "I just don't see any objective standards," he told the newspaper, which conveyed the smell of scandal under the headline: "Study Finds Hundreds of Highly Qualified Applicants Were Rejected in Favor of Freshmen Who Were 'Marginally Academically Qualified.'"[10]

Moores's villain was "comprehensive review," the new admissions policy that the UC system had adopted in 2001 during a relatively brief but tumultuous period in the university's history. Indeed, from 1995 through 2003, the university saw its Board of Regents abandon the consideration of race and gender in admissions; saw state voters do the same a year later by passing Proposition 209; and saw its president, Richard C. Atkinson, toss the biggest bomb of all by calling for the university to quit using the storied SAT I exam in its admissions process.

Unlike the old admissions system, which relied predominately on a mechanical sorting of applicants based on high school grades and SAT scores, comprehensive review called on admissions officials to consider a full range of factors that painted a portrait of a young person's academic promise. In fact, GPAs and test scores still topped the list of fourteen criteria in the revised process, but the difficulty level of high school courses, the student's talents and achievements on real-world projects, and the student's ability to overcome obstacles of poverty and social class were now integral to the new selection method.

Race, ethnicity, and gender were explicitly not to be considered, as a matter of state law. What's more, except for a small number of exceptions, no one could be admitted to the highly selective Berkeley campus or to any of the other eight UC undergraduate campuses who wasn't "UC-eligible"—that is, academically among the top 12.5 percent of California high school students, as established by the state's 1960 Master Plan for Higher Education.

No matter, though. The widespread impression conveyed by Moores's report and its subsequent coverage in the media was that comprehensive review was a fraud, allowing "unqualified" students, particularly underrepresented minorities, to gain admission to California's most prestigious public university. For Moores, the notion of comprehensive review reeked of conspiracy. He claimed that the university was doing an end run around voters' wishes on Proposition 209 by replacing affirmative action with a murky system that allowed the university to admit low-scoring minority students at the expense of white and Asian students with higher test scores.

"Defying voters, UC Berkeley is admitting kids with low SAT scores and rejecting high achievers," Moores later wrote in *Forbes* magazine. "The California electorate voted to stop racial preference in college admission in 1996. Since then UC administrators have been manipulating the admissions system and, I believe, thwarting the law."[11]

In *Forbes,* Moores noted, pointedly, that 231 of 359 students with SAT I scores below 1000 admitted to Berkeley were "underrepresented minorities—meaning blacks, Hispanics, and Native Americans. Only 19 of the low scorers were white." In a subsequent e-mail message addressed to fellow university regents that was leaked to the public arena, Moores claimed that university officials were withholding several "secret studies," the disclosure of which would challenge the legality of the UC admission process.[12]

"These admission results are difficult to understand unless perhaps it is the product of an academic bureaucracy that, for some reason or another, lost its way," Moores wrote in a letter that accompanied his report. In order to reform the allegedly illegal system, the report argued, UC Berkeley should have "compelling reasons" for admitting any student scoring less than 1200 on the SAT I (prior to the "new" SAT, when the maximum possible score was 1600) or with a high school grade point average of less than 3.8. Moores also called on the university to make the admissions process more "transparent" and "objective."[13]

––––––

Daisy Gonzalez surely would not pass academic muster in Moores's scheme for the University of California. She grew up in South Central Los Angeles, attending Catholic schools until ninth grade, when she entered the public school system at South Gate High School. Gonzalez's father made it to eighth grade, and her mother to the sixth grade. Her parents have variously worked in restaurants, printing shops, and furniture stores. She has one older sister, who has a high school diploma and now holds down a clerical job.

Once a largely white, industrial city that supplied workers to defense manufacturers during World War II, South Gate was largely Hispanic by the twenty-first century. Daisy's upbringing was fairly typical of South Gate's residents, who included many immigrants from Mexico and Latin America. Fully 36 percent of the city's adults had no more than a ninth grade education, in contrast to only 16 percent of Los Angeles County residents with that level of education. Nearly 81 percent of South Gate's adults had no more than a high school diploma. At just $10,000 annually, South Gate's per capita income was half that for Los Angeles County. A typical male worker in South Gate earned $25,000 a year, $10,000 less than the average wage for males in Los Angeles County; an average female worker in South Gate earned just $20,000.[14]

At South Gate High, Daisy found a "big, overpopulated high school," a dramatically different experience from the smaller, more intimate experience she had in Catholic school. The school mirrored the demographics of its surroundings. In 2005, 99 percent of its students were Hispanic. Of its nearly four thousand students, Daisy remembers just one white person at the school.

This was not a comfortable, middle-class school of high achievers bound for the University of California or Cal State. Some 70 percent of South Gate High's parents had just a high school education or less. More than eight out of every ten students were considered poor, eligible for federal lunch subsidies. Out of 803 graduates, only 62 South Gate students had completed the course requirements for Cal State or the UC system, a rate of 7 percent. In Los Angeles County, by comparison, almost 30,000 of some 85,000 graduates completed the UC course requirements, a rate five times that of South Gate High.[15]

I asked Daisy how she became interested in going to college and how she planned for it. While her parents encouraged her to go as far as possible with her education, they could offer little concrete knowledge or resources to help her. "Our parents were always telling us we had to go to college, or else we'd end up having to work really long days like them and do really hard labor," Daisy told me. "I always knew that I would go to college, but I never really thought about a plan or anything. It was always 'do good in school and then go to college.'"[16]

The school offered some help. Mainly, counselors told students about local community colleges, but that route held no interest for Daisy. "I didn't want to go to community college because I knew that, looking at a lot of my friends over there, a lot of students tend to slack off in community college. I was afraid that would be me, too," she said. Nor did Cal State interest her, but her reasons were admittedly nebulous. Nobody had really explained the differences, so she went by rumor. "Honestly, this sounds really dumb, but it seems like UC is better than Cal State."

According to John Moores, Daisy Gonzalez had no business going to UC Berkeley, whatever the hardships she had encountered growing up with immigrant parents in South Central L.A. The numbers were the numbers, and objective facts were facts. Despite Daisy's own sense that she would founder at a community college, girls like her should know their proper place. Students like her were the victims of the University of California's overzealous attempts to balance the scales of opportunity, leading astray overly ambitious and unqualified students like Daisy Gonzalez. According to Moores: "The victims are the kids who should have gone to one of California's outstanding community colleges, where they might have had the possibility of success and a chance to grow intellectually."[17]

In the backlash against the university's new admissions system, "hardship" became a dirty word, and the critics of comprehensive review oozed with sarcasm every time they uttered it. In Moores's report, he included an op-ed piece from the *Washington Post* by John McWhorter, a UC Berkeley professor (at the time) and an African American, who agreed with Moores that comprehensive review was "really just old wine in a new bottle." "The UC 'suits,' " he alleged, "have crafted a canny end run around 1996's Proposition 209." As McWhorter saw it, "At UC Berkeley, where I teach, we are awaiting the arrival of the first freshman class selected under a revised admissions policy for the University of California schools. All applicants are being evaluated according to whether they have survived 'hardships,' with those who have done so netting extra points. Under this policy, the student submitting a top-level dossier who has led a lucky life will often be less likely to get in than one whose dossier is just as good but also attests to suffering from family strife, the care of younger siblings, certified emotional problems or the like."[18]

In fact, Daisy Gonzalez did have an exceedingly difficult time competing with Berkeley's other applicants. Although she was legitimately among the qualified pool of high school graduates eligible for admission to any UC campus, she didn't have the numbers to get into Berkeley. This was despite all her "hardships," which, according to Moores and McWhorter, were supposed to allow her to sneak onto the Berkeley campus in violation of state law against affirmative action. Daisy's high school grade point average was only 3.3, a full point below the average for Berkeley's admitted freshmen in 2002, and her SAT I score, though well above the 1000-point threshold that was so important for Moores, still was "far below" the Berkeley average of 1343 (as the *Los Angeles Times* would put it).

Daisy wanted to attend UC Berkeley. Justifiably or not, she saw community colleges as a snare that would trap her in South Central L.A. She had a strong interest in politics and "social justice," as she told me, and she simply believed that she'd feel more at home at Berkeley than at the other UC campuses. "I really wanted to go to Berkeley because I had been there. I had visited the campus and knew how political the community is. I didn't get accepted."

By Moores's reasoning, Daisy also had little business going to the University of California at San Diego, whose freshman SAT averages and high school GPAs were only slightly below Berkeley's. In fact, at the San Diego campus, freshmen in 2002 averaged high school grades of 4.13 and SAT I scores of 1293. Nevertheless, Daisy did apply to UCSD, and the San Diego "suits" did admit her.

One wonders what the bureaucrats there possibly saw in a "victimized" student like Daisy. I wondered myself, and asked her what she did to prepare for the SAT exam, the test that affluent families routinely spend thousands of dollars prepping for, acquiring expertise from the most canny and experienced test-prep tutors and private consultants. And they do so in an effort to raise their scores the extra few hundred points that can elevate them from being community college bound to University of California material—*at a minimum*. While the University of California was a dream school for Daisy, for many well-off families in California, the UC system was a fallback position, as many set their sights on even more prestigious private colleges and universities beyond California's borders.

"So when you took the SAT, did you do any particular preparation for it?" I asked Daisy.

"No, I didn't," she answered. "They offered a small seminar at my school, like a three-week seminar for the SATs, but it was already full. I never did it."

"How did it go for you on the SAT?"

"I know that it was pretty hard. I didn't do too bad. I ended up with, like, an 1110."

"What's your favorite subject in school?"

"It would have to be math."

"How much math did you take in high school?"

"I went all the way to calculus."

When I spoke to Daisy, she was beginning her second semester at UCSD. From the clothes that her classmates wore to the cars they drove, she had become all too aware of her relatively impoverished background, compared to the relatively privileged backgrounds of many students she met on campus.

"I know one of my roommates went to a better high school here in San Diego. I see how well she does in school, and it just makes me think she had better teachers, smaller classes, and a smaller population in high school," Daisy recalled.

"I know that, in my school, books were a big deal. A lot of our books were old and outdated. Sometimes we didn't even have enough books. In English class, if a teacher wanted us all to read one book, we didn't have enough, so she would tell students to choose which one they wanted. In my high school, if you were doing poorly, you didn't have too many people to help you. A lot of people who were supposed to be seniors didn't have enough credits and just ended up dropping out. That was a very common thing at my school.

"And it makes me think my roommate just had a way better education."

There, then, was my answer. With no preparation whatsoever for the SAT and attending schools without enough books, where the main options for students were dropping out or, at best, attending a community college, Daisy Gonzalez still managed to do very well on the SAT and, more important, to succeed in advanced math courses. Her pluck got her into UCSD. With the demise of affirmative action at California's public universities, how did elite institutions such as UCSD and other UC schools come to this historical juncture that allowed students like Daisy to have that chance?

———

It's perhaps fitting that the first major skirmish of the post–affirmative action war in American higher education began at the University of California. Among the nation's most prestigious public universities in the largest and most diverse state, this institution has represented many sides of America's struggle with equal opportunity. From the beginning of the great idea that was the University of California in 1868, the school has struggled to balance its populist and democratic ideals against an elitism built into its very foundation. The university was supposed to be democratic and yet selective at the same time, charged with admitting top-tier students who were most likely to succeed.

In the early days, the university's faculty picked students based on oral interviews. Too, the university early on established a college preparatory curriculum that high school students would have to take to be eligible for admission. But even as far back as 1884, the university's leaders recognized that the institution wasn't immune to the inequality in the outside world: it was clear that some students had access to fine college preparatory schools, while others in the more remote parts of the state did not.[19]

For every forward stride in its historical mission to democratize a first-class higher education for Californians, the university also made regressive moves backward. In 1960, as the baby boomers began to reach college age, University of California president Clark Kerr pushed for the creation of the state's first Master Plan for Higher Education. While the Master Plan established the California State University and state community college systems, Kerr's grand design also cordoned off the University of California as the state's elite institution that would control all public rights to the granting of doctoral degrees in California.

Kerr, the son of an apple farmer, was a populist in many respects, who fought a losing battle to keep the university tuition-free for state residents. But one undeniable legacy of the Master Plan was that public higher education in California would become, in effect, quasi-officially stratified by social class and race. As the institution chosen to occupy the top of the educational pyramid, the University of California system would be protected from the biggest brunt of the baby boom wave, its pool of eligible students restricted to the top eighth of high school students statewide.

But even the UC system faced pressures to accommodate the baby boomers. By the mid-1950s, the university's faculty, who had been given broad powers to establish admissions standards, first entertained the notion of requiring standardized admissions tests for sorting through the ballooning eligibility pool. In particular, they focused on the SAT, then called the Scholastic Aptitude Test, the direct progeny of the IQ tests developed at the turn of the previous century. The SAT's backers at the College Board and the Educational Testing Service were pitching the exam as a superior alternative to subject-oriented achievement tests because the "SAT I," as it came to be called, a test of general academic "aptitude," was supposedly immune to specific preparation or study.

Prior to World War II, Harvard president James Bryant Conant was the most influential proponent of this view, believing that an intelligence test like the SAT would permit Harvard and other prestigious universities to identify the academically gifted, regardless of their family origins and regardless of whether they had attended Andover or public school in the Bronx.

After pilot-testing the SAT in 1960, however, the University of California faculty rejected it outright. Indeed, they discovered the flaw in the SAT that would continue to plague the exam for the next forty years, despite its continued commercial success in higher education. For all the SAT's benefits to colleges as a tool for sorting and ranking applicants, the University of California's experiment with the exam in 1960 showed that it simply wasn't a particularly effective predictor of how well students actually performed at the university.[20]

But, in the end, enrollment pressures won out. When studies indicated that California's eligibility pool had expanded to more than the legally permitted 12.5 percent of high school graduates, the faculty finally approved the SAT for selecting freshmen in 1968. According to one UC document on the history of the SAT at the university, "adopting an admissions test requirement was seen as a 'relatively easy' means of reducing the size of the pool."[21]

But questions about the SAT continued to nag at the university's faculty, acting through the Academic Senate and its influential systemwide committee known as the Board of Admissions and Relations with Schools. Over the years, the BOARS group had undertaken a series of remarkable studies about the SAT and the university's admissions practices in general. (UC's introspection about the fairness and validity of its admissions processes was carried out in public, with a degree of transparency that is rare in the often secretive world of elite college admissions.)

As doubts grew about the efficacy of the SAT I, the College Board's supposed "reasoning" test, BOARS began to focus increasing attention on a more obscure College Board product, the SAT II subject tests. As achievement tests, the SAT IIs sprang from a diametrically opposing cognitive theory, supported by convincing evidence, that college performance was not impervious to prior training and would be better predicted by assessing students on the content they had actually studied in high school. And so, in the late 1990s, the university faculty updated the UC eligibility formula to dramatically elevate the SAT IIs in the University of California's admissions process, making it carry twice the weight of the SAT I.[22] That proved to be the beginning of the end of the SAT I, not just at the University of California, but as all Americans had come to know it.

––––––

In the 1940s, Richard C. Atkinson—who would one day become president of the University of California system—was a high school sophomore in Oak Park, near Chicago. One Saturday morning, he and a buddy were supposed to get together to play basketball. Then came the knock on the front door. It was his friend, with his mother in tow. Apparently irritated that her son had made plans to play basketball, the boy's mother told Richard that her son couldn't play that morning because they were on their way to the University of Chicago campus, about an hour away, so the boy could sit for the university's college entrance examination.

"I was really depressed," Atkinson recalled. "I was walking down the driveway, and he called and said, 'Dick, Dick, don't go. Drive out with us, and I'll take the exam, and we can drive back, and we'll still have a good part of the day.' I'm sure his mother was upset about this."[23]

Atkinson was game. They drove out to the University of Chicago, got to Cobb Hall, and the man at the front desk asked the mother for her son's name. Then the man turned to young Dick. "And what's your name?" "Oh, I'm not here to take the exam," Atkinson told him. The man looked him over. "Well, you're here, you might as well take it." Atkinson took the test, which at that time consisted of a lengthy essay examination. A few weeks later, Atkinson was informed that, based on his examination results, he had been accepted to the University of Chicago. (His friend, however, wasn't as fortunate.)

If there is a single feature that characterizes Richard Atkinson's tenure as the president of the University of California, between the years 1995 and 2003, it would have to be serendipitous moments like the unusual way he entered the University of Chicago. In some respects, overseeing the downfall of the SAT I and the rise of a new admissions system at the University of California seemed to be Atkinson's destiny, changes that in all likelihood would not have come about with any other individual as president. But in other respects, the happenstance nature of the events leading up to those momentous changes was so extraordinary that, when Atkinson's legacy is finally written, he might well go down as the University of California's accidental revolutionary.

His credentials to lead the university in the effort to abolish the old SAT were sufficiently straightforward. He'd been trained in psychology and mathematics and began his teaching career at Stanford. He never considered himself a testing expert per se, but rather a cognitive scientist, who worked on theories of learning and memory. Still, during his career at Stanford, from 1956 to 1973, he associated with the likes of Fred Terman, the son of Stanford's Lewis Terman, who had been instrumental in the development of early IQ testing in the United States, which led to the creation of the SAT itself. Atkinson considered himself a close personal friend of many of the luminaries of the IQ testing movement, including Richard J. Herrnstein at Harvard, who would go on to co-author *The Bell Curve*.[24] After Stanford, Atkinson became the director of the National Science Foundation and chaired the NSF's Board of Testing and

Assessment, an influential policy group that evaluated the government's use of mental tests for employment, immigration, and the like.

But even in the 1940s at the University of Chicago, Atkinson was exposed to thinking that would lead to his growing doubts about the use of intelligence tests like the SAT for college admissions. When reporters and others asked Atkinson about his own SAT score, he was quick to tell them that he had never taken the SAT because the University of Chicago had its own written entrance examination, which was a far cry from a standardized, multiple-choice test. In fact, the testing experts at Chicago in those days—some of the early founders of a growing field known as psychometrics—had nothing but disdain for the SAT, an attitude that may have been exacerbated by the rivalry between Chicago and Harvard, where Conant was championing the SAT. "They had a big testing program, and some of the founders of psychometrics who were there were absolutely adamant that the SAT as it was being conceived was based on an outdated concept of intelligence," Atkinson told me. "They were strongly opposed to adopting the SAT."

If the University of Chicago planted Atkinson's doubts about the SAT and intelligence testing, then a book he read in the 1980s helped to reinforce them. That book was *The Mismeasure of Man,* by the late evolutionary biologist Stephen Jay Gould.[25] "That was a very important book for me," Atkinson said. "I mean, I'll never forget reading that. He was a biologist, and he really knew what he was talking about." After reading the book, and while working on testing issues at the National Science Foundation, Atkinson said, "I became very critical of any notions of measuring innate intelligence."

Sometime in 1999, Atkinson recalled, about four years into his presidency at the University of California, he attended a meeting in Washington, D.C., with representatives of the Educational Testing Service and the College Board. At the meeting, Atkinson wasn't liking what he was hearing from ETS and College Board officials. It was clear to him that these officials continued to believe in the SAT as a measure of general cognitive ability and, moreover, believed that it was impervious to training or preparation.

"I was very unhappy with their view about matters, that they really thought they were measuring aptitude in some pure sense," Atkinson told me. Even when I talked to him after his retirement from the university in early 2005, he remained diplomatic. When I asked him to elaborate, he would say only, "I was unhappy with it. I was unhappy with the whole analysis."

Instead of flying directly back to California from that meeting, Atkinson stopped in Florida to visit his daughter's family. At the time, his granddaughter was in sixth grade and attended a very good private school in Fort Lauderdale, where his daughter worked as a neurosurgeon and his son-in-law as a pediatric surgeon. One day, he saw his granddaughter poring over SAT-type vocabulary items, particularly the infamous verbal analogy questions that had consumed generations of young SAT takers with fear and loathing. "Every night she was studying vocabulary items, thousands of them," Atkinson said. "That's what kids at her school did. And I said to her, 'What are you doing?' And she said, 'I'm preparing for the SAT.' I was horrified at that."

That trip to the East Coast would prove to be a decisive event for the University of California, and the nation. On his flight back to California, Atkinson relaxed with a drink, pulled out a blank note pad and a pen, and started writing down his thoughts about admissions testing for university study. He returned to his office and shared the handwritten piece with just a few trusted colleagues, including Pat Hayashi, a former longtime admissions officer at UC Berkeley, whom Atkinson had brought in to work with him in the Office of the President. But he and Hayashi decided against going public.

In retrospect, the ideas on those handwritten pages weren't particularly dangerous. A good admissions test, Atkinson had written, would emphatically not be an aptitude test but an achievement test, based on the subject matter students learned in high school. It would include a writing assessment. And such a test would be rid of the horrible verbal analogies. But the timing wasn't right. "So I just tucked it away," Atkinson recalled.

That handwritten document had been sitting in Atkinson's desk drawer for some two years when a reporter learned of the draft from a conversation with someone in the president's office and requested the document under the Freedom of Information Act. Atkinson believed that the piece consisted of his own private musings, but the university's general counsel thought otherwise and told Atkinson he should release it. "I didn't like the idea of having to give up to the press a handwritten document, because, you know, I had had a couple of drinks and said some harsh things," Atkinson told me.

Then, in early 2001, Atkinson was asked to give the keynote address to the American Council on Education that February in Washington,

D.C. Hayashi suggested to Atkinson that, since the gist of his new think-ing on the SAT was leaking out anyway, he should use the handwritten draft as the core of his ACE speech. Atkinson trusted Hayashi's judg-ment, particularly because Hayashi himself was on the board of trustees of the College Board. "We had a very tight lid on this in the president's office," Atkinson explained. "People knew I'd be giving a speech, but only about four people actually read the speech ahead of time."

But even the events surrounding his fateful speech to the American Council on Education were full of serendipity. The text of his talk was a closely held secret because it contained a bombshell. Reflecting the next logical step of the evolution of Atkinson's thinking, his speech would propose that the University of California abandon the SAT I aptitude test and replace it with the SAT II subject tests until the university or some-body else could develop a suitable achievement test. He was to present the speech on a Sunday.

The event itself might well have received scant attention in the press but for another accident of circumstance. One of Atkinson's former em-ployees in the Office of the President, who was about to take a new job, knew of the speech and leaked it that Friday to several major national newspapers.

When Atkinson walked out of his D.C. hotel room, intending to spend Saturday visiting some art galleries, he was blasted by the page-one headline in the *Washington Post*: "Key SAT Test under Fire in Calif.; University President Proposes New Admissions Criteria." Every major paper in the country carried a similar headline, and a media frenzy en-sued, raising the interest level and expectations for his Sunday speech to unprecedented heights for an American Council on Education event.

"Saturday morning, it hit every paper in the country," Atkinson re-called. "I was really horrified. I thought, God, I'm going to give a speech, and the people in the audience are going to be disgusted with me because they've already read about it in the paper. When I got there, the place was packed, with news cameras everywhere. It was just a wild afternoon."

Several paragraphs into his speech, Atkinson mentioned, almost in passing, that the university had recently compiled some compelling data showing that the SAT I was, in fact, the weakest predictor of freshman performance among all academic measures in a student's application portfolio, behind high school grades and behind even the SAT II subject tests. Looking back, Atkinson told me that that one small paragraph may have been the most important part of the speech.

Indeed, the case for the university abolishing the SAT I had actually been building for some time, based on preliminary data showing that the SAT II subject tests were better predictors of UC freshman performance. But that information had gotten little traction within the UC system, particularly with the ten chancellors at the UC campuses, who served under Atkinson. Most of the chancellors believed that Atkinson was going off on a tangent to consider abolishing the SAT I. "Probably three thought it was the right thing to do," Atkinson told me. "The word was, leave it alone, everything's fine."

———

The months immediately following his speech were some of the most difficult of his presidency, Atkinson remembered, as he learned just how much power the College Board wielded. Put on the defensive in trying to protect its flagship product from the "California Problem," the College Board pulled out all the stops, said Atkinson, recruiting college admissions officials from around the country and even University of California faculty to discredit his proposal.

"If I had realized the obstacles that had to be overcome, I'm not sure I would have given the speech," Atkinson said. "The College Board is a big organization. . . . These admissions officers get together at conferences, and they're sort of in the [College Board's] pocket, and they did recruit a number of people to write incredibly hostile op-ed pieces."

But the nail in the SAT I's coffin came eight months after Atkinson's speech to the American Council on Education, when two researchers in the UC Office of the President, Saul Geiser and Roger Studley, published the full set of data that Atkinson had alluded to in the speech. The study was huge, based on some 78,000 student records for four years of admissions between 1996 and 1999, including students' SAT I and SAT II scores, their academic performance as UC freshmen, their high school grades, and their socioeconomic backgrounds.

Geiser and Studley found that high school GPA and the SAT achievement tests proved the most valuable predictors of academic performance at the university, explaining between 15 percent and 16 percent of the variance in freshman grades. High school GPA combined only with the SAT II exam accounted for 22.2 percent of the variation in UC performance. Adding the SAT I to that mix added a mere 0.1 percent to the amount of variance explained—in other words, the SAT I added little to no additional predictive value to what could be gleaned with only high school grades and SAT II scores (see appendix B, table B-4).[26]

When Geiser and Studley standardized their regression results using "beta weights," a statistical technique that permitted an apples-to-apples comparison of the relative predictive punch of grades and test scores, the results were even more astonishing. For the whole University of California system and all its campuses, the beta weights of high school grades and SAT II scores were about four times as powerful as SAT I scores in predicting freshman grades. At Berkeley, where, according to John Moores's reasoning, SAT I scores should be determinative, the predictive value of the SAT I relative to the other factors was essentially *zero* (see appendix B, table B-5).

But the kicker in the Geiser and Studley findings was an equity issue. The study showed unequivocally that the greater the weight a UC campus gave the SAT I in the admissions process, the more the university was rewarding students from advantaged family backgrounds. When the researchers controlled for students' family background, the predictive power of high school grades and SAT II subject tests actually improved, while the predictive power of the SAT I declined. "These findings suggest that the SAT II is not only a better predictor, but also a fairer test in college admissions insofar as it is demonstrably less sensitive than the SAT I to differences in family income and parents' education," Geiser and Studley explained.[27]

So startling and one-sided were the study's findings against the SAT I, perhaps the most widely used and commercially successful standardized test in history, that Atkinson feared that the researchers were simply trying to produce results that conformed to his view. "When he first gave me the results, I thought to myself, goddammit, these guys are trying to please me. I'm the president, they're just trying to tell me what I want to hear," Atkinson told me. "It's so amazing to me that it could have been that decisive. The results were so unquestionable."

Just eight months later, in June 2002, the College Board announced that it would, in effect, accede to the demands of its largest customer, the University of California, and create a new SAT I. The new test, to be rolled out in March 2005, would be stripped of some of the more cognitively dubious elements and supplied with new features to make it look more like an achievement test. Atkinson, when I spoke to him in early 2005, was pleased. The hated verbal analogies that he had seen his granddaughter mindlessly studying would be gone, replaced with a critical reading section. There'd be a writing test. The math section would be updated to include more of the real math that high school students were supposed to master, and tricky questions about simple mathematics would, he hoped, be eliminated.

"I think it will be better," Atkinson said. "The most important reason for the change is to send the message to the kids that certain things are important, that they've got to learn to write, and they should take eighth, ninth, and tenth grade mathematics seriously. I mean, there's no way you're going to prep for these tests except by writing essays and studying mathematics."

Disadvantaged students, especially, Atkinson suggested, would now have something concrete to prepare for. "It's very clear what you have to do now," he said. "You have to learn to write, and you have to learn to master some of the mathematics. Once [disadvantaged] kids know what's expected of them, they'll have a better chance of excelling. There will be less of this view that, 'Oh, well, this test is really an innate measure, so you can't prepare, and it doesn't matter.' For minorities, doing well on the test has to be viewed as a reachable achievement."

———

Prior to his recent retirement as chair of the University of California at Berkeley's math department, Calvin Moore helped to push the entire UC system to adopt the comprehensive review admissions system. Before meeting him, I thought he might be an old Berkeley radical out to raise a ruckus. But it was also plausible that, as a mathematician, he'd have more in common with John Moores than even he might admit, a true believer in all things quantitative who might dismiss all that mushy comprehensive stuff when deciding who belonged at Berkeley and who didn't.

When I found Calvin Moore in his quiet office in the math department at Evans Hall, I discovered a diminutive and soft-spoken man, a professor of the old-school kind, and hardly a firebrand. Nonetheless, he had a commanding perspective on the recent history of Berkeley's struggles to reform its admissions policies. Moore did believe in numbers, to be sure, but only to a point, and especially not to the exclusion of larger truths about a young person seeking admission to the university.

While Richard Atkinson was making headlines with his proposal to drop the SAT, Moore and his colleagues on the Berkeley faculty were quietly working behind the scenes, having become increasingly frustrated with the admissions system in general. When university regents abolished affirmative action with their own resolution, SP-1, in 1995, Berkeley and the other UC campuses were also required to adopt a so-called two-tiered admissions system, in which 50 percent to 75 percent of an applicant's score had to be based on test scores and high school grades alone, with the remaining 25 percent to 50 percent based on nonacademic, "supplemental" criteria.

Calvin Moore was no novice at the concept of comprehensive review. He personally had been reading entire admissions files since the 1980s for the limited number of marginal candidates whose questionable test scores and grades required a closer look at their complete files. But for the vast majority of Berkeley applicants, test scores and grades still ruled in the admissions process.

And that was the problem. As competition to get into the university heightened and as the university became more selective, the numbers-driven system became increasingly unsatisfactory and unreliable. By ignoring so much information in the applicant's file, was Berkeley really admitting the most promising students? "The dissatisfaction with this process was that small differences in test scores and grades could have big impacts," Moore told me.[28]

Also, the two-tiered process forced the admissions office, in essence, to split an individual in two, first looking at his or her academic side, marking the score, and then examining the "supplemental" side. The process assumed that academic accomplishments could be separated from the larger personal and social context in which the student had earned a certain GPA or a particular test score. For example, an SAT score for someone like Atkinson's own granddaughter, an upper-middle-class child of a neurosurgeon and a pediatric surgeon, who had grown up with every advantage, really did mean something different from an SAT score for a kid like Daisy Gonzalez, whose parents had no more than a ninth grade education.

The bifurcated review process struck Moore and other Berkeley faculty members as an arbitrary exercise. "It's almost as if you cover up one eye when you are looking at the kids, and you really need to look at them with both eyes," Moore explained.

As had long been the case under the shared governance procedures of the University of California, the admissions criteria for the entire university and all its individual campuses rested with the faculty. At Berkeley, the faculty's interest in admissions issues was represented by the Committee on Admissions, Enrollment, and Preparatory Education, which had been moving quietly toward a consensus that the Berkeley campus should adopt a "unitary" comprehensive review system to replace the two-tiered one.

The AEPE group wanted to do what was virtually without precedent for a large public university with a highly selective admissions process:

look at each applicant as a whole, and direct the admissions office to read each and every application file in order to glean as much useful information as possible about applicants to Berkeley.

But there was a major obstacle. In order to proceed, Berkeley needed permission from the university regents to be exempted from SP-1, which required the two-tiered review, including the 75–25 split on academics versus supplemental factors. On May 9, 2001, Berkeley chancellor Robert M. Berdahl, David Dowall, who was chair of the Berkeley Academic Senate, and Calvin Moore, the chair of AEPE, wrote to Richard Atkinson announcing Berkeley's intention to seek the exemption. Their timing proved to be good. By the spring of 2001, there were growing signs that SP-1 might be "in play." The regents had been considering nixing SP-1 in order to send a symbolic message that the University of California was open for business to citizens of all races and ethnic backgrounds.[29]

A week later, after Berkeley sent its letter to Atkinson, the regents did rescind SP-1, paving the way for the new comprehensive admissions system not only for Berkeley but also for the UC system as a whole. The new admissions system would be unprecedented for an institution the size of the University of California, which received some 78,000 applications in 2003. Admissions offices at every UC campus would read every file in its entirety, for every student who applied.

———

An effort of that magnitude was bound to bring out harsh criticism. John Moores and his allies believed that the university wasn't playing by the rules, particularly those barring special consideration for an individual's race or gender, nor was it being fair to some students with impressive academic credentials. When I asked Calvin Moore about John Moores's attacks on comprehensive review for denying some high-scoring students while admitting a small number of low-scoring applicants who "have no business going to Berkeley," the old-school professor's reply was uncharacteristically strong.

"Bullshit," he said. "They do just fine." He went on, "There's no one criteria that's going to get you into Berkeley."

In the world of prediction studies, which, for example, try to assess a student's chances of success in a demanding college environment, a growing body of evidence suggests that computer-based predictions of behavior or events can be consistently superior to predictions based on human judgments. But while such technological approaches are seductively attractive, the one catch is that the predictions are only as good as the number of useful variables accounted for in the model. The fact is, computer-driven models of college success haven't proven to be particularly good—they predict at most a quarter of the variability in student academic performance. That's because college admissions offices have been unable to account for many of the useful factors that create successful students. Truly important variables go unaccounted for in computer models because they are either not quantifiable or because no good measures yet exist.

"Admissions is a human process," Calvin Moore argued. "We shouldn't reduce it just to numbers. And, in fact, when you talk to kids and their parents, they don't like the idea that they are reduced to grades or test scores. They like the idea that they are being evaluated as a whole person. It's a very attractive and very powerful idea."

The one human trait that computer-based admission models have been unable to capture, and very likely the reason that their predictions have limited utility, is what Calvin Moore described as "that special spark," the thing about some individuals that shines above the GPAs and test scores.

For Moore, looking beyond the numbers, the essential questions he asks of any potential candidate are these: What have you done? What have you made of the opportunities you've had? "Above all, we're interested in kids who are taking advantage of all their opportunities," Moore emphasized. "If a kid growing up in an upper-middle-class family tells us about trips to Europe, we want to know, is that you or is that something that you've been given? We want to see what you have done. Don't tell us about your parents, tell us about yourself."

For kids who didn't have the advantages of growing up affluent, the same standard applied, Moore added. Disadvantaged students did not suddenly gain an edge in the UC admissions process by virtue of their disadvantage—despite what John Moores and John McWhorter have suggested. Quite the contrary: now all students admitted had to show something special.

"Special spark can pop out in an application when you see the incredible challenges that kids from broken families and dysfunctional families face, and how they got through that," Moore explained. "A girl becomes a surrogate mother to younger siblings at home. Another student has to work to help support the family, and they turn their earnings over to their parents for food. It's not so much that they had problems they faced, but how have they responded to them? How has the kid overcome these obstacles? How have they reflected on that? How have they matured? Tell us what you have done."

For many disadvantaged kids, that special spark that Calvin Moore speaks of could well be their one advantage in a highly selective admissions process. But that spark could easily have been ignored in the old admissions system, when numbers and formulas ruled the process. The numbers still counted in the new system—a lot, as a matter of fact. And the children born to wealthy families with highly educated parents continued to have enormous competitive advantages of their own at the University of California. But, in a post–affirmative action world, at least the kids growing up with so many strikes against them now had a fighting chance.

And, apparently, providing a fighting chance to economically disadvantaged students sits well with the American public, despite the views of those like Moores, McWhorter, and Wentworth, who argue that test scores should be some absolute measure of academic merit. In fact, according to recent public opinion polling, these critics are outliers.[30] While the public takes a dim view of race-based preferences in college admissions, almost two-thirds of Americans favor affirmative action based on economic disadvantage. Americans still think academic merit is important but don't see test scores as absolute, believing that one's accomplishments ought to be weighed against personal advantages or disadvantages—which are at the heart of programs like comprehensive review.

———

As I said, it's been a small revolution, all things considered. In truth, participants in the Moores-led backlash against the University of California's modest efforts at admissions reform, which even included elite parents whose high-scoring children were not admitted to Berkeley, have really had little to complain about in the final analysis, even by their own standards of what constitutes merit.

In 2003, 44,318 freshmen from public high schools were admitted to the University of California. Of this group, 57 percent, or 25,440 freshmen, had average SAT I scores of 1300 or above (see appendix B, table B-6). Just 10 percent of freshmen from public schools had SAT I scores of about 1000. What's more, the members of that high-scoring 57 percent, who clearly dominated the overall freshman class, were economically and socially an elite bunch, particularly compared with their lower-scoring counterparts who were admitted that year. The average family income of the dominant group was $98,000, nearly twice the family income for the relatively tiny number of students who scored below 1000 on the SAT I.[31]

Socially and economically, the University of California did not look much like the rest of California before the latest admissions reforms, and that remained the case afterward. With its pool of eligible students limited to the top 12.5 percent of students statewide, the UC system has always struggled with its elitist tendencies in the face of its public mission to serve all residents of California, and neither a new SAT nor comprehensive review would fundamentally change that (see appendix A, figures A-10, A-11, A-12, and A-13).[32] In the years just prior to the admissions reforms, about a third of UC freshmen were first-generation college students, and that remained the same in the first two years after the reforms. Both before and after the reforms, roughly 17 percent of new freshmen came from low-income families. The percentage of students from low-performing high schools also held steady. The percentage of underrepresented minorities in the freshman class did increase, but only slightly (see table 3).[33]

What's more, John Moores's speculations about monkey business at the university—that the "suits," as John McWhorter put it, were out to undermine Proposition 209 by relaxing academic standards for minorities—were decimated in the spring of 2005. That's when a UC Berkeley sociologist named Michael Hout issued his follow-up study for Berkeley's AEPE committee. In this quantitative study of the ratings that application readers gave to admitted freshmen, Hout found that race or ethnicity played virtually no role. "In the comprehensive review of 2004–05 freshmen applicants, academic considerations predominated," Hout wrote. "Grades and test scores settled most decisions." In an apparent reference to Moores's complaints, Hout concluded that the "subjective aspects" of comprehensive review, "long viewed with suspicion . . . do not generate ethnic disparity." In fact, "the effective aspects of comprehensive review are weakly correlated with ethnicity."[34]

Of all the University of California schools, the San Diego campus changed most after the admissions reforms. In 2001, about one-quarter of the campus's freshman class were the first in their families to attend college. Two years after the reforms, this figure had risen to nearly one-third. In the years prior to comprehensive review, from 15 percent to 17 percent of new freshmen came from low-income families; by the fall of 2003, almost 20 percent did. Even more noticeable, just 12.7 percent of UC San Diego freshmen had come from low-performing high schools in

**TABLE 3. UC SYSTEMWIDE FRESHMEN PROFILE, BEFORE
AND AFTER COMPREHENSIVE REVIEW ADMISSIONS POLICY**

	Before Comprehensive Review			After Comprehensive Review	
	1999	*2000*	*2001*	*2002*	*2003*
Mean high school GPA	3.86	3.87	3.83	3.82	3.81
Mean SAT I score	1210	1211	1209	1203	1205
First-generation college attendee	30.8%	31.1%	31.3%	32.0%	32.4%
Low family income (less than $30,000)	17.0%	17.5%	16.6%	16.5%	16.7%
Underrepresented minority	16.1%	16.7%	17.8%	18.3%	19.2%
From a low-performing school	15.6%	16.3%	15.5%	16.6%	15.9%

SOURCE: University of California, Office of the President, Eligibility and Admissions Study Group, *Final Report to the President,* Oakland, April 2004, p. 73, www.universityofcalifornia.edu/news/compreview/studygroup_final0404.pdf (accessed December 2005).

1999; in the first years after the reforms, 17 percent had attended such schools (see table 4).

For a young woman named Tiffany Nguyen, all those changes at UC San Diego portended well.

―――――

According to John Moores's standards of merit, by which students ought to be rank-ordered according to an index of grades and SAT scores, Tiffany Nguyen wasn't Berkeley material, either. Tiffany's parents came to Southern California from Vietnam when she was four, and she grew up in inner-city Pomona. Her mother never made it past middle school. Her father wasn't able to go to school at all either in Vietnam or in America, although schooling was something he had longed for his entire adult life. He had grown up in a family of eight children. When he was four, his father died, and he went to work to help support the family. In America, he worked as an auto mechanic, and then a trucker, the job he has now. Tiffany's mother worked as a manicurist.[35]

The family moved from place to place in Pomona, always in tough neighborhoods, with high rates of poverty and crime. Tiffany's first school was Alcott Elementary. In 2005, 76 percent of Alcott's parents

**TABLE 4. UC SAN DIEGO FRESHMEN PROFILE, BEFORE AND
AFTER COMPREHENSIVE REVIEW ADMISSIONS POLICY**

	Before Comprehensive Review			After Comprehensive Review	
	1999	*2000*	*2001*	*2002*	*2003*
Mean high school GPA	4.16	4.20	4.15	4.13	4.17
Mean SAT I score	1308	1313	1313	1293	1304
First-generation college attendee	24.5%	27.1%	25.7%	31.6%	31.5%
Low family income (less than $30,000)	16.3%	17.4%	15.2%	19.1%	19.1%
Underrepresented minority	10.4%	11.5%	11.1%	14.2%	14.5%
From a low-performing school	12.7%	14.7%	12.2%	16.6%	17.0%

SOURCE: University of California, Office of the President, Eligibility and Admissions Study Group, *Final Report to the President,* Oakland, April 2004, p. 79, www.universityofcalifornia.edu/news/compreview/studygroup_final0404.pdf (accessed December 2005).

had only a high school education or less; 90 percent of Alcott's students were considered poor, and 61 percent were classified as English-language learners. Then came San Jose Elementary, and then Barfield.

"Pretty much from elementary school to middle school, I grew up in really bad neighborhoods, and the schools that I went to—I don't think they were that challenging," Tiffany told me. "I didn't consider myself smart, but then, compared to the other students, I was doing pretty well, actually."

"When you say bad neighborhoods, what do you mean?" I asked Tiffany.

"There was a lot of poverty. Everything was very old, extremely old. There were always a lot of gangsters. The majority of the students at all of my schools were Hispanic and African American. It's just the way it was. There were a lot of *cholos,* they were called *cholos* around my neighborhood. It was just very common for them to be walking down the street. It was very dangerous to walk down the street. I used to walk home from school from the bus stop, and every single day, I would have men shout mean things at me. It was just—it wasn't the safest neighborhood."

But then Tiffany caught a break. Her uncle, who was a social worker, lived in Diamond Bar, a relatively well-off suburban area outside

Pomona. The neighborhoods there were served by Diamond Ranch High School, an architecturally magnificent new school that resembled a Frank Lloyd Wright design. Her uncle suggested that Tiffany register under his home address, which would allow her to commute to Diamond Ranch from Pomona, and she ended up doing so for three years.

Tiffany explained, "I guess my uncle saw potential in me, and he thought I would do well, so he convinced my parents to let me go to the school in his area with his kids. It was actually my uncle who talked them into it."

As Calvin Moore might say, Tiffany made the most of her opportunity. Going from schools in which she was an academic star to a high school in which she was far more average was something of a shock at first. But Tiffany told me that her peers had a profound influence on her. She found herself mimicking the behaviors of the middle-class students: how they studied, what they paid attention to, and how they generally carried themselves at school. When topics like the SAT came up, or which AP classes to take, Tiffany found herself in the game because friends she'd made were already talking about those things. "I met a lot of people who were school-oriented at Diamond Ranch, and I think that made all the difference, because that really inspired me to push myself harder to catch up to where they were," Tiffany told me.

I asked Tiffany who turned out to have the most influence on her at Diamond Ranch: counselors, or teachers, or even classmates?

"Counselors? No, I used to go see my counselor all the time. I would always come to him with questions, and he was not helpful at all," Tiffany said. "He really didn't know how to answer my questions and help me out. My teachers, I think I had very great teachers. I was very fortunate to have very great teachers.

"I think the one person that made the most impact was my friend Jolina. Her parents are really educated, and she and her sister are both incredibly smart, and she was taking really hard classes. I just admired her because I thought she was so incredibly smart, and then I hung out with her a lot. I wanted to be just like her, just be at her level, at least. That really pushed me. Even though she doesn't realize what she did, she really inspired me to work a lot harder because I admired her so much."

But there were cultural shocks. During the years that Tiffany commuted to school from Pomona, she told friends that she lived in Diamond Bar, afraid to tell them the truth about her family background and where she actually lived. At Diamond Ranch High, where she was surrounded by relative affluence and well-dressed classmates who lived in nice homes, being poor was something to be ashamed of.

"I was ashamed. I was really, really ashamed of where I was from," Tiffany admitted. "I went to great lengths to hide where I lived, even from my own friends. If they ever needed to pick me up, so we could go out or work on a project, or if I needed someone to drop me off, I would never have them drop me off at my actual house. I would have them drop me off at my uncle's, because his house is nice, and there was nothing to be ashamed of. So my friends, for a long time, thought that that was where I lived.

"Eventually, it was very hard to lie. Things came out, and then it was really hard to keep the same story all the time. I think I got caught, and I admitted it to my friends, and they found out eventually. When they did finally come to my house, their reaction really embarrassed me, because they were just shocked. They were just scared to be in my neighborhood, and that really embarrassed me."

In splitting her time between her middle-class surroundings at school and her real home, there was also the challenge of communicating with her parents about what she was going through in her other life. But she came to understand that her parents could offer little support. It was hardly possible, for example, for her parents to visit the school, to meet teachers, and to watch out for Tiffany's best interests. Tiffany had to depend on her own wit and pluck to adapt, to learn what was expected of a college-bound student, and to be assertive with teachers and counselors.

But she had been self-reliant for most of her life anyway. Growing up in America and more accustomed to its cultural norms than her mother and father were, Tiffany had been fending not just for herself but also for her younger brothers since she was a child.

"Actually, I got next to no support," she explained. "I pretty much had to do everything on my own. I made all my own decisions. They always treated me like an adult, I think. Ever since I was in eighth grade or ninth grade, I have been writing out all the checks, and I have been forging my parents' signatures on all the papers the schools needed. Pretty much whenever my brothers needed papers signed for the school, I would sign it. My parents didn't really pay much attention to those things; we just kind of did it ourselves.

"They never really told me to do my homework, because they always knew I'd have it done by the time they came home. I pushed myself, because my parents—I rarely interacted with them. I never really saw them, even when I was at home, because they went to work and they came home late."

Because Tiffany was fluent in English, her role in the family was to take care of family details that her parents were unable to handle or didn't have time for—doing the family's taxes, for instance, or taking her dad to the motor vehicles office to get his license or register the car. "I have been helping them with their taxes for a really long time," she told me. "Everything my parents do, they always need my assistance. My dad sometimes pulled me out of schools to help him if he needed to go somewhere or needed me to translate just in case he didn't understand.

"A lot of my parents' burdens were on my shoulders. I had to take on a lot of the responsibilities that they just didn't have time to look after. I thought it was really unfair. I had to take on a lot of adult responsibilities that I didn't want to have to worry about."

Meanwhile, Tiffany plugged along at Diamond Ranch High. The school divided students into different academic tracks, and in the beginning, she found herself in the regular classes, not yet familiar with honors, Advanced Placement, and the like. But she became more conversant with those things after getting to know Jolina and other more academically inclined kids.

Slowly, she added to her portfolio. "I really worked my way up," she recalled. "I worked my way up to college prep and honors, and then I moved up from honors to AP, and my senior year I took all AP classes. It was just little steps. It was a good challenge, I think, trying to catch up with all the other students. My goal was to catch up to everybody and be at their level. And once I was at their level, I wanted to be better than them."

I asked her where that inner drive came from.

"I think it came from my background. Every single day, I see all these people who haven't really accomplished much in their lives, and it pushes me to work harder because I know that that is not what I want to be. I ponder a lot about the way life works and the way the world works, and I know life is always going to be unfair. But then all you can do is just accept it and deal with it the best way you can, and make the most out of it, and that is what I am trying to do."

In the summer between her junior and senior years, Tiffany got another break, but it can easily be said that she made her own luck on this one. Talking to Jolina during her sophomore year, Tiffany had learned that the SAT was a requirement for applying to colleges. She borrowed self-help books from the school library and signed up for a free test-prep class offered at the school.

But she noticed that a lot of her peers were going several steps beyond her efforts, such as enrolling in very expensive SAT prep classes offered by private companies during the summer. One company popular with students at her school was Elite Educational Institute, which offered an intensive eight-week summer "boot camp" for students willing to devote their summers to raising their SAT scores. The course would be like going to school, with eight hours a day of classroom instruction, and Elite boasted impressive results in raising student scores. But for Tiffany, there was one very big catch.

Convincing her parents to help her pay the $2,000 for the boot camp was a hard sell. Tiffany's parents didn't know what the SAT was, let alone why she needed to pay extra money for studying something she was supposed to learn at that nice school in Diamond Bar.

"I begged my parents," Tiffany told me. "I actually begged them, and they agreed to pay two thousand dollars for that SAT prep class. Even though it was a lot of money, I told them it was for school, and I told them that it was really, really worth it. I felt like I really wanted it, and they supported that. I could have just gotten the self-help books and taught myself, but I really needed someone to push me, and I needed to have a schedule, and a class to go to, so I think it was really worth it."

Tiffany took the SAT three times, scoring about 890 on the first try. But by the third sitting, her score, on the old version of the exam, had improved some 300 points. "I only got an 1190, but it was a big improvement from before." Moreover, she added, "I got really good grades, actually. I graduated with a 4.2, and that is because I had honors and AP, and that's why it is over a 4.0. I got mostly As in high school—and a few Bs, but mostly As."

But even with the intensive test-prep course that raised her SAT score above John Moores's magical 1000 number, Tiffany still wasn't Berkeley material. In fact, she was rejected at both Berkeley and UCLA. And with an SAT score that was fully 200 points below the average at the San Diego campus, it can be argued that Tiffany wasn't UCSD material either, by Moores's reasoning. But because the new admissions system established a procedure that allowed admissions officials to see her as an individual, and not simply her test scores, she was admitted to UCSD. She was in her third quarter at the university when we spoke. During her first quarter, as a biology major, she took engineering-level calculus, chemistry, and writing courses, pulling a B– average. The following quarter, she took more calculus, anthropology, history, and more writing, earning As and Bs.

"I am making progress every quarter," Tiffany explained. "This quarter, I expect to do even better, because I am making improvements every quarter. That is just my goal right now, just to make improvements, even if it is a small improvement. I think I am doing better. I am doing much better."

Meanwhile, Tiffany has a job working in a medical laboratory on campus, helping to meet the college costs she couldn't cover from grants and a small amount of help from her family. Having already made the cultural leap from the inner city to a middle-class high school, the transition to UCSD for Tiffany hasn't been extraordinarily difficult. But making that transition is no small matter for many first-generation college students. Leaving behind their families and schools in poor urban neighborhoods, rural towns, or the rough edges of suburbia, they suddenly find themselves surrounded by affluent, culturally sophisticated, and highly competitive peers.

Tiffany told me that she has gotten somewhat accustomed to being the odd duck surrounded by well-to-do students, including her roommates, who drive nice cars, wear expensive clothes, and return to large and comfortable homes on weekends and holidays. She used to worry more about what she didn't have, but frankly, she said, she now has more pressing things to care about.

"I actually want to pursue a career in medicine, so I'm just trying to get the highest GPA that I can possibly graduate with. I feel like right now, as far as my rank with UCSD, I feel like I am just an average student. I would like to be at the top of the class, to be better than everybody else, I guess. Maybe not better than, but at least ranked a little higher. Right now, I am an average student, and I just don't think that's good enough."

Seeing what Tiffany had already accomplished after starting out at Alcott Elementary, making the most of every break she ever got to make the University of California a reality, I was thoroughly convinced that she would do what she set out to do.

I guess that's what's called "special spark." And to see it, you have to be willing to look for it.

———

But it's never simple. For all the visionary educators like Dayle Mazzarella, Calvin Moore, and Richard C. Atkinson, and for all the gutsy students like Tiffany Nguyen and Daisy Gonzalez who defy the odds against them, countless more students who come from similar backgrounds do fall through the cracks. Overcoming the class divide isn't easy, and hard cases abound. In the next chapter, we'll meet one of those hard cases, a young woman named Melissa Morrow.

TWELVE

"I ALWAYS IMAGINED MYSELF AS A ROCK"

Upon turning eighteen, Melissa Morrow promptly moved out of her house in Kevin, Montana, where she had lived with her mom and step-dad and her two younger siblings, about two hours' drive from Great Falls. Leaving behind her family and her small rural high school, she picked up and moved to Missoula. The adults who knew her were hoping for the best, that she would finish her senior year of high school in the western Montana college town. Though her family and support would remain in Kevin, Melissa's simple physical presence in Missoula would put her that much closer to the University of Montana, where she might be the first in her family to go to college.

In her heart and in her mind, Melissa Morrow was a gatecrasher, willing to do whatever it might take to go to college and improve her chances for a good and rewarding life. But for every student like Daisy Gonzalez or Tiffany Nguyen who defies the odds and makes it to a four-year college or university, scores more do not. Though their up-by-the-bootstraps stories are always inspiring, students like Daisy and Tiffany remain the exceptions, not the rule. Even with a fire in the belly that would have moved UC Berkeley's Calvin Moore to take notice, Melissa faced financial and cultural obstacles that were both numerous and formidable; and by the time she reached high school, there were no easy solutions to make the obstacles standing in the way of college less daunting.

For Christine Postma, Melissa's mom, getting out of Tacoma was a matter of simple survival. She'd grown up in Yelm, Washington, a small town in the foothills of the western slope of the Cascade Mountains, where the clear views of Mount Rainier were among the town's most treasured features. Christine was the youngest of ten kids. Her father was a Baptist minister, her mother a homemaker. "To be truthful, we were a bunch of hillbillies, basically, up on a mountainside," Christine told me. She was sixteen when she had Melissa. Then she got married, "popped out a couple more kids," got divorced, and moved up north to Tacoma to find work.[1]

Christine and her two daughters were living in a small apartment in an inner-city neighborhood of Tacoma in the early 1990s, when that gritty sister city of Seattle was best known as a haven for Crips and Bloods and crack cocaine. One day, while Christine was waiting for a bus with Melissa and Stephanie, her second oldest, a man stuck a knife in her face and demanded her jacket. This was no ordinary jacket—it was a Notre Dame team jacket that she had bought on sale for $53, the first present of any consequence Christine had ever bought for herself. She told Stephanie and five-year-old Melissa to run home.

"I'm standing there in the middle of the street with a knife to my throat, and he's pretty much saying, 'Give me your jacket or your life,' and you know, I gave him the jacket," Christine recalled. "And then I called the police, and the police are like, 'Yeah, well, stuff happens; it's the neighborhood you live in.'"

Montana seemed as good a place as any, and it was far from Tacoma. Christine and her young daughters landed in Shelby, in the oil patch of northwestern Montana. Her fiancé at the time got a job as the "city man" in Kevin (pronounced Kee-vin), a town of three hundred people, filling potholes, attending to water supplies, and performing other duties about town. Christine eventually broke up with the city man, but she stayed in Kevin. She met Bud Postma, a laboring man who worked on oil rigs in the Montana outback, married him, and had two more kids. Like Christine, Bud also came from a large working-class family. After five years with Bud, Christine would have six children in all, three of them living with her in Kevin. Melissa, almost eighteen when I met her, was the oldest. Bailey Jayne, almost two, was their youngest.

———

After a decade in Montana, Christine Postma could see her life repeating itself through Melissa, and she knew something had to be done. She saw her daughter struggling. A little bit rebel and a little bit urban punk, Melissa wasn't mixing well with the kids at school. Christine, who had never finished high school herself, agreed to pull Melissa out of school and home-school her. That lasted six months.

One day, Bud Postma was gone on one of his frequent working trips to the oil rigs, and mother and daughter were home with the small children. Christine remembers the day clearly, talking with Melissa in their living room. "I gave her a choice. And I said, 'You can either go make something of yourself, or you can end up just like me, in the middle of nowhere with all these children. Those are your choices. Those are your realistic choices. That's what you have to do. You either do something about it or you don't.' And she got up, and she done something about it."

"So Melissa is thinking about going to college?" I said to Christine. She replied with force: "She's going to college if I have to work twenty-five jobs to do it. She's *going* to college."

"Melissa would be the first in the family to go to college?" I asked.

"Yep, first in my entire family, and the second in my husband's family. And I am the youngest of ten kids, and he's got ten kids in his family, and only one of his sisters went to college. And graduated with a degree. This will be the first for any of my brothers and sisters and any of their kids. Yeah, so it's a huge deal."

———

I spoke with Melissa Morrow for the first time in late 2004. It seems that she had never quite fit into Montana, even as a young girl, and still thought of home as being near Tacoma and the Puget Sound, despite the fear of the city that had driven Christine to Montana. Her freshman year of high school was her lowest point. "I was just not happy at all," she told me. "My freshman and sophomore years weren't exactly great years for me. We didn't have much money. I was really, really sad, and I didn't talk to anybody. I didn't want nothing to do with anybody 'cause all I wanted to do was go back home."[2]

When the home schooling didn't work out, Melissa went back to North Toole County High School in Sunburst, Montana, about twenty-six miles from where she lived in Kevin. A little bit at a time, she started coming out of her private shell, and one day she started talking with North Toole County's longtime science teacher, Larry Fauque.

"I just started telling him about how my life was and everything, and he understood, and we became friends," she explained. "And he told me,

'You know, I see a fire in your eyes that I don't see very often, but when I see it, I know it.' "

So they talked about science, and they talked about a program that Fauque had started at the school that he called Individual Science Investigations (ISI), in which students learned science by doing it in the field and in the lab. After some thirty years of teaching, Fauque had earned a reputation as one of the state's most innovative science teachers, and North Toole County High, a tiny school "in the middle of nowhere," as Melissa said, was envied as a perennial powerhouse in state and regional science competitions—a rarity for schools serving significant numbers of disadvantaged students. Connecting with Larry Fauque was Melissa's first stroke of good luck.

But before Melissa could start on her ISI project, she needed some ideas and some preparation. Like many low-income kids who have few role models who have been to college, Melissa had little concept of how studying science might connect to the world of work or further education beyond high school. Few low-income students obtain these strands of cultural capital from family members, which leaves schools, teachers, and other outside benefactors to fill in the gaps. Understanding this, Fauque told Melissa about a regional program called Math and Science Upward Bound, which was run from the Dillon campus at Montana State University. Upward Bound was among the so-called TRIO programs created during Lyndon Johnson's Great Society era.

Melissa dove into Upward Bound that summer, spending six weeks in Dillon with the program's instructors and coordinator Mica Tommi-Slaven, an idealistic young New Yorker who had first made her way out west to work on a VISTA project on an Indian reservation aimed at preventing teen pregnancies.

Tommi-Slaven had grown up straddling two very different worlds of social class in New York City. A graduate of NYU and a college prep school, she was also a graduate of a community college in Kingsborough, New York. Her mother's family included salespeople, factory workers, and skilled crafts workers. Her father's family members were educated intellectuals. "My mom was the Italian-Catholic-Irish-Protestant working class, and my dad was the Russian-German-Jewish middle class. The people in his family were, like, jewelers and tailors, but they were also polyglots. They were oriented toward literacy and education, and they were in control of their destinies in a way that my mom's side of the family never was. It was probably because of money and education. It was all about social class. I lived both of those lives at different points."[3]

"On a whim," she moved to Paris for high school with her mother, the family's free spirit, who worked as an acupuncturist. In Paris, Tommi-Slaven attended both public and private schools. "I remember we lived in this one-room, really tiny apartment in not such a great part of town—and then I would go to friends' houses, and they lived in châteaus. And I never even noticed it. I felt comfortable in both worlds."

Her first realization of social class differences came when she returned to the United States, attending a New York prep school and visiting the homes of her affluent classmates' parents. Her second realization of the class divide came at the age of twenty-nine, when she left the city to go west and work with poor people on the VISTA project in Montana. She had taken a vow of poverty, leaving behind a job in New York that paid a modest five-figure salary and opting for a $6,000-a-year stipend in Montana. "It takes a while before your savings are gone, your car breaks, and you have to start from scratch, away from anybody who is supportive. But the poverty wage was just a gesture. You are not poor if you have an education and come from the middle class, and that is what most VISTAs do."

Yes, being poor was about money, Tommi-Slaven said. But after a few years of working with poor people, she discovered that being poor was less about money per se than about "fear and power." When social scientists talk about class, they typically speak of it in terms of the most readily measured attributes, such as parental education levels and economic factors such as income and wealth. But perhaps the most salient aspects of class differences aren't so easily measured—for example, the bold confidence with which the child of a wealthy family approaches the world, and how large and full of possibilities the world may be from that child's perspective. It is a sense of having the power to make your own choices, the power to control your own destiny. The flip side of power is fear. Choices are few and are grave. Wrong choices can mean devastating consequences. The world for the powerless is very small and potentially very cruel.

These attributes of the class divide made Tommi-Slaven's work at Upward Bound especially challenging. For most low-income students, going to college was an alien concept. There were few role models. Parents and siblings could offer little in the way of information, contacts, or resources. A simple desire on the part of the parents to help their children go further in life than they had was often the most families could offer. Even taking the affirmative steps to get to college, such as talking to somebody like Tommi-Slaven or filling out college applications, involved a process with which the parents and children of low-income families were not comfortable.

"The social currencies [for rich and poor] are completely different," Tommi-Slaven told me. "When I am talking to kids who are really poor, I have to think about what are those social currencies, and what are the obstacles they think about first before anything else. One of them, the first one that comes to mind, is financial aid. And, of course, the other thing is that poor people are caseworked to death. They have got welfare, and they have got caseworkers coming to their houses, so there is a lot of crisis. They are managed, but they kind of want to protect their freedom and their privacy. They don't have as much privacy because they need money, and they need food stamps, and they are getting a lot of their resources from a public entity. The last thing they want to do is submit a financial aid form, where they have to give all of their information all over again. They don't see it as, 'There is money in the system for me, and how am I going to get it?'

She went on, "They think the system is working against them, and the idea that they would choose to voluntarily go and have an interaction" with a social worker or a college counselor like herself "does not make any sense to them. The other thing is that in order to want to go to college, you have to understand what it is and what it does for you, or it just has to be in your DNA."

Simply put, Tommi-Slaven saw her job as instilling that college-going DNA into children who didn't have the opportunity to get it anywhere else, not from families, who struggled to provide for immediate needs of children, and often not even from schools, teachers, or counselors.

"The most obvious thing—and this isn't just true of rural kids—is that they have never been to a college," she said. "They have never seen a college. The parents don't have that experience to share with them. The only professional people these kids have met are the teachers in the high school. They don't know people who have been to college, and they have never seen a college. It's just 'that place over there.' It's like any unfamiliar situation: if you don't have any exposure to it, you are less likely to try, whether it is bungee jumping or anything else. College is not a familiar idea to them, and they are not invited. They are not invited to come and visit, and they don't have reasons to go onto campus. Their parents aren't telling them to go, because the parents don't know how to talk about it. It's not something they have to give their kids.

"Sometimes parents don't want their child to surpass them, because they are afraid it's going to take the child out of their own experience. I think some parents unconsciously are afraid; it is sort of a shame-based thing. I think that they are afraid if their child has an experience that they were not able to give them, that it takes their child away from them. So they tell their kids, 'If you want to go to college, you better start saving up money.' The parents don't know what else to tell them. All they know how to tell them is, 'I can't send you there.' If you don't know the color blue, you are not ever going to want it or want to see it. It is just so far away."

Colleges and universities, for the most part, are "rich-culture." "Poor-culture" people often find campuses to be unwelcoming places. For children who have no college-going in their families, these rich-culture institutions are full of people who talk differently, act differently toward each other, even walk differently. On a college campus, some people walk with eyes straight ahead, in a hurry to be somewhere else; others might relax by aimlessly playing in an open field—either behavior can be unsettling to a kid who's grown up in a small town or the inner city.

"All of the rules are different, and if they were to be on a campus, they would feel it immediately," Tommi-Slaven explained. "In a small town, for instance, poor-culture people are not rushing. They are rushing on a campus. People in a small town are walking around with their hands in their pockets, and they don't have stuff with them. Kids on campus have books and book bags. There is a uniform. There is a different way of using language. It is not inclusive. No culture is inclusive. If you take an extremely rich person and you drop them off in an extremely poor place, or you take a rural person and you drop them off in an urban place, they are not going to be like, 'Oh, I know what this is about, and I am going to fit in.' It is so much about fitting in."

As Tommi-Slaven sees it, her job with kids and families who have no knowledge of college culture is "to norm them to the experience so that it feels like something that can be of their kind, so that it is a thing or a place that they belong to. That is why we have our programs on college campuses. They eat the campus food, they get classes from professors, they are staying in the dorms where the college students are. They get to know the campuses. They will become familiar. It becomes part of their experience so that they can imagine themselves going there."

———

Melissa's six weeks in Dillon excited her brain in a way she had never before experienced. Her science project germinated in the estuaries along the Oregon coast, when Tommi-Slaven and the Upward Bound instructors took Melissa and the other students on a weeklong field trip. Melissa recalls wandering around the tidal waters where the Columbia River flushes into the Pacific, through the occasional farms blending with industrial development along the banks of the great river. Although Melissa had left Tacoma when she was just five, she still spoke fondly of the coast. "The ocean is basically my home, because that's where I grew up," she told me.

One day, while the group went tide-pooling, Melissa learned that sea urchins were key bioindicators of the ocean's ecological vitality—the ocean's equivalent of canaries in the coal mine. She saw the industrial development along the river and guessed that pollution dumping into the estuary could be harming the sea urchins. But how? She did a bit of background research, discovering that a common industrial pollutant, the chemical ethylbenzene, was harmful to estuaries; and she started putting the pieces together for her project. "It was a totally amazing experience," Melissa said of her six weeks in Dillon and her field trip to Portland. "I just loved it."

When I first spoke with Melissa, in a long-distance phone conversation in late 2004, I knew just a few bare facts about her. Tommi-Slaven had told me that Melissa's family income was sufficiently low to qualify for the federal Upward Bound program. And I knew that she'd be the first in her family to go to college. I also knew, vaguely, that she was doing something related to math and science. I was not prepared for the firecracker at the other end of the phone line.

"So, tell me how you discovered science?" I asked Melissa.

"Well, I have a teacher up at the high school, and his name is Mr. Fauque, Mr. Lawrence Fauque is what his name is, and he came up to me one day, and he said, 'You seem like you'd be a good person to maybe try out our science program.' He says there's a science program that is called Individualized Science Investigation, ISI, and I was like, 'Oh, well, my cousin Daniel was telling me about that, and he said that he had a blast.' And Mr. Fauque is like, 'Yeah, well, you're more than welcome to try it, and if you don't like it, you can just always drop it.' And so I tried it out, and I started really getting into it, and I was like, 'Wow, this is really great,' and I did a project on the effects of ethylbenzene on the sperm motility of sea urchins."

"Could you say that more slowly?" I asked.

"The . . . effects . . . of . . . ethylbenzene . . . on the sperm motility . . . of sea urchins," Melissa repeated. "And I went to regionals and got a first-place blue ribbon there. So I went on to state; and at state, I got a gold ribbon. And I was like, 'Yeah, I did a good job! Woo-hoo!' And so I am sitting there in the crowd, and all of a sudden, Melissa Morrow has third place in the entire state, and I'm like, what? I was freaking out, it was so cool.

"And then I went to internationals in Portland and competed with three thousand other kids in the entire world that got to go. It's a totally amazing experience. I was like, 'Whoa!' "

She was moving so fast and was so excited about science that I tried to slow her down in order to follow her narrative—and the science she was explaining to me.

"How did you pick that particular topic, since, obviously, there's no ocean in Montana?" I inquired.

"I love marine animals, and we went to an estuary, which is like the beginning of all the ocean; it's like the green ground of the ocean, and everything else goes out through the estuary. And I saw those factories lining this estuary, and I'm thinking that can't be good for this estuary. So I was thinking about it all summer, like, 'Okay, well, what kind of byproduct do these factories give off that could be harmful to the aquatics there, and how could I test for it? How could I, you know, legitimately test for it? Let me think about it. Okay, well, let's try ethylbenzene because it's a byproduct of styrene and rubber, which is basically toxic, and it's a huge byproduct of the factories all around the world. Basically, it goes up into the air and condensates when it falls down as acid rain into the water."

Melissa continued, "Sea urchins reproduce by just giving off their gametes into the water and letting the waves bring them together, so that means that the sperm and the eggs are in the water when the pollutant is there. So that means that the pollutant can get into the sperm and the eggs, causing mutations or, you know, reduced sperm motility. I proved, at a measurement of 0.25 parts per million, that the gametes are actually affected by 85 percent of them dying immediately. And I observed them at 0.5, 0.25, and 1 part per million immediately and at fifteen minutes. I measured the sperm motility at those levels, and the first one actually seemed to sort of help them out a little bit, but then the second one was worse, and then the third one, they were just dying immediately."

Then came the kicker.

"I was looking up on the Internet and seeing the regulations for ethylbenzene, and I found out to my surprise that it was 0.7 parts per million *for each factory*. They were able to put out 0.7 parts per million of ethylbenzene into the air. And that made my project really important, because I proved that at 0.25 parts per million that the sperm motility is dramatically reduced, and so if 0.7 parts per million is about halfway to 1 part per million, that meant if one factory is doing that and ten factories are doing that, then more than 1 part per million is going into the water. And that's really dangerous. Sea urchins are the bioindicators of the ocean, so they would go first."

"I loved it; I loved my project," Melissa said, finally pausing for a breath.

"How did you figure all this out?" I asked her.

"I just put it together," she answered. "I mean, it was common sense, and I just kind of put it together. I don't really know how I did it. I just did it."

And so, in late 2004, Melissa Morrow was on top of the world. She was going to college, she told me. She had plans to take the ACT college admission exam. She talked engagingly about the colleges she would apply to, or would like to apply to ($40 per application was a lot of money for her family, and might limit her number of applications). She wanted to major in marine biology and study microbiology. She wanted to find a college on the coast somewhere, maybe the University of Washington in Seattle or Reed College in Portland. But the University of Montana in Missoula seemed a more realistic possibility for her first year or so, and then she could transfer.

Seemingly overnight, with her great success in the science competitions, the people who hadn't believed in Melissa Morrow started to believe. Her high school counselor had written her off early. He hadn't informed her about some math courses she had missed during her troubled absence from school. "I missed like half a semester of classes, and he did not tell me until my junior year. I said, 'Well, why didn't you tell me that I had classes missing?' And he's like, 'Well, frankly, I didn't think you were going to graduate.' That doesn't make sense to me. I mean, if somebody is struggling, why wouldn't you want to help them? But I guess that's just me."

She wouldn't be the first struggling student to be forgotten, Melissa told me. There was her friend Troy, brilliant Troy, whose grades started dropping, probably because of a drug problem. "He just wasted away into nothing, and he's at the bottom of the class. It's really sad because nobody cares. It's like, 'Why don't you care?' I know what it's like not to be cared about," she said. "And it's really sad because Troy could be something really great someday." Until she became friends with Mr. Fauque, Melissa told me, "I was just this punk kid that nobody cared about."

During my conversations with Melissa, it seemed important to me that she was speaking about herself as a troubled young kid in the past tense. That was then. Now, she was a budding young scientist, and even in a remote corner of the country, she was becoming part of an international community of scientists. In fact, the Internet allowed her to write to scientists around the world. She had become friends with one female scientist in Switzerland, who seemed especially encouraging. "I love talking to scientists," Melissa declared. "I've talked to scientists from Sweden, New Zealand, in microbiology or marine biology, because I write them all the time. I look them up on the Internet, and then I write them, and then they write me back. They're really good about that, actually, writing me back, because you would think that, well, they're important people that would think, 'Oh, you're only a high schooler, and who cares about you?' But there are some people that are like, 'Wow, that's really interesting,' when I tell them about my projects."

I asked, "So would you say that science has been a kind of a savior for you?"

She answered, "Definitely. I feel like science has given me a reason to live and a reason to feel like I'm worth something and that my ideas are worth something. And that I really am here for a reason, and that reason is to make this world better. Totally better for everybody else—for me, for my brothers and sisters, for my mom and dad, and for my kids, and for my husband, and for everybody that I touch around me. I really believe that. I really believe that I'm here to make this world different and better. And science saved my life. I really do believe that. It saved me from myself."

Melissa seemed so confident about the changes she had made in her life, and her prospects for the future, that I surely did not want to raise any doubts. But I knew the data about the dismal college-going rate of lower-income students, and eventually I felt that I had to bring up the subject with Melissa.

"I hate to ask you this, but what happens if, you know, college doesn't work out? What are the obstacles ahead of you at this point?"

"No, nada," Melissa said emphatically.

"So failure is not an option?"

"No, that's not an option for me. I won't let it be an option. There is no option for me but to go to college, because I will not let myself fail. I won't let myself fail, and I don't care who tries to stand in my way. I don't care if it's money, I don't care if it's somebody who doesn't like me, I don't care if it's a professor. I don't care. I will push myself and make myself go that extra mile. . . . I will graduate from college, and I will be a productive member of this society if it kills me, because that's my goal in life."

"Melissa," I asked, "Where does this come from this, this amazing fortitude?"

"I don't know. I don't really know. It just comes from the way I was raised. I was raised in a little tiny apartment that got shot up every day from gangbangers, and we had no money, and my mom had to work every day. And the guy that we were living with would abuse us, and, you know, we had to be strong for that. And I figured, Hey, if I can go through all this other stuff, and if I can make it through that, I can do anything I want. Anything. Nobody's gonna stop me 'cause I'm—I'm way stronger than a lot of people think.

"Inside of myself, I always imagined myself as a rock, standing right where the tide comes in, and how it keeps crashing against that rock, and that rock isn't going anywhere. It'll stand there every day, even though it might get eroded a little bit, but it's still gonna be here for thousands and thousands of years—and so will I. That's what I want. And when I die, I want somebody to remember, 'Hey, you know that girl? Yeah, she may have had a few problems in her life, but she did some great things. She did some wonderful things for this world, and nobody's gonna forget her for that.' "

———

The next time I spoke with Melissa, there was something different about her, but it was hard to put my finger on. That top-of-the-world confidence was gone. Melissa struck me as distracted, perhaps even overwhelmed. I could hear her younger brother or sister crying in the background.

When I asked how her planning was going, I could sense that she was trying desperately to sound upbeat about the whole college thing.

"Let's see. I'm going to go to Missoula. That's pretty much all I know right now," she told me.

"What do you mean?"

"I'm going to go to college in Missoula. I have applied and everything, and I'm just waiting for a reply and stuff."

Despite Melissa's obvious brilliance, I couldn't help but remain unconvinced that she would really make it to the University of Montana. Sure, she tried to assure me, she was still planning on taking the ACT or SAT, but she seemed to believe that she could be admitted to the university without taking the test. She was waiting on her parents to file their income taxes so she could fill out the federal financial aid forms, and she did seem knowledgeable about Pell Grants, FAFSA forms, and the like. But there was still something out of balance in her voice, and I felt I wasn't getting the whole story.

"When I talked to you the first time, you were so adamant and positive about college and being able to go. Do you still feel that way?" I asked.

"Oh, yeah!" she reassured me. "The year's just drawing to a close, and there's just tons of things going on. And it's just stressful. Like, 'Oh, dear! I just want it to be over.' "

"What feels most stressful?"

"Just feeling like I'm on my own. I don't know. It's just like I know what I have to do, but it's just so much to do, it's just a little bit overwhelming. I mean, I have so much stuff going on. It's like—oh, God. . . . It's crazy! Crazy little brother and sister and just lots of stuff."

"Do you ever worry that things won't work out for college?"

"I always worry about that. I always think that I'm not going to be good enough, or they're not going to accept me, or something might go wrong. So . . . I always worry about that, but I try to be optimistic. I'm a pretty smart girl. I can get it all together."

"So, do you feel like you've pretty much figured things out with respect to the direction you're going in?"

"Oh, yeah. I had that figured out a long time ago. I'm not even worried about that. I know I'm going to be something great one day. It's just a matter of when. I can't let myself believe that I'm not going to succeed, because that's just not a possibility for me."

I asked Melissa about money for college and how much she was concerned about that.

"Yeah. It's an issue. But we're just going to have to deal with it. Do what we can. Take out loans. But it just stinks, you know, like when you're done with college, you have forty thousand dollars to pay right away. You're in debt. It's like, 'Oh, no!' It gives me a knot in my stomach."

"Does going into debt really concern you?"

"It does. Because it takes like eighteen years to get out of debt, and so I'm going to be thirty-five or forty years old before I get out of debt— and, you know, before I can start actually living my life the way I want to live it. . . . It still gives me knots in my stomach whenever I think about it. I mean, if by some extreme anomaly, I wouldn't finish because I got sick or hurt or something, I'd still have to pay that money. And that would stink! Especially if I got hurt or something and couldn't go to college 'cause I was hurt."

"When you talk about the money with mom and dad, how do those conversations usually go?"

"They're not going to be able to give much, but they're going to try to give as much as they can. But they still got two babies to take care of at home. And then there's child support and everything else."

I recalled my first conversation with Christine, Melissa's mom. She had been adamant that Melissa would turn out different and take a path in life that she had not been able to take.

"She's going to college if I have to work twenty-five jobs to do it. She's going to college," Christine had said, defiantly.

I replayed that conversation for Melissa. "When I talked to your mom, there was no question in her mind. You're going to college, she told me. But there still must be that little bit of feeling, with all the necessities to take care of, that college seems a little bit like a luxury. Does it sometimes feel that way to you?"

"Yeah, it does," she said. "It feels like if you don't bust your butt for it, you're not going to be able to get it, and college is just not something that I can take for granted. Somebody with a ton of money, they'd be like, 'Oh, I can just fail this semester. It's only ten thousand dollars.' No! I can't do that! I'm going to have to be pulling the grades, you know, 'cause I don't have a second chance. I don't have a reprieve. If I mess up, then that's it. It won't be, 'Oh, well, Mommy and Daddy will take care of me.' I got to work for it. College is a luxury. My grandma and grandpa, they didn't go to college. My mom didn't go to college. My dad didn't go to college. College is a luxury."

"But," I said, trying to sound hopeful, "going forward with your family and your kids, hopefully you'll be able to pass the idea of college on to them too."

Melissa replied, "Yeah. And, you know, be able to say, 'I did this and this and this. What do you think you can do?' Isn't that what generations are about, making each generation better? I'm trying to do that for my future generations."

———

That was the last time I spoke to Melissa. In March 2005, I received an e-mail from Mica Tommi-Slaven, Melissa's coordinator at the Math and Science Upward Bound program in Dillon. Apparently, after turning eighteen, Melissa had suddenly dropped out of school just a few months before graduating. Tommi-Slaven put the best spin she could on the turn of events. Melissa had gone to Missoula to live with a friend and finish school there, she said, offering the suggestion that the sheer physical proximity of the University of Montana would make Melissa's college dream seem more real. Tommi-Slaven said she'd know more in a few days after some student volunteers at Upward Bound reported back. They planned to go on the road to find Melissa, hoping to talk to her in person.[4]

I still hadn't heard any news after a few weeks. I called up Melissa's mom one morning to check up on how things were going. "Horrible," Christine said, and she told me the story. One day, probably not long after my last conversation with Melissa, she went to school and didn't come home. Without telling her mom, she took off for Missoula with her boyfriend. Missoula was a bust, because they couldn't find a place to live, and they found their way to Twin Falls, Idaho, where the boyfriend's family lived. Twin Falls was a small, working-class town amid the farm country in the southwestern part of the state. Melissa was now even farther away from the University of Montana, in more ways than one.

"Yeah, she's out of here," Christine told me. "She didn't finish school, she didn't even say goodbye." Christine was devastated. "I had everything set up for her to go to college. She was going to graduate with honors, and all of a sudden, she just left, four days after her birthday. It's a shame, because she had the world by the tail, and she could have done anything she really wanted."

I contacted Tommi-Slaven to tell her what I had found out, and I expressed how shaken I'd been by the news about Melissa. It made me angry that Melissa, who had so much promise, could behave so self-destructively. But that was from my perspective as a well-educated, fifty-one-year-old man steeped in middle-class values.

I confided my irritations about Melissa to Tommi-Slaven. As one who had been working with kids like Melissa for years, she helped me put Melissa's story into some context.

"I agree with you about Melissa," she sympathized. "Her story is important, period. I chose her to be an interviewee because she had so much promise *and* because she was so high risk, and I saw being interviewed as part of the intervention. If she had a comfy middle-class home, she'd be there right now, dutiful and focused."[5]

She continued, "I think low-income kids see no reason not to act directly on their unhappiness and boredom, because their potential success isn't real enough to them. Middle-class kids believe their reward is in the future. Poor kids know there's nothing waiting out there with their name on it."

Tommi-Slaven, too, never saw Melissa again. She had driven from Dillon to Melissa's high school to personally deliver some college application materials to Melissa and walk her through the process. There had been a blizzard that week, so Tommi-Slaven had made the drive at some personal risk. She had seen brilliant poor kids like Melissa fall through the cracks before, but each time was painful and seemed senseless.

"It just drives me nuts that I was on my way up to Sunburst with the [college] applications in hand the week after the blizzard, and she was gone. I don't kid myself that I was going to change her life, but I was really looking forward to taking some one-on-one time with her and trying to make her promising future more real than the crappy one."

As a promising young scientist, Melissa had so much going for her. She had adults who believed she could make it. She lacked money, for sure. But unlike Gillian Brunet in Santa Monica or Michael in West Palm Beach or the students at the Treasure Valley Math and Science Center, what Melissa also lacked was intangible: a deeply ingrained sense of confidence that the world was brimming with possibility for her. But one thing is clear: if the adult world waits until the end of high school to start closing the opportunity gaps for disadvantaged kids like Melissa, by then it may be too late.

————

Indeed, Melissa's circumstances and the opportunity structure she encountered can hardly be disconnected from the world beyond Montana. As we proceed to the final section of the book, we must examine how that opportunity structure came to be, and what must be done to make opportunities for kids like Melissa more than just an illusion.

PART 5

AMERICAN DREAMS

THIRTEEN

HOW WE GOT HERE

The educational opportunity structure for Melissa Morrow at the dawn of the twenty-first century was about far more than schools and colleges and individual families. It was also about the structure of the American economy. It was about winners—and losers. It was about the public and its problems.

When George W. Bush was sworn in for a second term as president, he spoke to Congress about his plans for war, for privatizing the Social Security system, for sweeping tax cuts, and for reductions in domestic programs on which many ordinary Americans depend. Bush and his neoconservative backers, stoking fears of terrorism breaching American borders, have nearly accomplished what would have seemed unthinkable just a few decades earlier: upending the relationship between government and citizens that has held American liberal democracy in balance since the end of the Second World War. A new bargain between citizens and government appears to be solidifying, a social compact resembling one that existed before the Great Depression, when the sanctity of private property and unbridled economic markets enabled some individuals to accumulate unprecedented wealth. During the decade preceding the 1929 crash, for example, the top 10 percent of American taxpayers earned almost half the nation's income.[1]

After the collapse of the American economy and the onset of the Great Depression, it took a scion of upper-class privilege, Franklin D. Roosevelt, to see that America's center would not hold unless the nation took drastic steps to mitigate the terrible damage of unfettered capitalism.

And thus a New Deal was born of economic calamity. This ensuing social compact between citizens and government held that people had certain rights to economic security against unemployment, hunger, and
predatory profiteering—the flotsam and jetsam of a capitalist economic
engine that created great wealth but also produced great inequality between rich and poor, and between those who labored and those who
owned wealth and paid the laborers. After the decade-long depression,
America was saved by the war against fascism in Europe and Asia—and
it was saved from itself. If the New Deal saved the American economy,
the Great War against fascism saved America's heart, a sense of its place
in the modern world as a defender of humanity. Quite true, the war created jobs. But in the end, this wasn't a war over land and resources and
material hegemony—it was a war against unthinkable evil.

Just as the New Deal provided an economic floor for Americans, pro-
tecting against our baser instincts and abuses of economic freedom, what
came to be called the Great Society during the Lyndon Johnson years
would both reinforce that floor and broaden it to attack poverty, racial
segregation, urban decay, and environmental damage and to extend the
dream of a college education to all who wanted it. Johnson told the nation in 1964: "Your imagination, your initiative, and your indignation
will determine whether we build a society where progress is the servant
of our needs, or a society where old values and new visions are buried
under unbridled growth. For in your time we have the opportunity to
move not only toward the rich society and the powerful society, but upward to the 'Great Society.' "[2]

The Great Society's Herculean effort, embodied in some one hundred
major initiatives to the 89th Congress and the 90th Congress, was
breathtaking in its scope. Any one of the Great Society programs, built
in a relatively short span of years, from 1964 through 1970, would be
considered a major achievement for a modern president: The Social Security Act of 1965, which ensured health care for the poor and elderly
by establishing the Medicaid and Medicare systems. The Higher Education Act of 1965, which provided grants and low-interest loans to
allow low-income students to attend college. The Voting Rights Act of
1965, which ensured that minorities would have the right to register
and vote. The Elementary and Secondary Education Act, which provided money for schools serving low-income children. The Food Stamp
Program. Head Start, Upward Bound. The National Endowment for
the Arts and Humanities. The Corporation for Public Broadcasting.
The Clean Air Act. The Wild and Scenic Rivers Act. The 1964 Civil

Rights Act. The 1968 Fair Housing Act. The Product Safety Commission. The National Transportation Safety Board. These and dozens of other programs amounted to nothing less than an idealistic nation's dream of making Aristotle's "good life" a tangible possibility for any citizen.

Then the 1980s happened, and Ronald Reagan happened, and he began his lifelong project to decimate, if not dismantle, the social compact established by the New Deal and the Great Society. As governor of California, Reagan, a self-proclaimed nonpolitician, seized on the political calculus that government wasn't the solution but the problem. Whether the social and economic ills were inflation, unemployment, bad schools, or crime, Reagan's political genius was to attribute all these problems—whether real or imagined—to the government itself, and to the morally corrupt nature of government solutions to public problems. His rhetorically forceful method, which he used repeatedly throughout his political life, was to make "the Government" into a welfare-maximizing force of its own, composed of faceless but self-interested automatons, whose agenda and interests stood apart from the very people the government was supposed to represent.

"The nine most terrifying words in the English language are, 'I'm from the government and I'm here to help,' " Reagan once said. "Government's view of the economy could be summed up in a few short phrases, 'If it moves, tax it. If it keeps moving, regulate it. And if it stops moving, subsidize it.' "[3]

While Reagan's stated mission from his first day as president was to reduce the size of the federal government, he established two fundamental parameters for fulfilling that pledge. He attacked government at every opportunity on the domestic side of policy, but his rabid anti-Communism in foreign affairs was such that federal military spending remained sacrosanct—spending that was sufficiently massive for the United States to bludgeon the Soviets into economic submission. In his reordering of the public good, Reagan thus exempted military spending from the same devastating spending cuts he applied to domestic programs.

And then there were the tax cuts, another pillar of Reagan's grand design to reduce the scope of government in virtually every aspect other than the military. The 1981 tax cuts were among the largest in the nation's history, relative to the size of the economy. "The American people now want us to act and not in half-measures," Reagan said in 1981, announcing his tax cut and economic program. "They demand and they've earned a full and comprehensive effort to clean up our economic mess. . . . And that cure begins with the federal budget. . . . Our government is too big, and it spends too much."[4]

But by his 1983 State of the Union address, when the federal budget deficits he had harangued against in his campaign speeches kept ballooning under his stewardship, Reagan defended himself against the increasingly clear budgetary arithmetic proving that outsized military spending and massive tax cuts were at the core of the growing federal deficits. "Let's be clear about where the deficit problem comes from," he said. "Contrary to the drumbeat we've been hearing for the last few months, the deficits we face are not rooted in defense spending. . . . Nor is the deficit, as some would have it, rooted in tax cuts. . . . The fact is, our deficits come from the uncontrolled growth of the budget for domestic spending."[5]

The Reagan deficits left the nation a terrible legacy of fiscal extravagance. The federal budget deficit rose from $74 billion in 1980 to $221 billion in 1986. As a percentage of the economy, the deficit ballooned from 0.7 percent in 1980 to a peak of 4.8 percent in 1986. In order to finance the deficit, the government was forced to borrow heavily, and the national debt rose from 26 percent of the gross domestic product in 1980 to almost 50 percent by 1993.[6]

According to the Reagan reformulation of government as the source of all ills, economic freedom meant fewer taxes, particularly for wealthy individuals and corporate entities, who could be counted on to create jobs (famously summed up as "trickle-down" economics); a reduced federal commitment to domestic programs such as education, highways, bridges, and health care; and an entrenched ideology, born from defeat in Vietnam, which held that defense spending was virtually untouchable and any and all appropriations sought by a U.S. president essentially were not open for debate. Repeated loudly and often enough, from the bully pulpit to U.S. Chamber of Commerce offices across the country, Reagan's ideology became settled truth among ordinary Americans. His anti-government views would henceforth shape acceptable bounds of public discourse for Republicans and Democrats alike. The New Deal? A feeble relic of history that no longer applied to the new economic and ideological order. And Johnson's Great Society? Worse than anachronistic, it was an invidious example of Big Government's crimes against people's right to live in economic freedom.

"If there is a prize for the political scam of the 20th century, it should go to the conservatives for propagating as conventional wisdom that the Great Society programs of the 1960s were a misguided and failed social experiment that wasted taxpayers' money," says Joseph A. Califano Jr., who served as secretary of Housing and Urban Development under Johnson. Califano asks, "Why . . . do Democratic politicians who battle to preserve Great Society programs ignore those achievements? For the same reason Bill Clinton came to the LBJ library on Johnson's birthday during the 1992 campaign and never spoke the name of Lyndon Johnson or recognized Lady Bird Johnson, who was sitting on the stage from which he spoke. The answer lies in their fear of being called 'liberal. . . .' In contemporary America politicians are paralyzed by fear of the label that comes with the heritage of Lyndon Johnson's Great Society."[7]

Ronald Reagan couldn't single-handedly dismantle the Great Society and the New Deal—the programs permeated much of American life; and seniors, the poor, college students, and cities continued to benefit from its programs, despite Reagan's harsh anti-government rhetoric. But he surely laid both the ideological and Machiavellian groundwork for quietly picking off domestic programs piecemeal.

Reagan realized that his hope of reducing the size of government lay in creating and sustaining the illusion of national impoverishment. Even in the midst of the Great Depression, FDR had persuaded Americans of the underlying wealth of the richest country on earth—a wealth that government could bring to bear on social and economic problems. But Reaganites took an opposite tack: what better means to create the illusion of scarcity than to slash taxes and allow the federal budget to bleed so much red ink that domestic spending seemed a luxurious waste, supporting bloated government programs?

Integral to Reagan's political calculus was the idea that tax cuts would bring progressively larger economic benefits as one climbed up the income ladder, with advantages accruing to the affluent taxpayers and corporations who were most likely to vote and exercise political power in Congress. Conversely, government programs that served the young and the poor could be cut; not coincidentally, these individuals were the least likely to vote and the least able to coalesce into an effective political force.

While Reagan was persuading Americans that the government could no longer afford to spend money on domestic programs, he got lucky. The underlying wealth of the nation expressed itself, despite periods of deep recession. Stock wealth accumulated. The financial, banking, defense, and technology sectors of the economy expanded. But, again, the darker sides of the nation's faith in free markets grew increasingly ominous. After a long period of relative stability in terms of economic equality, after the Second World War and through the Great Society years, a dramatic and disconcerting shift in the economic order became evident in the early 1980s. Economic inequality became far worse. By the end of the 1980s, the richest 10 percent of salary earners controlled about a third of the nation's salary income, up from the relatively stable 25 percent of incomes these individuals earned during the quarter century between 1950 and 1975 (see appendix A, figure A-14).[8]

Accompanying the growing income inequality during the Reagan years was a surge in wealth inequality. Between 1983 and 1989, the wealth of American households, indicated by financial holdings such as stocks, bonds, and other assets, grew by $4.9 trillion. Of that increase, 53 percent went to the richest 1 percent of households, New York University economist Edward Wolff discovered in his widely cited study. In contrast, the wealth of the bottom two-fifths of households actually declined by $300 billion during the 1980s. Wolff noted that the increase in wealth inequality during the 1980s "stands in sharp contrast" to the postwar years from 1962 to 1983, a period when all economic classes shared relatively equally in the nation's burgeoning wealth.[9]

Ronald Reagan's conservative genius paved the way for triangulating Democrats, shameless Republican excess, and a new Gilded Age that, for all the talk of culture wars, transcended political boundaries. After George W. Bush was reelected to office for a second term, his inaugural ceremonies, parties, and balls cost an estimated $40 million. As an Associated Press reporter wrote: "President Bush's second inauguration will cost tens of millions of dollars—$40 million alone in private donations for the balls, parade and other invitation-only parties. With that kind of money, what could you buy? Two hundred armored Humvees with the best armor for troops in Iraq. Vaccinations and preventive health care for 22 million children in regions devastated by the tsunami of 2004. A down payment on the nation's deficit, which hit a record-breaking $412 billion last year."[10] In one of its characteristically folksy pieces of Americana, National Public Radio interviewed fashion aficionados and inaugural ball watchers, and one longtime observer of style trends noted, without a trace of irony, that lots and lots of fur stood out as among the most notable trends of the 2005 inaugural parties.

In certain circles of wealthy and well-educated parents, there was no price too high to give their young ones a competitive start in life, including the perfect baby stroller. According to a *New York Times* account, one imported European model popular with some parents in New York, Los Angeles, and San Francisco, the Bébé Confort Elite with an

Opéra seat, ran a cool $850. Never mind, though. The Confort Elite conveyed the right cachet and social status.[11]

Social stratification in American society was being taken, quite literally, to new heights. At such American ski areas as Aspen, Beaver Creek, and Stratton Mountain, the affluent could avoid the hoi polloi altogether by paying upward of $50,000 to join private clubs with elegant lodging, choice parking, and exclusive, uncrowded lift-lines. Denny Lee of the *New York Times* wrote this about one such club member: "While others circled the parking lot, he drove his Lexus SUV directly into an underground garage. While others fumbled for quarters in the plebeian lodge, he rode an elevator up to his personalized locker. And while others waited for lift tickets, he finished his coffee, grabbed his Volkl skis from the valet, and was schussing down the slopes by 8 A.M., an hour before anyone else."[12]

As the inaugural minks shone and the sales of luxury goods soared, George W. Bush was proposing a federal budget and policy agenda that continued to redefine the government's increasingly stingy relationship with ordinary Americans. Following Reagan's formula, Bush proposed deep tax cuts for the wealthy and reductions in a wide array of domestic programs, from education to veterans' benefits.

Also following Reagan's script, Bush's military spending remained sacrosanct amid the U.S. military's ongoing occupation of Iraq and the administration's saber rattling toward Syria, Iran, and North Korea. The Bush tax cuts proved to be especially problematic for the economy—not merely for the health of the budget and the debt left for future generations, but also for economic equity. The deficit in 2004 surged to $412 billion, and the Congressional Budget Office estimated that cumulative deficits between 2006 and 2010 would climb to $1.2 trillion—not even counting costs for the military in Iraq and Afghanistan.[13] The war costs were hardly trivial. As of February 18, 2006, American taxpayers had spent more than $230 billion for military operations in Iraq, burning through money at a rate of $175 million per day. According to the Congressional Budget Office, military operations in Iraq and Afghanistan would increase total federal spending by more than $1.4 trillion over a ten-year period.[14]

As a percentage of the nation's economy, Bush's tax cuts rivaled the massive shrinkage of government revenues during the Reagan years—and were offered to the public in the same spirit of Reagan's discredited "trickle-down" theory of economic growth. Even more disturbing, the distribution of Bush's revenue cuts proved bountiful for just a tiny fraction of the nation's wealthiest taxpayers. According to the Tax Policy Center, a cooperative effort of the Urban Institute and the Brookings Institution, *fully 55 percent of the Bush tax cuts went to the 0.2 percent of American households earning more than $1 million a year.* Their average tax cut was more than $19,000—compared to an average tax reduction of less than $1 for the almost 90 percent of households earning less than $100,000 a year.[15]

While federal largesse flowed to support military programs and tax cuts for the wealthiest taxpayers, Bush called for spending reductions in education, health care, veterans' benefits, the environment, poverty programs, and the Justice Department, totaling 16 percent, in real dollars, or a reduction of $214 billion through 2010. In addition, his budget proposed, in effect, to cut federal spending on domestic programs by shifting $71 billion of costs to states and localities; and there was no telling how much of those costs states would actually decide to cover, given the choice of raising taxes or cutting services.[16]

Indeed, the ideology of scarcity had already swept the states, as state and local governments had been following the federal government's lead by dramatically shrinking financial expenditures—cutting taxes and rolling back state commitments to education, public safety, health care, and other services. During a twelve-month period ending in June 2003, state revenues—adjusted for inflation and population growth—were almost $60 billion less than they had been two years earlier. Relative to the size of the economy, state revenues were at their lowest level in thirty years.[17]

The states' disinvestment in higher education was particularly severe. State investments in educational institutions had climbed sharply through the 1960s and into the 1970s and stayed relatively flat between the peak in 1977 and 1980. Then, coinciding with a steep economic recession during Reagan's first term, in 1981, state support for colleges and universities began to fall dramatically and has been in decline since. With each cyclical economic downturn, the states ratcheted down their commitments to higher education throughout the 1980s and 1990s. In 1961, that commitment had averaged $3.59 per $1,000 of state personal income. Throughout the Great Society years, this figure grew steeply, as state policy makers recognized that public investment in higher education created public benefits far more significant than just the sum of the benefits that accrued to individuals. Such state investment peaked at $10.47 per $1,000 of personal income as the 1980s began, but by 2005, it had declined to $6.91.[18]

Accompanying this massive public disinvestment were large tuition hikes at public colleges and universities. Education costs were being shifted from the public to individuals and families: between 1976 and 2001, state support of higher education declined by $15.9 billion, while tuition at state colleges and universities surged by $9 billion (see figure 11).[19] As the new century unfolded, the long-term economic and social implications of this shrinking public effort were far from clear. It was clear, however, that the brunt of the privatization of state higher education systems would fall on the very individuals who would not be able to afford college without help from the public.

Meanwhile, George W. Bush was pushing hard for his domestic agenda, and his centerpiece proposal to privatize Social Security, a linchpin of the New Deal, captured the most headlines. What garnered far less public attention, however, were a few line items in the Bush administration's education budget for 2006 designed to eliminate several dozen programs aimed at helping students from disadvantaged backgrounds. At the top of Bush's hit list were the so-called TRIO programs, which included Educational Talent Search and Upward Bound. The intent of these programs is to nurture an interest in college among low-income students whose chances for college are otherwise poor, owing to poverty, lack of academic preparation, or lack of family awareness about college. Many of these students are the first in their family to attend college.

With roots going back to Lyndon Johnson's War on Poverty in the 1960s, the TRIO programs had long been targets of ideological conservatives. "The bad news," explained Thomas Wolanin of the Institute for Higher Education Policy, "is that TRIO programs are either the crown jewel of educational opportunity or some of those failed programs of the sixties, as some other people would think about them. To put it even more starkly, these are not Republican programs in their origin or in their continuation. So it's hard to expect a lot of sympathy for their future continuation."[20]

In the overall scheme of the federal budget, the cost of the Upward Bound program was minuscule—funded at $280 million a year, roughly a day and a half of expenditures for military operations in Iraq. The president's budget called for eliminating that $280 million along with the funding for other TRIO programs, including Gear Up ($306 million) and Educational Talent Search ($145 million). Those cuts and dozens more would pay for a modest increase in Pell Grants for low-income students going to college, in addition to a small increase in Title 1 funds—princi-

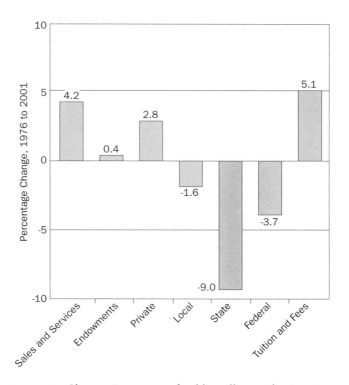

Figure 11. Changes in sources of public college and university funding, 1976 to 2001. Note: Sales and services include categories such as bookstore sales and the sale of other goods and services to the public. Source: Thomas Mortenson, "State Tax Fund Appropriations for Higher Education, FY1961 to FY2005," *Postsecondary Education Opportunity* 151 (January 2005): 1–2.

pally for the president's No Child Left Behind Act. Overall, the Bush education budget would decline by about $7 billion from the prior year.[21]

Millions and billions. Mere numbers that had come to mean increasingly less in the new Gilded Age and the great new inequality in America: brazenly inequitable distribution of tax cuts to the rich and powerful; a slow but steady dismantling of government help to the losers in a Darwinian economic competition whose rules systematically favored the wealthy few; massive retrenchment from public higher education; and an expanding sense of social and economic entitlement for the winners and just deserts for the losers. All this left America with many things, but mainly with an utter loss of shame and of outrage. In a nation where a salesman named Trump was the new role model for the young, who strove to become his "apprentices" in gold-plated surroundings in a Faustian bargain to win at any cost, there was no more outrage.

———

Throughout this book, we have examined the extent to which social class remains a formidable barrier throughout the American education system, dividing the nation into haves and have-nots. The claim that the advantages or disadvantages a child like Melissa Morrow has inherited from her family are fundamental to her life chances certainly runs counter to the tenet that the United States is a society where anything is possible with enough hard work and talent. In the following chapter, we examine some of the empirical support for that dearly held belief.

FOURTEEN

CLASS CONFUSIONS

Meandering into the cereal aisle at the grocery store, I happened to glance at a woman's grocery cart, and there lay the red and blue balloons of a Wonder Bread wrapper. Sometimes I do this, looking at people's grocery carts, merely curious about what they're buying, and it's usually a non-event. But that loaf of Wonder Bread somehow made a deeper imprint.

Of course, a loaf of Wonder Bread isn't commonly thought of as an especially noteworthy sight. But Wonder Bread is more than a package of processed white bread. It's more, even, than an icon of pre-VietGate, undeconstructed innocence, when a loaf of mass-produced bread was just that. It's just a loaf of bread, but one that nowadays often seems to announce that the buyer belongs to the class of working Americans who struggle to make ends meet.

I wasn't thinking about Wonder Bread as class symbolism when I first saw it in the woman's grocery cart. But I later reflected on my reaction. A part of me felt a smug superiority. Where was that coming from? What explained my vague sense of anxious shame about all this? I'd never explicitly confronted these questions before, although I think they had been lurking for some years. I began to think my class bigotry was the bizarre result of some brain implant that told people like me how to think about Kmart, *Guns & Ammo* magazine, NASCAR, and similar cultural artifacts.

I was reminded of a flyer that had been wending its way through the offices of doctors, lawyers, accountants, and others of the professional class in the city where I live. This Lettermanesque document was called

"You Might Be Considered a Redneck If . . . " and listed the supposed habits of rednecks. As I watched a table full of professionals laugh at the list, it seemed that its primary function was to allow them to revel—to bond, really—in their collective sense of class superiority, while never explicitly acknowledging why they were doing it. They didn't have to.

The landscape of class differences in the United States is littered with such Wonder Bread encounters. But the American class system that engenders such events rarely reaches the public's radar screen. The envy, shame, and bigotries aroused by class differences lurk anxiously between the main texts of American discourse, like ugly bugs beneath the green grass of a David Lynch film. Most Americans, in fact, are relatively blind to class, having faith in the upward mobility implicit in a supposedly classless society. Politicians can't abide raising the class question in public because it's a taboo subject. Besides, they're far more electable if they can view their constituencies through the lens of gender, age, race, red state or blue state, or other such commonly discussed and socially acceptable identities. Class, however, is the nation's mad aunt, a troubling part of our past safely stashed away in the historical archives.

As a result, most Americans—elites and Wonder Bread people alike—appear to embrace the prevailing view that class no longer matters much. Race matters. Gender matters. Religion and the question of whether Christmas should be merry or holidays should be happy do matter. Welfare and affirmative action also matter, but only when cast as issues of race or gender. But class barely registers in our collective consciousness, the social equivalent of a psychological disorder deeply buried in a patient's history.

This state of denial about class may be blinding the country to the unpleasant reality of an increasingly entrenched class system, one that pervades virtually every aspect of life in the United States, from separate schools and colleges to separate neighborhoods, shopping malls, TV shows, magazines, and even separate recreational pursuits. Despite its pervasiveness, the class divide in the United States is usually unacknowledged, mostly relegated to academic discussions and college courses in economic and political history. Americans sustain the belief that class conflict, biases, and privileges are at most a footnote of history, an interesting curiosity that has little or no bearing on current public problems.

Instead of doing something about brutal inequality, we simply embrace our national ideology, which, besides religion and money, is meritocracy. The backlash against college admissions reform in California and Texas illustrates this. Smacking of social Darwinism, the prevailing zeitgeist in twenty-first-century America, more than seventy-five years after the Great Depression almost destroyed American capitalism, is that what you get out of society is what you deserve. You're poor because it reflects the choices you've made in life. You're uneducated because of weakness and your addiction to the culture of poverty. Others are smart, well educated, and comfortably well off because they studied hard in school. Or, just as Tiger Woods was born to play golf or Michael Jordan to play basketball, some children are born to be high achievers. Born to do well on their LSATs, GREs, or MCATs and gain admission to a good graduate or professional school, these "cognitive elites" have worked hard to maintain their status on the proverbial bell curve, while others were born to join street gangs or attend community college.

Missing from that line of thinking are more salient pieces of background information that true believers in the supposed meritocracy prefer to ignore. What of a young person's family income and parents' educational background? What of the property values in the neighborhood where a child grows up—and their effect on the wealth and quality of the schools the child attends?

We've have seen how money, wealth, and family background are the most powerful predictors of a child's eventual success or lack of it in the American education system. As for those whose class backgrounds don't fit the prevailing rules of the meritocratic game—which largely benefit the children of well-educated and affluent professionals—they often don't make the Darwinian cut. For those who do make the cut, it's comforting to suspend any concerns that this brand of meritocracy might really be a game rigged in their favor.

———

But the meritocracy god may be just the modern version of the Horatio Alger notion of unbridled upward mobility, of an America that stands as the great exception to our highly stratified and class-bound cousins of Western Europe, the Old Europe that Tom Mortenson's ancestors abandoned for the limitless opportunities of the New World. The mobility myth has been such a deeply ingrained feature of the American character for so many generations that facts are unlikely to dislodge us from our collective dream state. After all, in what other country but America would 40 percent of adults believe that they either are or will be counted among the top 1 percent of the national income distribution?[1] While Americans hardly need to be reminded that wealth is unequally distributed among haves and have-nots, we seem certain that, eventually, we'll be among the haves. The social and economic fluidity of individual status and the possibility of reinventing ourselves, unshackled to the past, make up the quintessential American character. Of this, Alexis de Tocqueville observed in *Democracy in America*: "Among aristocratic nations, as families remain for centuries in the same condition, often on the same spot, all generations become, as it were, contemporaneous. . . . Among democratic nations [like the United States], new families are constantly springing up, others are constantly falling away, and all that remain change their condition."[2]

But much has happened, it seems, since the nineteenth century, and our collective self-image needs an extreme makeover. While de Tocqueville and other nineteenth-century observers were essentially correct that the new American nation was teeming with possibilities for upward mobility from one generation to the next, all that changed by the latter half of the twentieth century, when social class mobility in the United States began to look a lot like that in other industrialized nations. "Intergenerational occupational mobility in the U.S. clearly 'ain't what it used to be,' " economic historian Joseph P. Ferrie concluded after analyzing historical U.S. Census records for the National Bureau of Economic Research in 2005.[3]

Indeed, sociologists and economists now seem fairly certain that intergenerational mobility in modern times is even less dynamic than previously thought. For example, the Panel Study of Income Dynamics (PSID) is a rich database that has allowed researchers to follow the fortunes of a sample of some five thousand families since 1968. Until this information became available, researchers believed that only about 20 percent of the earnings of sons could be attributed to the economic status of their fathers, indicative of a relatively mobile society. But later measurements during the 1990s put the correlation between fathers' and sons' earnings at about 40 percent, suggestive of a moderately rigid class system.[4]

But even that number may be too low. Bhashkar Mazumder, an economist at the Federal Reserve Bank of Chicago, has analyzed an even richer source of generational income data from the federal government's Survey of Income and Program Participation, a nationally representative longitudinal survey of fifty thousand individuals and twenty thousand households. According to Mazumder, even the PSID was limited to just five years of income data for a given family, which meant that the numbers could be distorted by temporary financial shocks and setbacks. But the SIPP survey, which contains records on families' taxable income from 1958 through 1998, overcomes that problem, yielding a realistic picture of permanent income patterns and how the fortunes of one generation are connected to those of the next. If the economic fortunes of sons bore no relationship to their fathers—indicative of a perfectly mobile society—then the measured correlation between fathers' and sons' income would be zero. If American society were perfectly rigid and the fortunes of sons predetermined based on their fathers' social class, then the correlation would be 1. In fact, Mazumder found that the father-son income correlation was 0.6—indicating a society that is far more bound by social class than most Americans would dare to think.[5]

―――――

Add to the meritocracy myth and the upward mobility myth the happy talk of American popular culture, the grand sublimating force of our age, and you get the perfect formula for ensuring that class is kept in the closet of ancient and therefore irrelevant history.

Mass culture has functioned as a sort of decompression chamber for the release of American anxieties and bigotries about class, feelings that have virtually no other means for expression in U.S. society. Treatment of class in popular culture is often obtuse and passive-aggressive, but it's sufficiently entertaining and cathartic, and occasionally even funny enough, to disarm any serious confrontation of our growing class divide. Popular culture has co-opted the class question and trivialized it, making it just another small and endlessly amusing part of the spectacle. Mass culture imposes its own classless class system, where everyone, it seems, happens to be very well off. In the classless world, class isn't a matter of how much education you and your parents have or of the reach of your financial, social, and cultural capital—the hard assets of class status in the real world. Rather, class is what you consume. It's your Dodge Ram or your Audi Quattro. It's the *New Yorker* or *Guns & Ammo*. It's NASCAR or the PGA Tour. Class is a state of mind—or so we have been lulled into believing.

But then, in the fall of 2005, a hurricane hit Real America, and Happy America watched it on TV. Katrina hit with such ugly force in such a vulnerable place and time that, like a bucket of ice cold water viciously thrown at a slumbering and oblivious nation, we woke up to the strange and bizarre fact that, yes, Virginia, there are poor people. Possessing neither Dodge Rams nor Audis nor American Express cards, they were unable to escape the doomed city—and when Katrina hit, the impoverished residents of one of America's most storied cities looked on TV just like poor Africans or poor Mexicans. For the Happy American, who was pre-occupied with fear about whether the real estate bubble would pop investors' double-digit balloons, New Orleans was a curious, far-off spectacle that might just as well have been in Africa or Mexico.

Indeed, Happy America had already been successfully walled off from Real America, and one Category 5 storm wasn't going to disturb decades of tireless work by politicians, mass entertainment, and conventional news reporting, aimed at reinforcing the omnipresent and never-ending Huxleyan hypnopedia which maintains that America is a classless society, that anyone can become president with enough hard work and intelligence, that disadvantage in the free market economy is the result of not enough hard work and intelligence—and that it's taboo to question any of these propositions. And it's particularly taboo if you are running for political office. Of course, if you are a working-class white guy it *might* be in your best interest to question those propositions; and if you are rich and white, you'd better *not* question those propositions, lest you risk losing an awfully good gig.

Any hope that Happy America might actually have to confront the Real America laid bare by Katrina lasted about a day. "We've had a stunning reversal in just a few weeks," Robert Greenstein, director of the Center on Budget and Policy Priorities, told Jason DeParle of the *New York Times*. "We've gone from a situation in which we might have a long-overdue debate on deep poverty to the possibility, perhaps even the likelihood, that low-income people will be asked to bear the costs. I would find it unimaginable if it wasn't actually happening."[6]

Sorry to disappoint, Robert. But the new Gilded Age in America was just too much damned fun. For some of us, anyway. Indeed, the usual media accounts of the increasing concentration of wealth in the United States, released with predictable banality on page C-19 of the nation's leading newspapers, hardly conveyed the astounding sea change in the fortunes of the richest Americans.

The past two decades in particular have been the most beneficial to the wealthiest Americans, especially when they are compared to low-income and even middle-income Americans. In fact, when the population is sorted into five income quintiles, *all income groups except the top fifth saw their shares of the overall national income actually decline between 1977 and 1999* (see figure 12). For instance, the lower middle quintile of income earners saw their income shares decline from 11.5 percent in 1977 to 9.7 percent twenty years later. It was a far different story for the

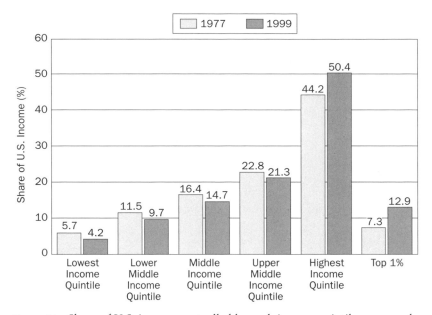

Figure 12. Share of U.S. income controlled by each income quintile, 1977 and 1999. Source: Isaac Shapiro and Robert Greenstein, "The Widening Income Gulf," Center on Budget and Policy Priorities, September 5, 1999, www.cbpp .org/9-4-99tax-rep.htm (accessed February 19, 2006).

richest Americans: the share held by the highest fifth jumped from 44.2 percent to 50.4 percent, and the income share of the top 1 percent nearly doubled, from 7.3 percent to 12.9 percent.[7]

Between 1970 and 1999, the average income of American taxpayers (adjusted for inflation) remained stuck between $30,000 and $35,000. In 1970, the average income of the top one hundred chief executive officers of U.S. corporations was approximately $125,000, about four times the U.S. average. While the average income of Americans didn't budge in real, inflation-adjusted terms during these years, CEO pay ballooned to 100 times the U.S. average in 1980 and 225 times the average in 1990. By 1999, the top one hundred CEOs averaged $40 million a year—1,142 times the salary of the average American.[8]

By the late 1990s, the United States had become the most unequal of all the advanced societies in the world, based on data from the Luxembourg Income Study, the definitive data source on household incomes for thirty-two nations between 1967 and 2002. According to Syracuse economist Timothy Smeeding's analysis of the LIS data:

- The average low-income American earned 38 percent of the U.S. median income. For the G-20 nations as a whole, in contrast, the equivalent figure was 49 percent. Sweden's typical low-income person earned 60 percent of that nation's median income.
- The average rich person in America earned 214 percent of the U.S. median income, while a rich person in Sweden earned 156 percent of the median.
- An individual in the top 10 percent of American income earners made almost six times as much money as a person in the bottom 10 percent—twice the same ratio in Sweden.
- The United States was more unequal than Britain, often held up as the class-bound society against which America represented the beacon of opportunity and egalitarianism.[9]

In addition to having the greatest income gaps between rich and poor among the advanced democracies, the United States also had the highest rates of poverty, particularly for children and older people. In a 2005 analysis of the LIS data, Smeeding concluded, "Comparative cross-national poverty rankings suggest that United States poverty rates are at or near the top of the range when compared with poverty rates in other rich countries. The United States child and elderly poverty rates seem particularly troublesome. . . . In most rich countries, the relative child poverty rate is 10 percent or less; in the United States, it is 21.9 percent." Smeeding also observed, "What seems most distinctive about the American poor, especially poor American single parents, is that they work more hours than do the resident parents of other nations while also receiving less in transfer benefits than in other countries."[10] Furthermore, according to a 2005 examination of the Luxembourg data by Lane Kenworthy at the University of Arizona and Jonas Pontusson at Cornell, between 1979 and 2000 not only did the United States have the highest disparity in income levels between the top 10 percent and the bottom 10 percent, but the growth of inequality in the United States was the greatest during that period.[11]

The principal rationalization for this level of disparity in the United States is that some inequality is a modest price to pay for the great economic efficiency and productivity that characterizes the American system. Indeed, America's gross domestic product per worker, the statistic most widely cited to illustrate U.S. economic prowess, is impressive compared to similar measures in other nations. But GDP per worker fails to account for joblessness and the number of hours that people in different countries actually work. When Harvard sociologist Christopher Jencks corrected for these problems, he found that America's real economic productivity was about the same as in France and Germany—two countries with significantly more economic equality than the United States.[12]

Smeeding and other economists point to the increasingly globalized world economy as a major reason why the affluent and highly educated in most advanced nations are getting richer while incomes of low-skilled and lower-income people stagnate. But that's not the end of the story. Scandinavian countries, in particular, have chosen to mitigate the economic losses at the bottom with gains from the top, leaving both groups still better off than they'd be without globalization. "Globalisation in rich nations," Smeeding writes, "appears to act more by raising incomes at the top of the income distribution than by lowering them at the bottom. Notwithstanding this influence, however, domestic policies—labour market institutions, welfare policies, etc.—can act as a powerful countervailing force to market-driven inequality. Even in a globalised world, the overall distribution of income in a country remains very much a consequence of the domestic political, institutional and economic choices made by those individual countries—both rich and middle-income ones."[13]

In their analysis of the Luxembourg data, Kenworthy and Pontusson looked at how the various advanced democracies responded to growing levels of "market inequality" created by the global marketplace. And they found that the U.S. response to growing inequality was virtually nonexistent, compared to the relatively aggressive moves made by many European nations to mitigate inequality. In other words, the United States had both the highest level of earnings inequality between rich and poor and the lowest percentage of GDP devoted to mitigating that inequality. Countries such as Denmark and Sweden were just the opposite, devoting the greatest percentage of GDP to social programs, thus creating societies with the lowest earnings gaps between rich and poor. "The American experience," Kenworthy and Pontusson explain, "appears to be exceptional" among advanced democracies in terms of responding to growing inequality. "The United States stands out as the one country in which increased market inequality did not produce any increase in redistribution."[14]

And that leaves us with the real legacy of Ronald Reagan, which has become a fixture of the U.S. political landscape: the ideology of scarcity. Its rationalizations ensure that Americans can't engage in a sustained conversation about class problems and simply cannot confront the dangerous levels of economic inequality that the market-based economy generates, even if we wanted to. Of course, we do want to. After all, our religious and moral beliefs tell us that we ought to. But we can't afford to. And even if we could afford to, we wouldn't want to, because helping the disadvantaged hurts the disadvantaged more than it helps them. In the richest nation on earth, when the question comes down to what our society is willing to expend to mitigate inequality—which we could easily afford if we made different choices with our vast wealth—then the false ideology of scarcity overtakes the political process. This myth of national impoverishment constricts the range of what is possible to what is politically expedient, from massive tax cuts for the wealthiest to merit scholarships to the children of the upper middle class.

Otherwise, triangulating Democrats might risk being called liberals or George W. Bush might be called not conservative enough and a traitor to the Reagan legacy.

The great charade, laid bare by the Katrina disaster, if only for forty-eight hours, is that Americans *perceive* the levels of inequality in our country to be modest compared to what they actually are. Chalk it up to the fact that we all wear the same designer jeans.

According to a 2005 study by the Organisation for Economic Co-operation and Development, citizens in various nations were asked about their perceptions of income inequality. The study compared those responses to actual measurements of economic inequality in the latter part of the 1990s. Among seventeen advanced nations, the Americans had the largest gap—by a wide margin—between the perception of inequality and its reality.[15]

And then there's this astonishing nugget. When Kenworthy and Pontusson, analyzing the Luxembourg data, plotted the degree of a nation's public expenditure on social programs against voter turnout, the United States essentially fell off the map, having both extremely low levels of voter turnout *and* low levels of social expenditure. The Netherlands topped all other advanced nations, with extremely high levels of both voter participation and social expenditure.[16]

But when you are among the 40 percent of American adults who believe they'll eventually rise to the top 1 percent of the economic heap, then voting—and voting one's interests—hardly seems necessary.

———

So where do we go from here? We've discussed what some institutions are doing to at least acknowledge the elephant in the room of educational opportunity. But breaking down the social class barriers in the education system is about far more than the isolated efforts of institutions and individuals. The final chapter broadens the focus to the nation at large. While individuals and institutions can continue to ignore the growing class divide—and perhaps even thrive in the ultra-competitive higher education marketplace by doing so—such a course could well lead to disaster for the nation as a whole. The question boils down to this: will we become a petrified, class-bound society in which only the privileged few can aspire to greater things, or will we truly become the beacon of opportunity that we now envision ourselves to be?

FIFTEEN

WHERE ARE WE GOING?

Forget the moral arguments about making America more socially and economically inclusive and less punitive to children who happen to have been born to poor parents. Forget the ideology of scarcity and the notion that colleges and universities, states and the federal government can't afford to embark on an ambitious strategy to diminish the widening opportunity gap between children born into privileged lives and those who are not. Instead, consider this simple truth: an untold amount of potential human talent in the United States is wasted as a consequence of an increasingly rigid class structure and the stagnant society it engenders.

But social class inequality isn't necessarily the problem. Inequality is inevitable. The problem is when public agencies, institutions, and enterprises, in addition to those private ones that owe their great wealth in part to the largesse of the public, systematically constrict educational opportunities for the disadvantaged while systematically enhancing opportunities for the already advantaged. The problem is when the public enterprise itself becomes subservient to elite interests.

As we've seen with kids like Ashlea Jackson and Melissa Morrow, part of this opportunity gap stems from the lack of cultural capital in families, the absence of basic knowledge and information about what it takes to succeed in school, get on the path to college, and stay on it. But the opportunity gap is rooted in economics. By the time children reach the end of middle school, they know where they fit in the class structure and what their opportunity horizon looks like. If they've never been given the assurance that graduating from a four-year college or university is a realistic financial possibility, they are not likely to take academics as seriously as they might otherwise. Many have never been allowed to dream that if they work hard in school and make good grades, they can earn a bachelor's degree at a minimum—or get equivalent vocational training—without having to face a lifetime of debt to do so. It may be, in the context of hundreds of billions of dollars in tax breaks to the wealthy and in the endless state of war the U.S. economy has been saddled with thus far in the twenty-first century, that the nation can't afford to close the opportunity gaps in the short run. But in the long run, the question becomes unavoidable: can the nation afford not to?

———

In March 2000, heads of state of the European Union met in Lisbon and declared that the EU would become "the most competitive and dynamic knowledge-based economy in the world" by 2010.[1] The purpose of what came to be known as the Lisbon Strategy was to join the European states around the common goal of making the collective economy more dynamic, more socially and economically inclusive, and less prone to the shocks that many European citizens have suffered from global competition. In addition to "a radical transformation" of the European economy, the heads of state said that by 2010 Europe "should be the world leader in terms of the quality of its education and training systems."[2]

Midway into this endeavor, in 2005, the novelty of a European Union was still evident, as recalcitrant member states were slow to get on board with the Lisbon Strategy, and the effort had achieved only patchy results. Still, in the spring of 2005, the European leaders reaffirmed and relaunched the Lisbon Strategy; and by October 2005, twenty-three of twenty-five member states had submitted their national plans for implementing the goal of overtaking the United States as the world's most dynamic economic force.[3] To be sure, the Lisbon Strategy is ambitious. But its fruition is hardly inconceivable. Just sixty years ago, after the Second World War, Europe was in tatters. Ever since, the prerogatives of shared economic well-being have slowly overcome sectarian national interests, and independent states have come together to methodically build a common European enterprise. The failure of the Lisbon Strategy to achieve its ambitious goals thus far should not be interpreted to mean that Europe lacks vast potential or that it can't supplant the United States over the next fifty years not only as the world's most dynamic economy but also as its most socially inclusive economy.

And it's not just the success or failure of the Lisbon Strategy that is important for Americans. The United States has reached a point in its economic and social history at which it seems legitimate to ask whether the American nation has reached its pinnacle. There are troubling signs that the United States at the turn of the new century is an increasingly stagnant, aging, and structured society. More so than we might care to think, America is looking a lot more like the Old Europe that Tom Mortenson's family left more than a century ago than the unwieldy, unpredictably egalitarian, and vibrant young nation that moved Alexis de Tocqueville to write *Democracy in America*. At the same time, there are indications that other countries with whom the United States must compete on the global stage are becoming more like America than America.

The Lisbon Strategy is just the tip of the iceberg. Consider what has already happened in recent years. In addition to intergenerational economic mobility—which, in America, seems to be diminishing, as the previous chapter points out—another measure of a society's economic and social dynamism, or stagnation, is the rate at which today's high school graduates go on to earn a college degree compared to the rate among older generations. Since World War II, the United States has led the world in graduation rates from four-year colleges. In the 1950s and 1960s, about 27 percent of young Americans—who reached ages fifty-five to sixty-four in 2003—earned bachelor's degrees. Among advanced nations, that was the world's highest rate of BA attainment at the time. In both Ireland and South Korea, in contrast, just 9 percent of those who turned fifty-five to sixty-four years old in 2003 had graduated from college.[4]

But U.S. rates of BA attainment have stagnated, while those of other advanced nations have flourished, catching up to the United States and, in some instances, exceeding it. Among Americans between the ages of twenty-five and thirty-four in 2003, 30 percent had earned at least a BA in the 1980s and 1990s—a gain of just 3 percentage points compared with the previous generation (see figure 13). In contrast, this same age cohort in some other nations showed dramatic increases in BA attainment: South Korea, where the college graduation rate went from 9 percent among the older generation to 30 percent today; Norway, whose graduation rate grew from 20 percent to 37 percent (the world's highest); Poland, which showed a rise from 11 percent to 20 percent; and Japan, whose rate increased from 12 percent to 26 percent. Among these and other countries belonging to the Organisation for Economic Co-operation and Development (OECD), only the United States, Germany, and Mexico recorded flat rates of BA attainment during these years.[5]

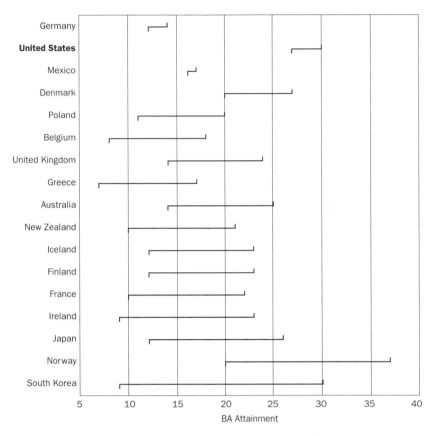

Figure 13. Earning college degrees: comparison of the previous generation with today's high school graduates, selected countries from the Organisation for Economic Co-operation and Development (OECD). Note: The previous generation is defined as those who completed high school during the 1950s and 1960s and reached ages fifty-five to sixty-four in 2003. The younger cohort is defined as those between the ages of twenty-five and thirty-four in 2003. Source: *Education at a Glance 2005*, Organisation for Economic Co-operation and Development, p. 36, www.oecd.org/document/34/0,2340,en_2649_201185_35289570_1_1_1_1,00.html (accessed October 12, 2006).

What's more, it is likely that in the years ahead, Americans will be less well educated than citizens in other advanced nations. As of 2001, 42 percent of American high school graduates continued on to four-year colleges and universities, well behind the average OECD college entry rate of 47 percent (see appendix A, figure A-15). In vivid contrast, 76 percent of New Zealand's high school graduates went on to four-year universities, as did 72 percent in Finland and 69 percent in Sweden. Even

Britain, the nation Americans like to portray as hobbled by the old habits of class, had higher rates of college-going than the United States.[6]

College-going rates at a given point in time are one indicator. But the changes in college-going rates among advanced societies since the late 1990s are even more ominous for the competitive position of the U.S. economy in the years ahead. Between 1998 and 2001, college-going among American high school graduates dropped 2 percentage points, compared to an average *gain* of 7 percentage points among all OECD countries. Iceland's college enrollment rate surged 23 points during that period, while such countries as Finland, Denmark, Australia, Hungary, and Sweden saw double-digit gains in rates of college entry (see appendix A, figure A-16).[7]

Then there's the rate of attaining degrees in natural science and engineering fields, which is considered a good indicator of a nation's potential capacity for future innovation. According to the National Science Foundation, the percentage of twenty-four-year-old Americans who earned science and engineering degrees has hardly budged in twenty-five years, going from 4 percent to 5.7 percent between 1975 and 2000. Compare that stagnation to rates in other advanced societies that Americans will have to compete against in the global economy for future employment and standards of living. For instance, Finland's number of science and engineering graduates as a percent of all twenty-four-year-olds rose from 4.1 percent to 13.2 percent; France's rate surged from 2.0 percent to 11.2 percent; and the United Kingdom's increased from 2.9 percent to 10.7 percent (see appendix A, figure A-17).[8]

Mathematics proficiency among high school students can also be seen as an indication of future innovation in science and engineering—and in this area, too, U.S. economic supremacy may be in its waning days. The Programme for International Student Assessment (PISA), undertaken by the OECD, shows that in 2003 just 10 percent of American fifteen-year-olds scored in the top levels in mathematics, considerably below the OECD average. Among the twenty-nine OECD countries that participated in the assessment, the United States ranked twenty-second. In contrast, almost a third of fifteen-year-olds in Belgium were assessed at the highest levels in math, as were at least 20 percent of students in countries such as the Netherlands, South Korea, Japan, Finland, Canada, and New Zealand (see appendix A, figure A-18).[9]

The PISA study also extensively analyzed the degree to which various countries have structured their education systems to mitigate the effects of a student's social class background. No matter the country, the data showed that socioeconomic background had a profound influence on the mathematics achievement of fifteen-year-olds. But high levels of academic achievement did not have to come at the cost of high levels of inequality. Indeed, some of the countries with the best-performing math students were also among the most equitable. By equitable, I mean that socioeconomic factors (such as parents' cultural, economic, and educational resources) contributed relatively less to students' academic achievement. To be sure, a few countries—Belgium, Germany, and the Slovak Republic—produced both relatively high achievement with relatively more inequality. But many more states had both high achievement levels and education systems that were relatively more equitable—including countries such as Australia, Finland, Japan, Norway, Spain, Hong Kong–China, Iceland, Canada, and, to a lesser extent, Italy and Russia. For its part, the United States earned its relatively weak performance in math achievement with a level of inequality that was about average for all OECD countries, placing it on a par with Luxembourg, Poland, and Portugal.[10]

Can a nation in which educational attainment is increasingly concentrated among the elite continue to reproduce a middle-class standard of living for the majority of citizens?

Revisit for a moment the extent of that concentration (as shown in figure 14):

- An American eighth grader in 1988 whose family was in the lowest socioeconomic quartile had only a 6.9 percent chance of earning a bachelor's degree twelve years later and almost a zero percent chance of earning a master's degree. That eighth grader had nearly a 50 percent probability of not going to college at all.
- An eighth grader in 1988 in the highest socioeconomic quartile had a 51 percent chance of completing a BA twelve years later and an 8.6 percent chance of earning at least a master's degree. That eighth grader had just a 4.4 percent chance of not going to college.[11]

An astonishing aspect of these disparities is that the economic payoffs for educational achievement, both to individuals and to society, have been large and growing larger since the mid-1970s. For instance, from 1975 through 1999, Americans with bachelor's degrees earned incomes

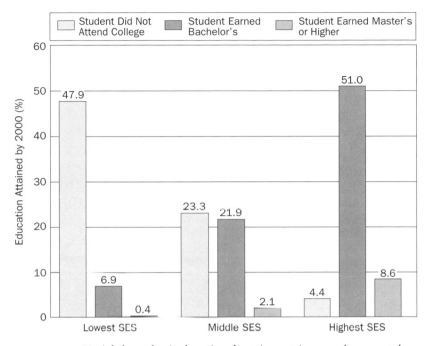

Figure 14. 1988 eighth graders' educational attainment in 2000, by parental socioeconomic status. Source: U.S. Department of Education, National Center for Education Statistics, *Coming of Age in the 1990s: The Eighth-Grade Class of 1988, 12 Years Later,* by Steven J. Ingels, T. R. Curtin, Phillip Kaufman, Martha Naomi Alt, Xianglei Chen, and Jeffrey A. Owings, NCES 2002–321 (Washington, D.C.: U.S. Government Printing Office, 2002), p. 43.

between 1.5 and 1.7 times the earnings of a person with a high school diploma. And the more education, the bigger the gap. In 1977, Americans with advanced degrees earned about 1.7 times what those with a high school diploma earned. In 1994, the gap peaked: people with advanced degrees earned almost 3 times the salary of a high school graduate.[12] In dollar amounts, a high school diploma in 2003 could produce median earnings of $30,800. That figure, according to recent calculations by the Economic Policy Institute, was about $4,000 less than a family of four living in Baltimore would need to cover just basic needs and live in safe and decent surroundings. In contrast, a professional degree yielded a median salary of $95,700 (see figure 15).[13]

What accounts for such huge pay disparities between the educated and the uneducated in a nation of supposedly limitless opportunity, where, according to conventional wisdom, anybody who wants an education

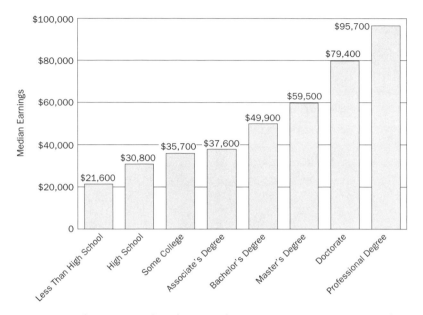

Figure 15. Median earnings by educational attainment, 2003. Source: Sandy Baum and Kathleen Payea, *Education Pays 2004: The Benefits of Higher Education for Individuals and Society* (Washington, D.C.: College Board, 2004), p. 10, www.collegeboard.com/prod_downloads/press/cost04/Education-Pays2004.pdf (accessed February 19, 2006).

can get one? Either disadvantaged children and their parents don't understand how significantly their prospects are diminished without higher education, or they do understand but don't take the steps necessary to get on the path to higher education because of financial, cultural, informational, and other intangible barriers. In either case, these large and growing earnings gaps tied to educational level—earnings that can lead either to a middle- or upper-middle-class existence or to a subsistence-level lifestyle, at best—reveal a human capital economy that is burdened with excessive "friction," as economists say, lacking sufficient institutional grease to permit human talent to reach its full potential.

This is not rocket science. A society can rationally choose to create the necessary institutional arrangements up front, in ways that enhance creativity, innovation, and, ultimately, economic well-being for the most people possible. Or that society can pay even more on the back end for maintaining institutions that subtract from economic productivity, preoccupied with cleaning up the social problems associated with treating precious human capital like so many cattle.

A nation of highly educated citizens isn't a zero-sum game—gains at the bottom of the income distribution don't have to come from losses at the top. More highly educated people contribute to the whole, and, what's more, they help to grow the entire national enterprise. Call it "trickle-up economics": educated people behave in ways that reflect a middle-class life in the real world, not the happy-face world of an illusory middle class in which all who passively partake in the spectacle of popular and consumer culture can count themselves as part of the American mainstream because they can buy designer jeans on credit or worship an *American Idol* on TV. As Tom Mortenson argues, we're better off when we're all better off. Educated people are jobless less often. They receive public assistance far less often. They report better health at all ages throughout their lifetimes and are incarcerated at a fraction of the rate of less educated people. And educated people vote. They vote at far higher rates than less educated people in all age groups. Fully six in ten American young people eighteen to twenty-four years old who graduated from college voted in 2000. That was almost three and a half times the voting rate for those of the same age with less than a high school diploma.[14]

Policy makers, of course, know these things. But when it comes to education reform and public policy priorities, they have often acted in recent years as if they know nothing about these issues.

––––––––

In April 1983, the Reagan administration issued a prominent report titled *A Nation at Risk: The Imperative for Education Reform.* This effort got some things right, recommending, for instance, that high school students be required to take a more challenging and comprehensive curriculum in order to prepare for higher education and the world of work. The *Risk* report surely fed into a dissatisfaction about the state of the U.S. education system, appealing to Americans' sense that the system wasn't working as it should.

Risk essentially was the launching point of the modern standards and accountability movement as Americans know it today, culminating in George W. Bush's No Child Left Behind Act, which Congress overwhelmingly approved in 2001. But by targeting academic performance and standards—relying on widespread standardized testing of schoolchildren to achieve its objectives—*Risk* and its progeny failed to produce genuine change because they committed a cardinal sin of policy reform: both focused on the effects of an education system at risk, and not on the root causes of the problem.

The standards movement, as it came to be called, got off on the wrong track from the beginning. It has failed to understand that, at its highest levels, the American school system is among the best in the world because affluent parents ensure that their children have access to the best schools, the most experienced teachers, the most well-informed college counselors, and all the best of everything else that money really can buy, despite the assertions of conservatives that money doesn't matter when it comes to school improvement. The standards movement remains insufficiently comprehensive. The cultural and financial capital that families provide children at home contributes as much or more to the academic success of schools and children than anything schools themselves could provide alone. And no amount of standards and testing can change that.

Indeed, the standards movement has its eyes on the wrong prize. By narrowly focusing on test results and standards, it fails to define the problem in the clearest possible terms: for the sake of the nation's future economic productivity, for the sake of individual children making the most of their natural talents, schools need to provide disadvantaged children what they are often unable to get from home. Children need a *reason* for wanting to go to school, to do well in school, and to go as far in school as their skills and talents permit. For the nation, the real prize would be getting more disadvantaged children interested in higher education and aware that more education would lead to better lives. The standards movement, in the end, fails to comprehend that traditional American schools, permeated with a middle-class mindset and middle-class pedagogy, lack the intellectual tools and resources to do that job. And even when schools have the intellectual tools, inspired by innovative administrators and teachers who motivate kids to a genuine love of learning, their efforts get beaten down by NCLB's federally imposed imperative to raise test scores or else.

Finally, the standards movement has failed to recognize that educational inequalities have been a direct result of America's growing economic divide. For instance, in a series of working papers examining the relationship between the nation's growing economic disparities and educational attainment, Susan E. Mayer of the University of Chicago writes that greater economic inequality, operating through increased economic segregation between rich and poor neighborhoods, has produced educational gains for affluent children and educational losses for children from low-income families.[15]

This carries the profound implication that economic policy and educational policy can't be separated. It means that budgetary and taxation measures that exacerbate economic inequality, such as those enacted under the administration of George W. Bush, may be working at cross-purposes with educational programs that hope to diminish the achievement gaps between advantaged and disadvantaged groups. Thus, without complementary economic policies that reduce economic inequality between haves and have-nots, educational policies like No Child Left Behind are tantamount to foolishly running on a treadmill.

It's time to fix what *Risk* and No Child Left Behind got wrong. And doing that requires nothing less than a Sputnik-like commitment to the nation's investment in higher education, making a four-year college degree the requisite credential for full participation in the American experience in the twenty-first century. The United States needs its own Lisbon Strategy, and the educational component must be aimed at children who, without such a national effort, *will* be left behind in the global economy. Of that, we can be certain.

I don't mean to suggest that higher education should be a universal attainment. But it should be a universal opportunity. After the Second World War, the notion of equality of educational opportunity became a linchpin of higher education policy in the United States. It has been one of the few features of American social policy that historically has worked as a progressive check against the deleterious effects of market capitalism. The United States has never been like Sweden or Denmark, both social democratic states in which citizens are entitled to a humane and decent standard of living. America's social humanity has come not from universal health care or income-maintenance programs. Rather, it has come from the ability of have-nots to rise in the world through education. But that ideal of equal opportunity is in danger because the United States is rapidly becoming a petrified society where only the affluent can get ahead. When that happens, we all lose, because the nation will be left behind in the global marketplace, surpassed by the more dynamic, educated, innovative—and equitable—societies that are now rapidly advancing on the world stage.

Making higher education a universal opportunity means educating at-risk children and their families about what it will take to get to college, and doing so from sufficiently young ages to make a difference.

It means creating schools that promote a lifelong love of learning, not schools that simply prep kids for the next standardized test.

It means overhauling the admissions procedures of colleges and universities, not rigging admissions rules so that affluent students almost always win and disadvantaged students almost always fail.

It means ensuring that college financial aid systems provide an adequate floor of support based on *actual need,* not on social class disguised as merit.

And it means confronting some cold, hard demographic facts. In the years ahead, according to widely acknowledged population trends in American society, groups of people now at the bottom of the nation's social, economic, and educational hierarchy will come to dominate the nation's population growth. People who are now underrepresented in American colleges and universities will make up much higher percentages of high school graduates. Should college attendance and educational attainment among these growing groups continue to stagnate, the nation can fully expect to suffer the brutal economic consequences. As more disadvantaged people go through the educational pipeline without graduating from high school or earning a college degree, total incomes and salaries will stagnate or decline, state budgets will have to be cut in response to declining tax bases, and public services from health care to education will need to be reduced in a vicious cycle of diminishing resources.

For example, accounting for population trends of various underrepresented ethnic groups and their current rates of educational attainment, Patrick J. Kelly of the National Center for Higher Education Management Systems projects that between 2000 and 2020, the number of Americans with less than a high school degree will surge by an additional 7.3 million; and those with just a high school diploma will grow by almost 5 million, dwarfing the 2.3 million additional people earning a bachelor's degree during that period. Because less educated people earn less money, national personal income will take a hit of some $400, on average, for every person in the country, translating to a $1.2 trillion loss for a nation of 300 million people. Several states in which the demographic challenges are most severe will suffer staggering declines in per capita personal income: almost $2,500 in California; nearly $1,200 in New York; and about $1,000 per person in states such as Texas, Connecticut, and New Jersey. "Given these conditions, it is highly improbable that 'business as usual' will get us where we need to be," Kelly's report concludes. "State policymakers not only must become more aware of these disparities but they also must understand what is likely to happen if they are not addressed. They must grasp the social and economic impacts of ignoring the problem."[16]

To be sure, there are some promising developments. Clearly, some educational leaders have recognized that the deepening class divide at their own institutions reflects some ominous trends that don't portend well for the country. Despite their perceived need to build empires and place highly in the *U.S. News* rankings game, some institutions are trying to confront this emerging crisis. In recent years, several elite institutions with enormous endowments have decided to use a portion of their wealth to reduce the financial burden to students from lower-income families. At Harvard, for instance, families earning $60,000 or less will no longer be expected to contribute to their child's college costs. Yale and Stanford have adopted similar programs, but with lower income cut-offs. Princeton, the University of Pennsylvania, and Brown have replaced loans with grants for some students from lower-income families. MIT created an aid program that matches the $4,050 Pell Grants of its low-income students.[17] With a $75 million private donation, Duke University will designate that money for need-based financial aid, and the university hopes to double the amount in future fund-raising.[18] Other programs are even more ambitious. The University of North Carolina at Chapel Hill has created the Carolina Covenant, which promises to pay 100 percent of a needy student's college costs in the form of grants and work-study, allowing lower-income students to obtain their degrees without going into debt. The University of Virginia has set up a similar program called Access UVa.

As important as such programs are, they address only one aspect of the increasing class stratification in American higher education. In order to qualify for debt-free aid from a university such as Duke, the University of North Carolina, or Harvard, one must, of course, be admitted to these institutions. And the fact remains that, under the entrenched rules of academic merit, disadvantaged students have but a small chance of being admitted unless colleges and universities become far more aggressive at challenging the *U.S. News and World Report* mentality regarding academic quality and institutional prestige. Median SAT scores should not be the last word in evaluating an institution's academic quality and the sorts of learning and teaching experiences one is likely to find there.

Along these lines, the *U.S. News* emperor is being defrocked on a number of new fronts, and it may be just a matter of time before some sanity is restored to the higher education rankings game. For instance, the news magazine *Washington Monthly* launched its own college rankings issue in September 2005, one that assesses how well colleges and universities serve some larger public good, including a university's community service and enrollments of lower-income students. "Of course universities ought to be judged," the magazine's editors wrote in unveiling the first rankings issue. "The key is judging the right things."[19] Indeed, the *Washington Monthly* ranking revealed some interesting departures from its *U.S. News* counterpart. MIT, which ranked seventh in *U.S. News* rankings, jumped to the top slot under the *Monthly*'s new paradigm. UCLA, which *U.S. News* ranked twenty-fifth, climbed to the second spot; and two other University of California campuses, at Berkeley and San Diego—both well down on the *U.S. News* list—jumped into the top ten. Losers under the *Monthly*'s methodology were several elite private institutions that have a bleak record of serving lower-income students. This included Harvard, which fell from first to fourteenth.

Another important challenge to prestige-driven ranking systems is a survey known as the National Survey of Student Engagement, known as "Nessie." The annual survey, based at Indiana University, attempts to answer a basic question: what do students actually gain from spending four or more years at a school in terms of their personal and intellectual development? That's a far different question than the premise of the *U.S. News* survey, in which the most important predictor of a college's rank is the median SAT scores of its entering freshmen—the institution's selectivity. In fact, according to academic studies, once an institution's freshman SAT scores are accounted for, all remaining fifteen or so "quality" factors in the *U.S. News* ranking system are virtually meaningless in explaining where an institution ranks on the list. Using the Nessie survey, scholars have been able to demonstrate quite clearly that institutional selectivity, and therefore how a college performs on the *U.S. News* list, bears almost no relationship to the personal and intellectual development of students at a given institution. "National magazines that purport to identify the nation's 'best' colleges are essentially ranking institutions by their selectivity, not by the likelihood of their exposing students to the most effective educational practices," write George Kuh, who directs the Nessie survey at Indiana, and his co-author Ernest T. Pascarella. "Given the challenges facing the nation and the higher education system, it's time for some straight talk about the deleterious grip that selectivity has had on our perceptions of what constitutes collegiate quality. It's bad public policy and educationally indefensible."[20]

The Nessie survey, the *Washington Monthly* approach, and a growing number of independent efforts, including a new database developed by the Institute for College Access and Success that tracks economic diversity at educational institutions, are potentially powerful resources for helping the public hold colleges and universities accountable to the public good.

———

I must make a final, mighty tilt at the windmill by suggesting that for any educational reform to really happen, in earnest, America will have to confront its class problem. And, like an alcoholic who must first admit that he or she is an alcoholic, part of America's class problem is that Americans collectively believe that there is no class problem. There's a conspiracy of silence about class among opinion leaders, politicians, and policy makers that is perpetuated by both the political left and right. Whether progressive Democrats or right-wing Republicans, these opinion shapers and agenda setters effectively suppress the discussion of class because neither side sees such a debate as serving its best political interests.

Indeed, Republicans' suppression of economic inequality has been a finely tuned political art since the late 1960s. Recall Richard Nixon's so-called southern strategy, which converted longtime Democratic strongholds in the South into bastions of Republicanism. This strategy appealed to festering white anger and racism in the wake of the historic civil rights movement that turned the segregated South upside down. As a political strategy, the southern strategy was more than a success; it was a revolution. And Republicans from Nixon to Reagan to George W. Bush have employed its racially loaded code of "states' rights" and "cultural values" to keep working-class and poor southern whites from talking about such nasty topics as jobs, income inequality, health care, and education and to prevent them from voting in ways that would be more consistent with their own economic well-being.

By continuing to use race as a wedge between southern whites and blacks, the Republican strategy has kept at bay a potential time bomb that would truly upend the American political landscape: a potent coalition of disadvantaged whites and blacks in the South who realize that they have far more in common with one another than not, especially in a global economy where American jobs are being shipped out to such faraway places as India and China.

The Republican Party has masterfully turned economic despair into a nonissue in much of the South and the West. Consider the southern and western states that voted overwhelmingly for George W. Bush in the 2004 presidential election, and then consider the impoverished social and economic circumstances in those states.

- Among the ten poorest states in terms of median income between 2002 and 2004, all but two—Montana and New Mexico—were southern states; and all ten were easily carried by Bush in his contest with John Kerry.

- Of the ten states with the highest rates of poverty, seven were southern; and all of them voted overwhelmingly for the Republican.

- Of the ten states with the poorest records of health insurance coverage for their citizens, all were in the South and the West; and all of them except California voted for Bush.[21]

- Of the ten states with the nation's lowest percentages of low-income students attending college in 2004, all were in the South and the West; and all of them were squarely in the Republican camp.[22]

But when it comes to confronting class questions, the elites in the Democratic Party are often just as willing as the elites of the Republican Party to change the subject. The Democratic blind spot toward class came into sharp focus in the 2004 presidential primary season. That is when former Vermont governor Howard Dean, in an interview published in the *Des Moines Register* in the fall of 2003, said this: "I still want to be the candidate for guys with Confederate flags in their pickup trucks. We can't beat George Bush unless we appeal to a broad cross-section of Democrats." In fact, he had been saying similar things throughout his upstart campaign. In an earlier speech to the Democratic National Committee, for instance, Dean said, "White folks in the South who drive pickup trucks with Confederate flag decals on the back ought to be voting with us, and not [Republicans], because their kids don't have health insurance either, and their kids need better schools too." He received a rousing ovation.[23]

But it was only after Dean became the frontrunner that his rivals in the Democratic primary pounced. While Dean was making a powerful point about the politics of class in America, the Democratic establishment immediately turned it into a tiff about race. John Edwards, a North Carolinian, took Dean to task for stereotyping southern whites. Al Sharpton all but called Dean a racist. Of course, none of Dean's competitors really believed any of their own posturing, but their theatrics raised enough of a ruckus, feeding into the horse-race mentality of the media's election coverage, that they damaged Dean badly; and the potentially explosive debate about class inequality, which might have upended the balance of political power in the Republican South and West, got buried.

Dean's political ear was tin, but his analysis was spot on. Democrats, who claim they care about economic inequality, health care, good jobs, and educational opportunity for all, will continue to have a difficult time making that message stick in the parts of white, black, and brown America that are in most desperate need until the party can moderate its instinctive need to frame social and economic inequality strictly along racial lines. Even though race still plays an undeniably powerful role in economic inequality, as the TV images of African American families baking in the sun on New Orleans's rooftops so potently illustrated after Hurricane Katrina, race as a political strategy may have run its course. Not since the 1960s civil rights movement, when blacks had the backing of educated whites and idealistic white college students, has race been an effective means to leverage political power. In the past few decades, many of those same whites have virtually disappeared as potential allies of the disadvantaged. At best, elite whites have become indifferent to economic and educational inequality. Or worse, they challenge attempts to equalize educational opportunity because that is seen as a threat to their own entitlements in the new Gilded Age. They have circled their baby strollers and turned inward, consumed with their stock portfolios, their gated communities, and how to get their kids into Harvard.

Since disadvantaged minorities can no longer depend on white idealism or altruism, other allies are necessary; and their most natural political allies are the disadvantaged whites who share their economic misfortune. Ironically, the most productive way for racial minorities to advance their economic interests may be to reach out to disenfranchised whites, talk a bit less about America's race problem, and start talking a lot more about America's class problem. The reverse also holds true.

If Howard Dean became a dangerous man when he started to talk about the common interests of poor people, he wasn't the first to pay a price for doing so. Martin Luther King Jr. and Robert F. Kennedy, of course, paid the ultimate price. Both men were killed at a time when they began to talk far more pointedly about economic inequality as the root cause of America's racial problems. "Always," writes Richard D. Kahlenberg, "Kennedy emphasized the common ground between poor and working-class blacks and whites." The astonishing aspect of

Kennedy's success, Kahlenberg notes, is that Kennedy was able to forge this coalition at the most racially turbulent moment in U.S. history in the late 1960s.[24]

Dean's analysis was nearly identical to what King himself was saying in some of his later speeches and sermons before he was assassinated on April 4, 1968. King, who was becoming increasingly radical in his analysis of the U.S. economic system, told the convention of the Southern Christian Leadership Conference in August 1967, "We must honestly face the fact that the movement must address itself to the question of restructuring the whole of American society. There are forty million poor people here, and one day we must ask the question, 'Why are there forty million poor people in America?' And when you begin to ask that question, you are raising a question about the economic system, about a broader distribution of wealth. When you ask that question, you begin to question the capitalistic economy."[25] Then, in February 1968, in his famous sermon "The Drum Major Instinct," King spoke of his time in a Birmingham jail, chatting with his white wardens, and how he got to "do a little converting" while he was in prison. King told his parishioners at Atlanta's Ebenezer Baptist Church:

> So I would get to preaching, and we would get to talking—calmly, because they wanted to talk about it. And then we got down one day to the point—that was the second or third day—to talk about where they lived, and how much they were earning. And when those brothers told me what they were earning, I said, "Now, you know what? You ought to be marching with us. You're just as poor as Negroes." And I said, "You are put in the position of supporting your oppressor, because through prejudice and blindness, you fail to see that the same forces that oppress Negroes in American society oppress poor white people. And all you are living on is the satisfaction of your skin being white, and the drum major instinct of thinking that you are somebody big because you are white. And you're so poor you can't send your children to school. You ought to be out here marching with every one of us every time we have a march."[26]

As I write this, another Martin Luther King Jr. holiday has just passed, and the local university in the town where I live has just had another day of remembrance with films, speakers, and presentations. These events pass by, year after year, with predictable regularity, as King's words are memorialized and ossified into beautiful shrines that permit the well-educated and relatively affluent people who attend the ceremonies to feel good about themselves.

One can't help but feel that something is missing, something true and vital about how King's life might apply to the here and now. These remembrances of King's past don't even take up where King himself left off, when he brought his project to the brink of being a genuine poor people's movement that would tear down color and class lines. That project is still not done, and it remains to be seen whether America's loss of King and Kennedy was the end of our last best hope. If America's problem of the last century was the problem of the color line, as W. E. B. DuBois put it, then America's problem of the twenty-first century is the problem of the class line.

APPENDIX A

SUPPLEMENTARY FIGURES

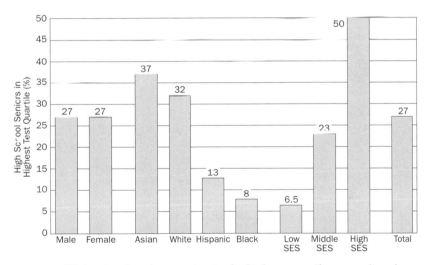

Figure A-1. High school seniors scoring in the highest quartile on math and achievement tests, by gender, race, and socioeconomic status, 1992. Source: U.S. Department of Education, National Center for Education Statistics, *National Educational Longitudinal Study 1988: Trends among High School Seniors, 1972–1992*, NCES 95–380 (Washington, D.C.: U.S. Government Printing Office, 1995), http://nces.ed.gov/pubsearch/pubsinfo.asp?pubid=95380 (accessed September 2006).

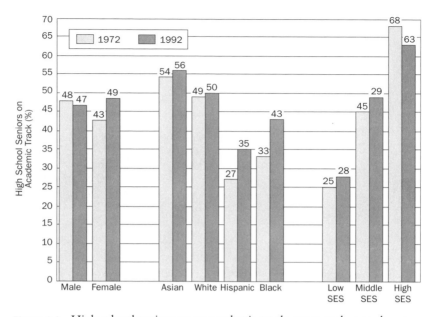

Figure A-2. High school seniors on an academic track, 1972 and 1992, by gender, race, and socioeconomic status. Source: U.S. Department of Education, National Center for Education Statistics, *National Educational Longitudinal Study 1988: Trends among High School Seniors, 1972–1992*, NCES 95–380 (Washington, D.C.: U.S. Government Printing Office, 1995), http://nces.ed.gov/pubsearch/pubsinfo.asp?pubid=95380 (accessed September 2006).

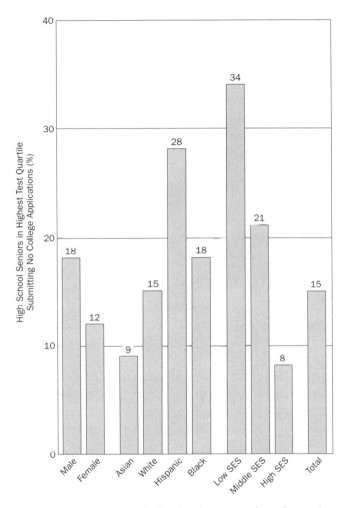

Figure A-3. High-scoring high school seniors who submitted no college applications, by gender, race, and socioeconomic status, 1992. Source: U.S. Department of Education, National Center for Education Statistics, *National Educational Longitudinal Study 1988–1994: Descriptive Summary Report,* by Allen Sanderson, Bernard Dugoni, Kenneth Rasinsky, John Taylor, and C. Dennis Carroll, NCES 96–175 (Washington, D.C.: U.S. Government Printing Office, 1996).

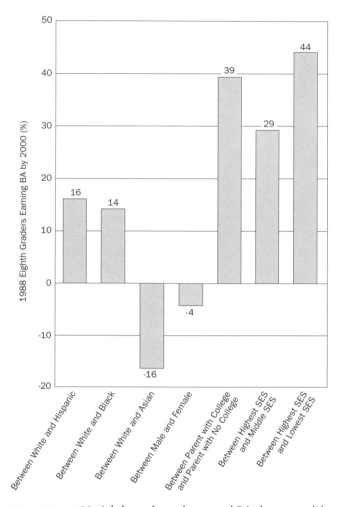

Figure A-4. 1988 eighth graders who earned BAs by 2000, differences between paired demographic groups. Source: U.S. Department of Education, National Center for Education Statistics, *Coming of Age in the 1990s: The Eighth-Grade Class of 1988, 12 Years Later,* by Steven J. Ingels, T. R. Curtin, Phillip Kaufman, Martha Naomi Alt, Xianglei Chen, and Jeffrey A. Owings, NCES 2002–321 (Washington, D.C.: U.S. Government Printing Office, 2002).

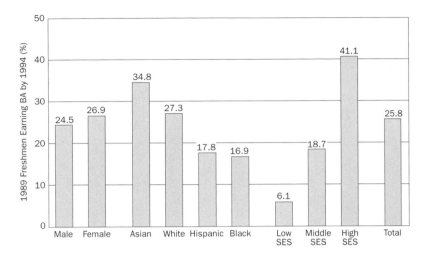

Figure A-5. 1989 college freshmen who earned BAs by spring 1994, by gender, race, and socioeconomic status. Source: U.S. Department of Education, National Center for Education Statistics, *Descriptive Summary of 1989–90 Beginning Postsecondary Students: Five Years Later—Statistical Analysis Report, March 1996,* by Lutz K. Berkner, Stephanie Cuccaro-Alamin, and Alexander C. McCormick, NCES 96–155 (Washington, D.C.: U.S. Government Printing Office, 1996), table 1.3, p. 34, http://nces.ed.gov/pubs/96155all.pdf (accessed February 14, 2006).

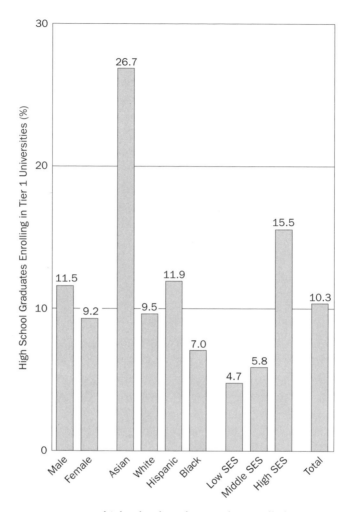

Figure A-6. 1992 high school graduates who enrolled in U.S. Tier 1 universities, by gender, race, and socioeconomic status. Source: U.S. Department of Education, National Center for Education Statistics, *Who Goes to America's Highly Ranked National Universities?* by Jeffrey Owings, Timothy Madigan, and Bruce Daniel, NCES 98–095 (Washington, D.C.: U.S. Government Printing Office, 1998).

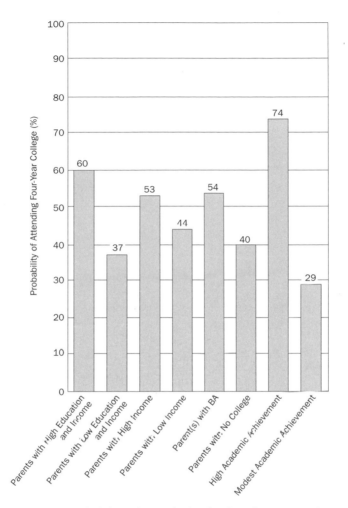

Figure A-7. Probability of 1992 high school graduates attending a four-year college, by socioeconomic factors and academic achievement. Source: David T. Ellwood and Thomas J. Kane, "Who Is Getting a College Education? Family Background and the Growing Gaps in Enrollment," in *Securing the Future: Investing in Children from Birth to College*, ed. Sheldon Danzinger and Jane Waldfogel (New York: Russell Sage Foundation, 2000), pp. 283–313.

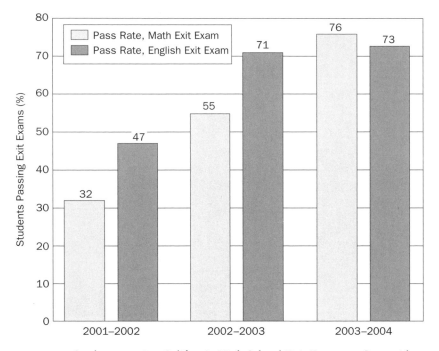

Figure A-8. Students passing California High School Exit Exams at Oceanside High School, 2001–2002 to 2003–2004. Source: Dayle Mazzarella, Oceanside High School, unpublished summary data provided to author.

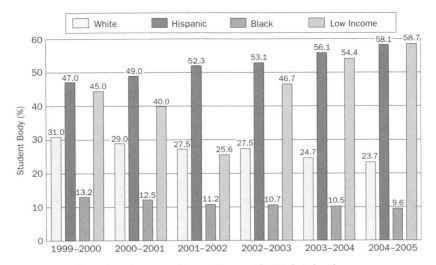

Figure A-9. Changing demographics at Oceanside High School, 1999–2000 to 2004–2005. Source: California Department of Education, "School Demographic Characteristics: 2004–05 Academic Performance Index (API) Growth Report," http://data1.cde.ca.gov/dataquest/, report generated by author, December 2005.

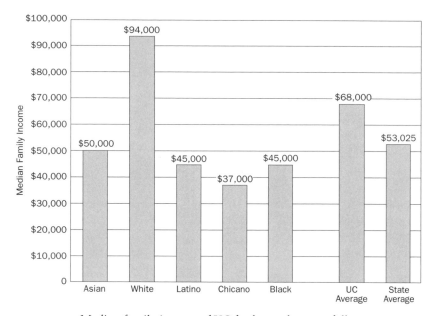

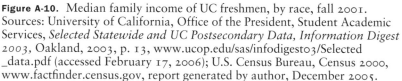

Figure A-10. Median family income of UC freshmen, by race, fall 2001. Sources: University of California, Office of the President, Student Academic Services, *Selected Statewide and UC Postsecondary Data, Information Digest 2003*, Oakland, 2003, p. 13, www.ucop.edu/sas/infodigest03/Selected _data.pdf (accessed February 17, 2006); U.S. Census Bureau, Census 2000, www.factfinder.census.gov, report generated by author, December 2005.

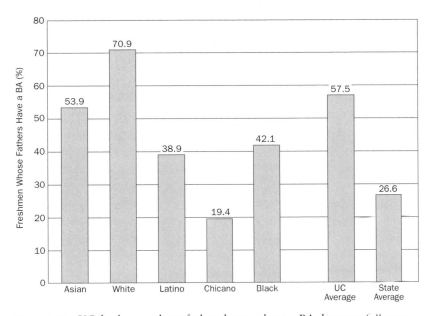

Figure A-11. UC freshmen whose fathers have at least a BA, by race, fall 2001. Sources: University of California, Office of the President, Student Academic Services, *Selected Statewide and UC Postsecondary Data, Information Digest 2003,* Oakland, 2003, p. 13, www.ucop.edu/sas/infodigest03/Selected _data.pdf (accessed February 17, 2006); U.S. Census Bureau, Census 2000, www.factfinder.census.gov, report generated by author, December 2005.

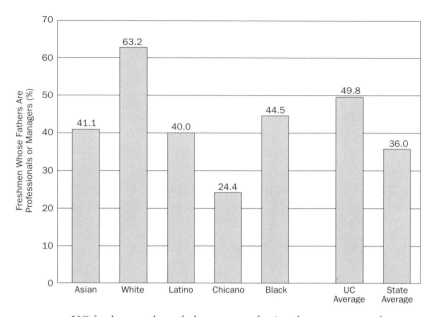

Figure A-12. UC freshmen whose fathers are professionals or managers, by race, fall 2001. Source: University of California, Office of the President, Student Academic Services, *Selected Statewide and UC Postsecondary Data, Information Digest 2003,* Oakland, 2003, p. 13, www.ucop.edu/sas/ infodigest03/Selected_data.pdf (accessed February 17, 2006); U.S. Census Bureau, Census 2000, www.factfinder.census.gov, report generated by author, December 2005.

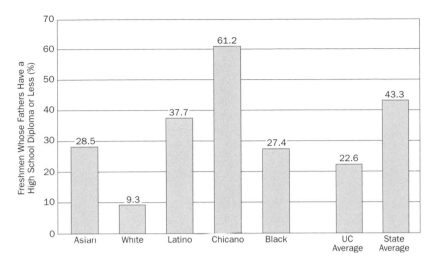

Figure A-13. UC freshmen whose fathers have only a high school diploma or less, by race, fall 2001. Sources: University of California, Office of the President, Student Academic Services, *Selected Statewide and UC Postsecondary Data, Information Digest 2003*, Oakland, 2003, p. 13, www.ucop.edu/sas/infodigest03/Selected_data.pdf (accessed February 17, 2006); U.S. Census Bureau, Census 2000, www.factfinder.census.gov, report generated by author, December 2005.

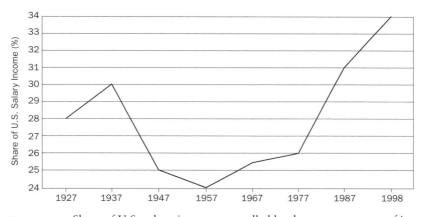

Figure A-14. Share of U.S. salary income controlled by the top 10 percent of income earners, 1927 to 1998. Source: Thomas Piketty and Emmanuel Saez, "Income Inequality in the United States, 1913–1998," National Bureau of Economic Research, NBER Working Paper 8467, September 2001, p. 74, fig. 13, www.nber.org/papers/w8467 (accessed January 2005).

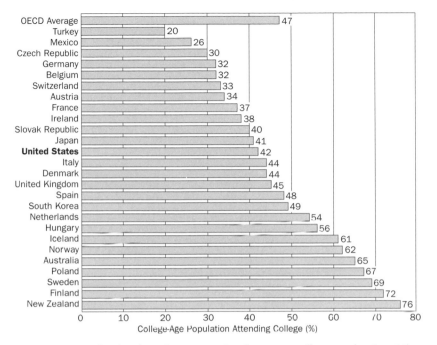

Figure A-15. High school graduates entering four-year colleges and universities, selected countries from the Organisation for Economic Co-operation and Development (OECD), 2001. Source: Thomas Mortenson, "International Comparisons of 4-Year College Continuation Rates, 1998 and 2001," *Postsecondary Education Opportunity* 144 (June 2004): 11.

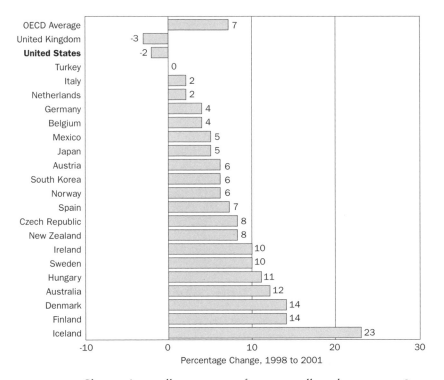

Figure A-16. Changes in enrollment rates at four-year colleges between 1998 and 2001, selected countries from the Organisation for Economic Co-operation and Development (OECD). Source: Thomas Mortenson, "International Comparisons of 4-Year College Continuation Rates, 1998 and 2001," *Postsecondary Education Opportunity* 144 (June 2004): 11.

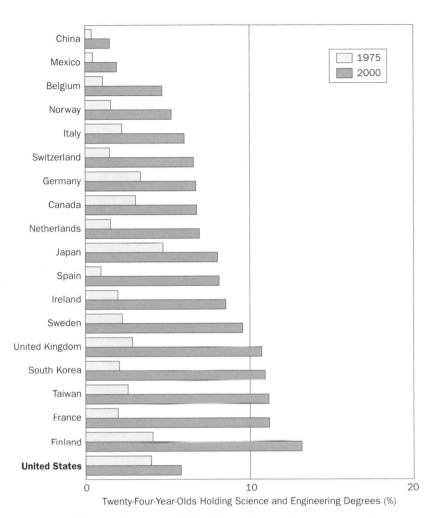

Figure A-17. Twenty-four-year-olds holding science and engineering degrees, selected countries, 1975 and 2000. Source: National Science Foundation, Division of Science Resources and Statistics, *Science and Engineering Indicators 2004*, Arlington, Va., 2004, www.nsf.gov/statistics/seind04/c0/fig00-20.htm (accessed January 2006).

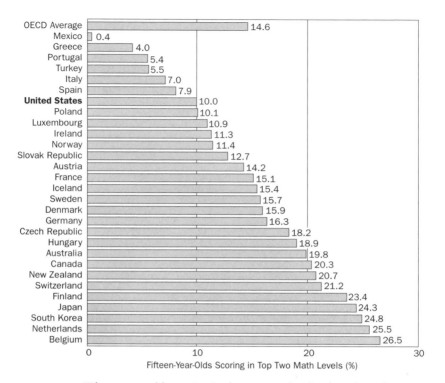

Figure A-18. Fifteen-year-olds scoring in the top two levels of math proficiency, selected countries from the Organisation for Economic Co-operation and Development (OECD), 2003. Source: *Education at a Glance 2005*, Organisation for Economic Co-operation and Development, p. 68, table A4.1, www.oecd.org/document/34/0,2340,en_2649_201185_35289570_1_1_1_1,00.html (accessed January 2006).

APPENDIX B

SUPPLEMENTARY TABLES

**TABLE B-1. PERFORMANCE ON THE AP U.S. HISTORY TEST,
OCEANSIDE AND EL CAMINO HIGH SCHOOLS, 2003**

	Oceanside High		El Camino High	
Test Score	Number of Test-Takers	Percentage of Test-Takers	Number of Test-Takers	Percentage of Test-Takers
5	1	1.7	10	7.2
4	2	3.4	27	19.4
3	7	12.0	34	24.5
2	26	44.8	52	37.0
1	22	37.9	16	11.5
Total	58	100.0	139	100.0

SOURCE: Dayle Mazzarella, "2003 AP U.S. History Results," unpublished Oceanside High School documents provided to author.

TABLE B-2. DISTRIBUTION OF GEOMETRY GRADES, OCEANSIDE HIGH SCHOOL, 2003 AND 2004

Grade	2003	2004
A	55	110
	10.8%	10.9%
B	96	211
	18.8%	20.9%
C	98	296
	19.2%	29.5%
D	126	258
	24.7%	25.7%
F	136	130
	26.6%	12.9%
Total	511	1,005
	100%	100%

SOURCE: Dayle Mazzarella, Oceanside High School, unpublished data provided to author.

TABLE B-3. GRADE POINT AVERAGES OF UNIVERSITY OF TEXAS FRESHMEN, 2003

	Average GPA	
SAT Range	Students from Top 10% of High School Class	Students Not from Top 10% of High School Class
900–990	2.71	2.46
1000–1090	2.90	2.79
1100–1190	3.09	2.94
1200–1290	3.26	3.02
1300–1390	3.51	3.15
1400–1490	3.66	3.30
1500+	3.81	3.51

SOURCE: University of Texas at Austin, Office of Admissions, *Implementation and Results of the Texas Automatic Admissions Law (HB 588); Demographic Analysis of Entering Freshmen, Fall 2004; Academic Performance of Top 10% and Non-Top 10% Students, Academic Years 1996–2003*, Austin, 2005, http://www.utexas.edu/student/admissions/research/HB588-Report7.pdf (accessed October 2006).

TABLE B-4. PREDICTORS OF ACADEMIC PERFORMANCE OF UC FRESHMEN, 1996–1999

Predictor Variables	Percentage of Variance in Freshman Grades Attributed to the Variable(s)
High school GPA	15.4
SAT I	13.3
SAT II	16.0
SAT I + SAT II	16.2
High school GPA + SAT I	20.8
High school GPA + SAT II	22.2
High school GPA + SAT I + SAT II	22.3

SOURCE: Saul Geiser and Roger Studley, University of California, Office of the President, *UC and the SAT: Predictive Validity and Differential Impact of the SAT I and SAT II at the University of California,* Oakland, October 29, 2001, www.ucop.edu/news/sat/boars.html (accessed December 2005).

TABLE B-5. RELATIVE POWER OF HIGH SCHOOL GPA, SAT I, AND SAT II IN PREDICTING UC UNDERGRADUATE ACADEMIC PERFORMANCE, 1996–1999

Groups of Undergraduates	High School GPA	SAT I	SAT II
1. 1996–1999 UC	.27	.07	.23
2. UC Berkeley	.21	−.02	.27
3. UC Riverside	.31	.16	.10
4. UC San Diego	.27	.03	.25
5. UC general/undeclared	.27	.08	.22
6. UC social sciences/ humanities	.28	.11	.20
7. UC biological sciences	.31	.12	.25
8. UC physical sciences/ math/engineering	.28	−.05	.30

SOURCE: Saul Geiser and Roger Studley, University of California, Office of the President, *UC and the SAT: Predictive Validity and Differential Impact of the SAT I and SAT II at the University of California,* Oakland, October 29, 2001, www.ucop.edu/news/sat/boars.html (accessed December 2005).

NOTE: Standardized regression coefficients for high school GPA, SAT I scores, and SAT II scores. Regression equation: UC GPA = high school GPA + SAT I + SAT II.

TABLE B-6. CHARACTERISTICS OF SELECTED GROUPS OF UC FRESHMEN ADMITTED FROM PUBLIC HIGH SCHOOLS, BY AVERAGE SAT SCORE, FALL 2003

Average SAT I Score	Number Admitted	Percentage of Admissions	Average High School GPA	Percentage of Underrepresented Minorities	Average Family Income	Percentage Whose Parents Lack BAs	Percentage from Low-Performing High School
816	118	0	3.61	38	$40,116	79	61
904	511	1	3.57	35	$49,782	70	51
960	1,167	3	3.57	32	$59,085	61	40
1030	2,907	7	3.59	33	$67,414	56	34
1132	5,904	13	3.67	25	$79,964	46	24
1300	25,440	57	3.86	12	$98,309	29	11

SOURCE: University of California, Office of the President, Eligibility and Admissions Study Group, *Final Report to the President*, Oakland, April 2004, p. 39, www.universityofcalifornia.edu/news/compreview/studygroup_final0404.pdf. Partial data from the original source.

Notes

INTRODUCTION

1. The actual names of students, teachers, interviewees, and others are used in this book, unless specifically noted otherwise.

2. David Brooks, "The Triumph of Hope over Self-Interest," *New York Times*, January 12, 2003, sec 4.

3. Thomas Mortenson, "Family Income and Higher Education Opportunity, 1970 to 2002," *Postsecondary Education Opportunity* 143 (May 2004): 1–13.

1. ASHLEA AND GILLIAN

1. Ashlea Jackson, student, interviews by author, Boise, Idaho, October 15, 2004; November 2, 2004; and December 24, 2004.

2. Debbie Bailey, principal of Whittier Elementary, interview by author, Boise, Idaho, October 25, 2004.

3. James S. Coleman, "Equality of Educational Opportunity," in *Equality and Achievement in Education,* ed. Marta Tienda and David B. Grusky (Boulder, Colo.: Westview Press, 1990), p. 119.

4. Meredith Phillips, Jeanne Brooks-Gunn, Greg J. Duncan, Pamela Klebanov, and Jonathan Crane, "Family Background, Parenting Practices, and the Black-White Test Score Gap," in *The Black-White Test Score Gap,* ed. Christopher Jencks and Meredith Phillips (Washington, D.C.: Brookings Institution Press, 1998), p. 138.

5. Pierre Bourdieu and Jean-Claude Passeron, *Reproduction in Education, Society and Culture* (1977; London: Sage Publications, 1990), pp. 72–76.

6. Patricia M. McDonough, *Choosing Colleges: How Social Class and*

Schools Structure Opportunity (New York: State University of New York Press, 1997), pp. 8–9.

7. Coleman, "Equality of Educational Opportunity," p. 114.

8. Tiffani Chin and Meredith Phillips, "Social Reproduction and Child Rearing Practices: Social Class, Children's Agency, and the Summer Activity Gap," *Sociology of Education* 77 (July 2004): 185–210.

9. Yang Yang and Jan-Eric Gustafsson, "Measuring Socioeconomic Status at Individual and Collective Levels," *Educational Research and Evaluation* 10, no. 3 (2004): 259–288.

10. Amy J. Orr, "Black-White Differences in Achievement: The Importance of Wealth," *Sociology of Education* 76 (October 2003): 281–304.

11. Gary Jackson, interview by author, Boise, Idaho, November 15, 2004.

12. Elizabeth L. Useem, "Middle Schools and Math Groups: Parents' Involvement in Children's Math Placement," *Sociology of Education* 65 (October 1992): 263–279.

13. Jim Brunet, telephone interviews by author, November 15, 2004; November 19, 2004; and November 21, 2004; Gillian Brunet, telephone interview by author, December 13, 2004.

14. McDonough, *Choosing Colleges*, p. 9.

15. Pierre Bourdieu, *In Other Words: Essays towards a Reflexive Sociology* (Cambridge: Polity Press, 1990), p. 190.

16. Jim Wolfreys, "In Perspective: Pierre Bourdieu," *International Socialism Journal,* no. 87, Summer 2000, http://pubs.socialistreviewindex.org.uk/isj87/wolfreys.htm (accessed May 2006).

17. According to Smith College, the institution offers a "limited" number of scholarships based on merit, while 60 percent of students receive need-based financial aid. See Smith College, "Just the Facts," www.smith.edu/about_justthefacts.php (accessed May 24, 2006).

2. "DO WE LOOK INTIMIDATING?"

1. Becky Parkinson, parent of Highlands Elementary School student, interview by author, Boise, Idaho, April 1, 2005.

2. U.S. Census Bureau, Census 2000, Data Sets with Quick Tables, http://factfinder.census.gov, report generated by author, July 2005.

3. Sally Skinner, principal of Highlands Elementary School, interview by author, Boise, Idaho, November 14, 2004.

4. Independent School District of Boise City, "Boise School District Statistics—Low-Income," www.boiseschools.org/district_info/distses.html (accessed February 13, 2006).

5. Independent School District of Boise City, "Highlands Elementary School Performance Report 2004–05," www.boiseschools.org/performance/highlands.pdf (accessed February 13, 2006).

6. Skinner interview.

7. Holly MacLean, principal of Treasure Valley Math and Science Center, interviews by author, Boise, Idaho, October 22, 2004; and November 1, 2004.

8. Eric Fruits and Alec Josephson, "Economic Impacts of Micron's Idaho Operations," ECONorthwest, February 18, 2005.

9. Independent School District of Boise City, "Treasure Valley Mathematics and Science Center Design," 2003, p. 15.

10. Ibid., p. 9.

11. Independent School District of Boise City, "Boise School District Statistics—Low-Income," www.boiseschools.org/district_info/distses.html (accessed August 17, 2005).

12. Dan Spangler, university relations manager for Micron Technology Inc., telephone interview by author, December 10, 2004.

13. Joe Gordon, e-mail to author, November 29, 2004.

14. Holly MacLean, e-mail to author, January 19, 2005.

15. Otis-Lennon School Ability Test, 8th ed., http://harcourtassessment.com/hai/images/dotCom/olsat8/OLSAT_Brochure.pdf (accessed October 2006).

16. Lizanne DeStefano, "Test Review of the Otis-Lennon School Ability Test, Seventh Edition," in *The Fourteenth Mental Measurements Yearbook*, ed. B. S. Plake and J. C. Impara (Lincoln, Neb.: Buros Institute, 2001); electronic version available at www.unl.edu/buros.

17. Bert A. Goldman, "Test Review of the Otis-Lennon School Ability Test, Seventh Edition," in Plake and Impara, *The Fourteenth Mental Measurements Yearbook*.

18. Lewis M. Terman, *The Measurement of Intelligence* (Boston: Houghton Mifflin, 1916), pp. 6–7.

19. Carl C. Brigham, A *Study of American Intelligence* (Princeton: Princeton University Press, 1923), p. 119.

20. Robert J. Sternberg, *Encyclopedia of Human Intelligence* (New York: Macmillan, 1994), pp. 509–510.

21. Independent School District of Boise City, "Micron Technology Foundation Grant Agreement," Boise, Idaho, 2003; provided to author by Holly MacLean.

22. Mike Wiedenfeld, interview by author, Boise, Idaho, December 14, 2004.

3. BERKELEY HIGH AND THE POLITICS OF EXCLUSION

1. Hasmig Minassian, teacher, Berkeley High School, telephone interview by author, December 14, 2004.

2. U.S. Census Bureau, Census 2000, Data Sets with Quick Tables, www.factfinder.census.gov, report generated by author, April 20, 2005. I have used the location of elementary schools in the analysis of economic segregation in Berkeley as a convenient marker, though it should be noted that Berkeley has endeavored to rectify geographic segregation by voluntarily integrating its schools via a comprehensive school assignment policy that has been in effect since 1995. For a summary of the legal issues regarding the Berkeley plan, see the NAACP Legal Defense and Educational Fund Web site at www.naacpldf.org/content.aspx?article=284 (accessed May 2006).

3. Ibid.

4. Western Association of Schools and Colleges, Berkeley Unified School District, Berkeley High School, "Self-Study 2005," April 2005, pp. 36–40.

5. Ibid.

6. Ibid.

7. Cindy Peng, "A Struggle for Berkeley High's Choice Classes," *Daily Californian*, September 27, 2004, www.dailycal.org/article.asp?=16245.

8. Jim Slemp, principal, Berkeley High School, interview by author, Berkeley, Calif., January 30, 2005.

9. Karen Hemphill, telephone interview by author, December 17, 2004.

10. Berkeley High School Academic Choice, "Program Proposal," http://bhsacademicchoice.com/propose (accessed February 2005).

11. Jessica Seaton, e-mail to Berkeley High School Academic Choice newsgroup, September 5, 2004, BHSAcademicChoice@yahoogroups.com.

12. Nancy Feinstein, telephone interview by author, December 18, 2004.

13. Jessica Seaton, telephone interview by author, December 14, 2005.

14. Ibid.

15. Doug Powers, interview by author, Berkeley, Calif., January 30, 2005.

16. Dibsy Matcha, telephone interview by author, December 19, 2004.

4. "DO I MAKE THE KIDS SMART OR GET THEM INTO COLLEGE?"

1. Doug Powers, interview by author, Berkeley, Calif., January 30, 2005.

2. Nina Robinson, telephone interview by author, January 18, 2005.

3. Ellen Cushing, telephone interview by author, January 23, 2005.

4. Author's class visit on January 28, 2005.

5. Ibid.

6. Jessica Quindel, interview by author, Berkeley, Calif., January 28, 2005.

7. Mark Tatz, e-mail to Berkeley High School Academic Choice newsgroup, September 11, 2004, BHSAcademicChoice@yahoogroups.com.

8. Rick Ayers, interviews by author, Berkeley, Calif., January 15, 2005; and January 28, 2005.

5. PUBLIC SCHOOLS, PRIVATE PRIVILEGE

1. Adrian Raftery and Michael Hout, "Maximally Maintained Inequality: Expansion, Reform, and Opportunity in Irish Education, 1921–75," *Sociology of Education* 66 (January 1993): 41–62.

2. Ellen A. Brantlinger, *Dividing Classes: How the Middle Class Negotiates and Rationalizes School Advantage* (New York: Routledge-Falmer, 2003), p. 30.

3. Christopher Jencks, *Inequality: A Reassessment of the Effect of Family and Schooling in America* (New York: Basic Books, 1972), p. 135.

4. U.S. National Commission on Excellence in Education, *A Nation at Risk:*

The Imperative for Education Reform (Washington, D.C.: U.S. Government Printing Office, 1983).

5. Pierre Bourdieu, "Cultural Reproduction and Social Reproduction," in *Power and Ideology in Education,* ed. Jerome Karabel and A. H. Halsey (New York: Oxford University Press, 1977), pp. 487–488.

6. Brantlinger, *Dividing Classes,* p. 1.

7. Elizabeth L. Useem, "Middle Schools and Math Groups: Parents' Involvement in Children's Math Placement," *Sociology of Education* 65 (October 1992): 263–279.

8. John O'Neil, "On Tracking and Individual Differences: A Conversation with Jeannie Oakes," *Education Leadership* (October 1992): 18–21.

9. Ronald H. Heck, Carol L. Price, and Scott L. Thomas, "Tracks as Emergent Structures: A Network Analysis of Student Differentiation in a High School," *American Journal of Education* 110, no. 4 (August 2004): 321–353.

10. Samuel R. Lucas and Mark Berends, "Sociodemographic Diversity, Correlated Achievement, and De Facto Tracking," *Sociology of Education* 75 (October 2002): 328–348.

11. Adam Gamoran, "Is Ability Grouping Equitable?" *Educational Leadership* 50, no. 2 (October 1992): 11–17.

12. Adam Gamoran, "The Stratification of High School Learning Opportunities," *Sociology of Education* 60 (July 1987): 135–155.

13. Elizabeth L. Useem, "Getting on the Fast Track in Mathematics: School Organizational Influences on Math Track Assignment" (paper presented at the annual meeting of the American Educational Research Association, Boston, Mass., April 16–20, 1990), ED318624.

14. U.S. Department of Education, National Center for Education Statistics, *Highlights from the Trends in International Mathematics and Science Study (TIMSS) 2003,* by Patrick Gonzales, Juan Carlos Guzman, Lisette Partelow, Erin Pahlke, Leslie Jocelyn, David Kastberg, and Trevor Williams, NCES 2005–005 (Washington, D.C.: U.S. Government Printing Office, 2003), http://nces.ed.gov/pubsearch/pubsinfo.asp?pubid=2005005 (accessed October 2006).

15. U.S. Department of Education, National Center for Education Statistics, *Mathematics and Science in the Eighth Grade: Findings from the Third International Mathematics and Science Study,* NCES 2000–014 (Washington, D.C.: U.S. Government Printing Office, 2000), p. 83, http://nces.ed.gov/pubsearch/pubsinfo.asp?pubid=2000014 (accessed October 2006).

16. Ibid., p. 27.

17. U.S. Department of Education, Office of Educational Research and Improvement, *To Sum It Up: Case Studies of Education in Germany, Japan, and the United States,* by Harold W. Stevenson and Roberta Nerison-Low, undated document, www.ed.gov/pubs/SumItUp/SumItUp.pdf, p. 50 (accessed July 2005).

18. Ibid., p. 54.

19. Ibid., p. 52.

20. Ibid., p. 76.

21. U.S. Department of Education, National Center for Education Statistics, *Using TIMSS to Analyze Correlates of Performance Variation in Mathematics,*

by Daniel Koretz, Daniel McCaffrey, and Thomas Sullivan, Working Paper no. 2001–05 (Washington, D.C.: U.S. Government Printing Office, 2001).

CHAPTER 6. CLASS MATTERS

1. *Grutter v. Bollinger* et al., 02–241, Sup. Ct. 20 (2003).

2. *Gratz v. Bollinger* et al., 02–516, Sup. Ct. 3 (2003); Peter Schmidt, "Affirmative Action Survives, and So Does the Debate," *Chronicle of Higher Education,* July 4, 2003, http://chronicle.com/weekly/v49/i43/43s00101.htm (accessed February 13, 2006).

3. Thomas Mortenson, "Pell Grant Share of Undergraduate Enrollment at the 50 Best National Universities, 1992–93 and 2001–02," *Postsecondary Education Opportunity* 141 (March 2004): 18; Thomas Mortenson, "Economic Segregation of Higher Education Opportunity, 1973 to 2001," *Postsecondary Education Opportunity* 136 (October 2003): 3.

4. In the figures that accompany this discussion (both in the chapter text and in appendix A), families designated as low SES are typically those in which neither parent has attended college and family income is in the lowest quartile. The highest SES category typically means that both parents have at least a bachelor's degree and that the family's income is in the highest quartile. Middle SES typically means that one parent has a bachelor's degree or higher and family income is in the middle two quartiles of the income distribution.

5. U.S. Department of Education, National Center for Education Statistics, *National Educational Longitudinal Study 1988: Trends among High School Seniors, 1972–1992,* NCES 95–380 (Washington, D.C.: U.S. Government Printing Office, 1995), http://nces.ed.gov/pubsearch/pubsinfo.asp?pubid=95380 (accessed September 2006).

6. Ibid.

7. Ibid.

8. Piper Fogg, "Harvard's President Wonders Aloud about Women in Science and Math," *Chronicle of Higher Education,* January 28, 2005, http://chronicle.com/weekly/v51/i21/21a01201.htm (accessed September 29, 2006).

9. U.S. Department of Education, National Center for Education Statistics, *National Educational Longitudinal Study 1988–1994: Descriptive Summary Report,* by Allen Sanderson, Bernard Dugoni, Kenneth Rasinski, John Taylor, and C. Dennis Carroll, NCES 96–175 (Washington, D.C.: U.S. Government Printing Office, 1996).

10. Ibid.

11. U.S. Department of Education, National Center for Education Statistics, *Coming of Age in the 1990s: The Eighth-Grade Class of 1988, 12 Years Later,* NCES 2002–321 (Washington, D.C.: U.S. Government Printing Office, 2002).

12. U.S. Department of Education, National Center for Education Statistics, *Descriptive Summary of 1989–90 Beginning Postsecondary Students: Five Years Later—Statistical Analysis Report, March 1996,* by Lutz K. Berkner, Stephanie Cuccaro-Alamin, and Alexander C. McCormick, NCES 96–155 (Washington, D.C.: U.S. Government Printing Office, 1996), table 1.3, p. 34, http://nces.ed.gov/pubs/9615 5all.pdf (accessed February 14, 2006).

13. Lawrence E. Gladieux, "Low-Income Students and the Affordability of Higher Education," in *America's Untapped Resource: Low-Income Students in Higher Education,* ed. Richard D. Kahlenberg (New York: Century Foundation Press, 2004), p. 25.

14. Thomas Mortenson, "Segregation of Higher Education Enrollment by Family Income and Race/Ethnicity, 1980 to 2004," *Postsecondary Education Opportunity* 160 (October 2005): 8.

15. Thomas Mortenson, "Underrepresented Minorities' Share of Undergraduate Enrollments at State Flagship Universities, 1992 and 2001," *Postsecondary Education Opportunity* 146 (August 2004): 10.

16. Jane R. Porter, "State Flagship Universities Do Poorly in Enrolling and Graduating Black Men, Report Says," *Chronicle of Higher Education,* September 29, 2006, http://chronicle.com/daily/2006/09/2006092901n.htm (accessed September 2006).

17. Bill Ruben, telephone interview with author, December 18, 2004.

18. U.S. Department of Education, National Center for Education Statistics, *Digest of Education Statistics 2003,* by Thomas D. Snyder, Alexandra G. Tan, and Charlene M. Hoffman, NCES 2005-02 (Washington, D.C.: U.S. Government Printing Office, 2004), table 246, "Degree-Granting Institutions by Control and Type of Institution, 1949–50 to 2002–03," http://nces.ed.gov/programs/digest/d03_tf.asp (accessed February 14, 2006).

19. Thomas Mortenson, "Bachelor's Degree Attainment by Age 24 by Income Quartile, 1970–2002," *Postsecondary Education Opportunity* 143 (May 2004): 1.

20. Mortenson, "Economic Segregation of Higher Education Opportunity," p. 1.

21. Ibid.

22. U.S. Department of Education, National Center for Education Statistics, *Community College Students: Goals, Academic Preparation, and Outcomes — Postsecondary Education, Descriptive Analysis Reports,* by Gary Hoachlander, Anna C. Sikora, and Laura Horn, NCES 2003–164 (Washington, D.C.: U.S. Government Printing Office, 2003).

23. U.S. Department of Education, National Center of Education Statistics, *Community College Transfer Rates to 4-year Institutions Using Alternative Definitions of Transfer,* by Ellen M. Bradburn and David G. Hurst, NCES 2001–197 (Washington, D.C.: U.S. Government Printing Office, 2001).

24. Martin Trow, "The Second Transformation of American Secondary Education," in *Class, Status, and Power,* ed. Reinhard Bendix and Seymour Martin Lipset, 2nd ed. (New York: Free Press, 1966); quoted in Jerome Karabel, "Community Colleges and Social Stratification: Submerged Class Conflict in American Higher Education," *Power and Ideology in Education,* ed. Jerome Karabel and A. H. Halsey (New York: Oxford University Press, 1977), p. 234.

25. Karabel, "Community Colleges and Social Stratification," p. 248.

26. Anthony P. Carnevale and Stephen J. Rose, "Socioeconomic Status, Race/Ethnicity, and Selective College Admissions," in Kahlenberg, *America's Untapped Resource,* p. 106.

27. William Bowen and Derek Bok, *The Shape of the River: Long-Term Con-*

sequences of Considering Race in College and University Admissions (Princeton, N.J.: Princeton University Press, 1998), p. 49.

28. Alexander W. Astin and Leticia Osegueva, "The Declining Equity of American Higher Education," *Review of Higher Education* 27, no. 3 (2004): 321–341. This study is especially noteworthy because the authors drew from the Cooperative Institutional Research Program database. Since 1966, the CIRP survey has included some seven hundred institutions, covering approximately four hundred thousand freshmen, and is considered a nearly universal sample of college freshmen over time.

29. Ibid., p. 338.

30. Carnevale and Rose, "Socioeconomic Status," pp. 107–114.

31. Astin and Osegueva, "Declining Equity."

32. U.S. Department of Education, National Center for Education Statistics, *Who Goes to America's Highly Ranked National Universities?* by Jeffrey Owings, Timothy Madigan, and Bruce Daniel, NCES 98–095 (Washington, D.C.: U.S. Government Printing Office, 1998).

33. James C. Hearn, "Academic and Nonacademic Influences on the College Destinations of 1980 High School Graduates," *Sociology of Education* 64 (July 1991): 158–171.

34. David Karen, "Changes in Access to Higher Education in the United States, 1980–1992," *Sociology of Education* 75 (July 2002): 191–210.

35. David T. Ellwood and Thomas J. Kane, "Who Is Getting a College Education? Family Background and the Growing Gaps in Enrollment," in *Securing the Future: Investing in Children from Birth to College,* ed. Sheldon Danzinger and Jane Waldfogel (New York: Russell Sage Foundation, 2000), pp. 283–313.

36. Ibid., p. 313.

37. David Karen, telephone interview with author, March 4, 2005.

7. PART CHURCH, PART CAR DEALER

1. Louis Menand, "The Thin Envelope: Why College Admissions Has Become Unpredictable," *New Yorker,* April 7, 2003, www.newyorker.com /critics/atlarge/?030407crat_atlarge (accessed October 1, 2006).

2. Patricia M. McDonough, *Choosing Colleges: How Social Class and Schools Structure Opportunity* (Albany: State University of New York Press, 1977), p. 28.

3. Thomas Mortenson, telephone interview with author, January 23, 2005.

4. Thomas Mortenson, "Average Family Income by Educational Attainment, 1967–2002," *Postsecondary Education Opportunity* 142 (April 2004): 6.

5. "Facts and Figures: 746 College and University Endowments, 2004–2005," *Chronicle of Higher Education,* http://chronicle.com/stats /endowments (accessed February 16, 2006).

6. Gordon C. Winston, "Differentiation among U.S. Colleges and Universities," *Review of Industrial Organization* 24 (June 2004): 331–354.

7. Dominic J. Brewer, Susan M. Gates, Charles A. Goldman, *In Pursuit of Prestige: Strategy and Competition in U.S. Higher Education* (New Brunswick, N.J.: Transaction Publishers, 2002), p. 28.

8. Ibid., p. 43.

9. Ibid., p. 57.

10. Noel-Levitz, 2004 *National Enrollment Management Study: Key Findings for Two-Year and Four-Year Institutions,* 2005, www.noellevitz.com/Papers+and+Research (accessed October 2005).

11. Education Systems Inc., "Education Management Action Systems for Professionals," www.ese.org (accessed October 2005).

12. National Research Center for College and University Admissions, "Programs and Services for College Admissions Professionals," www.nrccua.org/educator/admit/index.asp (accessed October 2005).

13. College Board, "Enrollment Planning Services," www.collegeboard.com/highered/ra/eps.html (accessed October 2005).

14. U.S. Securities and Exchange Commission, *Annual Report, Princeton Review, Inc., for the Fiscal Year Ended December 31, 2004,* 20549 Form 10-K H, May 2, 2005, Washington, D.C., p. 1.

15. Princeton Review, "Enrollment Management on the Princeton Review," www.princetonreview.com/educators/enrollment/applicant.asp (accessed October 2005).

16. Princeton Review, "Counselor-O-Matic," www.princetonreview.com/college/research/advsearch/match.asp (accessed October 2005).

17. Princeton Review, "Embark Apply Online," http://apply.embark.com/profile.asp (accessed October 2005).

18. Princeton Review, "Privacy Policy," www.princetonreview.com/footer/privacy_policy.asp (accessed February 15, 2006).

19. College Board, 2005 *College Bound Seniors, National Report,* www.collegeboard.com/research/home/ (accessed October 2005).

20. Ibid.

21. Matthew Quirk, "The Best Class Money Can Buy," *Atlantic Monthly,* November 2005, www.theatlantic.com/doc/200511/financial-aid-leveraging (accessed February 15, 2006).

22. Gordon C. Winston, "The Positional Arms Race in Higher Education," *Forum Futures 2001 Papers,* Forum for the Future of Higher Education, April 2000, www.educause.edu/apps/forum/index.asp, pp. 19–22 (accessed February 15, 2006).

23. Jerry Sheehan Davis, *Unintended Consequences of Tuition Discounting,* Lumina Foundation for Education, New Agenda Series, vol. 5, no. 1, May 2003, www.luminafoundation.org/publications/Tuitiondiscounting.pdf (accessed February 15, 2006).

24. Christopher Avery, Andrew Fairbanks, and Richard Zeckhauser, *The Early Admissions Game: Joining the Elite* (Cambridge, Mass.: Harvard University Press, 2003).

25. Ibid., p. 66.

26. Ibid., pp. 69, 157.

27. Ibid., pp. 149, 67.

28. Ibid., p. 197.

29. Ibid., p. 74.

30. Ibid., p. 83.

31. Scott Jaschik, "Princeton Ends Early Decision," *Inside Higher Ed,* Sep-

tember 19, 2006, http://insidehighered.com/news/2006/09/19/princeton (accessed September 2006).

32. Thomas Mortenson, "Admissions Selectivity of 4-Year Colleges and Universities, 1986 to 2003," *Postsecondary Education Opportunity* 136 (October 2003): 1–3.

33. David A. Hawkins and Jessica Lautz, *State of College Admissions,* National Association for College Admission Counseling, March 2005, p. 10, www.nacacnet.org/MemberPortal/ProfessionalResources/Research/2004–05+Annual+State+of+College+Admission+Report.htm (accessed October 2006).

34. Ibid., pp. 39–40.

35. Hunter Breland, James Maxey, Renee Gernand, Tammie Cumming, and Catherine Trapani, *Trends in College Admission 2000: A Report of a National Survey of Undergraduate Admission Policies, Practices, and Procedures,* Association for Institutional Research (with ACT Inc., the College Board, Educational Testing Service, and the National Association for College Admission Counseling), March 2002, p. 61.

36. Hawkins and Lautz, *State of College Admissions,* p. 39.

37. Breland et al., *Trends in College Admission 2000,* p. 72.

38. Hawkins and Lautz, *State of College Admissions,* p. 43.

39. Jacques Steinberg, *The Gatekeepers: Inside the Admissions Process of a Premier College* (New York: Viking, 2002).

40. Reshma Memon Yaqub, "Getting Inside the Ivy Gates," *Worth,* September 2002, www.electricprint.com/edu4/classes/readings/edu-eliteschools.htm (accessed February 16, 2006).

41. Ibid.

42. Hawkins and Lautz, *State of College Admissions,* p. 126.

43. Ibid., p. 13.

44. Erin Strout, "Private Giving to Colleges Is Up, But Fewer Alumni Made Donations," *Chronicle of Higher Education,* February 24, 2006, http://chroncle.com/weekly/v52/i25/25a02701.htm (accessed April 25, 2006); William G. Bowen, Martin A. Kurzweil, and Eugene M. Tobin, *Equity and Excellence in American Higher Education* (Charlottesville: University of Virginia Press, 2005).

45. Daniel Golden, "Many Colleges Bend Rules to Admit Rich Applicants Seeking Big Donors," *Wall Street Journal Online,* http://online.wsj.com/public/resources/documents/Polk_Rich_Applicants.htm (accessed April 25, 2006).

46. Duke University, *Development Annual Report: 2004–05,* www.dukecomm.duke.edu/development/AnnualReport/AnnualReport.pdf (accessed April 25, 2006).

47. Golden, "Many Colleges Bend Rules."

48. Thomas Mortenson, "Segregation of Higher Education Enrollment by Family Income and Race/Ethnicity, 1980 to 2004," *Postsecondary Education Opportunity* 160 (October 2005): 13.

8. A SOCIAL COMPACT BROKEN

1. Carnegie Mellon University, "History of Carnegie Mellon," www.cmu.edu/home/about/about_history.html (accessed February 16, 2006).

2. A. Gabor, "Best Big Universities," *U.S. News and World Report,* October 15, 1990, p. 118; and "America's Best Colleges," 2006 edition, *U.S. News and World Report,* June 1, 2006, pp. 80–81. Pell Grant data comes from Thomas Mortenson, "Pell Grant Shares of Undergraduate Enrollments in Postsecondary Institutions, 1992–93 and 2001–02," *Postsecondary Education Opportunity,* January 2005, www.postsecondary.org/archives/Reports/Spreadsheets/Master Document.htm (accessed October 2005).

3. Carnegie Mellon University, *Self-Study Report, 1998,* February 22–25, 1998, www.cmu.edu/splan/index.html (accessed October 2005).

4. Ronald G. Ehrenberg, Liang Zhang, and Jared M. Levin, "Crafting a Class: The Trade Off between Merit Scholarships and Enrolling Lower-Income Students," National Bureau of Economic Research, NBER Working Paper no. 11437, June 2005, pp. 13–14, www.nber.org/papers/w11437 (accessed October 2005).

5. University of Wisconsin-Madison, Office of the Provost and the Office of Budget, Planning, and Analysis, *Data Digest, 2004–2005,* www.bpa.wisc.edu/datadigest (accessed September 2006); College Board, "Mean SAT Scores of College-Bound Seniors, 1967–2005," www.collegeboard.com/prod_down loads/about/news_info/cbsenior/yr2005/table2-mean-SAT-scores.pdf (accessed February 16, 2006).

6. Thomas Mortenson, "Pell Grant Share of Undergraduate Enrollment at the 50 Best National Universities, 1992–93 and 2001–02," *Postsecondary Education Opportunity* 141 (March 2004): 2–13.

7. Ibid.

8. Ibid.

9. Thomas Mortenson, "Pell Grant Enrollment at State Flagship Universities, 1992–93 and 2001-02," *Postsecondary Education Opportunity* 140 (February 2004): 1.

10. Ibid.

11. "Best National Universities, 1996," *U.S. News and World Report,* September 18, 1996, p. 126; University of Michigan-Ann Arbor, Office of Budget and Planning, "Common Data Set, 2004–2005," http://sitemaker.umich.edu/obpinfo/common_data_set (accessed October 2006).

12. University of Michigan-Ann Arbor, Office of Budget and Planning, "Common Data Set, 1998–1999," and "Common Data Set, 2004–2005," http://sitemaker.umich.edu/obpinfo/common_data_set (accessed October 2006).

13. Mary Sue Coleman, "Building on Our Diversity" (keynote address, Society for Advancement of Chicanos and Native Americans in Science, October 1, 2005), www.umich.edu/pres/speeches/051003diverse.html (accessed October 24, 2005).

14. University of Michigan-Ann Arbor, Office of Budget and Planning, "Facts and Figures," http://sitemaker.umich.edu/obpinfo/, under "Facts and Figures" (accessed October 2005).

15. Mortenson, "Pell Grant Share of Undergraduate Enrollment at the 50 Best National Universities," pp. 12–13.

16. Hunter Breland, James Maxey, Renee Gernand, Tammie Cumming, and Catherine Trapani, *Trends in College Admission 2000: A Report of a National Survey of Undergraduate Admission Policies, Practices, and Procedures,* Associ-

ation for Institutional Research (with ACT Inc., the College Board, Educational Testing Service, and the National Association for College Admission Counseling), March 2002, pp. 103–104.

17. Ibid., p. 122.

18. Eugene Tobin, "The Supply Side Block in Higher Education: Attainment, Equity, and Social Class" (keynote address, College Board Colloquium, Refocusing on the Common Good: Advancing Equity and Access in Higher Education, January 8–10, 2005, Bal Harbour, Fla.); William G. Bowen, Martin A. Kurzweil, and Eugene M. Tobin, *Equity and Excellence in American Higher Education* (Charlottesville: University of Virginia Press, 2005).

19. Michael Arnone, "The Wannabes: More Public Universities Are Striving to Squeeze into the Top Tier; Can States Afford These Dreams?" *Chronicle of Higher Education,* January 3, 2003, http://chronicle.com/weekly/v49/i17/17a01801.htm (accessed February 16, 2006).

20. Thomas Mortenson, "State Tax Fund Appropriations for Higher Education, FY1961 to FY2005," *Postsecondary Education Opportunity* 151 (January 2005): 1–5, 5–7.

21. University of Wisconsin-Madison, *Data Digest, 2004–2005,* pp. 56–72; University of Wisconsin-Madison, Office of the Chancellor, *Points of Pride, Causes for Concern,* February 2, 2005, http://www.chancellor.wisc.edu/pdf/72575_UWMadison.pdf (accessed October 2005).

22. University of Wisconsin-Madison, *Data Digest 2004–2005,* pp. 56–72.

23. Graham B. Spanier, "The Privatization of American Public Higher Education" (presentation to the Pennsylvania State University Faculty Senate, March 16, 2004, University Park, Penn.), http://president.psu.edu/sou/articles/151.html (accessed October 2005).

24. Erin Strout, "U. of Virginia Unexpectedly Opens $3-Billion Campaign to Become a 'Private' Public University," *Chronicle of Higher Education,* July 25, 2004, http://chronicle.com/weekly/v50/i42/42a03302.htm (accessed October 2005).

25. John T. Casteen III, "The New Deal: Why the University Needs Charter Status," *Alumni News,* Winter 2004, University of Virginia, Office of the President, www.virginia.edu/president/spch/04/newdeal04.html (accessed September 16, 2005).

26. Washington State University, *Strategic Plan, 2002–2007,* www.wsu.edu/StrategicPlanning/plan-detail.html (accessed October 2005); Washington State University, *University Relations Strategic Plan, 2002–2007,* www.wsu.edu/university-relations/strategic-plan.html (accessed October 2005).

27. Washington State University, "Regents Scholarship Program," http://regents-scholarship.wsu.edu/index.html (accessed October 2005).

28. V. Lane Rawlins, Washington State University, Office of the President, "State of the University Address" (September 15, 2004, Moscow, Idaho), www.wsu.edu/president/powerpoints.html (accessed October 2005).

29. Mortenson, "Pell Grant Shares of Undergraduate Enrollments in Postsecondary Institutions, 1992–93 and 2001–02"; and Thomas Mortenson, "Pell Grant Shares of Undergraduate Enrollments at Universities and 4-Year Colleges by Athletic Conferences, 1992 and 2001," *Postsecondary Education Opportunity* 147 (September 2004): 4.

30. Washington State University, Office of the President, "Update from President V. Lane Rawlins for the Faculty, Staff, and Graduate Assistants of Washington State University," September 7, 2005, www.wsu.edu/president/update32.html (accessed February 16, 2006).

31. University of Memphis, "History," www.memphis.edu/history.htm (accessed February 16, 2006).

32. University of Memphis, Office of Institutional Research, *Common Core Data*, http://oir.memphis.edu/cds/cds_index.html (accessed February 16, 2006).

33. Joe LaPointe, "For the People or the Powerful? Skybox Plan Divides Michigan," *New York Times*, April 9, 2006, http://select.nytimes.com/search/restricted/article?res=F20E15FF35540C7A8CDDAD0894DE404482# (accessed April 2006).

34. "Say No to Private Luxury Boxes in Michigan Stadium," Save the Big House, www.savethebighouse.com/index.html (accessed April 17, 2006).

9. GOVERNMENT GIFTS TO THE RICH

1. Bonnie Butler, telephone interview by author, September 25, 2005.

2. College Board, *Trends in Student Aid 2004*, p. 7, www.collegeboard.com/research/home/ (accessed November 2005).

3. The 1976 Pell Grant statistics are found in Lawrence E. Gladieux, "Low-Income Students and the Affordability of Higher Education," in *America's Untapped Resource: Low-Income Students in Higher Education*, ed. Richard D. Kahlenberg (New York: Century Foundation Press, 2004), p. 29. On the income levels of Pell Grant recipients, see Susan Dynarski, "The Consequences of Merit Aid," Harvard University, Kennedy School of Government and National Bureau of Economic Research, December 2002, p. 2, www.nber.org/papers/w9400 (accessed November 2005).

4. College Board, *Trends in Student Aid 2004*, p. 4.

5. Ibid., p. 7.

6. Michael S. McPherson and Morton Owen Schapiro, "Changing Patterns of Institutional Aid: Impact on Access and Education Policy," in *Condition of Access: Higher Education for Lower Income Students*, ed. Donald E. Heller (Westport, Conn.: Praeger, 2002), p. 80.

7. Lawrence E. Gladieux, "Federal Student Aid in Historical Perspective," in Kahlenberg, *America's Untapped Resource*, p. 54.

8. College Board, *Trends in Student Aid 2004*, p. 7; Thomas Mortenson, "Need-Based Student Financial Aid, 1964 to 2001," *Postsecondary Education Opportunity* 119 (May 2002): 1.

9. U.S. Department of Education, National Center for Education Statistics, *Access to Postsecondary Education for the 1992 High School Graduates: Statistical Analysis Report, October 1997*, by Lutz Berkner and Lisa Chavez, NCES 98 10 (Washington, D.C.: U.S. Government Printing Office, 1997), p. iii, http://nccs.ed.gov/pubsearch/pubsinfo.asp?pubid=98105 (accessed February 17, 2006).

10. Edward P. St. John, *Refinancing the College Dream: Access, Equal Op-*

portunity, and Justice for Taxpayers (Baltimore: Johns Hopkins University Press, 2003), p. 152.

11. U.S. Congress, Advisory Committee on Student Financial Assistance, *Empty Promises: The Myth of College Access in America* (Washington, D.C., 2002), p. 22, www.ed.gov/about/bdscomm/list/acsfa/emptypromises.pdf (accessed February 17, 2006).

12. Ibid., p. v.

13. National Association of State Student Grant and Aid Programs, *35th Annual Survey Report on State-Sponsored Student Financial Aid, 2003–2004 Academic Year,* p. 3, www.nassgap.org/viewrepository.aspx?categoryID=3 (accessed October 2006).

14. Ibid.

15. Donald E. Heller, "State Merit Scholarship Programs: An Introduction," in *Who Should We Help? The Negative Social Consequences of Merit Aid Scholarships,* ed. Donald E. Heller and Patricia Marin, Harvard University, Civil Rights Project, 2002, p. 17, www.civilrightsproject.harvard.edu/research/meritaid/fullreport.php (accessed November 2005).

16. National Association of State Student Grant and Aid Programs, *35th Annual Survey,* p. 10.

17. Susan Dynarski, "Race, Income, and the Impact of Merit Aid," in Heller and Marin, *Who Should We Help?,* pp. 80–82.

18. Christopher Cornwell and David B. Mustard, "Race and the Effects of Georgia's HOPE Scholarship," in Heller and Marin, *Who Should We Help?,* pp. 61–64.

19. Ibid., p. 71.

20. U.S. Department of Education, National Center for Education Statistics, *Paying for College: Changes between 1990 and 2000 for Full-Time Dependent Undergraduates,* NCES 2004–075 (Washington, D.C.: U.S. Government Printing Office, 2004), pp. 32–33, http://nces.ed.gov/pubsearch/pubsinfo.asp?pubid=2004075 (accessed September 2006).

21. College Board, *Trends in College Pricing 2004,* p. 18, www.collegeboard.com/research/home/ (accessed November 2005).

22. Interviews by author, October and November 2004. (These names have been changed. All other details are factual.)

10. A DANGEROUS MAN

1. Dayle Mazzarella, interviews by author, Oceanside, Calif., November 28, 2004; and February 20, 2005.

2. California Department of Education, "School Demographic Characteristics: 2004–05 Academic Performance Index (API) Growth Report," http://data1.cde.ca.gov/dataquest/, report generated by author, December 2005.

3. Ibid.

4. Ibid.

5. Ibid.

6. California Postsecondary Education Commission, "Freshmen at Public

Institutions/College-Going Counts," www.cpec.ca.gov/OnLineData/OnLine Data.asp, report generated by author, November 25, 2005.

7. Sherry Parmet, "Firm Push for College," *San Diego Union-Tribune*, September 15, 2004, www.signonsandiego.com/news/education/20040915-9999-1mi15college.html (accessed November 2005).

8. Kimo Marquardt, interview by author, Oceanside, Calif., February 20, 2005.

9. Dayle Mazzarella, Oceanside High School, "2003 AP U.S. History Results," unpublished data provided to author.

10. Robert Driscoll, interview by author, Oceanside, Calif., February 20, 2005.

11. Michael Lewis, *Moneyball: The Art of Winning an Unfair Game* (New York: Norton, 2003).

12. Robert Mueller to Staff, memorandum, December 3, 2004.

13. Robert Mueller to Staff, memorandum, January 20, 2005.

14. Robert Mueller, interview by author, Oceanside, Calif., February 20, 2005.

15. Oceanside High School, "Geometry Statistics, 2003–2004," unpublished document provided to author.

16. David Kalt, interview by author, Oceanside, Calif., February 20, 2005.

17. California Department of Education, "Course Enrollments by School," http://data1.cde.ca.gov/dataquest, report generated by author, November 21, 2005.

18. Oceanside High School, "Preliminary SAT Tests, 2001–2004," and "Students Passing the California High School Exit Exam," unpublished summary data provided to author by Dayle Mazzarella.

19. California Department of Education, "High School SAT/ACT/AP Test Results," http://data1.cde.ca.gov/dataquest, report generated by author, December 2005.

20. Oceanside High School, "Oceanside High AP Politics, 2003–04," unpublished data provided to author. (Student names are pseudonyms.)

21. Student interview by author, Oceanside, Calif., February 20, 2005; the student is identified by a pseudonym.

22. California Department of Education, "School Demographic Characteristics."

11. THE GATECRASHERS

1. University of Texas at Austin, Office of Admissions, *Implementation and Results of the Texas Automatic Admissions Law (HB 588); Demographic Analysis of Entering Freshmen, Fall 2004; Academic Performance of Top 10% and Non-Top 10% Students, Academic Years 1996–2003*, Austin, 2005, www.utexas.edu/student/admissions/research/HB588-Report7.pdf (accessed October 2006).

2. University of Texas at Austin, Office of Admissions, *Access to the University of Texas at Austin and the Ten Percent Plan: A Three-Year Assessment*, by David Montejano, Austin, 2001, www.utexas.edu/student/admissions/research/montejanopaper.html (accessed October 2006).

3. Karin Fischer, "Class-Rank Plan Faces Trouble in Texas," *Chronicle of*

Higher Education, April 22, 2005, http://chronicle.com/weekly/v51/i33/33a02501.htm (accessed October 2006).

4. Ibid.

5. Marta Tienda and Sunny Niu, "Texas' 10-Percent Plan: The Truth behind the Numbers," *Chronicle of Higher Education,* January 23, 2004, http://chronicle.com/weekly/v50/i20/20b01001.htm (accessed October 2006).

6. Rose Gutfeld, "Ten Percent in Texas: The Jury Is Still Out on an Alternative to Affirmative Action," Ford Foundation Report, Fall 2002, www.fordfound.org/publications/ff_report/view_ff_report_detail.cfm?report_index=355 (accessed April 27, 2006).

7. Marta Tienda, Kevin T. Leicht, Teresa Sullivan, Michael Maltese, and Kim Lloyd, *Closing the Gap? Admissions and Enrollments at the Texas Public Flagships before and after Affirmative Action,* Office of Population Research, Princeton University, p. 2, www.texastop10.princeton.edu/reports/wp/closing_the_gap.pdf (accessed April 27, 2006); emphasis in original.

8. John Moores, *A Preliminary Report on the University of California, Berkeley, Admission Process for 2002,* University of California, Board of Regents, October 29, 2003, p. 2, www.universityofcalifornia.edu/news/compreview/moores-report.pdf (accessed December 2005); Rebecca Trounson, Tony Perry, and Stuart Silverstein, "UC Berkeley Admissions Scrutinized: Study Finds Hundreds of Highly Qualified Applicants Were Rejected in Favor of Freshmen Who Were 'Marginally Academically Qualified,'" *Los Angeles Times,* October 4, 2003, p. B1.

9. Tanya Schevitz, "UC Admissions under Fire Again," *San Francisco Chronicle,* October 10, 2003, www.sfgate.com/cgi-bin/article.cgi?f=/c/a/2003/10/10/MN92829.DTL&hw=Schevitz+Admissions&sn=007&sc=572 (accessed December 2005).

10. Trounson, Perry, and Silverstein, "UC Berkeley Admissions Scrutinized."

11. John Moores, "College Capers," *Forbes,* March 29, 2004, p. 1, https://www.keepmedia.com/Auth.do?extId=10022&uri=/archive/forbes/2004/0329/040.html (accessed December 20, 2005).

12. Ibid.; John Moores, e-mail message addressed to the Regents of the University of California, March 25, 2004, *Daily Bruin Online,* www.dailybruin.ucla.edu/news/articles.asp?id=28153 (accessed December 2005).

13. Moores, *Preliminary Report,* pp. 147, 25.

14. U.S. Census Bureau, Census 2000, Data Sets with Quick Tables, www.factfinder.census.gov, report generated by author, July 2005.

15. California Department of Education, "School Demographic Characteristics," http://data1.cde.ca.gov/dataquest, report generated by author, December 2005.

16. Daisy Gonzalez, telephone interview by author, March 11, 2005.

17. Moores, "College Capers," p. 1.

18. John McWhorter, "Victims Hed *[sic]* Here," *Washington Post,* August 4, 2002; included in Moores, *Preliminary Report,* p. 183.

19. University of California, Office of the President, Eligibility and Admissions Study Group, *Final Report to the President,* Oakland, 2004, p. 74, www.universityofcalifornia.edu/news/compreview/studygroup_final0404.pdf (accessed December 2005).

20. University of California, Board of Admissions and Relations with Schools, *The Use of Admissions Tests at the University of California,* Oakland, 2003, pp. 4–6, www.universityofcalifornia.edu/senate/committees/boars/admissionstests.pdf (accessed February 17, 2006).

21. Ibid., p. 6.

22. Ibid., p. 8.

23. Richard Atkinson, interview by author, La Jolla, Calif., February 18, 2005.

24. Richard Herrnstein and Charles Murray, *The Bell Curve: Intelligence and Class Structure in American Life* (New York: Free Press, 1994). As the title suggests, *The Bell Curve* argued that intelligence, measured by IQ tests, strongly predicts an individual's place in the social and economic hierarchy of American life. As a close cousin to the eugenics movement, the book contained inflammatory arguments about intelligence and race. Because "intelligence" and academic achievement were impervious to schooling, the authors argued, public policies that attempted to rectify educational imbalances between disadvantaged groups of people were a waste of money. Numerous scholars have rebutted the book's claims: see, for example, Joe L. Kincheloe, Shirley R. Steinberg, and Aaron D. Gresson, eds., *Measured Lies: The Bell Curve Examined* (New York: St. Martin's Press, 1996).

25. Stephen Jay Gould, *The Mismeasure of Man* (New York: Norton, 1981). Gould's classic was a devastating attack on IQ testing in the United States, particularly the belief that human intelligence was a biologically based quantity that could be precisely measured with IQ tests.

26. Saul Geiser and Roger Studley, University of California, Office of the President, *UC and the SAT: Predictive Validity and Differential Impact of the SAT I and SAT II at the University of California,* Oakland, October 29, 2001, www.ucop.edu/news/sat/boars.html (accessed December 2005).

27. Ibid., p. 11.

28. Calvin Moore, interview by author, Berkeley, Calif., January 29, 2005.

29. University of California, Berkeley, Committee on Admissions, Enrollment, and Preparatory Education, *A Report to the Berkeley Faculty on Undergraduate Admission and Comprehensive Review: 1995–2002,* Berkeley, 2002, pp. 5–16, http://academic-senate.berkeley.edu/archives/documents/Moorereport.pdf (accessed February 17, 2006).

30. Anthony P. Carnevale and Stephen J. Rose, "Socioeconomic Status, Race/Ethnicity, and Selective College Admissions," in *America's Untapped Resource: Low-Income Students in Higher Education,* ed. Richard D. Kahlenberg (New York: Century Foundation Press, 2004).

31. University of California, Office of the President, Eligibility and Admissions Study Group, *Final Report to the President,* Oakland, April 2004, p. 39, www.universityofcalifornia.edu/news/compreview/studygroup_final0404.pdf (accessed December 2005).

32. University of California, Office of the President, Student Academic Services, *Selected Statewide and UC Postsecondary Data, Information Digest 2003,* Oakland, 2003, p. 13, www.ucop.edu/sas/infodigest03/Selected_data.pdf (accessed February 17, 2006).

33. University of California, Office of the President, Eligibility and Admissions Study Group, *Final Report to the President,* p. 73.

34. Michael Hout, University of California, Berkeley, Academic Senate, Berkeley Division, *Berkeley's Comprehensive Review Method for Making Freshman Admissions Decisions: An Assessment,* Committee on Admissions, Enrollment, and Preparatory Education and the Associate Vice Chancellor, Berkeley, 2005, http://academic-senate.berkeley.edu/committees/pdf_docs_consolidate/ Hout_Report.pdf (accessed February 18, 2006).

Although comprehensive review has not dramatically changed the socioeconomic composition of the UC system, it should be noted that several of the UC campuses lead the nation among top universities in terms of the percentage of undergraduates who receive Pell Grants. This can be attributed to several reasons, including a historically strong state grant program and UC's traditional focus on enrolling state residents. See University of California, Office of the President, "UC Is Best Top-Ranked University at Enrolling Low-Income Students, Study Says," press release, January 28, 2004, www.ucop.edu/news/archives/ 2004/apr28.htm (accessed May 23, 2006).

35. Tiffany Nguyen, telephone interview with author, April 8, 2005.

12. "I ALWAYS IMAGINED MYSELF AS A ROCK"

1. Christine Postma, telephone interviews by author, December 6, 2004; and March 14, 2005.

2. Melissa Morrow, telephone interviews by author, December 8, 2004; January 6, 2005; and March 14, 2005.

3. Mica Tommi-Slaven, telephone interview by author, October 25, 2004.

4. Mica Tommi-Slaven, e-mail to author, March 17, 2005.

5. Mica Tommi-Slaven, e-mail to author, March 18, 2005.

13. HOW WE GOT HERE

1. Thomas Piketty and Emmanuel Saez, "Income Inequality in the United States, 1913–1998," National Bureau of Economic Research, NBER Working Paper 8467, September 2001, p. 60, fig. 1, www.nber.org/papers/w8467 (accessed January 2005).

2. Lyndon B. Johnson, "Remarks at the University of Michigan," May 22, 1964, *American Presidency Project,* University of California, Santa Barbara, www.presidency.ucsb.edu/ws/index.php?pid=26262&st=michigan&st1=great +society (accessed February 18, 2006).

3. Ronald Reagan, "Address before a Joint Session of Congress on the State of the Union," February 4, 1986, Ronald Reagan Presidential Library, National Archives and Record Administration, www.reagan.utexas.edu/archives/ speeches/1986/20486a.htm (accessed February 18, 2006).

4. Ronald Reagan, "Address before a Joint Session of the Congress on the Program for Economic Recovery," April 28, 1981, Ronald Reagan Presidential Library, National Archives and Record Administration, www.reagan.utexas .edu/archives/speeches/1981/42881c.htm (accessed February 18, 2006).

5. Ronald Reagan, "Address before a Joint Session of the Congress on the State of the Union," January 25, 1983, Ronald Reagan Presidential Library, National Archives and Record Administration, http://www.reagan.utexas.edu/archives/speeches/1983/12583c.htm (accessed February 18, 2006).

6. Peter R. Orszag, "How the Bush Tax Cut Compares in Size to the Reagan Tax Cuts," Center for Budget and Policy Priorities, www.cbpp.org/2-6-01tax2.htm (accessed October 2006).

7. Joseph A. Califano Jr., "What Was Really Great about the Great Society," *Washington Monthly,* October 1999, www.washingtonmonthly.com/features/1999/9910.califano.html (accessed February 2005).

8. Piketty and Saez, "Income Inequality in the United States," p. 74, fig. 13.

9. Edward N. Wolff, "Trends in Household Wealth in the United States, 1962–83 and 1983–89," *Review of Income and Wealth,* series 40, no. 2 (June 1994): 171–172.

10. Will Lester, "Some Question Propriety of High Inaugural Costs," Associated Press, January 14, 2005, www.sfgate.com/cgi-bin/article.cgi?file=/news/archive/2005/01/14/national0319EST0428.DTL (accessed October 2006).

11. Dan Berrett, "These Days, It Has to Do a Lot More Than Roll," *New York Times,* July 3, 2005, sec. 3, p. 5.

12. Denny Lee, "The New Art of Coddling V.I.P. Skiers," *New York Times,* February 18, 2005, p. D9.

13. U.S. Congressional Budget Office, "The Budget and Economic Outlook: Fiscal Years 2006 to 2015," Statement of Douglas Holtz-Eakin, Director, before the Committee on the Budget, U.S. Senate, February 1, 2005, www.cbo.gov/showdoc.cfm?index=6065&sequence=0 (accessed February 18, 2006).

14. Center for American Progress, "Cost of Iraq War," www.americanprogress.org/site/pp.asp?c=biJRJ8OVF&b=171440 (accessed February 18, 2006); U.S. Congressional Budget Office, "The Budget and Economic Outlook."

15. Robert Greenstein, Joel Friedman, and Isaac Shapiro, "Two Tax Cuts That Benefit *Only* High-Income Households," Center for Budget and Policy Priorities, February 24, 2005, www.cbpp.org/2-4-05tax.pdf (accessed February 18, 2006).

16. Sharon Parrott, Jim Horney, Isaac Shapiro, Ruth Carlitz, Bradley Hardy, and David Kamin, "Where Would the Cuts Be Made under the President's Budget?" Center for Policy and Budget Priorities, February 28, 2005, www.cbpp.org/2-22-05bud.htm (accessed February 18, 2006).

17. Nicholas Johnson, Jennifer Schiess, and Joseph Llobrera, "State Revenues Have Fallen Dramatically," Center for Policy and Budget Priorities, October 22, 2003, www.cbpp.org/10-22-03sfp.htm (accessed February 18, 2006).

18. Thomas Mortenson, "State Tax Fund Appropriations for Higher Education, FY1961 to FY2005," *Postsecondary Education Opportunity* 151 (January 2005): 1–2.

19. Ibid.

20. Thomas Wolanin, "TRIO Is Educational Opportunity for Low-Income and Disabled Americans," Council for Opportunity in Education, December 1996, www.coenet.us/whatisTRIO_History.html (accessed February 18, 2006).

21. U.S. Department of Education, *Fiscal Year 2006 Budget Summary,* Sec-

tion III, Programs Proposed for Elimination, www.ed.gov/about/overview/budget/budget06/summary/edlite-section3.html (accessed February 18, 2006).

14. CLASS CONFUSIONS

1. David Brooks, "The Triumph of Hope over Self-Interest," *New York Times,* January 12, 2003, sec. 4 , p. 15.

2. Alexis de Tocqueville, *Democracy in America,* trans. Henry Reeve (Cambridge, Mass.: Sever and Francis, 1864); quoted in Joseph P. Ferrie, "The End of American Exceptionalism? Mobility in the U.S. since 1850," National Bureau of Economic Research, NBER Working Paper 11324, May 2005, p. 4, www.nber.org/papers/w11324 (accessed January 2006).

3. Ferrie, "The End of American Exceptionalism?" p. 14.

4. Bhashkar Mazumder, "Earnings Mobility in the US: A New Look at Intergenerational Inequality," Federal Reserve Bank of Chicago, Working Paper 2001–18, December 2001, pp. 3–4, www.chicagofed.org/economic_research_and_data/publication_display.cfm?Publication=6&year=2000%20AND%202005#2001 (accessed January 2006).

5. Ibid., pp. 34–35.

6. Jason DeParle, "Liberal Hopes Ebb in Post-Storm Poverty Debate," *New York Times,* October 11, 2005, p. A1.

7. Isaac Shapiro and Robert Greenstein, "The Widening Income Gulf," Center on Budget and Policy Priorities, September 5, 1999, www.cbpp.org/9-4-99tax-rep.htm (accessed February 19, 2006).

8. Thomas Piketty and Emmanuel Saez, "Income Inequality in the United States, 1913–1998," National Bureau of Economic Research, NBER Working Paper 8467, September 2001, p. 79, fig. 18, www.nber.org/papers/w8467 (accessed January 2005).

9. Timothy M. Smeeding, "Globalisation, Inequality, and the Rich Countries of the G-20: Evidence from the Luxembourg Income Study," Reserve Bank of Australia 2002 Conference: Globalisation, Living Standards, and Inequality: Recent Progress and Continuing Challenges, May 27–28, 2002, www.rba.gov.au/PublicationsAndResearch/Conferences/2002/smeeding.pdf (accessed January 2006).

10. Timothy Smeeding, "Poor People in Rich Nations: The United States in Comparative Perspective," Luxembourg Income Study, Working Paper 419, October 2005, p. 19, www.lisproject.org/publications/liswps/419.pdf (accessed February 19, 2006).

11. Lane Kenworthy and Jonas Pontusson, "Rising Inequality and the Politics of Redistribution in Affluent Countries," Luxembourg Income Study, Working Paper 400, January 2005, www.lisproject.org/publications/liswps/400.pdf (accessed February 19, 2006).

12. Christopher Jencks, "Does Inequality Matter?" *Dædalus* 131, no. 1 (Winter 2002): 49–65, http://mitpress.mit.edu/catalog/item/default.asp?ttype=6&tid=13200 (accessed January 2006).

13. Smeeding, "Globalisation," p. 23.

14. Kenworthy and Pontusson, "Rising Inequality," p. 19.

15. Michael Förster and Marco Mira d'Ercole, "Income Distribution and Poverty in OECD Countries in the Second Half of the 1990s," Organisation for Economic Co-operation and Development, OECD Social, Employment, and Migration Working Papers 22, March 10, 2005, p. 12, http://oberon.sourceoecd .org/vl=29109703/cl=20/nw=1/rpsv/workingpapers/1815199X.htm (accessed January 2006).

16. Kenworthy and Pontusson, "Rising Inequality," p. 32, fig. 9.

15. WHERE ARE WE GOING?

1. Barry McGaw, "OECD Briefing Note for United States," *Education at a Glance 2005*, Organisation for Economic Co-operation and Development, September 13, 2005, www.oecd.org/dataoecd/41/13/35341210.pdf (accessed January 2006).

2. European Union, European Commission, Education and Training, *Education and Training 2010: Diverse Systems, Shared Goals,* http://europa .eu.int/comm/education/policies/2010/et_2010_en.html (accessed January 2006).

3. "Commission Has Received All But Two Lisbon National Action Plans," EurActiv.com: European Union News and Policy Positions, November 30, 2005, updated January 19, 2006, www.euractiv.com/Article?tcmuri=tcm:29-150135–16&type=News (accessed February 19, 2006).

4. *Education at a Glance 2005,* Organisation for Economic Co-operation and Development, p. 36, www.oecd.org/document/34/0,2340,en_2649 _201185_35289570_1_1_1_1,00.html (October 12, 2006).

5. Ibid.

6. Thomas Mortenson, "International Comparisons of 4-Year College Continuation Rates, 1998 and 2001," *Postsecondary Education Opportunity* 144 (June 2004): 11.

7. Ibid., p. 12.

8. National Science Foundation, Division of Science Resources and Statistics, *Science and Engineering Indicators 2004,* Arlington, Va., 2004, www.nsf.gov/ statistics/seind04/c0/cos1.htm (accessed January 2006).

9. *Education at a Glance 2005,* p. 68, table A4.1.

10. *Learning for Tomorrow's World—First Results from PISA 2003,* Organisation for Economic Co-operation and Development, Paris, p. 183, www.pisa.oecd.org/document/55/0,2340,en_32252351_32236173_33917303 _1_1_1,00.html (accessed January 2006).

11. U.S. Department of Education, National Center for Education Statistics, *Coming of Age in the 1990s: The Eighth-Grade Class of 1988, 12 Years Later,* by Steven J. Ingels, T. R. Curtin, Phillip Kaufman, Martha Naomi Alt, Xianglei Chen, and Jeffrey A. Owings, NCES 2002-321 (Washington, D.C.: U.S. Government Printing Office, 2002), p. 43.

12. U.S. Census Bureau, *The Big Payoff: Educational Attainment and Synthetic Estimates of Work-Life Earnings,* by Jennifer Cheeseman Day and Eric C. Newburger (Washington, D.C.: U.S. Government Printing Office, 2002), www.census.gov/prod/2002pubs/p23–210.pdf (accessed February 19, 2006).

13. Jared Bernstein, Chauna Brocht, and Maggie Spade-Aguilar, *How Much Is Enough? Basic Family Budgets for Working Families* (Washington, D.C.: Economic Policy Institute, 2000), p. 2, www.epinet.org/content.cfm/books_howmuch (accessed January 2006).

14. Sandy Baum and Kathleen Payea, *Education Pays 2004: The Benefits of Higher Education for Individuals and Society* (Washington, D.C.: College Board, 2004), pp. 16–25, www.collegeboard.com/prod_downloads/press/cost04/EducationPays2004.pdf (accessed February 19, 2006).

15. Susan E. Mayer, "How Economic Segregation Affects Children's Educational Attainment," Working Paper Series 01.18, Harris School of Public Policy, University of Chicago, July 2001, http://harrisschool.uchicago.edu/About/publications/working-papers/pdf/wp_01_18.pdf (accessed May 18, 2006).

16. Patrick J. Kelly, *As America Becomes More Diverse: The Impact of State Higher Education Inequality,* National Center for Higher Education Management Systems, Boulder, Co., November 2005, www.higheredinfo.org/race ethnicity/InequalityPaperNov2005.pdf (accessed May 16, 2006).

17. Karen Arenson, "Harvard Extends Breaks for Low-Income Parents," *New York Times,* March 31, 2006, www.nytimes.com/2006/03/31/education/31harvard.html?ei=5102&en=b58ae36d3f22b92e&ex=1146462318&adxnnl=1&partner=vault&adxnnlx=1145412332-MrF084lRYKygn38VwXE-bGw&pagewanted=print (accessed April 20, 2006).

18. Erin Strout, "Duke U. Gets $75-Million Pledge for Financial Aid," *Chronicle of Higher Education,* October 4, 2005, http://chronicle.com/daily/2005/10/2005100406n.htm (accessed April 20, 2006).

19. The Editors, "The *Washington Monthly* College Guide," *Washington Monthly,* September 2005, www.washingtonmonthly.com/features/2005/0509.collegeguide.html (accessed April 20, 2006).

20. George D. Kuh and Ernest T. Pascarella, "What Does Institutional Selectivity Tell Us about Academic Quality?" *Change,* September-October 2004, pp. 53–58.

21. U.S. Census Bureau, *Income, Poverty, and Health Insurance Coverage in the United States: 2004,* by Carmen DeNavas-Walt, Bernadette D. Proctor, and Cheryl Hill Lee (Washington, D.C.: U.S. Government Printing Office, 2005), p. 83, www.census.gov/prod/2005pubs/p60–229.pdf (accessed February 19, 2006); CNN.com, "2004 Election Results," www.cnn.com/ELECTION/2004/pages/results/president/ (accessed February 19, 2006).

22. Thomas Mortenson, "College Participation Rates for Students from Low Income Families by State, 1992–2002," *Postsecondary Education Opportunity* 150 (December 2004): 3.

23. Associated Press, "Dems Battle over Confederate Flag," November 2, 2003, CNN.com, www.cnn.com/2003/ALLPOLITICS/11/01/elec04.prez.dean.confederate.flag/ (accessed January 2006).

24. Richard D. Kahlenberg, *The Remedy: Class, Race, and Affirmative Action* (New York: Basic Books, 1996), p. 194.

25. Martin Luther King Jr., "Where Do We Go from Here?" annual report delivered at the Eleventh Convention of the Southern Christian Leadership Conference, August 16, 1967, Atlanta, Georgia, Martin Luther King Jr. Research and

Education Institute, Stanford University, www.stanford.edu/group/King/mlk papers/ (accessed January 2006).

26. Martin Luther King Jr., "The Drum Major Instinct," sermon delivered at Ebenezer Baptist Church, Atlanta, Georgia, February 4, 1968, Martin Luther King Jr. Research and Education Institute, Stanford University, www.stanford .edu/group/King/mlkpapers/ (accessed January 2006).

Index

Hispanics, 11, 172, 251; bachelor's degrees and, 115; at Berkeley High School, 65–66, 84; at elite universities, 122; improvement in educational opportunities, 113; in Los Angeles, 231–35; at Oceanside High, 219–20, 222
history classes, 82–83, 99, 100
home-schooling, 260
Hong Kong, 104, 304
HOPE Scholarship program, 184, 185–86
Hopwood v. Texas, 225
Horatio Alger ideal, 2, 290
Hout, Michael, 94, 249
human capital, 6, 12, 92; concentration of private power and, 98; economic productivity and, 306; loss of, 182; "market value" of children and, 96; transmission from parent to child, 41. *See also* cultural capital
Hungary, 303

Iceland, 303, 304
immigrants, 121, 134, 135; Hispanic, 219–20, 222; IQ tests and, 229; Vietnamese, 250–57
income distribution, 7, 115–16, 156, 332; achievement of bachelor's degree and, 118, 119; education level and, 134–35; growth of inequality, 293–95; SAT scores and, 146, 248–49, 250
Indians, American, 203–4, 231
inequality, 6, 121; fatalism about, 5; ideology of scarcity and, 296–97; increase in, 282–87; maximally maintained, 94; reproduction of, 32, 225; tracking system and, 101
Inequality: A Reassessment of the Effect of Family and Schooling in America (Jencks), 96
information economy, 134
In Pursuit of Prestige (Brewer, Gates, Goldman), 137
Inside Higher Ed, 151
Institute for College Access and Success, 312
intelligence, measurement of, 239, 357nn24–25
Internet, 2, 143, 144, 266, 268
internships, 34
IQ (intelligence quotient) tests, 32, 55, 57, 357nn24–25; ideology about merit and, 229; SAT built upon, 236; tracking and, 98

Iraq war, 283
Ireland, 94, 301
Italy, 304
Ivy League, 3, 33, 149

Jackson, Ashlea, 1–2, 3, 4, 19–20, 45, 122; Big Sister of, 1, 12, 13–14; brothers of, 11, 12–13, 20; college prospects, 18, 22, 31, 34–35; family lack of cultural capital and, 299; interest in journalism, 1, 18–19; in math classes, 22–23; precarious family situation of, 35–36
Jackson, Gary, 19–21, 29, 34, 35–36
Jackson, Patty, 19–21
Japan, 103, 104–6, 301, 303, 304
Jefferson, Thomas, 169
Jencks, Christopher, 15, 96, 296
John Muir Elementary School (Berkeley), 64–65
Johns Hopkins University, 160, 164
Johnson, Lyndon, 164, 167, 177, 278; heritage of Great Society and, 281; on Higher Education Act, 175; War on Poverty, 285
Joint Center for Political and Economic Studies, 117
Jones, Marilee, 156
juvenile detention, 1, 12

Kahlenberg, Richard D., 315–16
Kalt, David, 214–15
Kane, Thomas J., 127–28
Karabel, Jerome, 121
Karen, David, 127, 128–29
Katrina, Hurricane, 292–93, 297
Keeping Track (study), 99
Kelly, Patrick J., 310
Kennedy, Robert F., 315–16, 317
Kenworthy, Lane, 295, 296, 297
Kerr, Clark, 236
Kerry, John, 314
kindergarten, 2, 14, 76, 102, 105
King, Martin Luther, Jr., 133, 315, 316–17
Korea, 103, 104, 106, 301, 303
Koretz, Daniel, 106
Kuh, George, 312
Kurzweil, Martin, 155, 166

languages, foreign, 30
Lautz, Jessica, 154
lectures, classroom, 46
Lee, Denny, 283
legacy preference, 155, 166
Levin, Jared M., 160

Text:	10/13 Sabon
Display:	Franklin Gothic
Compositor:	Binghamton Valley Composition, LLC
Indexer:	Alexander Trotter
Illustrator:	Bill Nelson
Printer and binder:	Maple-Vail Manufacturing Group